I0833304

PROCEEDINGS

OF THE

LYCEUM OF NATURAL HISTORY

IN THE

CITY OF NEW YORK.

PROCEEDINGS

OF THE

LYCEUM OF NATURAL HISTORY

IN THE

CITY OF NEW YORK.

SERIES I. (April 4, 1870, to December 4, 1871).
Pages 1 to 300.

SERIES II. (January 6, 1873, to June 1, 1874).
Pages 1 to 156.

NEW YORK

PUBLISHED BY THE SOCIETY.

OFFICERS OF THE LYCEUM.

1873–1875.

President:

John S. Newberry.

Vice-Presidents:

Thomas Egleston.
Henry Morton.

Corresponding Secretary:

Robert Dinwiddie.

Recording Secretary:

Robert H. Brownne.

Treasurer:

John H. Hinton.

Librarian:

Bernard G. Amend.

Curators:

William J. Hays, Henry Wurtz,
Lewis Feuchtwanger, William H. Leggett,
John J. Stevenson.

Committee on Nominations:

Charles A. Joy, *Chairman;*
Robert Dinwiddie, Charles A. Seeley,
Benjamin N. Martin, Albert H. Gallatin.

Committee on Publications.

Thomas Bland, *Chairman;*
John S. Newberry, George N. Lawrence,
Daniel S. Martin, H. Carrington Bolton.

Finance Committee.

Benjamin N. Martin, *Chairman;*
J. Carson Brevoort, D. Jackson Steward.

Library Committee:

Robert H. Brownne, *Chairman;*
Louis Elsberg, Oran W. Morris.

TABLE OF CONTENTS.

BUSINESS PROCEEDINGS.

SCIENTIFIC PROCEEDINGS.

PAPERS READ BEFORE THE LYCEUM.

SERIES I.

P. T. AUSTIN.

THOMAS BLAND AND W. G. BINNEY.

H. CARRINGTON BOLTON.

FRANCIS COLLINGWOOD.

ARTHUR M. EDWARDS.

SERIES II.

W. G. BINNEY.

H. CARRINGTON BOLTON.

THOMAS BLAND.

THOMAS BLAND AND W. G. BINNEY.

FRANCIS COLLINGWOOD.

A. K. EATON.

THOMAS EGLESTON.

LOUIS ELSBERG.

HERMAN ENDEMANN.

The second fasciculus of the Proceedings, Series II., which should have been paged from 33 to 64, was, by an unfortunate oversight, renumbered 1 to 32. In the present contents and index, to avoid confusion, these misnumbered pages are considered and placed as if they were paged correctly; *e. g.*, a title referred to page 45, in the index, is found on the second page 13 (45—32) of the Proceedings.

INDEX OF PROCEEDINGS.

SERIES I.

SERIES II.

PROCEEDINGS

OF THE

LYCEUM OF NATURAL HISTORY

IN THE

CITY OF NEW YORK.

April 4, 1870.

The President in the chair. Eight persons present.

The President, as chairman, reported from the Committee, on the publication of the proceedings of the Lyceum, that arrangements had been made to carry out the wishes of the society, and that the first number would shortly appear; Prof. Edwards having charge of the reporting.

Dr. L. Feuchtwanger sent, for exhibition, some fine specimens of crystallized Quartz and Arkansite, from the Hot Springs of Arkansas. The Quartz was mostly in curious flattened crystals, arranged in cockscomb form, and the Arkansite in remarkably perfect crystals.

Prof. A. M. Edwards described a late addition to the Micro-Spectroscope, contrived by Mr. John Browning, of London, with which, by projecting a ruled scale into the field, reflecting its image from the upper surface of the compound prism, the lines in the spectrum under examination may be readily registered.

Dr. J. S. Newberry read a paper

On the Earliest Traces of Man found in North America.

Dr. Newberry stated that the human relics for which the highest antiquity had been claimed were the Natchez bone and Table Mountain (California) skull. If it could be shown beyond question, that these bones really occurred in the positions to which they had been referred, we should have evidence that man existed on this continent as a contemporary with the mammoth, mastodon and other extinct mammals, and at a period so remote that all the topographical features of the surface have since changed—in the case of Table Mountain the bottom of a valley having become a mountain summit. As regards the Natchez bone, geological changes have been effected since the date assigned it, which, in Sir Charles Lyell's judgment, must have required a hundred thousand years. In neither of these instances, were the human remains actually found by credible persons in strata of high antiquity, and no dependence whatever can be placed upon inferences made from this material in the solution of the question of the antiquity of man. We may to-morrow obtain indubitable evidence of the occurrence of the remains of man in the Table Mountain tertiaries and the Vicksburg bluff; but until such evidence be discovered we must discuss the question, leaving these hypothetical cases entirely out of view. No solid and enduring scientific fabric can be reared on doubtful premises.

The caves of our country have as yet scarcely been entered upon as ground for archæological research. But one cavern has been examined with any care—that of Carlisle, Pa., by Professor Baird—and this may be said to have been but partially explored. Human remains were found in it, but not of special interest. The fauna represented by the great number of bones collected there, is essentially the same with that which occupied the country on the advent of the whites. This remarkable fact, however, is reported by Professor Baird, that all the species represented in the collections made in the Carlisle cave, have degenerated in size, and this modern degeneracy ranges from ten to twenty-five per cent.

The shell mounds on the Atlantic Coast north and south have been partially investigated by Professor Wyman, Professor Baird, and others. In these mounds human remains are constantly met with, but none which can serve as proof of great antiquity. Perhaps the best evidence that these shell mounds are of ancient date, is furnished by the facts reported by Professor Baird, that those of Maine contain the bones of the great Auk (*Alca impennis*) and those of the walrus. Of these the first is supposed to be entirely extinct, and both in modern times have been confined to higher latitudes.

The mounds of the western states, the copper mines of Lake Superior, the old oil wells of Pennsylvania, and the lead mines of Kentucky, really afford us the only traces of human occupation yet found within our territory, which have a respectable antiquity, and one which can be measured even negatively in years. All these traces of the ancient semi-civilized people that once inhabited the Mississippi valley, are found overgrown by what we term the "primeval forest," in which are trees five hundred years old; and these trees in some instances, are growing on the prostrate trunks of individuals of equal size, belonging to a preceding generation. This, then, is the record. We can positively assert that the works of the mound builders were abandoned and overgrown by forests a thousand years ago; how much before that time we have no means of knowing. We may fairly infer that some hundreds of years were consumed in the multiplication of this ancient people, in their spread over and subjugation of the country they occupied, in the substitution of cultivated farms for the pre-existent forest, in the construction of towns so numerous as to thickly dot all the surface, in the thorough exploration and extensive working of the mineral districts and oil fields, in the acquisition of the degree of civilization they attained, in their gradual reduction in numbers to their total extinction.

In New Mexico, Mexico, Central America and Peru, we have countless monuments of a civilization generically the same throughout this great area, and a civilization which was indigenous to America. For the rise, culmination and decline of this civilization—for it was in its decadence when Columbus discovered America—we must allow two thousand or three thousand years. Perhaps they occupied much more time than this; but all these changes could hardly have been effected in less than two thousand years. Whether there was any relationship between the ancient Mexicans and the mound-builders is a question yet to be decided. They had this in common, that both were sedentary and agricultural; were miners and builders. But the Mexicans and the Incarial race were famous masons, and built huge structures of dressed stone which scarcely suffer in comparison with our finest architectural monuments. The mound-builders, on the contrary, built in earth and wood, and the structures they raised have little in common, so far as plan is concerned, with those of the southern nations. No geographical connection has been traced between these ancient civilizations. The one seems to have been strictly confined to the Valley of the Mississippi, the other to the high table lands lying between the Rocky Mountains and the Sierra Nevada.

In answer to inquiries, Professor Newberry stated that the inscriptions which covered the monuments of Central America and Peru, like the arrowhead characters of Assyria, and the hieroglyphics of Egypt, were destined to be read. Indeed, it might be said that many of these inscriptions could now be read. But little was to be expected, however, in the way of historical facts, from a perfect translation of all these records. They were apparently, for the most part, local and personal in character, and like the Egyptian and Assyrian records, consisted mostly of religious invocations, laudation of persons or celebrations of local and temporary political triumphs, which to us have no special significance or value.

The mining operations of our ancient Americans were so extensive, that most of the important deposits of copper on Lake Superior, had been not only discovered, but worked by them.

The working of the oil wells by the mound-builders, had not perhaps been noticed by others, but Professor Newberry asserted it from observations he had himself made. On the bottom lands of Oil Creek, below Titusville, he had, in 1860, noticed that the ground in the primeval hemlock forest was pitted in a peculiar way, the pits two or three feet deep, eight or ten feet in diameter, and almost contiguous. These were proved (by excavations made preparatory to boring oil wells) to be the remains of ancient wells or pits sunk in the alluvial clay. One of these, opened to the depth of twenty-seven feet, was cribbed up with timber, and contained a ladder like those found in the ancient mines of Lake Superior, formed from the trunk of a tree on which branches were left projecting six or eight inches. Professor Newberry had subsequently seen similar pits to these, around the oil springs of Mecca and Grafton, Ohio, and at Enniskillen, Canada West. In the latter locality, a modern oil well cut into the circumference of an ancient one, and this was found to be filled with sticks and rubbish. A pair of deer's horns were taken out thirty-six feet below the surface.

The lead vein in Kentucky, to which reference had been made, had been worked by an open cut several hundred yards in length. This was now a ditch some feet in depth, with a ridge of material thrown out on either side, the whole was covered by forest, and trees three feet in diameter were growing upon the ridges of rejected rubbish.

Dr. Tellkampf and the President, made some further remarks relative to the celebrated "Hydrachos," exhibited many years since by Dr. Koch, and spoke of the hesitancy with which any evidence coming from that quarter should be received.

April 11, 1870.

The President in the chair. Eleven persons present.

The President, to whom the subjects had been referred, reported that he had not deemed it advisable for the Lyceum, to take any action in the matters of the Arctic Expedition and Yosemite Valley.

He also read a letter from a member of the Darien Expedition, giving an account of the many difficulties to be encountered by any parties undertaking the survey of that country.

Prof. T. Egleston, Jr., read a letter received from Dr. Eulenstein, of Berlin, speaking of his forthcoming revised edition of Pritchard's Infusoria, and asking for contributions of specimens for the purpose of furthering that undertaking.

Mr. O. Loew read a paper

On Hydrogenium-Amalgam.

He showed that when Zinc-amalgam is agitated with a weak solution of Bi-Chloride of Platinum, a spongy mass forms upon the surface of the Zinc-amalgam, having buttery consistence, and strongly resembling in physical characters, the well-known Ammonium-amalgam. This body he considers to be an amalgam of Hydrogenium and Mercury. To prepare it on a large scale, he shakes thoroughly Zinc-amalgam, containing three per cent. of Zinc, with an equal volume of a solution of Bi-Chloride of Platinum, containing ten per cent. of the salt. The mass becomes warm, and must be cooled from time to time, by plunging the flask, in which the reaction is carried on, into cold water, and also takes on a black color from the finely-divided Platinum which is reduced. The mixture is then thrown into moderately dilute Hydrochloric acid, by which the excess of Zinc and Oxychloride formed is dissolved. Unless thus treated, the amalgam is rapidly decomposed with evolution of Hydrogen. The Platinum is, for the most part, removed with the excess of mercury. The body thus prepared, has the consistency and appearance of Ammonium-amalgam, as obtained by acting upon an Ammonium Salt with Sodium-amalgam. At ordinary temperatures, several days are required for its complete decomposition. It possesses the marked reducing power peculiar to Hydrogenium, reducing Ferricyanides to Ferrocyanides, Per Salts of Iron to Proto Salts, decolorizing Permanganate of Potassium, &c. This Hydrogenium-amalgam also absorbs Ammonia, and the resulting body resembles Ammonium-amalgam as otherwise obtained.

Since Graham compared Hydrogenium with the active modification of oxygen, Mr. Loew proposed to consider the following series as parallel.

Antozone.	Common Oxygen.	Ozone.
Nascent Hydrogen.	Common Hydrogen.	Hydrogenium.

And he further suggests the representing of these three states of Hydrogen, by formulæ in the following manner.

[H]	[H H]	[H H] H
Nascent Hydrogen.	Common Hydrogen.	Hydrogenium.

He performed the experiment as described, in a most satisfactory manner, producing a large mass of the supposed Hydrogenium-amalgam. The reading of this paper elicited considerable discussion. Dr. I. Walz, spoke in high terms of Mr. Loew's ingenious experiment, but opposed his theoretical views; especially the comparison of nascent Hydrogen and Antozone, the existence of which he denied. He exhibited the action of Bi-Chromate of Potassium and Zinc-amalgam when shaken together, whereby the former is reduced, and apparently a compound of Hydrogenium and Mercury obtained, which differed in characters somewhat from that exhibited by Mr. Loew.

Prof. C. A. Joy, referred to the experiments of Schönbein, which conclusively prove, he considered, the existence of Antozone. Schönbein agitated Zinc-amalgam with water, and examined the solution obtained. This did not act upon Iodide of Potassium and Starch, until a trace of a Proto-salt of Iron was added, when immediately the blue color of Iodide of Starch appeared. The use of Bi-Chloride of Platinum for assisting the evolution of Hydrogen, originated with De la Rive. He thought that Mr. Loew had gone a step farther than either Schönbein or Graham in this most important discovery.

Prof. C. A. Seely differed in his views from the gentlemen preceding him. He thought the conclusions not warranted by the facts. He doubted the existence of Hydrogenium or Hydrogen as a metal, and claimed that the facts could all be satisfactorily explained, as phenomena of adhesion or absorption, and he suggested a theory for the present case in accordance with these views.

Dr. Paul Schweitzer read a

NOTICE OF RECENT INVESTIGATIONS ABROAD IN CHEMISTRY.

He gave an abstract of Mohr's investigations on the analysis of mineral waters, and Liebig's paper on Fermentation and the source of muscular power. He also referred to Rammelsberg's classification of meteorites. In conclusion he presented the results of some analyses of pure lead which he had made, and in which he had endeavored to determine the small amount of impurities with the greatest possible accuracy.

One of the analyses was as follows:

Iron	0.0008
Nickel	0.0001
Zinc	0.0001
Cadmium	0.0001
Bismuth	0.0111
Copper	0.0030
Silver	0.0041
Antimony	0.0012
Arsenic	Trace
Lead	99.9775
	100.

Prof. Joy exhibited some of the double Iodide of Silver and Mercury, received from Prof. W. Gibbs. It is a yellow salt, and one of the most sensitive to heat known, turning red on warming, and returning to its original yellow color on cooling, thus changing tint very much after the manner of Bin-Iodide of Mercury.

April 18, 1870.

The President in the chair. Twelve persons present.

Prof. D. S. Martin, exhibited a specimen of Copper Pyrites from Central Texas. This ore is worked, and reported to be very rich, yielding as much as 62 per cent. of copper; and is smelted with great ease. It is frequently found as a pseudomorph replacing wood.

The President remarked upon this specimen, that the deposit from which it was procured, was a very extensive one, being found in the same horizon in New Mexico and Arizona. These deposits have been very extensively worked by the Spaniards, and some of the ancient workings are at the present time in a state about as perfect as when abandoned by these ancient miners. They are now the abode of multitudes of bats. Specimens of wood ten feet long, and two feet in diameter occur, in which the woody fibre has been completely replaced by the Pyrites, besides which are found accumulated at the bottom of the cliffs, large quantities of silicified wood.

Prof. C. A. Seely remarked upon the occurrence of Nitre in the caves in Arkansas, and attributed its origin to the excrements and remains of the bats inhabiting those places.

The President stated that these caves were found in many places in the West, and it was to be regretted, that as yet, no systematic examination of them and their contents had been made.

The President then made some remarks on the Metalliferous deposits of the West, stating it as his opinion, that the production of Gold had passed its climax; giving his reasons for so believing. Gold is found disseminated over vast regions in the West; the accumulations in the placers having been worked for ages. He then entered into a description of the manner in which the accumulation of metal had taken place. There is still plenty of gold everywhere, but it is very difficult to separate it from the associated rock in which it is imbedded. Those deposits where it could be readily procured, are beginning to be exhausted. The mountain system of the West, considered with respect to the mineral wealth of that portion of the country, he considered divisible into belts, the Westernmost or Coast Range producing Mercury, the next Eastward or Sierra Nevada Range, is very rich in Gold. In the Rocky Mountains, the Gold is associated with Copper and Iron Pyrites. In Montana, the Gold-bearing veins are extremely rich in that metal, but very difficult to work. Between the Rocky Mountains and the Sierra Nevada, there occurs an Argentiferous belt stretching through Idaho, Nevada and Montana; it is in this region that the celebrated Comstock Lode is situated, which, up to the present time, has yielded $75,000,000. The agricultural portions of California, and the region eastward of the mountains, is of little value except for its mineral wealth, and, if it ever becomes important, it will be by the development of these deposits.

April 25, 1870.

The President in the chair. Twenty persons present.

Mr. W. J. Hays presented, in behalf of Mrs. Say, a large collection of shells contained in a Mahogany case of twenty-four drawers. This collection is a very valuable one, consisting as it does of several hundred specimens, and was made by the late Thomas Say, the husband of the donor.

On motion, the thanks of the Society were voted to Mrs. Say, for her valuable donation.

Mr. A. J. Cotheal read a letter from Mr. Archbald, at present in Italy, soliciting exchanges of the shells of the United States, and the West Indies, for those of Italy and the Mediterranean.

Prof. O. W. Morris, exhibited a portion of the stem of a Cornus, which broke in a remarkable manner in consequence, probably, of the borings of the larva of an insect present in it. On examination, Prof. D. S. Martin pronounced the larva to be that of Caladium violaceum. He also exhibited a number of fresh water shells from the Monongahela River, near Morgantown, and remarked that the shells found in the rivers east of the Alleghany Mountains were, as a general thing, elongated in outline, and thin in texture, while those west of the mountains are mostly rounded in form and thick. Dr. R. P. Stevens, remarked that the Unios of Western New York, and west of that state, present very great differences of character in the same species. The specimens found on the bar of Mud Creek are beautifully colored, while those found in other parts of the same stream are nearly devoid of color.

Prof. O. W. Morris stated that the Unios found in the Holston River, have the nacre highly colored, while those from the Clinch and Little Tennessee are colorless.

The President remarked that the fossil fresh water shells of the West, present a very great variety in form and other characters, in the earlier formations; but from the Whealden to the present time, the shells have preserved their characteristic forms throughout the whole period. The marine shells, on the contrary, have changed very greatly. In many instances whole genera have died out.

Mr. W. H. Leggett exhibited a specimen of Anemone nemorosa from Bergen Point which had the leaves covered upon the under side with a minute fungus. He remarked that this fungus is not found upon any of the fertile leaves. On motion the specimen was referred to Prof. Edwards for examination and report.

Prof. A. M. Edwards read a paper

ON THE PRESENCE OF LIVING INSECTS IN THE HUMAN BODY,

showing that several such cases were on record.

In one case a fly had been reared from a larva ejected from the human intestines. As such larva are found mostly in decayed fruit, the plan to be followed by means of which the unpleasant results sometimes, although not always, arising from the introduction of such insects by the mouth, is to avoid eating such fruit or vegetables in a raw condition, which are at all decayed.

Mr. W. J. Hays made some remarks upon the remarkable anatomy of a Currasowa dissected by him. The bird itself was only twenty-two inches in length, but the trachea being bent upon itself, was found to measure thirty inches.

May 2, 1870.

The President in the chair. Twenty-three persons present.

The Corresponding Secretary announced the decease of Dr. Gustav Magnus, of Berlin, Prussia, a Corresponding Member of the Society.

Prof. T. Egleston, Jr., exhibited a very fine cut specimen of genuine Topaz, and made some remarks with regard to that mineral. Genuine Topaz is a Silico-Fluoride of Aluminium, but the substance generally found replacing it as a gem is merely colored Quartz. The Topaz is not often found in large masses clear enough to cut, and the false

Topazes or Quartz may be distinguished where, as in the specimen exhibited, slight cleavage plains are seen; the cleavage of the two minerals being very different. Otherwise they are not readily distinguished, and on that account false Topazes are very common. White Topazes of large size and clear enough to cut are rare.

Prof. A. M. Edwards read a

Report upon a Specimen of Anemone nemorosa infested by a Fungus.

This fungus is a species quite common both in this country and Europe, upon the true leaves of the *Anemone* in early spring, and has been named *Puccinia Anemones.* In Ray's "Synopsis," (3d edition, 1724,) it is described in company with true ferns, and was for a long time supposed that the deeply cleft leaf of the *Anemone* with the brown spots upon its under side was a fern with sori. As Ray says, "this capillary was gathered by the Conjurer of Chalgrave," hence it has come to be known as the Conjurer of Chalgrave's fern. This fungus like the other microscopic parasitic ones, grows beneath the surface of the plant, throwing out its threads of mycelium among the cells, until it develops the brownish colored bodies, known as *spores* (perhaps incorrectly), and it is by the peculiar characters of these that species have been distinguished; although there seems two good reasons for supposing that these plants are not only dimorphous, as has been stated, but polymorphous, assuming different forms according to the habitat in which they are found.

In reply to the question, as to whether it was true, as was stated by farmers, that Barberry bushes infested with fungus, or mildew, conveyed that mildew to fields of wheat adjoining, which then showed the presence of "brand."

Prof. Edwards remarked that such might very likely be the case, as very little certain is known respecting the life history of these minute plants, and he was now carrying on some experiments, by infesting different plants with fungi taken from others, so as to see if the host which they inhabited modified their characters materially. He described and illustrated by means of diagrams, the characteristics of the Wheat Brand, *Puccinia graminis*, and other fungi, and expressed a hope that the Botanical members would contribute specimens of such plants, as they found to be infested by mildews, brands and smuts, for the Society's collection.

Prof. B. N. Martin exhibited several specimens of fossils, from the celebrated Phosphatic beds of South Carolina. They included a rib, vertebræ, a tooth, several shark's teeth and others. They had been taken from a portion of the stratum, covered by a branch of the Cooper River, and were secured from the bed of the stream.

The President remarked that the vertebræ and rib, were probably those of the Manatee, which had been found in this stratum. The teeth were of the Carcarodon and other extinct sharks. In this bed were found associated together, Tertiary fossils from the Eocene, Miocene and Pliocene formations, with even, perhaps, still more recent forms, as human remains had been found, which doubtless had been washed in from surface deposits. In fact this Phosphatic bed seemed to have received contributions from several strata around, whose fossils had been washed out in the course of time. Such admixture of fossils from old or even more recent strata, in portions of a particular bed were not uncommon, as in England, where Cretaceous and Triassic forms were found mingled. Prof. Shaler had recently published his investigations into these South Carolina beds, which were very extensive, and reached all along the coast, from North Carolina around into the Gulf in Georgia.

The President made some further remarks on the existence of human remains in caves in this country, in continuation of his communication at a recent meeting. He alluded to the well-known cave at Carlisle, Penn., which had been very carefully searched by Prof. Baird, of the Smithsonian Institution, whose investigations would be, it was hoped, shortly published. Beside the human remains there were found many of various mammals identical specifically with those now or lately living in the vicinity. But one remarkable fact had been developed; viz.: that in every case they were at least one quarter larger in dimensions, so that these particular animals at least would seem to have degenerated in size during the lapse of time. Thus, for instance, numerous remains of Foxes were found, have characters identical with those now living with the exception of the size. Prof. Shaler's explorations at Big Bone Lick, recently had also brought to light facts of great interest which showed that the Deer and Buffalo were comparatively new comers upon this portion of the continent. He, Dr. Newberry, had found the bones of a Buffalo on the west side of the Rocky Mountains although they were not to be seen living there at the present time. The Indians of that district had traditions of the Buffalo existing there at a recent period. All of which illustrated the change of fauna which had been for a long time and still was taking place upon this continent.

Prof. O. W. Morris read an

ABSTRACT OF THE COMPARATIVE METEOROLOGY OF THE MONTH OF MARCH FOR THE YEARS 1869 AND 1870 AND OF THE MONTH OF APRIL, 1870,

Showing that in 1869 the lowest daily mean for March was 13.76°, and for 1870 it was 24.80°, or 11.04° lower. The mean temperature for March, 1869, was 34.10°, and for 1870 it was 35.55° or 1.45° warmer. The mean of the Barometer for March, 1869, was 29.834 in., and for 1870 it was 29.772 in. The mean humidity for March, 1869, was 49.50°, and for 1870 it was 54.85°. The month of March, 1870, was thus shown to be warmer than in 1869; the Barometric pressure was a little less; and the humidity greater, although there was not so much rain. March, 1870, kept up its old reputation as the "windy month."

He also quoted from tables, prepared to show some other important facts in Meteorology. Thus, examination of the records kept for the last sixteen years, (1854—69, both inclusive) shows that the temperature during that time did not vary much, as the mean, for the sixteen years, is 52.60°, giving eight above and eight below the mean, and a range of 7° only; 1859 having the highest mean (55.66°) and 1868 the lowest (48.67°). The year 1869 was 1.1° below the average; the maximum of 1869 was nearly that of 1855; the minimum was greater than of any in the series, being 85° above zero, while 9 of the years it was below, and in 1866 it was 13° below, and in that year also the thermometer rose to 98.8°, the highest in the series.

He also read from abstracts of the temperature, &c. kept by C. Bogert, in New York city, from 1816 to 1853.

May 9, 1870.

The President in the chair. Twenty-five persons present.

Mr. R. Dinwiddie exhibited a photograph of Sir James Young Simpson, recently deceased, and made some remarks on his contributions to Medical Science.

Prof. Chas. A. Seely read a paper

On the Constitution of Ammonium-Amalgam.

He began by referring to its original discovery in 1808, by Berzelius and three other chemists, almost simultaneously. Davy's reduction of Potash and Lime, by means of the Galvanic battery, whereby the metallic base of those substances was demonstrated, preceded this presumed discovery of Ammonium-Amalgam, and probably led the way for other researches in this direction. Berzelius on this discovery of his, founded the Ammonium radicle theory, which at the present time is very generally accepted. Prof. Seely stated that he differed in opinion from most chemists as to the constitution of this Amalgam; he thought that the gases

Ammonia and Hydrogenium are only intimately mixed with the Mercury. The peculiar buttery consistence of the Amalgam he attributed to inflation or frothing of the Mercury. If this theory be a correct interpretation of the facts the gases being uncombined should obey Marriotte's law of condensation. This he considered would be the *experimentum crucis* in this case. He then prepared some of the Ammonium-Amalgam in a glass tube closed at one end and submitted it to considerable pressure by means of a piston. The contraction and expansion of the Amalgam was very clearly and evidently seen, which was apparently proportioned to the pressure exerted. On increasing the pressure to six or eight atmospheres the Amalgam became liquid like Mercury and on removing the pressure it resumed its pasty condition.

Prof. G. F. Barker, of Yale College, being called upon, offered some remarks. He thought Prof. Seely's experiment exceedingly interesting and a valuable contribution to our knowledge of Ammonium-Amalgam. He questioned, however, Prof. Seely's hypothesis as to its constitution. He asked in what condition the gaseous Hydrogen and Ammonia might be while under pressure? There was no visible escape of the gases during the compression; and the fact that on removing the pressure the Amalgam resumed its bulky nature, was opposed to Prof. Seely's physical theory.

Mr. O. Loew thought it possible to calculate the amount of Hydrogen developed by a certain quantity of Sodium, and if a portion was united with the Mercury, it would become evident by measuring the free Hydrogen evolved. He thought that Prof. Seely's experiment proved conclusively that the Amalgam was a chemical compound, and not a physical or mechanical mixture.

Dr. I. Walz remarked, that if we adopt the physical theory, we must agree that a decomposition and recomposition takes place, each time that the pressure is applied and removed.

Dr. Isidor Walz presented the following

Notes on the Extinction and Reducing Power of Mercury.

At the last meeting of the Chemical Section of the Lyceum, I drew attention to the conversion of liquid Zinc-Amalgam to a gray powder, when shaken with a solution of Potassium Bichromate. Subsequently I became convinced that this phenomenon was solely due to the extinction of the Mercury, and have made a number of experiments regarding the phenomenon of which I present the following results. It is hardly necessary to state that the Mercury used was absolutely pure. It is very difficult, but essential, to use chemically pure Mercury, as even a very small trace of a foreign metal is often sufficient to influence the results materially. The experiments were made in ordinary test-tubes, in which the materials were shaken a length of time varying from a few seconds to 10 minutes. I believe that we ought to distinguish between two methods or kinds of extinction, namely the mechanical and the chemical. The former is effected by a very large number of solutions of neutral salts, which exert no chemical action on Mercury, and even by pure water, if shaken long enough. The extinction of the Mercury in this case, is produced simply by the interposition of fine films of the liquid between the globules, into which the Mercury is separated by the mechanical agitation, and which are thus prevented from running together again. By mechanical extinction, Mercury is converted into what appears to be a fine powder, which, however, never loses its white color and metallic appearance, and under the lens its globular structure is clearly seen. Quite interesting in many cases, are the reactions which accompany the chemical extinction of Mercury, which takes place when the metal is shaken with a solution of a salt, by which it is chemically affected. In these cases, the newly-formed Mercury compounds act in the same way as the films of liquid in the former instance, preventing the separate globules from re-uniting. A finer division of the metal is obtained in less time than by the mechanical method, and the resulting metallic powder is generally of a dull gray leaden color. When a solution of Potassium Bichromate is poured upon mercury, the convexity of the surface is at once destroyed; presently the surface is tarnished and begins to look wrinkled, while at the same time a greenish-black powder commences to deposit itself. This greenish-black powder is a mixture of Chromic and Mercurous Oxide; it is formed abundantly when the two liquids are agitated more or less strongly; the Mercury is at the same time completely extinguished, and at the end of the reaction neutral Potassium Chromate alone remains in solution, which is not acted upon by Mercury. Ferric Chloride extinguishes Mercury; Ferrous and Mercurous Chlorides are formed. Potassium Permanganate also acts upon the metal; Manganic and Mercurous Oxides are deposited, while Potassic Hydrate remains in solution. Mercury shaken with Fehling's solution, is simply extinguished mechanically, when all the reagents used are pure; but when a very small quantity of Zinc-Amalgam is added, Cu_4O is reduced from the solution.

A solution of Potassium Ferricyanide does not affect the fluidity of Mercury; but when the two are shaken together, a green powder is formed in large quantities, which if allowed to stand, changes to a dark, and later still to a light blue color. Potassium Ferrocyanide appears to be formed at the same time. I am still engaged in studying this interesting reaction, and will endeavor to determine if this blue powder is Prussian blue or not. Sodium Hyposulphite, also, does not affect the Mercury physically; on agitation, however, a heavy black powder, Mercuric Sulphide, is formed. Its amount increases with the lapse of time, and in one of my test-tubes which has hardly been disturbed for weeks, the original black Sulphide has assumed a yellowish red color.

I conclude from these observations that the reducing power of pure Mercury is greater than is generally supposed, and I expect to be enabled to obtain some interesting results from an extension of these experiments.

I have repeated some of Loew's experiments, which he described at our last meeting, and can state that similar results are obtained by substituting Palladium Bichloride for the Platinum salt. I cannot, however, yet coincide with him in considering his final product as Hydrogenium-Amalgam, as by every method by which it has yet been made, it contains another metal besides Mercury and Hydrogen, namely, either Platinum, Palladium, Gold or Silver, in no inconsiderable proportion.

May 16, 1870.

The President in the chair. Thirty-seven persons present.

Prof. D. S. Martin exhibited a series of fossils from the Phosphate beds of South Carolina, consisting of vertebræ, of fish, sharks' teeth, a reptilian tooth, besides mollusca, all in a good state of preservation, and illustrating in a marked manner the mingling of remains from various strata, ranging from the Eocene to the present day, which is characteristic of of these beds.

Prof. B. N. Martin, exhibited a very fine crystal of gold from California, being remarkable as a singularly distorted hemitrope.

Prof. A. M. Edwards, exhibited a fine series of crystallized micas from New York Island, in some of which the black and white varieties were mingled in the same crystal.

Prof. B. N. Martin, called attention to a case of the sudden simultaneous discharge of pollen, from all parts of a large bush of Paper Mulberry, (*Broussonetia papyrifera*).

Dr. H. Carrington Bolton, read a paper entitled :

RISE AND FALL OF THE DEFUNCT ELEMENTS.

A complete catalogue of so-called "Defunct Elements," is nowhere found, but notices of their *rise* and *fall* are scattered throughout periodical literature; from these the following list has been compiled, which, if incomplete, is still comparatively full. Within the limits of this abstract, little more than the date, name of discoverer, and references can be given. Taking them up in chronological order, the first is

TERRA NOBILIS, discovered in 1777, by Tobern Bergmann, who extracted it from diamonds.

HYDROSIDERUM, discovered by Meyer, in 1780, and obtained by dissolving crude Iron in acids, the residue being the new element. It is called in German *Wassereisen*. Klaproth showed that it consisted of Iron combined with Phosphorus. (Schrift. Ges. Nat. Freunde, Berlin, II. 334 and III. 380.)

SATURNUM, discovered in 1784, by Monnet. (Journal de Physique, XXVIII.)

DIAMANTHSPATHERDE, discovered in 1788, by Klaproth, in corundum. (Beschäft. Ges. Nat. Freunde, Berlin, VIII. St. 4.)

AUSTRALIA, discovered in 1790, by Wedgewood, in Sand from Australia, and examined by Hatchett, who pronounced it a mixture of Aluminia, Iron Oxide, Silica and Graphite.

NAMELESS EARTH. Fernandez, 1799. (Scherer's Allg. J.)

AGUSTERDE was extracted from the mineral known as *sächsische-beryll*, by Trommsdorff, in the year 1800. Vauquelin showed it to consist of Phosphate of Lime, the mineral being now known as apatite. (Scherer's Allg. J., IV. 312; also Gehlen's Allg. J., I. 445.)

SILENE, Proust, 1803. (Journal de Physique.)

PNEUM ALKALI, discovered by Hahnemann in 1801. It was sold at the price of one gold Frederic the ounce, but eventually proved to be Borax.

NICCOLANUM, was found in Cobalt ores by Richter, in 1805,

but was shown to consist of a mixture of Nickel, Cobalt, Arsenic and Iron. (Gilb. Ann., XIX. 377.)

ANDRONIA, an earth which existed only in the imagination of J. J. Winterl, of Pesth. He prepared it by igniting charcoal with saltpeter and exhausting with water, the residue consisting of *Andronia.* His statements excited much controversy; a committee of the French Academy of Sciences appointed to examine it, proved that it was but a mixture of Lime, Alumina, Iron Oxide and Silica, which materials it was suggested, came from the earthen crucibles in which Winterl conducted the experiments. (Gehlens J. und Gilberts Annalen.)

THELIKE, discovered by Winterl.

NITRICUM, is the imaginary body, which according to Berzelius, united to Oxygen formed Nitrogen.

ARAEON, is in accordance with Meissner's views, *ponderable caloric;* thus Hydrochloric acid is composed of two equivalents of Oxygen and one of water, combined with ARAEON and the imaginary radical MURIUM. (Handwörterbuch.)

JUNONIUM, discovered by Thomson, in 1811, but its identity with Cerium was soon proved by Wollaston. (Phil. Mag., XXXVI. 278, also Gilb. Ann., XLIV. 113.)

THORIUM; the first element known by this name, proved to be Phosphate of Yttria. (Schweigg., XXI. 15; Pogg. Ann., IV. 145.)

VESTIUM, discovered in 1818, by von Vest. Faraday showed that it consisted of a mixture of Iron, Nickel, Sulphur and Arsenic. (Gilb. Ann., LIX. and LXII.)

WODANIUM, extracted from the so-called *Wodankies* by Lampadius, 1818, but shown by Stromeyer to consist of Nickel, Arsenic, &c. The mineral is now known as Gersdorffite. (Gilb. Ann., LX. and LXIV.)

CRODONIUM, discovered by Trommsdorff in 1820, was found in an incrustation, on a carboy of Sulphuric acid imported from England. Its name is derived from *Crodo,* an idol held in veneration by the ancient people of Thuringia. Trommsdorff afterwards showed that it was but Lime and

Magnesia, rendered impure by Copper and Iron. (Gilb. Ann., LXV. and LXVI.)

APYRE, Brugnatelli, 1821. (Gilb. Ann., LXVII.)

PLURANIUM, POLINIUM and RUTHENIUM, all three discovered by Osann, (1828), in Platinum ores from the Ural Mts. (Pogg. Ann., XIII. and XIV.)

DONIUM, discovered in 1836, by Richardson, in a mineral from Aberdeen, but its identity with Glucinum was afterwards established by Heddle. (Ann. Chem. Pharm., XIX. and XXIII.)

TREENIUM, discovered by Boase, in 1836, and partly supposed identical with Donium. (Thomson's Records Gen. Sci., IV. 20.)

TERBIUM, found accompanying Erbium in Gadolinite, by Mosander (1843), but pronounced by Berlin (1860), to have no existence. (Ann. Chem. Pharm., LXVIII. CXXXI. CXXXVII, &c.

PELOPIUM, discovered by Rose, in 1846, and supposed to accompany Niobium (Columbium). Rose has shown that Pelopic acid is convertible into Niobic acid, and this into Hyponiobic acid. (Pogg. Ann., LXIX. and XC.)

ILMENIUM, discovered in 1846, by Hermann. (Journ. pr. Ch., XXXVIII. and XL. also Pogg. Ann., LXXIII.

ARIDIUM, discovered in 1850, by Ullgren. Journ. pr. Ch., LII. Ann. Ch. Pharm., LXXVI. and LXXXVIII.)

DONARIUM, discovered in 1851, by Bergemann. (Ann. Ch. Pharm., LXXX. and LXXXIV.)

THALIUM, discovered in 1852, by Owen. (Am. J. Sci., (2) XIII. XVI. and XVII.)

NAMELESS METAL of Platinum group, discovered by Genth, in 1853. (Am. J. Sci., (2) XV.)

DIANUM, extracted from Tantalite from Finland, by von Kobell, (1860). H. Rose questioned its identity, also St. Claire-Deville and Herrmann. Von Kobell distinguished it from Niobic and Tantalic acids, by the formation of a deep blue solution, when treated with Tin and Hydrochloric acid. (Ann. Ch. Pharm., CXIV. and CXXXVI.)

Wasium, discovered by Bahr, in 1862. (Pogg. Ann., CXIX. 572; Journ. pr. Ch., XCI. 316.)

Nameless earth of the Calcium group, Dupré, 1861.

Nameless metal of Platinum group, Chandler, 1862. (Am. J. Sci., (2) XXXIII.)

Jargonium; under this head are collected the various oxides supposed to accompany Zirconia; it appears that six chemists have independently suspected the compound nature of Zirconia, as follows:

(1) *Norium*	in	1845,	by Svanberg.
(2) *Nameless earth*	in	1854,	" Sjögren.
(3) *Nameless earth*	in	1864,	" Nylander.
(4) *Nigrium*	in	1866,	" Church.
(5) *Jargonium*	in	1869,	" Sorby.
(6) *Nameless earth*	in	1869,	" Loew.

The references are as follows:

(1) Berz. Jahresb., XXV. Journ. pr. Chem., LVII. and XCVII. (2) Journ. pr. Ch., LV. and LVII. (3) Acta Univers. Lundensis, 1864. (4) Chem. News, 1869. (5) Idem. (6) Annals. N. Y. Lyc. Nat. Hist., IX. 211.

Summing up all the reactions, by which these unknown Oxides are distinguished from Zirconia, we have the following table.

(1) Great variation in atomic weight of Oxide, Svanberg.
(2) Solubility of Oxide in Oxalic Acid, Svanberg, Sjögren, Loew.
(3) Solubility of Chloride in Hydrochloric Acid, Svanberg & Forbes.
(4) Precipitation by Ferrocyanide of Potassium, Sjögren.
(5) Insolubility of Tartrate in Tartaric Acid, Forbes.
(6) Solubility of double Potassium Sulphates, Nylander.
(7) Variation in nature of Sulphates, Loew.
(8) High. Sp. Gr. of Oxide (5·5 instead of 4·3), Sjögren.
(9) Black absorption bands of spectrum, Church, Sorby.

(2) Some misapprehension exists on the second point, owing to the fact that most text books state that Zirconia is *insoluble* in Oxalic Acid, whereas, Berlin, in 1853, showed on the con-

trary that Zirconia is readily and completely *soluble* in Oxalic Acid.

In Finkener's revised edition of H. Rose's work, the error contained in earlier editions is corrected.

(8) Berlin found the Sp. Gr. of Zirconia from Catapleite =4.9, precisely the mean of the other two.

(9) The manner in which Sorby has explained the last point is familiar to all.

Frederick Prime, Jr., read a paper

On the Metallurgy of Argentiferous Galenas,

giving details of the several processes at present in use, with their various advantages and disadvantages. He entered into a detailed account of the methods put into practice in Freiberg, and showed how these could and would be used in the United States.

Dr. J. S. Newberry read a paper on

The Ancient Lakes of Western America, their Deposits and Drainage.

He first alluded to the wonderful collections of fossil plants and animals, brought by Dr. Hayden from the country bordering the upper Missouri, which are from deposits made in extensive fresh-water lakes which, at one time, occupied much of the region lying immediately east of the Rocky Mountains. The water of these lakes was first salt or brackish, as the remains of oysters and similar estuary forms show. By continental elevation the whole country west of the Mississippi, was raised out of the Cretaceous sea, and these estuaries became lakes inclosed by raised dry land. The knowledge of this country from the Mississippi to the Pacific Ocean, has been accumulated by various explorers besides himself, as Dr. Hayden, Mr. George Gibbs, Professors W. P. Blake and Thomas Antisell, and Prof. J. D. Whitney and the state Geological Survey of California, and Baron Richtofen, the lamented Rémond, Drs. Shiel, Wislizenus and others. Besides Mr. Clarence King has explored a large tract of this country but his very important contributions have not, as yet, been made public.

The general character of the topography of the region west of the Mississppi has been given by these great lines of elevation traversing the country from north to south. There are the Rocky Mountains, the Sierra Nevada and the Coast Ranges. The last is the most modern, and is composed, for the most part, of Miocene Testiary rocks. Parallel with this lies a narrow trough, in California traversed by the Sacramento and San Joachin Rivers, encroached on by the mountains at places, but still in Oregon and Washington, traversed by the Willamette and Cowletz Rivers. These two sections are drained through the Golden Gate and Columbia. The mountain barriers formerly caused the valleys to consist of great inland lakes which are now only represented by the chain of small pieces of water still to be seen in that region of country.

East of the Sierra Nevada and between it and the Rocky Mountains is another still larger basin. For a thousand miles it has no openings to the westward which are less than five thousand feet above the sea, but at three points there are gate-ways, which may be passed, but little above the sea level. These are the *Cañons* of the Sacramento (Pit River) the Klamath and the Columbia. These have been cut through by the drainage of the interior of the continent. The former beds of the lakes have thus been left dry and waste—the only real desert on the North American continent. The Sierra Nevada is older than the Coast Ranges and projected above the ocean, though not to its present altitude, previous to the Tertiary and even Cretaceous ages. This we learn from the fact that strata belonging to these formations cover its base. The mass of the Sierra Nevada is granitic rocks and metamorphic slates, proved by the California Survey to be Triassic and Jurassic. These slates are traversed by the gold-bearing Quartz.

East of the Sierra Nevada is a high and broad plateau five hundred miles wide, and from four to eight hundred feet in altitude and reaches south into Mexico. This mountain belt was once the margin of the Pacific ocean. Its crest is crowned by volcanic cones like gigantic towers of a fortification. The central portion of this plateau was called by Fremont "the great basin" as it forms a hydrographic basin drained by the Columbia and Colorado. The former makes its way to the ocean through a gorge in the Cascade Mountains, whilst the latter escapes to the south through a series of Cañons, of which the most important is nearly a thousand miles in length, and from three to six thousand feet deep. In Vol. VI. of the Pacific Rail Road Reports the country of the Columbia is described and the reasons for concluding that it had cut its way through the Cascade Mountains, and similar facts were observed in the district drained by the Klamath and Pit Rivers. Certain peculiarities are to be seen in the country between the Sierra Nevada and Rocky Mountains. In the northern and middle portions of the great table lands the surface is somewhat thickly set by short and isolated mountain ranges, sometimes called "the lost mountains." These rise like islands above the level of the plain, and are generally composed of volcanic or metamorphic rocks. The spaces between them are level desert surfaces. Towards the north and west, on the tributaries of the Columbia, Klamath or Pit Rivers, the plateau is cut by these streams, and the deposit can be examined. The rocks are nearly horizontal, some are coarse volcanic ash, with fragments of pumice and scoriæ. Others denominated "concrete" resemble the old Roman Cement. Many are quite white and are generally known as "chalk-beds" though they contain no lime. The late Prof. J. W. Bailey determined these to consist of the remains of fresh water species of Diatomaceæ. The stratification and horizontality of these beds show them to have been thrown down from great bodies of water which once covered the greater part of these level plains.

From south-western Idaho and eastern Oregon, have lately been brought large collections of animal and vegetable fossils, of great variety and interest. The plants were mostly collected by Rev. Thomas Congdon, of the Dalles, Oregon, at great risk of life and while exposed to great hardships, on the flanks of the Blue Mountains. They are apparently Miocene, forming twenty or thirty species, nearly all new, and which represent a forest growth as varied and luxurious as can be found on any portion of the continent. The animal remains came mostly from the banks of Castle Creek in the Owyhee district, Idaho. These were sent by Mr. J. W. Adams of, Ruby City. They consist of bones of the Mastodon, Rhinocerous, Horse, Elk and other large mammals of which the species are probably in some cases new, in others identical with those obtained from the deposits examined by Dr. Hayden. There are also bones of birds and great numbers of the bones and teeth of fish. These last are Cyprinoids applied to *Mylopharodon*, *Milocheilus*, *&c.*, some three feet and more in length. Also many fresh water shells as *Unio*, *Corbicula*, *Melania* and *Planorbis.* These illustrate the inhabitants of the extinct lakes which were of a much larger size and greater depth than the great fresh-water lakes which now lie upon our northern frontier. Between these were areas covered with a luxuriant and beautiful vegetation and inhabited by herds of elephant and other great mammals. In the streams were numbers of fish and mollusks of species now extinct. Gradually these lakes evaporated and at last became dry. In the Klamath lakes and Suisun bay we have their remanants, whilst on the Columbia the drainage streams have cut cañons two thousand feet deep. At times the peace and quiet of this country, was disturbed by violent volcanic eruptions from the peaks of the Sierra Nevada, which ejected showers of ashes covering the land and filling the lakes, as is seen in the strata now existing, some ten and twenty feet thick. Sometimes lava was thrown out and covered hundreds of miles of surface, and is now seen as solid basalt. Then quiet reigned, and new fresh water deposits were formed, only to be succeeded by other volcanic disturbances. Some parts of this plateau have not been drained, and the remains of the ancient lakes now exist as Salt lake, Pyramid lake and others. These are gradually diminishing, as is to be seen by indications all around their borders, where we can trace ancient shore lines. The alkali plains and salt flats, mark the places of dried up lakes; all of these still existing being excessively salt. This is the state of things at the north. In the south, the great Colorado plateau is without mountain barriers or local basins, and there are few traces of extinct lakes. This arid district was once a beautiful and fertile plain, drained by the Colorado which, on the western margin poured over a precipice five thousand feet or more high, into the Gulf of California, which then reached several thousand miles farther north than it does now. In time the river cut its way farther back through the subjacent rocks, and at last formed that remarkable gorge, nearly a thousand miles long and three to six thousand feet deep. As the channel deepened, the country around became dryer, until it was the arid plain we find it now. Almost no rain falls on this plain, therefore the walls of the cañon remain sharp-cut precipices unaffected by moisture.

On the east of the Rocky mountains, is the great plateau country of the plains, which differs from the country to the west, by not being bordered on its east by a mountain chain, but sloping gradually to the Mississippi. Its surface was also covered by great fresh water lakes, larger if not more numerous than those now existing on our northern boundary. From the northern portion of this plateau, Dr. Hayden has brought his specimens, and he has there obtained a harvest of scientific truth, which will form for him an enduring and enviable monument. He has studied the deposits which accumulated in these lakes, and they are very rich in specimens of both animal and vegetable life. The vertebrate remains have been studied by Dr. Leidy, who has published his investigations in the splendid monograph so well known, and which forms a contribution to palæontology, not second in value or interest to that made by Cuvier, by his illustrations of the fossils from the Paris basin, nor to that of Falconer and Courtly, descriptive of the Sewalik hills of India. The first instalment of the plants have been described by Dr. Newberry, in the Report of Col. W. F. Reynolds, U. S. A., not yet published. The descriptions are published, in the

Annals of the Lyceum of Natural History of New York, Vol. 9, 1868.

The general conclusions from these examinations have greatly enlarged the flora of the Tertiary and Cretaceous periods. Since then largely additional material has been collected by Dr. Hayden, Mr. Congdon and Dr. Le Comte, and Dr. Newberry; and in Alaska by Mr. W. H. Dall and Capt. Howard, and by others in Greenland.

The flora and fauna of the lake deposits on both sides of the Rocky Mountains apparently belong to one and the same geological age, and tell the same story as to topography, climatic conditions and development of animal and vegetable life. There is a striking difference in one particular between the deposits east and west. In Oregon, Idaho and Nevada, volcanic material has accumulated in the lake basins to a much greater extent than on the east of the mountains. The deposits of the Upper Missouri region are shales, marls and earthy limestones, with immense quantities of Lignite and almost no traces of volcanic material. The animals and vegetables of the Tertiary here were in much greater number than now. This existed long enough for thousands of feet to accumulate in the lake basins, and sometimes these deposits are found turned up on edge on the flanks of the mountains, showing that this chain although existing in embryo from the earliest palæozoic ages, has been subjected to great modifications. The collections made by Dr. Hayden at various points differ among themselves. In every bed are new species, and between some deposits there are no connecting links. In the beginning of the Cretaceous the land surface and climate of this continent was similar to the present period, the trees for the most part belonged to the same genera. Then the most of the region west of the Mississippi sunk beneath the ocean and the Cretaceous deposits were made containing more tropical species. There were islands in this western sea, and the gulf stream had a course north and west from the Gulf of Mexico, to the Arctic Sea. In the earlier Tertiary ages the continent here emerged from the ocean and approached the previous and present conditions, indicated by the flora. In this category is to be placed the Green River Tertiary beds, those of Mississippi studied by Lesquereux, and those of Brandon, Vermont. In the Miocene the continental surface was broader, the western lakes were fresh and the vegetation very much like that of the present day. A few palms then grew as far north as the Yellow Stone River, and a flora flourished in Alaska and Greenland as varied and as luxuriant as now grows along the fortieth parallel. At this time land connected Europe, this continent and China, as the flora in this region was essentially the same, a large number of plants being common to the three continents. The mammals were peculiar; over our western plains rolled herds of great quadrupeds rivaling in number and variety those of southern Africa at the present time. This state of things continued during the Pliocene age and up to the ice period. In the middle Tertiary the climates of Alaska and Greenland were those of New York and St. Louis at present. Then came the Glacial epoch, and the climate of Greenland of the present time is brought down to New York and all the northern portion of the continent is wrapped in ice. This change of climate was gradual, but the animals and vegetables were driven southward until the glaciers reached the thirty-eighth or fortieth parallel when a temperate climate prevailed in Mexico and only on the southern border would the temperature be what it had previously been on our northern border. Thus nearly all the animals were exterminated or forced into very narrow limits in southern Mexico.

Plants bore their expatriation better, and as a consequence we find the present flora of our continent much more like that of the Miocene than is our fauna, though most of the forest-trees have become extinct. Of these the Glyptostrobus is an example, which grew all over our continent and northern Europe. In the glacial period it was exterminated except in China where it now grows. So when we compare the present flora of China and Japan with that of the eastern half of our continent we find the strongest proofs of their relationship; many species are identical, while others are but slightly changed. Some of the great mammals of the preglacial period bade defiance to these changes, as the Mastodon and Elephant, both of which could endure great changes of climate, and the Mammoth, we know, was defended from cold by a thick coat of hair and wool. We find its remains imbedded in peat-bogs and marshes where they were mired and suffocated and it is even claimed that here, as in Europe, it was contemporaneous with man.

After the conclusion of the reading of Dr. Newberry's paper, Prof. A. M. Edwards made some remarks on the microscopical examination of the fresh water Infusorial deposits of the west, and classification of these and the marine strata, containing microscopical organisms which he had adopted. Besides the recent deposits, made up for the most part of muds of both marine and fresh water origin, we have Lacustrine sedimentary deposits, now forming in lakes and ponds, and which belong to the present or Post Tertiary Period. The Sub-Plutonic or lake deposits of the west, only found as yet in that part of our continent where volcanic action has prevailed, and the marine deposits of the coast Range in California, Virginia and Maryland on the Atlantic coast, Japan, Payta in Peru, Moron in Spain, the Island of Jutland in Denmark, and the Islands of Trinidad and Barbadoes, all of which were Miocene Tertiary. A full exposition of this subject, would be published in a future volume of the California Geological Survey, upon which he was now engaged.

May 23, 1870.

The President in the chair. Twenty-two persons present.

Prof. A. M. Edwards, reported upon two specimens of plants referred to him, and supposed to have growing upon them microscopic Fungi. On one of them he had seen indications of *Æcidium* which looked like *Æ. Berberidis,* found on the Barberry. This plant, he remarked, was of interest at the present time as De Bary has ascertained that the spores of the Wheat blight, *Puccinia graminis* do not germinate when sprinkled upon the leaves and stalks of the cereals, which this must infests, while they will germinate on the leaves of the Barberry, and there give rise to the *Æcidium Berberidis.* The spores of this again will not grow upon the Barberry but on the wheat produce *Uredo* and thereafter *Puccinia.* This proves that these hitherto supposed distinct genera are but stages of one species.

Prof. T. Egleston Jr. exhibited a fine suite of crystallized diamonds including about all of the known forms in which this gem is found. They varied in color as well as form and many were curiously distorted as well as twins. The distortions of this mineral are very numerous and of great interest to the mineralogist, as well as dealer in gems. The cube is always opaque. Even if the crystaline form were not well marked, yet a diamond could be told from its peculiar cleavage, which was unmistakable. This cleavage was taken advantage of often in preparing gems for cutting, but sometimes it could not be employed on account of the shape of the stone which would be injured in such cases.

Prof. A. M. Edwards read a

Note on Itacolumnite.

To those accustomed to the use of the Microscope it is not a matter of surprise that persons who do not commonly employ that instrument in research should make very serious mistakes in interpreting what they think they see by means of it; the more especially when high powers of magnification are made use of. The delicacy of manipulation necessary to work with the microscope at all satisfactorally and the education of the eye required for the proper seeing by means of it are not generally understood, so that those who are not skilled microscopists are extremely liable to be led into error.

What I am inclined to consider a case of this kind has lately been brought to my attention and I am persuaded to make a note of it the more for the purpose of correcting a grave error in investigation and one which is, strange to say, readily demonstrated to be an error.

In 1867 (Amer. Jour. Science, Vol. XLIV.) Dr. C. Wetherill published a well-written and seemingly-exhaustive paper setting forth some "Experiments on Itacolumnite with the explanation of its flexibility and its relation to the formation of the diamond." In attempting to elucidate the flexibility of this rock he has made use of the microscope and, in fact, mainly draws his conclusions from the revelations which he supposes that instrument makes. Some specimens of Italcolumnite, varying in tint from almost pure white to a rusty red tint and in texture from finely granular to coarse and distinctly laminated, having come into my hands, I have been enabled to examine into this point of structure and attendant flexibility, which I have done with some care.

It is well known that Itacolumnite is the accompanient and often the matrix of the diamond, hence the interest which attaches to its peculiarities, as it would seem in some way to be connected with the occurrence or formation of that gem. Detecting dark colored grains in it Dr. Wetherill considers them to be black diamonds and doubtless he is correct in his supposition, but with this portion of his paper I do not desire to deal at the present time. It is with regard to the structure of the sandstone whereby it becomes flexible to the remarkable degree so evident when thin slabs are examined. The stone is plainly laminated and has clearly been thrown down beneath water, it being readily cleavable into more or less distinctly marked laminæ.

Almost universally the flexibility is attributed to the presence of Mica but the brighter-colored specimens which I have
ˆn no Mica and yet possess the property of
ənt to a very marked degree. Even in the
ıens there are large portions in which no Mica
Wetherill says that by examining the Ita-

columnite by means of the microscope he has been enabled to ascertain that the "flexibility is due to *small and innumerable ball and socket joints* which exist throughout the mass of the stone very uniformly. Each joint permits a slight movement which is always greater in one direction." Now I must say that, though I have come to the investigation prepared with considerable faith, yet, after many careful examinations, I was never able to force my imagination to the extent of getting it to show me anything resembling ball and socket joints. The examination need not always be made of the opaque sandstone, but portions can be roughly crushed and mounted in Canada Balsam so that light may be transmitted through them and the mode of their interlocking plainly made evident. The fact is that the rock is made up of small, broken, irregular masses of transparent sand which evidently have not been carried any great distance by water, as their sharp edges have not been at all abraded, but, on the contrary, remain, but they have evidently been broken off from a rock which had a conchoidal fracture, they being little plates of extremely irregular outline. Thus when they settled in the liquid in which we can suppose them to be thrown down they naturally, for the most part, distributed themselves with their greatest axes in the same direction, and hence the lamination and cleavage of the rock itself. We can readily understand that in such a rock, if the particles were not strongly held together, that they would possess a certain amount of motion one over the other, and this motion would be most marked in a direction at right angles to the lamination, which is the case. But, also, such a rock would not be elastic, only flexible, and gradually, after several times bending, be broken. Such is exactly the case with Itacolumnite. In fact any one possessing a microscope and a fragment of this rock, can readily verify my observations and demonstrate that Dr. Wetherill's proposed name of Articulite is inappropriate for Itacolumnite. In conclusion, I would mention that grains of the crushed rock when put up in Canada Balsam become very beautiful objects for examination by means of the Micro-Polariscope, exhibiting a gorgeous display of colors when the interposing Selenite film is used.

Dr. T. A. Tellkampf read a paper on *Ascidia Manhattensis*, describing its anatomy, habits and mode of reproduction in detail. This paper is to be published in full in the Annals of the Lyceum.

May 30, 1870.

The President in the chair. Twenty-four persons present.

Dr. L. Feuchtwanger exhibited a well-preserved specimen of *Icthyosaurus tenuirostris* nearly three feet in length, from the Lias of Wurtemburg. Also a specimen of Dendritic Manganese from the Hot springs of Arkansas and a remarkable specimen of the same upon the rounded surface of a pebble from the bed of the Stanislaus River, California. He remarked that he considered that the mode of formation of these Dendrites had not been satisfactorily explained as yet; the specimen upon the rounded surface not being explainable by the means usually employed.

Dr. J. S. Newberry called attention to some curious facts with regard to the red-colored sedimentary rocks; illustrating his remarks with specimens of Potsdam Sandstone from Lake Superior and Red Shale of the Onondaga Salt group, from near Syracuse. All of these sedimentary deposits, which are strongly colored with the Red Oxide of Iron have been found to be singularly wanting in fossiliferous remains and this is the more remarkable as it can hardly be supposed that the seas from which they were thrown down were so destitute of organic life as this fact would lead us to suppose. On the specimens exhibited there were circular spots, often over an inch in diameter, the prevailing color of which was either whitish or greenish, but at the centre was always a seeming nucleus of a darker tint. This central spot was undoubtedly of organic origin and was the last traces left of the living being whose carbonaceous material had reduced the Peroxide of Iron to a Proto-compound, showing itself in the change of color from red to white or green. The same oxidizing agency which had Peroxidized the Iron had decomposed the organic form, which had hence disappeared, as these deposits were doubtless thrown down from a slowly retreating sea the animal remains being thus gradually and slowly exposed to the disintegrating and oxidizing effect of the atmosphere. A similar instance of the obliteration of organic remains on the shores of a sea teeming in animal life was to be seen in the mud-floats of the Bay of Fundy, where the great tides laid bare extensive tracts in which few traces of organisms were to be found. The Medina Sandstone, which is also red in color, contains no fossil remains, only casts which have been left to show where organisms once existed.

Mr. George Gibbs said that he had remarked the fact of the paucity in organic remains of red colored rocks in the deposits of the Rocky Mountains and other points along the 49th parallel. Ripple marks and rain-drop impressions were common, showing the exposure of the deposits previous to, and during hardening. The red jaspers of this region, however, had the impressions of bi-valve mollusca scattered throughout them.

June 6, 1870.

Prof. B. M. Martin, Vice President, in the chair. Twenty-one persons present.

Dr. L. Feuchtwanger exhibited a remarkably-fine specimen of crystallized Cinnabar from California, and some crystals of Quartz from the Hot Springs of Arkansas, showing marked Striæ upon the prismatic faces.

Dr. Isidor Walz exhibited to the Lyceum a fungus which grows on the calcareous rocks of Florida. It is said to possess narcotic properties and is used by the natives to some extent as a substitute for tobacco. He next showed a specimen of metallic Manganese and of the slag, obtained by reducing the Oxide of Manganese with coal in a Siemen's furnace. The Manganese shown resembled white iron to a considerable extent and contains a large quantity of carbon. Four and a half pounds of metallic regulus were obtained from ten pounds of ore. The production of this metal is part of a new process for the manufacture of steel, invented and patented by Mr. Chas. Bain, of Brooklyn. A small quantity of Manganese is added to iron and after fusion has taken place the latter is converted into an excellent steel.

The speaker also passed around a specimen of

ARTIFICIAL ALIZARINE,

In the shape of a yellowish-green paste manufactured by a process somewhat differing from those published heretofore. He also exhibited crystals of Alizarine obtained from this mass by sublimation, mordanted cloth dyed in a bath of artificial Alizarine, solutions of the substance in Alkalis and other proofs of the identity of the artificial product with that derived from the madder plant. In connection with these specimens he made the following remarks:

Alizarine was first obtained from madder by Robiquet and Colin in 1826 by sublimation. Schenck gave it the formula $C_{14}H_{10}O_4$, according to which it would be derived from Anthracene, while Wolff and Strecker proposed $C_{10}H_6O_3$, referring it to Naphthaline. Debus proposed the formula $C_{30}H_{20}O_9$, Rochleder $C_{60}H_{30}O_{19}$. Schützenberger doubled Strecker's formula and writes $C_{20}H_{12}O_6$. The dispute about the true formula of Alizarine gave rise to many investigations on the subject by a large number of chemists and was finally settled by Messrs. Græbe and Liebermann, who succeeded in obtaining Anthracene by heating Alizarine with powdered Zinc. They addressed themselves after this discovery to the synthesis of Alizarine from Anthracene and succeeded in this about a year and a half ago.

Anthracene $C_{14}H_{10}$, is a carburetted Hydrogen, obtained from coal tar and belonging to the same type as Benzole; in fact it may be considered as being formed by the *condensation* of three molecules of Benzole into one, as illustrated in the following graphic formula:

```
CH—CH=CH              CH—CH=C—CH=C—CH=CH
||    |               ||    |    |    |
CH—CH=CH              CH—CH=C—CH=C—CH=CH
```

Benzole C_6H_6 Anthracene $C_{14}H_{10}$

In 1838 Woskressensky obtained a substance, called Quinone by distilling Quinic Acid with Sulphuric Acid and black Oxide of Manganese. Its formula is $C_6H_4O_2$. A similar substance, Anthraquinone was obtained by Laurent, derived from Anthracene. They are constituted as follows:

```
CH—CH=CO              CH—CH=C—CH=C—CH=CO
||       >            ||    |    |       >
CH—CH=CO              CH—CH=C—CH=C—CH=CO
```

Quinone $C_6H_4O_2$ Anthraquinone $C_{14}H_8O_2$

Græbe and Liebermann conceived the opinion that Alizarine, whose properties as a weak Acid have long been recognized, might be the Quinone Acid of Anthracene and could be obtained by substituting two Hydrogen atoms in Anthraquinone by the Hydroxyl group, OH. Strictly speaking Alizarine, according to this formula and the manner of its formation, is not an Acid, as it does not contain the group COOH, but it must be considered as a diatomic Phenol. In the constitutional formula given above I have assigned the two Hydroxyls to contiguous Carbon atoms because this explains on the simplest manner the compounds which Alizarine forms with diatonic metals, Ba, Ca, &c. By treatment with Bromine they first obtained the Bibromide of Anthraquinone:

$$C_{14}H_8O_2 + 4\,Br = C_{14}H_6Br_2\,O_2 + 2\,HBr.$$

This Bromide heated with potassic Hydrate yielded Alizarate of Potassium:

$$C_{14}H_6Br_2O_2 + 4\,KOH = C_{14}H_6K_2O_4 + 2\,KBr + 2\,H_2O.$$

This Alizarate may be decomposed by Acids by which a flocculent yellow precipitate is formed, which is Alizarine, $C_{14}H_8O_4$. The following graphic formula may represent its constitution for the present.

```
HOC—CH=C—CH=C—CH=CO
 ||      |      |    | >
HOC—CH=C—CH=C—CH=CO
```

Alizarine.

Science had thus presented to the world for the first time an artificial method of preparing a natural dye-stuff; but in order to make the process practically applicable some cheaper substitute for the too expensive Bromine had to be found. This was discovered in Sulphuric Acid which gives with Anthraquinone Disulphoanthraquinonic Acid $C_{14}H_8(SO_3)_2O_2$. With caustic Potash this yields Sulphite and Alizarate of Potassium, by a reaction similar to that by which the Bibromide of Anthraquinone is converted into the Potassium Salt of Alizarine.

After this theoretical disquisition the speaker dwelt on the question of the identity of artificial and natural Alizarine and gave a brief summary of the opinions arrived at by prominent European chemists. The attention of the Lyceum was called to the fact, that a Potassic solution of the artificial Alizarine exhibited had a very slight purplish tinge compared with a similar solution of the product obtained from madder, which was also shown. The colors obtained from artificial Alizarine are as fast and far brighter than these obtained from madder. The speaker concluded by pointing out the consequences which the introduction of artificial Alizarine as a substitute for madder would be likely to produce in the art of dyeing and printing cloth and the difficulty which at present seemed to render unprofitable its manufacture on a large scale, namely a limited supply of Anthracene, saying that it would be well for American chemists to examine our natural bituminous and resinous deposits for this substance, which is probably destined to play a great rôle in the technology of the future.

Prof. O. W. Morris read a

REPORT ON METEOROLOGY FOR THE MONTH OF MAY, 1870.

He showed that the Barometer had been highest at 9 A. M. on the 18th, when it reached 30·245 inches; and lowest at 7 A. M. on the 7th, when it was 29·356 inches. The monthly rain had been 889 inches.

The Thermometer was highest at 2 P. M. on the 16th, when it stood at 83° F., and lowest at 7 P M. on the 11th, when it was 47° F. These observations were taken under the Northernmost portico of the Cooper Union building, at a point where the sun never reached. The warmest day was the 16th, when the mean temperature was 75°16 F., and the coldest the 11th, when the mean temperature was 47°50 F. There had been rain on 17 days and the depth was 3.08 inches. There were six thunder showers during the month.

Prof. A. M. Edwards read the following paper:

ON THE PREPARATION OF SPECIMENS OF SOUNDINGS FOR THE MICROSCOPE.

In the course of his gatherings it not unfrequently happens that the microscopist acquires specimens of the bottom of the ocean, from various localities, which, if properly prepared furnish him with many beautiful objects for observation and study. And the beauty of these objects, the remains of once-living organisms, are of such a marked character and present so many points for admiration that even to the unscientific observer they become sources of pleasure often leading to farther enquiry into their life-history, so that imperceptibly almost and by gradual degrees the possessor becomes a student in fact and is induced to follow up his investigations to some practical end.

At the present time such specimens are of especial interest on account of the remarkable revelations made by the deep-sea dredging lately carried on upon our coast and in Europe and the bearing of these specimens upon Geology, Zoology as well as other branches of science. The immense tracts covered by what Dr. Carpenter has characteristically termed "Globigerina-mud," on account of it teeming with Foramenifera so called and the connection of Prof. Huxley's "Coccoliths" and Coccospheres" with the formation of the chalk-beds of the Cretaceous open up to the microscopists an universe of new facts for investigation. Added to these Calcareous organisms the specimens of sea-bottom present us with siliceous forms, both animal and vegetable, of surprising delicacy and beauty of outline and structure and it was to these last named that my attention has been more particularly turned.

Among such specimens of sea-bottom the soundings taken at different times and at various points on the coast of the United States by the Coast Survey have been subjects of extreme value to the scientific observer, while they have, at the same time, furnished many unscientific possessors of microscopes with matter for admiration, wonderment and joy; the graceful Diatomaceæ, the symmetrical Radiolaria and marvelous Foramenifera often present in such profusion serving to enable the preparer to put up slides of surpassing beauty.

One of these soundings, for which I am indebted to the Smithsonian Institution, was of such a character that I was extremely desirous of studying as completely as possible the forms presented in it, belonging as they did to all of the three families mentioned, besides which it contained several minute mollusca and the remains of sponges and other organisms. It was, as is shown by the remains present of such a character as to consist essentially of Calcium Carbonate, commonly known as Carbonate of Lime, and Silicon Dioxide, (Silica) built up into the skeletons of dead organisms. The problem, then, presented to me was to prepare it in such a way, if possible, first, to show all of these objects at the same time or, second, to separate it into calcareous and siliceous specimens, and this last method I found, after trial, to be the best. As my mode of manipulation may hereafter be of value to others possessing similar gatherings, I will give it in detail.

The sounding, being in the shape of a dry powder of a light greyish-green color was placed in a suitable glass vessel and moderately strong Liquor Potassa poured upon it. It was now boiled for a few moments until I saw that the lumps present in it were broken up and a light mud-like sediment was the result. The solution of Potassa must be, of course, apportioned in strength to the specimen under manipulation, such as consists of many lumps and much organic matter will require it of greater strength than that which is mostly calcareous and siliceous. If it be used too strong some of the more delicate siliceous forms will be attacked or even, as I have occasionally found, entirely dissolved. After it had boiled for a short time, as I have said, I allowed it to stand until the mud had settled and a tolerably clear solution was left above it. I now poured off most of the Liquor Potassa and replaced it by a strong solution of Chloride of Soda, so-called. That sold by apothecaries under the name of "Labarraque's Solution" will answer generally and is readily procured. This I now boiled until I found its action to cease. By this means the mud is so much bleached as to become almost white. The Potassa at first has the effect of dissolving much of the organic matter present and, thus, breaking up the lumps and setting the shells free, and the Chloride of Soda solution bleaches them so that we have them clean and separated to such an extent that under the microscope the individual shells are easily recognised. I now proceeded to separate the larger from the smaller forms by means of the "Elutriation" process, which consists in first washing off thoroughly all the Potassa and Chloride of Soda with pure filtered or distilled water and shaking up the sediment in a glass about two inches high filled also with water. If now permitted to stand for a few seconds the larger forms and coarser sand settles and the supernatent liquid can be poured off into another larger vessel. Again water is added to the first sediment and, in turn, removed and this is done as many as six or eight times until we see that the coarse sediment is not contaminated by finer particles by the water it is shaken in remaining almost clear. The same process is carried out with the sediment in the second vessel, only permitting each charge of water to stand longer than in the first case, as the forms are now much smaller and require longer to settle. In this way we may get three or four densities of sediment, although I found that my specimen yielded but two which contained anything of interest of a calcareous nature. After, then, setting aside the two first sediments, I carefully acted upon what was left with Hydrogen Nitrate (Nitric Acid) and procured a small quantity of a sediment consisting for the most part of nothing but the siliceous lorica of Diatomaceæ. They were very few, however, so, to procure all the remains of Diatomaceæ and other siliceous organisms present in the gathering, I took a quantity in the rough state and, after breaking it down by Potassa, acted on it with boiling Hydrogen Nitrate. Thus I found that I had good representatives of all the gathering contained. Some specimens, however, are not thoroughly cleaned by boiling, even for a considerable length of time in strong Hydrogen Nitrate. To such I add either Hydrogen Chloride alone or a few grains of finely-pulverized Potassium Di Chromate. In this way, and after thoroughly washing with pure water I have been enabled to obtain extremely beautiful specimens of Diatomaceæ, Radiolaria and other siliceous organisms in a good condition for studying them. This I am engaged upon at the present time and intend before long to lay the results before the Lyceum.

Mr. S. F. Mackie made some remarks, illustrated by means of diagrams, upon the construction of ancient ships; showing that the principles of construction and to a great extent of managing sailing vessels has remained essentially the same from the earliest dates up to the present time.

October 3, 1870.

Mr. J. W. Ward in the chair. Twelve persons present.

The Librarian laid upon the table a large number of books, consisting for the most part of the proceedings and transactions of native and foreign societies, received in exchange since the last meeting.

DR. H. C. BOLTON presented a number of **Specimens in Ethnology** consisting of portions of a human skull of considerable size and thickness, vertebræ, arrow-heads, axe-heads, a pipe and fragments of utensils, some of pottery, and one carved from a talcose rock; all from a mound in the Mississippi Valley, the exact locality uncertain. He made some remarks upon the points of interest presented by these specimens, and pointed out that the talcose vessel was of uncommon occurrence.

PROF. A. M. EDWARDS announced that Prof. C. H. Hitchcock, State Geologist of New Hampshire, had written to him within a few days, that he had made an important discovery. Throughout the State of New Hampshire, hitherto no traces of undoubted fossils had been obtained, the rocks being Granites, Schists and the like. On the 28th of last month, September, however, he had been enabled to detect **Crinoidal Fragments in a supposed Quebec Group Limestone** band. This fact was of interest and desirable to be recorded at this time.

Prof. O. W. MORRIS read a

Meteorological Report for the Month of Sept., 1870.

(All temperatures are Fahrenheit.)

The mean temperature for the month had been				68·91°
Maximum	"	"	on the 25th	83·50°
Minimum	"	"	" 12th	55·40°
Range				28·10°

In 1867 the mean was	64·202°=4·708° lower than this year.		
1868	"	64·362°=4·548° "	"
1862	"	68·951°= ·041 higher	"
1865	"	72·714°=3·804° "	"

With these exceptions, it has been warmer than any year for the previous ten years. The maximum was higher also in 1870. The minimum lower in four out of the ten. The highest temperature reached in the sun was 100°. The prevalent wind was S. W. Lightning occurred on the 3d, but no thunder. Meteors, on three evenings, two of them were brilliant. The Aurora Borealis was observed eight times, that on the evening of the 24th was very fine; a beautiful corona was formed about 11 P. M. and continued for some time, the colors of the massed clouds varying, whilst the beams shooting through them were white, many reaching to the zenith.

It rained in appreciable quantities on six days, and on one very slightly; the quantity was 2·38 inches. The only equinoctial storm before the 30th, was on the 17th, and then it lasted only a few hours.

The mean of the Barometer was			29·968	inches.
Maximum	"	" on the 8th	30·284	"
Minimum	"	" " 4th	29·603	"
Range			·681	"

On the 14th, three days before the equinoctial storm, (?) the barometer was 30·222 in., on the day of the storm it was from 29·901 in. at 7 A. M., to 29·969 in. at 2 P. M. It fell a little on the next day, (18th) and rose again from that time to the morning of the 22d, when it was 30·265 in. After that it fell again.

The mean of the barometer for the month of September.	
in 1868 was	29·879 in.
in 1869 "	30·025 in.

The Chairman, Mr. J. W. Ward, said he had observed that Prof. Morris had used the term "**Equinoctial Storm,**" and in relation thereto, he would like to ask if he believed that there was such a thing as an Equinoctial storm, or a prevalence of stormy weather peculiar to the Equinoxes. For his part, his opinion, from considerable observation continued over some length of time, was that no such thing existed. In fact, he was under the impression, that the same was the conclusion which scientific observers had come to, from careful and protracted observation and comparison of records. In short, that the facts were, that there was no prevalent storm confined or peculiar to the Vernal or Autumnal Equinox.

PROF. MORRIS replied that he had come to a like conclusion, from his observations carried on through a considerable number of years. Therefore it must be considered as pretty well settled, that the "Equinoctial storm" had no existence separate and distinct.

The following paper was read.

On some Facts connected with the Occurrence of Deposits of Fresh Water Diatomaceæ commonly known as Infusorial Earths.

BY PROF. A. M. EDWARDS.

These deposits are of great interest to the geologist, as well as to the biologist, and occur largely disseminated all over the world. They can, however, be very properly divided into two classes, and it is for the purpose of pointing out some points in which these two classes vary, the one from the other, and, at the same time, to call the attention of scientists to the importance of devoting more time to their study, that I publish this short paper. For several years I have been engaged in employing the microscope, for the purpose of studying our native and certain foreign "Infusorial earths," as they are commonly termed. These earths, or as they sometimes appear as rocks, are either of marine origin, consisting almost entirely of the siliceous remains of Diatomaceæ, minute aquatic organisms which Biologists are now in the habit of considering as belonging to the vegetable kingdom, intermixed with a smaller number of the skeletons, also siliceous, of Radiolaria and Spongida. All of these marine deposits which I have examined or heard of, were fossil in character, and all of those whose geological position has been determined with exactness, are considered as belonging to the Miocene Tertiary.

But besides the marine deposits, we have others which occur much more commonly all over the world. These I am now in the habit of calling "Lacustrine Sedimentary" deposits, in preference to "Sub-Peat," a term I proposed for them some years since, and which has come into very general use. This term had been suggested by the finding of most such fresh-water deposits beneath peat, but of late years, several have been discovered at the bottoms of ponds and lakes where no peat exists, and the Diatomaceous stratum makes itself evident as an almost white cloud, when the bottom of the pond is stirred by means of a pole or the oar of a boat. But, as it appeared to be necessary that there should be a considerable extent of comparatively still water for the formation of such deposits, the term "Lacustrine Sedimentary" had been chosen as more appropriate. Such deposits are extremely common in this country, as well as in Europe, and are generally of a light grey color, or perfectly white, and extremely light and pulverulent in texture. On our Western coast, through California, Oregon, Washington Territory and Nevada, there exist vast tracts covered by fresh water deposits of Diatomaceæ, which are hard and stony. They have become so by the action of superimposed lava and basalt. Now it is a remarkable fact, that there have come to light two deposits from our Atlantic coast, possessing very much the same physical characters as these Western strata; that is to say they are hard and stony, and almost white in color. One of these was presented at a meeting of the Lyceum some time since, by Dr. L. W. Feuchtwanger, but, unfortunately its exact locality has not been ascertained. The other is from New Hampshire, and all of the facts connected with its manner of occurrence, doubtless will be brought to light, as I am at present engaged on the microscopical department of the geological survey of that state, now being prosecuted under the superintendence of Prof. C. H. Hitchcock. A very extensive Lacustrine Sedimentary deposit of the pulverulent kind, and almost white in tint, has been discovered on the shores of Lake Umbagog, in New Hampshire, and there were indications that it extends beneath the waters of the lake, perhaps over the whole bottom. These deposits are of interest, geologically and microscopically, but at the same time commercially, as they have been used to some extent, not only as polishing powders, but as a source of very finely divided silica, of which the skeletons of the Diatomaceæ they contain are made up, for the manufacture of soluble Silicates, or "Soluble glass" as it has been called, which is now a considerable article of trade. Although existing for the most part, in strata of no very great thickness, or usually covering no more than a few acres of ground, yet, as the number of localities from which they have already been procured in the Atlantic states is over a hundred, the supply for commercial purposes is amply sufficient, without having to draw upon the vast tracts covered by the lake deposits of the Pacific coast, or the marine strata of California and Virginia. In a forthcoming volume of the Report on the Geology of California, the whole subject of these deposits, their mode of formation, with descriptions and figures of the organisms found in them, will be published, when will be cleared up several points of interest with regard to them. They must not be confounded as they often are, with the marine strata containing the remains of Diatomaceæ, which occur in various parts of the world, and of which I have already spoken. That constituting the major part of the Coast Range of Mountains running down our Pacific Coast through California, is now undergoing investigation, and the results arrived at, will be shortly made public. It is known as the "Bituminous Shale," as it is associated with the Bitumen of the Pacific Coast, and there, and elsewhere, it has been proved to be of Miocene Tertiary origin. The deposits containing the remains of fresh-water Diatomaceæ, are evidently of more recent formation; those of our Atlantic Coast being very recent, and in fact now undergoing deposition. By means of an extended and careful examination many of these Lacustrine Sedimentary deposits as well as the hardened fossil fresh-water deposits of our Western states, which I have called, from their mode of formation, Sub Plutonic, and comparison of the forms they contain, I have been enabled in several cases, to determine the character of the piece of water in which the organisms grew and were deposited. Thus distinct forms appear to be peculiar to still and to running water, to lakes near the surface of the sea, and to those from greater altitudes. These, as well as other similar points, doubtless will hereafter be comparatively easy of settlement, when our knowledge of the life-history of these minute organisms is more perfect. Already a systematic study of them has proved of great value to the geologist, and the student of biological metamorphoses has in them, as seemingly simple unicellular, plants, whose position would seem to be close upon the border line, where the animal merges into the vegetable kingdom, excellent opportunities for investigating many points which the more complex forms of life do not present. At some future time I will lay before the Society some of the results which I have arrived at, in studying the Diatomaceæ in this connection.

October 10, 1870.

The President in the chair. Twenty-eight persons present.

Dr. L. W. Feuchtwanger exhibited some very distinctly striated **Crystals of Iron Pyrites** from Roxbury, Conn. and made some remarks on striated crystals, to which subject he had given considerable attention of late.

Mr. T. Bland exhibited a specimen of **Magnetic Iron** in the form of a sand **from Santa Martha, New Granada,** where it occurs in large quantities contiguous to means of transportation so that if, upon analysis, it were found to be of good quality, it could be readily supplied in abundance.

The President, Dr. J. S. Newberry, made some remarks upon this specimen, and said that doubtless it would prove to be similar in character and belonging to the same geological position as the Magnetic Iron of this country, as existing along our Atlantic sea-board. He had received fine specimens of Magnetite from the region of the Rocky Mountains where it is abundant in what are there known as the "Black Hills;" even being said to constitute whole mountains. At some future time, doubtless, these vast deposits will present to the manufacturing industry of this continent a source of supply for iron of almost inestimable extent. When the West has been more fully settled and rail-road communication is more extended, then will come a demand for iron which the Magnetic beds will amply meet; and this the more surely and readily as it is in that region that the vast layers of lignite are found which will serve as fuel for the reduction of the ores. With regard to the use of this lignite as fuel in furnaces, some doubts have been entertained as to its value but recent experiments tend to show that it will serve admirably for that purpose. There is one drawback in connection with the use of these Magnetic ores as at present manipulated and that is that that they are universally accompanied by compounds of Titanium, which interferes very materially with their employment in the manufacture of steel.

Dr. I. Walz reported that he had examined the Santa Martha Magnetite chemically and had found that, like the United States mineral it contained Titantium. Otherwise it was remarkably pure.

Prof. B. N. Martin exhibited specimens of the, so called, "steel ore," known commonly as the **Codorus Ore,** from Pennsylvania and concerning which and its use in the direct manufacture of steel much had been published in the public prints. This ore is being worked very extensively in furnaces at York, Pa., and apparently successfully. It looks like Mica-schist with dark, evidently crystaline granules disseminated throughout the mass. Where it is mined it is reported to occur in the form of hills of two to three hundred feet in height and readily accessible. When analyzed it is found to contain about forty per cent. of Magnetic Oxide of Iron with ten per cent. of the Peroxide. Ordinarily to convert it into steel, Cast Iron in certain proportions is mixed with it, and in this way it would appear that some of the oxygen of the ore is used to burn off a portion of the carbon present in the Cast Iron and leave sufficient to render the resulting compound still of good quality.

Dr. Walz remarked that he had examined three analyses of the Codorus ore made by separate chemists and they agreed very closely, showing it to be remarkably free from both Phosphorous and Sulphur, which substances the metallurgist finds it at present impossible to remove economically from Iron ores; hence many ores which occur in abundance are useless for the manufacture of steel; those two substances being extremely deleterious. The Codorus ore contains, however, Chromium.

Prof. H. Morton exhibited two **Photographs upon Glass of Sun Prominences,** taken by Prof. C. A. Young, of Dartmouth College, Hanover, N. H., by means of the spectroscope; the first time that this remarkable feat has been accomplished. He also exhibited photographs of the instrument employed by Prof. Young. It consists of a spectroscope attached to the Equatorial telescope, and furnished with a battery of six prisms and a half prism. That is to say, after the ray of light proceeding from the sun's prominence, passes through the six prisms of the instrument, and then the half prism at the end, it is caught by a right-angled reflecting prism, thrown back, and made to traverse again the half prism, and six following whole prisms. In this way the dispersion of fourteen prisms is made use of, and the results obtained superior to what has been got in any other manner. Although somewhat indistinct in detail, the photographs show the prominences in a satisfactory manner, as to outline.

PROF. C. A. SEELY called attention to a property of **Gun Cotton** which he considered new, or at least, unrecorded. It was well known, that Gun Cotton was soluble to a very considerable extent in alcohol, which held Gum Camphor in solution. A knowledge of this fact had been made use of in the arts, for the manufacture of an artificial ivory, which was reported to be fully equal, if not superior, to the genuine article. In making this substance, the Gun Cotton is ground up with the Gum Camphor, by means of water into a pulp, and then pressed into a solid mass, whilst being heated to a temperature of about 300° F. Taking this fact into consideration, he had thought of ascertaining what would be the effect of exposing Gun Cotton to the action of the vapor of Gum Camphor. Therefore a small quantity was thus exposed in a glass tube; the Camphor being heated to a temperature just high enough to volatilize it. He was surprised to find that after a short time the tube became filled with red vapors, aud ultimately the Gun Cotton exploded. Now, as in the manufacture of the artificial ivory mentioned, the mixture of Gun Cotton and Camphor is exposed to a much higher heat than that he had made use of, it was a fact worth taking into consideration, as to whether there might not be danger of explosion resulting. It is true, that ordinarily there is water present, but towards the end of the process this is all pressed out, and a dry mass is left. Therefore as a precaution, it is as well to remember this fact thus ascertained.

The following paper was read

On the Question of the Existence of Antozone.

BY O. LOEW.

Engler and Nasse published a few months ago in the Annalen der Chemie u. Pharmacie, a very able paper on the questionable existence of Antozone. They have shown that the mist, which appears according to Meissner, when electrified Oxygen is passed through a solution of Iodide of Potassium, was due to the presence of Peroxide of Hydrogen, which they condensed in strongly-cooled U tube. Further, they stated that no Antozone, but only vapors of Peroxide of Hydrogen appear, when Peroxide of Barium is heated with concentrated Sulphuric Acid. For these two special instances, it is proved that the supposed Antozone was only Peroxide of Hydrogen. But there are several other instances, for which this proof is wanting; among them are certain peculiarities of some essential oils, especially Oil of Turpentine, and of the Fluorspar from Woelsendorf, Bavaria.

We know from the interesting researches of Schoenbein, that Spirits of Turpentine, which has been for a long time exposed to the influence of the air, possesses bleaching and oxidizing properties, and that such spirit when shaken with water, produces therein a certain quantity of Peroxide of Hydrogen. There are good reasons for believing that the oxidizing agent contained in the Spirits of Turpentine, is neither common Oxygen nor Ozone, but it remained to be proved whether the Peroxide of Hydrogen was contained in the Spirits before contact with water, or was produced by the action of a peculiar modification of oxygen contained in the Spirits upon the water. The following experiments proves that the original bleaching and oxydizing agent in the Spirits was not Peroxide of Hydrogen, but Oxygen in a peculiar condition, which we may call if we please "Antozone."

It is well known that Peroxide of Hydrogen, when in a

perfectly neutral solution, is not able to yield with Iodide of Potassium and Starch the familiar blue reaction, but that this reaction makes its appearance when some acid or traces of Protosulphate of Iron are added.

Old Spirits of Turpentine always contains some Formic Acid, and hence the blue color with Iodide of Potassium and Starch can be traced to the simultaneous presence of Acid and Peroxide of Hydrogen. If it could be proved that this reaction appears, even when the spirit contains not the slightest trace of an acid, and without any addition of Protosulphate of Iron, then the active agent is surely not Peroxide of Hydrogen. I shook Spirits of Turpentine with caustic lye thoroughly, whereby every trace of an acid was perfectly removed. The thus treated Spirits, showed not the slightest acid reaction with wet test-paper, did not decompose Iodide of Potassium and Starch, and shaken with water did not yield Peroxide of Hydrogen; the acid as well as the active Oxygen was therefore thoroughly removed; the latter probably forced to go into chemical combination with the Hydrocarbon and Potassa. The Spirits was then poured into a capacious flask, covering the bottom to a depth of about one half an inch, and left standing three days in common daylight. Then it was shaken with Iodide of Potassium and Starch, when a slight reaction appeared. The flask was now exposed for three hours in the direct sunlight, when a portion of the contents shaken with Iodide of Potassium and Starch, produced at once an intense blue color, although not the slightest trace of any acid could be detected. Another portion was shaken thoroughly with about one quarter its volume of water, which was then poured off and filtered. This water had a perfectly neutral reaction, and an odor of Spirits of Turpentine. After addition of Iodide of Potassium and Starch, only a slight blue color made its appearance, but after addition of a trace of Protosulphate of Iron, an intense blue tint appeared at once. These observations show plainly, that (1) the active principle in Spirits of Turpentine is not Peroxide of Hydrogen, and (2) that the effect upon the reagent used, was only produced after shaking with water. We know that Ozone, by simply shaking with water, does not produce any trace of Peroxide of Hydrogen, therefore we must conclude that another modification of Oxygen is contained in the Spirits of Turpentine. The most reasonable supposition is, that the molecule of common Oxygen in contact with the essence, was split up into its two atoms and these, yet surrounded by their heat-sphere, formed a loose, more physical than chemical combination with the molecules of the Hydro-carbon; as we are acquainted with analogous instances in chemistry. This atomistic Oxygen may be called "Antozone." I thoroughly agree with Engler and Nasse, in their view that the hypothesis of positive and negative Oxygen has no foundation whatever, and that there is not any reason for distinguishing different Peroxides of the metals as "Ozonides" and "Antozonides," but what I undertook to prove is, that Oxygen may exist as yet another modification, which however has nothing to do with an especially electric character.

PROF. HENRY WURTZ read

A Preliminary Note on the Chemical Geogony of Silica,

Of which the following is an abstract. As long ago as 1854, he took occasion, in the report upon the Geology of New Jersey for that year, page 37, to insist on the importance of Silica in soils in the soluble form, thus:

"It is the ingredient in soils which furnishes to many plants, especially to the cereals, such as corn, wheat, etc., the *silica*, which is absolutely necessary to the formation of their stalk or stem. Silica, which is the most abundant of all mineral substances, forming certainly more than one half of the mass of the earth, so far as the latter is known, occurs in soils in three different forms; first, in the crystalline form, as quartz, sand, etc., in which form it is wholly insoluble, and may be considered inert, so far as the nutrition of plants is concerned; secondly, in combination, in fragments of feldspar, hornblende, and other silicates, in which it is also comparatively inactive; and thirdly, as amorphous or *soluble* silica, or *opal*, as it is called by mineralogists, the only form of much importance in agriculture, since in this form it is soluble in the liquids of the soil. Far too little attention has been paid in analyses of soils and fertilizing minerals to their content of opal or soluble silica, whereas a soil may be rich in every other necessary ingredient, and yet, if deficient in this respect, be perfectly sterile for many crops.

"An analysis of the straw of wheat, made by Weber, in the laboratory, and according to the method of H. Rose, showed 3·82 per cent. of total ash and in this, ·68 per cent. of soluble silica. A ton of such straw must therefore obtain from the soil not less than 50 lbs. of silica."

The importance of the function of soluble and hydrated forms of silica in mineral fertilizers, like green sand, has been underrated. Though some vegetable spongioles *may* be able to cause quartz to pass into solution in the sap, yet it is of course the soluble forms that are thus chiefly taken up, constituting the vegetable skeleton, as phosphate of lime the animal. Silicic acid, though so minute an ingredient in actual animal nutrition is indirectly as essential to animal life as even carbonic acid. The author has presented to the Lyceum and to the American Association, peculiar views of the relations of oxygen and carbon to life, arrived at by the *a posteriori* method of studying the chemical changes now going on, and tracing them backwards throughout their anterior stages. By the application of the same process to the past history of silicic acid, equally curious generalizations regarding the relations of this material (which next to oxygen is the most abundant of all) to zoic history in the past and the present are pointed to with greater or less probability. The study is, however, as yet, far more difficult and uncertain than in the case of carbonic acid, for the reason that the facts as yet established by chemical research regarding the habitudes and migrations of silicic acid, and the parts which it sustains in the grand drama of Life, are comparatively few.

The pervading idea has been that this acid was pre-eminently the mineral acid, and that its study belonged therefore to mineralogy, a science in itself so great and complex that it has, as yet, scarcely advanced beyond the first stage, namely that of provisional classification.

He believes, however, that his studies have unmistakably tended towards the conclusion, which will be startling to many, that silicic acid *as such*, that is, in isolated forms, *appertains, in origin at least, altogether to the vegetable kingdom;* and that the tendency of chemical investigation and discovery is to confirm this conclusion. He presented, to illustrate this and other related generalizations, the following diagram, which was prepared in substance nearly a year since, and of course before the announcement of the discovery by PAUL THENARD of the nitrohumic solvents of silicic acid. This discovery serves now to illustrate the agencies concerned in the second stage of migration, in the diagram, that which involves the transfer by condensing atmospheric waters, of the soluble silica of soils of the external continental *cuticles* (so to speak) to the fluviatile systems of drainage. As illustrations of the general neglect that the whole subject has received from chemists hitherto, it may be mentioned that almost the only analyses of the waters of first-class river systems, in which the amount of soluble silica present has been determined separately, are those of STERRY HUNT. In his analysis of the waters of one of the great rivers of the world, the St. Lawrence, he found the relative properties of carbonates of lime and silica to be, in 10·000 parts 0,8083 and 0·37; or as 100 to 45·77. A comparison of this result with others recently published by JOHN HUNTER, of Atlantic deep-sea ooze, from 14,600 feet deep (See *Am. Chemist* for October, 1870, p. 138) is instructive. HUNTER found for the relative proportions of carbonate of lime and silica in this, 100 to 39·10; and this notwithstanding that we have scarce an analysis of oceanic water indicating silica as a constituent.

He finds also that an analysis made by himself very carefully of the waters of the Delaware River collected just above tide water at Trenton, in 1856, (See *Am. Jour. of Science*, xxii, 154,) gave the proportions when all the lime was calculated as carbonate, of 100 of the latter to 31·7 of silica. Doubtless the great difference in the geological surfaces of drainage systems of the St. Lawrence and Delaware will serve to explain the variation from HUNT'S results.

The following paper was read,

On Volatile Liquids suitable for Ice Machines.

BY PROF. CHARLES A. SEELY.

The Twining ice machine comprises three essential parts, which may be called the freezer, the vapor pump and the condenser. These are arranged in the order named, and the condenser is joined with the freezer, so as to form the series into a closed circuit. When the machine is in action, the volatile substance continually flows or circulates in the circuit, taking away heat from the water of the freezer, and giving it up at the condenser; the volatile substance is the conveyor or vehicle for heat, loading at the freezer, and discharging its burthen at the condenser.

The power consumed in working the ice machine, may be divided into two parts, that which is directly and only concerned in the freezing, and that which is used in meeting what are termed practical difficulties. The calculation of the first is the simplest of problems, for its terms and conditions are few, well known and invariable. A unit of heat or of cold if one chooses, measured by gravity, is 772 foot pounds, that is, to heat or to cool one pound of water, one degree requires a force equivalent to 772 ft. lbs. The freezing of a pound of water at 32° to ice at 32° represents (143.772) 110,396 ft. lbs. One pound of pure Carbon develops 8,000 heat units in its combustion, and this amount of energy expended directly in freezing water, will produce 56 lbs. of ice;

a ton of coal will make over 50 tons of ice, except for the practical difficulties.

The practical difficulties are many, and greatly differing from each other; that they are formidable is apparent, when we observe that in practice, instead of getting 56 tons of ice by the use of one ton of coal, we think we do pretty well when we get ten per cent. of that amount, and the coal furnishes only a moiety of the energy consumed; we waste nearly all our force in meeting practical difficulties. We may well be abashed, when we observe that these practical difficulties, and indeed all others, are incident only to the ignorance and want of skill of men. The only one of these which the author proposes to discuss, was that pertaining to the degree of volatility of the vaporizing substance of the ice machine. Aside from practical difficulties, one volatile liquid is as good as another; it would cost no more of the direct force to make ice by the evaporation of Mercury or water, than by the evaporation of Ether or Ammonia.

What is the precise degree of volatility, of a liquid best suited for use in the practical machine? Mercury and liquid Nitrous Oxide may be taken as the extremes, quite unsuited for use and for opposite reasons; what liquid is the proper mean? The author here exhibited a chart of curves, representing the tensions and temperatures of the saturated vapors of water, Ether, Sulphurous Acid, Ammonia and Carbonic Acid. The ordinates of the curve represented temperatures, and the abscissas the tensions.

In order that the curves might be easily comparable by inspection, they were all commenced from the same point of tension, namely, atmospheric pressure, 760 m m. The chart was drawn on engineers' profile paper, about a yard long, and the data of the most recent experiments were used.

The author continued the discussion by going considerably into detail, all illustrated by the chart, or having direct reference to it. This part of the paper is unsuited for abstract, without the assistance of engravings. The conclusion arrived at, was that a liquid boiling about midway of

0° and 32° F. would be of suitable volatility. Such a liquid avoids on the one hand the inconveniently large evaporating surface, and on the other the excessive pressure.

Attention was called to the fact that the chart of curves, besides illustrating the subject of the paper, also was a compact substitute for the ordinary tables of tension, and representing in a very clear manner, some of the laws pertaining to saturated vapors. For example, a simple inspection teaches that the tensions increase more rapidly than the temperatures, and on comparing the different curves, it appears that the rate of increase is greater for the liquids of lowest boiling points, and that there may be some exact relation between volatility and the rate of increase of tension.

October 17, 1870.

The President in the Chair. Twelve persons present.

MR. R. DINWIDDIE exhibited specimens of crystallized **Green Colored Feldspar** from what is known as the Sea Wall of Mount Desert Island, Maine, where it occurs not very commonly in scattered particles or cavities. Many of the crystals were remarkably perfect and appear upon superficial examination to be peculiar. The color in most of them is very bright; often light but brilliant, and frequently not extending throughout the crystal.

PROF. D. S. MARTIN exhibited a series of very fine specimens of Magnetite from Cornwall, Penn., constituting the "**Codorus Ore**" alluded to at the last meeting. Magnetite is pervaded with Cobaltiferous Iron Pyrites and has associated with and often encrusting it masses of Brochantite, essentially a Silicate of Copper, containing sometimes, a little Zinc and Lead. Also there was present on some of the specimens incrustations of Allophane.

The President, DR. J. S. NEWBERRY, exhibited a series of specimens of White Statuary Marble from Vermont, as well as true Carrara Marble, and made some remarks upon the **Marble Beds of Vermont.** The particular specimens shown, were from a quarry which has been lately opened, and is now being successfully worked, for the most part, by Boston Capital, at Middlebury, in Vermont. The marble extracted is shown to be of a very superior quality, both as regards texture and color; whilst the strength is also very great. At Rutland, marble has been worked, and one layer of five feet in thickness, out of the whole series, which extends over sixty feet, yielded good statuary marble, but for the most part, the stone quarried there was not of a pure color. At Sutherland's Falls, marble of excellent quality, somewhat mottled, was found. At Brandon, marble is worked, but the surface rock is found to be very much shattered. The color and grain of the stone are excellent, but sound marble, such as can be worked in large blocks, has not yet been found there.

South of these localities, and in other states, the continuation of these beds of marble, wherever they crop out, have been found to become more and more granular and coarse as we proceed southward. The well-known Sing Sing Dolomite of New York State, which is being extensively employed in this city, more particularly by Mr. A. T. Stewart, in building his magnificent residence on the corner of Fifth Avenue and Thirty-fourth Street, and in the construction of the Catholic Cathedral on Fifth Avenue, is made up of large crystals, thus being coarse in texture, and not adapted to fine work. Besides, it often contains Pyrites and other minerals, which very materially deteriorate its quality. The Potomac marble, again, is of a coarse texture and inferior quality. So that it would seem, that we would naturally expect to find an improvement in quality in this stone, as we travel to the Northward. And this is the case, as the Vermont excavations show. The ancients used for the construction of their statuary, more particularly two kinds of marble. The Parian which was fine grained and waxy in appearance, and of a yellowish-white color. The texture is composed of fine shining scales or crystals, lying in all directions. This the ancients knew as *lychnites*, on account of its quarries being worked by means of lamps. Of this they did not carve their finest statuary, although the Medicean Venus is composed of it. They had also the white marble of Carrara, between Spezia and Lucca, which was of an excellent quality and fine white color, although it is frequently traversed by grey veins, which have to be avoided when statuary is cut from it. It is not apt to turn yellow in tint, as is the case with the Parian marble. This quarry is still worked, and yields some of the finest statuary marble in use.

The quarry at Middlebury, Addison County, Vermont, yields a marble of an almost white color, having however, an extremely delicate flesh tint, which strikingly contributes to its value as a statuary marble. Mr. Grenough, the sculptor, has pronounced it of very superior quality, and, in fact, the best in the world. One face of it which lies upon the side of the hill, through which it extends, dips at an angle of about forty-five degrees, and is of a considerable extent, and smoothly polished by glacial action. At some places grooves have been ploughed out by the ice, but one large face is as flat and polished, as if done by art for a special purpose. A fragment chipped out from this plane with some difficulty was exhibited, and it was of such thinness, as to permit light to pass through it, and demonstrate the very superior texture of the stone. At Middlebury, a series of marble beds are exposed in the quarry, having an aggregate thickness of over 150 feet, the strata varying from 5 to 12 feet each, the greater portion being pure white in color, and much of it of the very finest quality. Thus it is seen that we have in this country, ample supplies of the very best quality of statuary marble.

The following paper was read.

Notes of some Observations made in Dakota, during two Expeditions, under Command of General Alfred Sully against the Hostile Sioux, in the Years 1864 and 1865.

By Charles Froebel.

Both of the expeditions in question started from Sioux City, Iowa, in the beginning of the summer, and followed the general course of the Missouri River, on its eastern shore, to a point at the mouth of Long Lake Creek, and a few miles above the mouth of the Cannonball, a small tributary affluent from the west. At this point the first expedition crossed the Missouri and encamped on the site of the military fort, then projected, and built during the same summer, known as Fort Rice. Leaving their camp on or about the 10th of July, 1864, the expedition followed for a number of days the course of the Cannonball, then passed to the northward crossing the Big Knife and Heart Rivers and encountering the hostile Sioux, in a wide, dry valley, on the southern flank of the Takaokutah Mountains on the 29th of July. Returning thence to the camp before occupied on Heart River, the expedition pursued the course of this stream to its source, crossed the valley of the Little Missouri des Gros Ventres on the 8th and 9th of August, and some smaller streams, and reached the banks of the Yellowstone, 35 miles above its mouth on or about the 13th day of the same month. Following the western bank of the Yellowstone to its confluence with the Missouri and fording the latter, the expedition returned homeward by way of Fort Berthold and Fort Rice, on the eastern shore of the Missouri Valley. The second expedition left their camp at the mouth of Long Lake Creek about the 20th of July, 1865, traversed the high plateau frequently designated on maps as the "Prairie du Coteau du Missouri," and reached the shores of Mini-Wakan (Mini-Water; Wakan-Medecine, t. i. mystic influence, &c. or better "Fetish") or Devil's Lake, on the 29th day of the same month. Starting from the eastern extremity of the lake on the 2d of August, the expedition passed in a north-westerly direction, in sight of British Territory, touched the banks of the Mouse River, a tributary of the Assineboine, and thence southerly to Fort Berthold, from where it turned its face to the point of starting.

The valley of the upper Missouri is bounded on both sides by table lands, which rise from the alluvial plain, in many places very abruptly and often to heights of probably from 300 to 800 feet, giving to the country, as seen from the banks of the river, here and there quite a mountainous aspect. It is only when the explorer has ascended the sides of this trough, that he is undeceived by seeing the approximate levels of a great plateau spreading before him, broken, only now and then by water courses or capped by hills, whose, occasionally flat, heads remain as monuments of another higher plateau, now almost entirely gone.

The table-land to the west of the Missouri Valley forms an inclined plain, which rises gently from the border of the trough rim, apparently attaining its greatest elevation in the immediate vicinity of the Little Missouri des Gros Ventres, or between this stream and the Yellowstone, and is intersected by two systems of watercourses, the streams of one of which, flow, generally speaking, from west to east and enter the Missouri below Fort Berthold, while those of the other system pursue a direction from south to north and join the great Water-Artery of the country above the point mentioned. The action of the streams of the first system on the physical outlines of the country has generally been but slight, that of those of the second system at times very powerful.

The contrast between the resulting effects, leaves a very vivid impression in the mind of the observer, who pursues the route of the expedition of 1864. Following the courses of the Cannonball and Heart Rivers, the eye is met everywhere by the same gently undulating plain, in which the river valleys form but slight indentations, and above which the ridge of the Takaokutah Mountains rises in the North, to an elevation of perhaps from 800 to 1000 feet. About three hundred miles of this plain, may have been traversed from east to west, the source of one of the little water-courses, here dry, is reached, and a slight elevation, two or three hundred yards distant, seems merely to hide from view another portion of the same uniform landscape. But a few steps more, and the ground opens before our very feet, and we stand on the brink of a valley-gorge, 10 to 15 miles in width, almost the entire space of which is covered with innumerable hills and hillocks, from the size of a baker's oven to that of a mountain, the smaller of these being generally of the shape of a Beehive, Mushroom or "Glacier-table," the largest of similar form, but with flat tops, the levels of which correspond to the levels of the plain, in which the valley has been ploughed by the waters of the Little Missouri des Gros Ventres. The number of the hills filling the bottom of the valley is immense. Standing on the brink of the gorge, the eye takes in, in all probability, more than a thousand at one glance, on a section perhaps 30 miles in length and 15 miles in width. The general configuration of the surface, is however unlike that of a rocky mountainous country; the hills and hillocks form no, or only indistinct chains, but stand more or less isolated. Some of the valleys or gorges are so narrow, that wagons get jammed between the two sides, some of them even end in sacs. Others, that connect with the main valley of the Little Missouri, show a water-course, but no running water, only here and there a puddle of the appearance of strong coffee. The main valley of the Little Missouri, is, at the point, where it was crossed by the Expedition, about half a mile in width. The elevation attained after crossing, say 300 miles of inclined plain, from the Missouri to the eastern brink of the valley-gorge, appears to be from 1500 to 2000 feet, the descent from this brink to the banks of the Little Missouri, leads in 6 to 7 miles to a level 800 to 1000 feet lower than the surrounding plain. The elevation of the plateau between the western brink of the valley gorge, and the valley of the Yellowstone, appears to be a trifle higher than that to the east of this Gap.

The inclined plain between the Missouri River and the Little Missouri, is covered for the greater part by Drift, the river courses cutting here and there, through this into the Tertiary Formation of the "Bad Lands." Thus the Cannonball near its mouth. At the camp on Heart River, mentioned above, specimens of marine shells were found, at an elevation not over 50 feet above the stream, still preserving their pearly appearance, but rapidly crumbling by exposure. In the creek-bed itself, a ledge of limestone with beautifully preserved impressions of the leaves of dicotyledonous plants crops out, apparently unconformable and inclined at a steep angle, to the superincumbent formations. Between the Cannonball and Heart Rivers, a very fine bed of apparently Basaltic Lava, black and full of cavities, covers the Plateau, whether above or below the Drift was not ascertained. This Lava Bed was the only exhibition of volcanic formations noticed on either of the two expeditions. It has the external appearance of a tolerably recent flow, the surface being piled near its margin with frothy blocks. The Takaokutah Mountains, whose ridge intersects the plain from east to west, about 70—90 miles (?) north of the camp on Heart River, and about due south of Fort Berthold, is composed entirely of a greyish green sandstone, which also covers the greater portion of the plateau between the Little Missouri and the Yellowstone, and probably forms the masses of all the hills rising above the general level of the plateau. The formation of the hills and hillocks of the Little Missouri Bad Lands is highly peculiar. As seen from the edge of the plateau, the landscape is at once characterized by the singular shapes of the hills, whose summit flanks are often painted in red, yellow, blue, and other ochreous colors, and by a sharp black line, which goes through the entire view, like a knife-cut, and is due to a lignite bed. Other lignite beds crop out in the beds of the water-courses. Generally speaking, the body of the hills shows a bed of very friable sandstone, or rather of loose sand forming their base, to the rapid destruction of which the oft-recurring mushroom or glacier-table-like shapes are due. On this bed rest solid sandstones, which form the rim-base of the mushroom and the tops of the tables. Above this come formations not remembered, followed by a bed of beautifully silicified stumps of trees in position, and immediately above these the great black line or chief lignite bed, probably about two feet thick and still higher, painted formations, of unascertained character. In places marine shells were found, in which of the beds cannot now be stated, but probably in the higher, above the "Black Line." In many places of varying position, painted masses sometimes resembling dykes, and composed of fragments of the surrounding rocks, cemented with ferruginous matter, and having the taste of sulphates, were found. Most of the little water-courses tributary to the Little Missouri are dry, with here and there a puddle of clear but dark brown water, tasting of sulphates and humus substance. Even the running water of the Little Missouri is straw or wine-colored, with a strong inky flavor. The beds of all the streams are covered with fragments of surrounding formations. Among the fragments were noticed a great number of pieces of agates, chalcedonies, wood-opal, silicified wood, and other silicious rocks; also red pipe or clay-stones, and geolithic minerals. It should be added, that the formations of the Little Missouri, of the Yellowstone, and of the Missouri Valley between Fort Union and Fort Rice are identical, the developments on the two latter streams being however not so bold or extensive as on the Little Missouri.

The plateau to the east of the Missouri River rises gradually towards the Mini-Wakan or Devil's Lake, where it attains its greatest elevations in the summit of Chantee Hill on the immediate south-eastern shore of the lake, and in the Dog House Butte, situated south-west or west of the lake and probably 60 to 70 miles distant. The Big Chyenne River (there are several streams of this name in the West) a small running brook, whose source lies probably near the Dog House Butte, encircles the lake on the South about 20 miles away, flowing in an easterly direction towards the Red River of the North, to which it is tributary, and to the north-west about 70 or 80 miles distant, the Mouse River, a small bright stream enters the United States from the North, describes a short curve, and again crosses the boundary line on its way to its confluence with the Assineboine. The water-courses to the south of the Big Chyenne, chief among which is the James River, all point to the south, and are so far as observed in their upper courses, marked by valleys of considerable width,—sometimes of several miles—but forming only shallow depressions in the face of the plateau. None of those observed contained running water, but are generally characterized by "chains" of lakes of variable size, from that of small ponds, to those many miles in length. Almost all of these are very shallow. Not only the valleys mentioned, but also the entire face of the country is covered with these shallow lakes, ponds and puddles, many of which are, however, dry or undergoing a process of gradual drying out. This can be seen from the fact that some of the dry lakes are full of decaying fresh-water molluscs of species still living in wet lakes near by, while others show only bleached shells, and still others not even these. Many of the lakes are very round, the central portion of the dry lakes is generally covered with fine white sand with a few isolated Salsolas or Salicornias. Around this sand-bed is a circle of larger stones, and around these concentriccircles of different species of plants. The water of all the lakes is charged with salts, probably mostly sulphates.

Mini-Wakan, to judge from its taste and strong action on the kidneys, seems to contain Nitrates, some of the ponds are also charged with Sulphuretted Hydrogen, and a small lake between Mini-Wakan and Mouse River showed strong reactions of a solution of Alkaline Sulphurets. The waters of the Mouse River and of the Big Chyenne, are fresh and limpid.

The entire surface of the eastern plateau is covered by the Drift, apparently of northern source, characterized by the predominence of boulders of a white, very hard and solid siliceous rock, of perfectly homogeneous texture, which becomes enameled by exposure to the atmosphere. At the Mini-Wakan one piece of Drift Rock, containing fossils (*Strophonema?*) was noticed. In the southern portion of the plateau, below Port Rice, Hills of the Green Sandstone formation, mentioned above, are frequent, and the Dog

House Butte, which was not examined, but only seen from the distance, probably belongs to the same. Near the Missouri Valley, the water-courses and lake valleys are cut down to lower strata, and in the bottom of one lake, not far from Fort Berthold, a lignite bed was noticed. Chantree Hill on the southern shore of Mini-Wakan appears to be Drift also, or is perhaps, in part at least, an artificial mound, as a large double cross of stone flags was found on its summit.

The Organic forms which inhabit the plateaus on the two sides of the Missouri Valley do not differ much in character. In midsummer, when the expedition of 1864 crossed the inclined plain between the Missouri and the Little Missouri des Gros Ventres, the gentle undulating hillsides were covered almost exclusively with the well-known Buffalo-Grass, then maturing its seed, and waving like a golden field of dwarfed grain only two feet high. The banks of the small running streams as the Cannonball, Big Knife, and Heart Rivers, are fringed with little groves and copses, principally of the Box Elder, *Negundo Aceroides*, while the sides of the Takaokutahs is covered with a very fine, dense growth of timber, Oak, Ash, Elm, Maple, Cherry, &c., and various other kinds. Two characteristic plants, the Cottonwood-poplar and the Wild Grape, are not to be seen on this inclined plain. On descending into the Bad Lands of the Little Missouri, the character of the Flora is slightly changed. The Cedar, Juniper, and a creeping Lycopodium-like dwarf-species of Juniperus, the Choke-Cherry and Plum Bushes, clothe the smaller gorges, while the hill-sides are almost entirely bare of vegetation, showing only here and there a Cactus, Artemisia or pyramidal, white-flowering Argemone. Further down on the banks of the Little Missouri, the Cottonwood and the Bull Berry, a thorny shrub, with very astringent reddish yellow berries, both plants characteristic of the valley of the Missouri and the Yellowstone, appear. At the time the expedition passed, the plateau between the Little Missouri and the Yellowstone was almost completely stripped of its grass by a devastating army of Orthoptera, of which grasshoppers formed the van, and crickets the rear

Guard. Only the grass-root remained where they had passed. The table lands to the east of the Missouri River, are characterized principally by the very great scarcity of trees of any kind, and by the somewhat peculiar vegetation on the banks of the innumerable lakes, whose flora consists chiefly of a considerable variety of species of Chenopodium, Rumex, Salsola or Salicornia, Polygonum, Burlap, white-flowered Euphorbia and others. The shores of the Devil's Lake show a very fine body of Oak timber, besides this the white-barked so-called Quaking Asp or Mountain Poplar, and the usual Box Elder Maple, while the banks of the Mouse River are inhabited by still more northern or subalpine plants as Parnassia, Sphagnum, and the elegant little one-flowered Lobelia, (*Clintonia?*) The groves on the banks of the Mouse, consist chiefly of Elm and Box Elder; on the Alkaline Sulphuret Lake above mentioned, a Balm of Gilead Poplar was noticed, and generally the country between Devil's Lake and the Mouse, is richer in trees than any other portion of the territory visited by the two expeditions, always excepting the well-timbered Missouri Valley, where the Cottonwood, Oak, Ash, Maple, Box Elder, Hackberry, Willow, Cedar, Bull-Berry and Wild Grape, Poison Ivy, Choke Cherry, Plum and June Berry, (*Amelanchier?*) The latter plant is also found at Devil's Lake, and in the lower courses of most of the tributaries of the Missouri. The plateaus and untimbered valleys are everywhere characterized by the Buffalo Grass, and other grasses, Sunflower, Artemisia, Aster Finnia, and other Composites, Roses and Cactacea in the Opuntia, and globular form. One of the globular species is a representative spring-flower of this section, each Cactus appearing on the ground like an inverted saucer, and being covered by many pink blossoms, soon after the snows have disappeared. The berries of the same species, ripening in September, are edible, much resembling Gooseberries in flavor.

The entire section of the country visited by the two expeditions, is inhabited by the Buffalo, Antelope, Elk Deer, Wolf, Coyote, Lynx, Badger, Otter, Mink, Ermine, Beaver,

Prairie Dog, Gopher, Mushrat, numerous small Rodents, &c., the Buzzard Prairie Owl, many species of Hawks, the Prairie Chicken, Frogs, Toads, Garter-snake, Massasauga Rattlesnake and King-snake. In the small streams and pools in dry creeks, the Sun Perch and small species of Cat Fish, are frequent; in the Lakes of the Eastern Plateau, Salamander Ichtyoid Batrachians abound, though fish are sometimes or often absent. In Devil's Lake, Pickerel are found, while the Missouri contains large Catfish, several species of Sturgeon, &c., but apparently only small numbers of these. The Fauna of the Plateau on the East of the Missouri, is specially distinguished by the immense numbers of water-fowls, Ducks, Geese, Water-hens, Divers, Snipes, Cranes, Plover, Bitterns, &c., found everywhere. The more extensive waters of Devil's Lake abound in these, and besides in Swans, Pelicans, Herons, Recurvirostras, Fish-hawks and Gulls. On the western side of the Missouri, insect-life is very highly developed in innumerable forms, the orders of Orthoptera (Grasshoppers, Crickets and Phasmas) Diptera, Hymenoptera, Neuroptera, Hemiptera and Coleoptera appearing to predominate. The small creeks and ponds show but very few forms of Mollascs, only *Physa* (*heterostropha?*) *Limnea* (*stagnalis* and *desidiosa*) a *Planorbis*, a *Cyclas* and an *Anodon* being observed, none of these so far as remembered, on the shores of the Mini-Wakan.

The difference in the climate of the Plateaus on the two sides of the Missouri Valley is very remarkable. The western side is in part at least, exceedingly arid, dry and hot, so much so, that western winds passing the Missouri Valley between Fort Sully and Fort Rice, feel as if they had passed through an oven. Yet in the middle of August on the Yellowstone, 35 miles above its mouth, the expedition of 1864 experienced heavy frosts. The Eastern Plateau is very wet, and when the expeditions of 1864 and 1865 crossed it, cold rains were very frequent, chilling men and animals, causing the death of some of the horses in the month of September. The Western side, the Missouri Valley, and especially the Bad Lands of the Little Missouri, are very subject to hailstorms, often resulting in sudden inundations. Such an inundation was observed by the expedition in 1865, near Fort Berthold, a wall-like mass of water ten to fifteen feet high, rushing down a small dry watercourse, on which the expedition was camped. In the narrow gorges of the Bad Lands of the Little Missouri, the effect of these floods was observed by the presence of tree-trunks and brush-wood, at a height of fifty feet above the level of the then dry water-courses. During both expeditions, the nights were bright with auroras, sometimes for weeks in succession, and especially is this the case between Fort Berthold and Devil's Lake, and in the neighboring sections of country.

October 24, 1870.

The President in the chair. Twenty-four persons present.

DR. L. FEUCHTWANGER, exhibited a specimen of a mineral which has gone by the name of **Onoprite**. It is a Selenio-Sulphide of Mercury, and was first obtained by Del Rio near San Onopre, in Mexico. H. Rose has made an analysis of it showing it 6·49 per cent. of Selenium, 10·30 of Sulphur, and 81·33 of Mercury. The specimen exhibited was not from the original locality in Mexico, but from the Santa Clara Mine, in Lake County, California, near Clear Lake. It was of particular interest, on account of its locality, being associated with the Cinnabar of California. Lately it has had the name of Tiemanite bestowed upon it.

He also exhibited specimens of **Stream Tin Ore from Durango, Mexico.** This resembles so closely the Stream Tin of Cornwall, England, that they cannot be distinguished. Unfortunately labor is so precarious, and other attendant circumstances are so unpropitious, that the working of this ore at Durango, has not been prosecuted so that the English mines still continue to supply the major part of the Tin of commerce; although the new Missouri mines promise very well, ores yielding as high as eight per cent. having been lately reported from there.

He also exhibited specimens of **Black Band Iron Ore from Pottsville,** where it occurs in large quantities.

DR. J. S. NEWBERRY, remarked that in Ohio beds of the Black Band Iron Ore, have been found of at least sixteen feet thick, but these are not common, thinner beds are frequently worked, and very advantageously, as this ore is an easy one to smelt, and at the same time, one which, as a general rule, yields a very superior quality of metal.

PROF. O. W. MORRIS, presented specimens of **Fossils** from **Webster Tunnel, Colesville, Broome County, N. Y.** These are much weathered, but can be distinguished as coming from the sandstones of the Chemung group.

PROF. D. S. MARTIN, exhibited specimens of **Cassiterite from San Jacinto, San Bernadino County, California,** and of the Tin smelted from the ore. The metal on analysis, is shown to consist of Tin 99·78. Iron 0·11. Copper 0·11. The ore is reported to yield 13·37 per cent. of metal. It is being worked very extensively and successfully.

He also exhibited a fine specimen of **crystallized Cinnabar from Napa County, California.** The crystals were of remarkable perfection of form and good size.

He also exhibited a specimen of **Copper Glance,** replacing woody-fibre from the three forks of the Little Washita River, Archer County, Texas. This was a remarkable specimen, inasmuch as the texture of the wood was very perfectly retained, whilst its original constituents had been entirely replaced by the copper compound. On analysis it was found to contain 55·44 per cent. of Copper, with a little Malachite and Carbonaceous matter.

DR. NEWBERRY remarked that specimens of this kind, in which the woody tissue has been replaced by Copper compounds, are extremely common all over that section of country from which this was obtained. They are from the

Permian formation, generally in Sandstone, and in some of the old Spanish mines, are to be seen excavations which have been made for the purpose of coming at these trunks of trees, which has been converted into cupiferous ore. Some of these mines have been, in former times, worked to a considerable extent, but now are neglected.

Dr. Newberry exhibited a specimen of a **Fossil** of considerable interest. It was obtained at **Long Branch,** below the water-mark, by a gentleman whilst in bathing setting his foot upon it. On being brought to the surface, and subsequent careful examination, it proved to be a very strongly-silicified specimen of the anterior portion of the **Craniun of a Walrus.** Only three other similar specimens are known to have been found, and all of them from this same locality. Dr. Leidy, who has examined and reported upon these specimens, has determined them to be crania of the existing species of Walrus or Morse (*Trichecus rosmarus*). This specimen exhibited a portion, broken off of one of the so-called tusks which are so conspicuous in the head of this animal. These are really the upper canine teeth produced to this extraordinary extent, the other teeth being very small in comparison, and in number exceedingly variable, according to the age of the animal. On account of the development of these teeth, which furnish a very fine quality of ivory, the animal is hunted. The upper jaw is, at the muzzle, much enlarged, and hence the nostrils are removed from their usual position, to a higher locality than that which they occupy in other Seals, to which family the Walrus belongs. The fossil specimens are either Tertiary, being washed out of the beds contiguous to the spot where they have been found, by the action of the waves, or they are of recent origin, but they would seem to be most likely Tertiary, as we can hardly imagine several individuals of Walrus being carried so far South as Long Branch, on the New Jersey coast, either by means of ice, or in any other way. Similar crania have been found in the shell-heaps which occur upon the coast of Maine, but none of them are silicified.

MR. J. HYATT made some remarks on **Auroras.**

On this evening, Monday, October 24, 1870, a very remarkable Auroral display has been observed over New York city. In the North, at first, was seen an obscure segment, low towards the horizon, surmounted by a pale glow of light. Later in the evening, this was replaced by an extensive manifestation of beautiful streamers.

But the most notable part of the phenomenon, was a band of brilliant red light varying in its different parts, constantly throughout the evening, in brilliancy, definition and breadth, but in general some ten degrees wide. It was seen early in the evening, and could be traced from within fifteen degrees of the horizon in the East and the West, extending entirely across the sky, south of the Zenith.

The position of this rosy red band, viewed from the southeast corner of the Central Park, was from 8.15 to 8.30 P. M. N. York City mean time about as follows:

In the East it could be seen just above the horizon, passing centrally and diagonally through the figure of *Cetus*, say be tween *delta and zeta Ceti;* thence going westward, it lay between *Piscis occidentalis and gamma Aquarii* and between *Altair and Delphinus*, often expanding in width beyond their boundaries. Thence it extended westward to the stars in the heads of *Hercules* and *Serpentarius*, nearly to the horizon.

In all its splendid variations throughout the evening, this red band maintained its position in regard to the horizon of the observer standing in the locality before mentioned, the diurnal motion of the earth carrying the stars past it.

Mr. W. H. LEGGETT, called attention to some of the wonderful provisions in the vegetable kingdom, by means of which the seeds of plants are distributed; the seed-case often holding the seed until the period of its ripening, when it is cast out in ways particular to the species of plant and specially provided therefor.

MR. J. W. WARD, called attention a remarkably fine exhibition of the results of glacial action, now to be seen upon New York Island, and laid bare in consequence of excavations made for the extension of streets in the upper part of the city.

The following paper was read:

The Geological Position of the Remains of Elephant and Mastodon in North America.

By Dr. J. S. Newberry.

The genera *Elephas and Mastodon* existed on the globe during the Miocene Tertiary Epoch and were represented by various species from that time to the advent of man. The question before us is, when the two species *Elephas primogeneus* and *Mastodon giganteus* are first met with in ascending the geological scale? In Europe it is claimed that remains of these species are found in the true Bowlder Drift and in California in the Pliocene Tertiary deposits. Whether either of these statements is strictly true remains to be decided by future investigations. In central and eastern North America the remains of Elephant and Mastodon are found abundantly in Peat Bogs and other superficial and recent deposits, also in some strata of unconsolidated material which are considered as belonging to the Drift, although there has been much difference of opinion whether these beds form part of the true undisturbed Drift, or whether they consist of re-arranged drift-materials or what is called "Modified Drift." The facts now offered, seem to prove conclusively that the remains of Elephant and Mastodon are found in the true and unchanged Drift, but only in the more recent of the Drift-deposits.

The presence of these great mammals must therefore be considered as one of the incidents in the history of the Drift; but as incidents belonging only to the last chapters in this long and somewhat eventful history.

In order that the advent of the Elephant and Mastodon may be properly placed in the sequence of phenomena embraced in the Drift period, it will be necessary to make a brief review of these phenomena so far as they are known to us.

The geological periods immediately antecedent to the Drift are the Cretaceous, which was a period of marked continental submergence, when the ocean covered most of the Western half of the continent and reached several hundred feet higher than now over the basis of the eastern highlands; and the Tertiary with its three subdivisions Eocene, Miocene and Pliocene. The Eocene was a period of continental progressive emergence—land area gradually expanding, climate subtropical. In the Miocene and Pliocene epochs the topography was in a general way what it is now, but in detail the surface was considerably more diversified, especially by the presence of great fresh-water lakes which occupied much of the surface on both sides of the Rocky Mountains. At this time there was probably a land connection between the northern part of North America and Europe on the one hand and Asia on the other. The climates of Alaska and Greenland were then as mild as that of Virginia now; the flora was luxuriant and varied, and was common to Europe, Iceland, Spitzbergen, Greenland, our continent and North-eastern Asia; palms grew further north than the Canadian line. The fauna was much richer than now, including Elephant, Rhinoceros and many other animals not now living in either of the Americas, and indeed as large a number of the great mammals as are now found in Africa.

This picture which geology gives us of our continent—the picture of a country more beautiful and fertile than now, covered with a more luxuriant and varied vegetation and with a much nobler fauna, is followed by another almost its opposite in all things. This is the Ice period, when the present climate of Greenland was brought down to New York, when the continent was several hundred feet higher than now and a large part of the surface covered with glaciers as far down as the line of the Ohio. This period continued long enough to produce a general planing down and grinding off of the surface rocks, and long enough for the draining streams to cut their valleys to a much greater depth than they now exhibit.

The mouth of the Hudson was then eighty miles south and east of its present position and six-hundred feet lower. The Mississippi discharged itself into the Gulf through a valley of its own making, bordered by bluffs as bold and picturesque as those between which it flows in the vicinity of St. Paul. In process of time the continent sank at least a thousand feet. The glaciers retreated northward leaving behind them water basins of great extent in which were deposited the older Drift strata, the Erie clays in the interior, the Champlain clays on the coast, both fine stratified deposits the clay flour ground by the glaciers. In these clays, so far as yet known, no remains of Elephant and Mastodon have been found. In Canada and New England the clays contain large numbers of arctic marine shells, in the interior some fresh-water shells have been reported in them, but it is not certain that they have not been derived from overlying and more recent beds. In the Western States the lower drift clays are covered by beds of sand and gravel of considerable thickness, and these in turn are strewed over with innumerable bowlders, many of large size, for the most part granites, greenstones, &c., transported from the Canadian and Lake Superior highlands. Among these bowlders or in the superficial gravel some hundreds of masses of native copper have been found, brought, without question, from the Kewanaw copper range.

Still more recent than the latest Drift deposits, there are found running through the Drift-covered area, terraces and beach-lines which prove that the water-level of the great Lakes was once more than three hundred feet higher than now.

The superficial bowlders and gravels of the Drift, are clearly the result of iceberg action. It is proven by the undisturbed condition of the clays below, that they must have been *floated* to their present resting places just as boulders, sand and gravel are floated from Greenland to the banks of Newfoundland and there spread broadcast over the sea bottom.

In the Drift deposits above the blue clay, remains of Elephant and Mastodon have been repeatedly found still more frequently in the Peat-bogs of the present surface, and the much-discussed question has been, whether these mammalian remains were deposited with the upper layers of the Drift or were buried in them by subsequent shifting, as in the valleys of streams. The facts to which attention is now specially directed would seem to decide that question.

It has long been known that in many parts of the valley of the Mississippi, wells penetrating twenty, thirty or more feet, the superficial accumulations of *drifted* materials—clays and sands with gravel and bowlders brought from the far north—encounter sticks, logs, stumps and sometimes a distinct carbonaceous soil. Combining facts of this character, of which records have been accumulating from year to year, with those brought to light by recent investigations directed specifically to this object, it is proven that over a great area at the West a sheet of buried timber, a vegetable soil, beds of peat covered with sphagnous moss, erect stumps, and in some cases standing trees,—form a distinct line of demarcation between the older and newer drift deposits.

In or above the horizon of this ancient soil have been found numerous animal remains: *Elephas*, *Mastodon*, *Castoroides* (the great extinct beaver) and some others.

All these facts show that in the sequence of events included in our Drift period there is a marked break, a middle period, during which, over most of the north-western states, no Drift deposits were made and when most of this area was covered with a forest growth and sustained many and large animals. At a subsequent period, all parts of this area, less than 500 feet above the highest of our present great lakes, was submerged, and most portions of it covered to a greater or less depth, with new Drift deposits, clays, sands, gravel and bowlders, a large part of northern and remote origin. Nearly all the large bowlders of the Drift belong to this later epoch, are sometimes of great size, (100 tons) and have been *floated* to their present positions, as they overlie undisturbed stratified sands and clays, which would have been broken up and carried away by glaciers or currents of water, moving with sufficient velocity to transport these blocks. Hence they must have been floated from the Canadian highlands, the place of origin of most of them, by *icebergs.*

This epoch of the Drift period I have therefore termed the Iceberg Epoch. During this epoch the submergence of the land in the interior of the continent, was greater than in the epoch of the deposition of the Champlain and Erie clays, and all the area north of the Ohio was covered with water up to a height of over 500 feet above Lake Erie, or 1100 feet above the Ocean level. The highlands of south-eastern Ohio, and most of the country South of the Ohio river, were not covered by this flood, and now bear no Drift deposit of any kind. Tracing out the line of ancient water-surface, we find that the depression was greater toward the North, so that the Alleghanies and their foot-hills, and also a wide area of comparatively low country in the Southern states, formed not only a shore, but a continental limit to the great interior iceberg-ridden sea of the later Drift Epoch.

In the western reaches of this sea, which was of fresh water, in the later centuries of its existence, was deposited the Löes or "Bluff" which I have elsewhere designated as the later lacustrine, non-glacial Drift. During the deposition of the Löes, the interior sea was already narrowing and growing shallower by the cutting down of its outlets, or by continental elevation or both. The descent of the water-level, and decrease of water-surface, have been going on perhaps constantly but not uniformly, to the present time, when the area of the great lakes is the insignificant 85,000 square miles it now is. In the descent of the water-level, retarded at certain periods, Terraces and beach lines were formed at various places by the shore waves. With these the history ends.

This then is the classification I would suggest of the Drift deposits, as they occur in the valley of the Mississippi, premising that here as in other geological periods, the column is nowhere absolutely complete.

Period.	Epochs.	Strata.	Notes.
Quaternary.	Terrace.	Terraces, Beaches, Löes.	Sand and gravel beaches with logs, leaves and fresh-water shells. Löes with fresh-water and sand shells.
		Iceberg Drift, Löes.	Bowlders, gravel, sand and clay, drifted logs, elephant and mastodon teeth and bones.
		Forest Bed.	Soil-peat with mosses, leaves, logs, stumps, branches and standing trees, mostly red cedar. Elephas, mastodon, castoroides, &c.
	Glacial.	Erie Clays.	Laminated clays with sheets of gravel, occasional rounded and scratched northern bowlders, many angular fragments of underlying rocks.
		Glacial Drift.	Local beds of bowlders and gravel and rarely bowlder clay resting on the glaciated surface.

From the above table, it will be seen that the remains of Elephant, Mastodon and the gigantic Beaver, occur in the Forest-bed and in all the succeeding Drift deposits. It should also be said that they are found in still greater abundance in peat-bogs and alluvial deposits, which belong to the present epoch.

We have seen that the submergence of the later Drift epoch, though so wide-spread, left a large part of the area lying between the Mississippi and Atlantic uncovered. This area the Elephant, Mastodon, Great Beaver, &c., inhabited during the continuance of the flood that covered the Forest-bed. From this retreat they issued with the subsidence of the water, following the retreating shore-line, till they occupied all the region now exposed about the great lakes. By what influence they finally became extinct, we cannot yet say. It has been claimed that they continued to exist down to the advent of man, and that he was an agent in their destruction. This statement may be true, but requires further proof before it can be accepted with confidence.

The vegetation of the Forest-bed indicates a cold climate, thus confirming what we had otherwise learned of the habits of the extinct elephant. He was clothed with long hair and wool, was capable of enduring, and probably preferred a subarctic climate, and was associated in this country as in Europe, with the musk ox and the reindeer. We may therefore infer that a progressive increase in the animal temperature, drove most of the animals of the Forest-bed northward, and caused to gather on the shores of the Arctic sea, the herds of Elephants whose remains so much impress all travelers who visit that region.

This was probably the scene of the last vigorous and abundant life, and of the death of the species; an event consequent perhaps on the action of local causes, which we shall comprehend when we have opportunities of studying the record.

One remarkable statement in regard to the Forest-bed requires notice. In more than one instance, parties digging wells in South-western Ohio, have reported not only that they found a black soil and logs, but that "*some of these logs bore marks of the axe, and were surrounded with chips.*" These stories I formerly rejected as pure fabrications, but in the light of recent observations, they seem to me to be in part true, and not difficult of explanation.

Prof. Orton reports the finding of the teeth of *Castoroides*, in connection with the peat bog of which he has given an interesting description in the Journal of Science, for July, 1870. Now we know that the great dental chisels of *Castor* and *Castoroides* are exclusively employed in felling and cutting up timber, and wherever these animals have lived, some traces of their work must almost necessarily be found. In Arizona at one of our camps on the San Juan River, I measured three cottonwood trees cut by beavers, within fifty feet of our camp-fire. All these were over two and a half feet in diameter above where cut. In the vicinity were acres of bottom-land, once heavily timbered, now cleaned as if by the hand of man. There the logs and chips quite covered the ground. As the *Castoroides* was more than double the size of the largest living beaver, his prowess as a wood-cutter must have been proportionably greater, and I am disposed to make him responsible for the "cut-logs and chips" reported to have been found in the Forest-bed.

October 31st, 1870.

The President in the chair. Fourteen Persons present.

PROF. O. W. MORRIS presented a mass of brown sandstone full of **Fossils from Colesville, Broome County, N. Y.**

THE PRESIDENT said that this specimen was from a stratum of the Hamilton period which is largely represented in this state and includes the Marcellus shales, the Hamilton formation and Genessee shales. Some of these rocks occur as thin limestone beds, which, where they are not exposed to the action of the weather are hard, compact rocks and then the fossils which they may contain are not readily distinguishable. But, on exposure to the atmosphere, the Lime, of which they are for the most part made up, is acted upon by the Carbonic acid and thereby rendered soluble and washed away. The material of the fossils themselves seems to consist of a harder substance, which is less readily acted upon, therefore often remarkably perfect specimens are thus excavated through the weathering action and drop out. The specimen under consideration is one of the sandstones of this group and is almost entirely made up of individuals of *Spirifer mucronatus*, or rather casts of that Brachiopod as the material which constituted the shell is entirely removed leaving cavities to represent it, and which exhibit the beautiful sculpture of the *Spirifer* in a remarkably fine manner.

With regard to the rocks belonging to this group, the flagging stones of our streets come from a thin layer belonging to the Hamilton epoch. At one point in the state, east of the centre, these rocks attain to a thickness of about 1200 feet and extend to the south-west into Pennsylvania and

Virginia, and westward through Michigan, Illinois, Iowa and Missouri.

DR. L. FEUCHTWANGER exhibited an interesting specimen of **Wolfram from Trumbull, Conn.** It consists for the most part Scheelite, Tungstate of Lime, but at places this mineral has been replaced by the Wolfram, Iron and Manganese taking the place of the Lime, but the crystaline form of the Scheelite has been retained so that we have a remarkable example of pseudomorphism where large crystals appear having the form of Scheelite, but composition of Wolfram. This is stated by Dana to take place by the action of a solution of Bicarbonate of Iron and Manganese, or perhaps mainly through Sulphate of Iron arising from the decomposition of Pyrites. He also exhibited a finely crystalized specimen of Pyrargyrite, a Sulphuret of Antimony and Silver, containing from 58 to 60 per cent. of the latter metal, from Germany.

DR. NEWBERRY presented a **Preliminary Geological Map of Ohio,** constructed by himself and exhibiting the progress of the survey, now being carried on, of that state under his superintendance. A more complete, and larger map will be hereafter published as the survey progresses in its work.

The following paper was read:

On the Colors of Metals.

BY PROF. C. A. SEELY.

Of all the metals two only, Gold and Copper are distinctly colored. When nicely polished the surfaces of all metals become nearly perfect mirrors, reflecting almost all the light, whatever be its tint, which falls upon them and the chemically clean mat surfaces of all metals except gold and copper appear white to the eye. Yet the white light from such surfaces is invariably contaminated with a small amount of colored light, and this colored light is without doubt the result of a normal and ordinary decomposition of the incident white light. If the greater part of the incident white light were in the same way, decomposed, the metals instead of appearing to us white, would shine with splendid colors. The colors of natural objects are always mixed with white light, that is, the white light falling on the surfaces of natural objects is never completely decomposed, and in this regard the case of the metals shows a difference in degree and not in kind. To the eye of the scientist then, all the metals may be colored; the colors are ordinarily invisible simply because they are diluted or overpowered by the white light with which they are mingled. With the explanation thus given I assume in this paper that all metals are colored.

The most satisfactory method of rendering the colors of metals apparent, heretofore proposed, consists in repeatedly reflecting a beam of white light from the metallic surface under examination. A convenient arrangement is two parallel plates of the metal between which the light is reflected from one to the other at a small angle of incidence.

At each incidence the white light is partially decomposed and if the number of incidences be sufficiently multiplied, all the white light will have disappeared, and only the pure colored rays be visible. In this way the colors of most of the metals have been exactly determined. The actual experiment, however, is not a very brilliant one, inasmuch as the larger part of the light with which it begins is lost by gradual diffusion; especially the colored light is so lost, probably for the reason that the decomposition of the white light takes place within the reflecting surface.

Another method of developing the true colors of metals, has recently occurred to me, and it is the main purpose of this paper to describe it. I present first a few theoretical considerations.

When white light is decomposed by a colored body, the reflected colored ray is complementary to that part of the white light which is transmitted or absorbed; if a colored body be seen both by reflected and transmitted light, the colors so seen should be complementary, or an approach to being so. These statements seem to have many exceptions; as, for example, the colored transparent salts of metals, show the same color by reflected as by transmitted light. But I am persuaded that a careful discussion of the case would show that such exceptions are not well taken, and that this apparent discrepancy with the statements may be consistently explained away; thus it may be shown that the supposed reflected light of the exceptions is really a part of the transmitted light which has been returned by internal reflection; such mixture of the transmitted with the reflected light, implies a considerable degree of transparency of the substance under test. The lustre and whiteness of metals have a close relation to their opacity and density; perhaps the relation is that of effect and cause. If the opacity and density of metals be progressively decreased the optical metallic character will in the same ratio be diminished; the true color by reflected light would become brighter and freer from white light till it come to be contaminated with more and more of the returned transmitted light. Such changes are beautifully exemplified by the gradual additions of a solvent to Fuchsine or other Aniline colors in crystals. Aniline colors, Prussian Blue, Indigo, Carmine and all other dye-stuffs which have very great tinctorial powers, have the metallic lustre, and their color by transmitted light is nearly complementary to that by reflected light.

In their relation to light I suggest that metals are closely analogous to those dye-stuffs which show a bronzed surface by reflected light. Metals are more perfectly bronzed because their opacity and density are greater, or in other words their tinctorial powers are greater.

It will be seen that the above theory requires for its demonstration a transparent diluent or solvent of metals, which shall have no chemical action on them. Such a solvent, for a few of the metals, is anhydrous liquid Ammonia. If this menstrum be gradually added to the silver-white alkali metals, the whiteness disappears, is replaced by copper-redness which at last gives place to the blue of transmitted light. The changes of tint in this case from copper-redn ess to the transparent blue may be exactly repeated by treating pure Aniline blue with alcohol. The alkali metals are then copper-red in reflected light, and by transmitted light blue. In this connection, the fact that the salts of Copper are blue, is, perhaps, of some significance.

The solution of metals without definite chemical action, is almost a new idea in chemistry. Faraday made the first approach to it by showing that the color of ruby glass is due to metallic Gold; and it received a final and definite shape in a demonstration of the solvent properties of anhydrous liquid Ammonia, which I made at the late Troy meeting of the American Association for the Advancement of Science.

The tinctorial power of metals appears to be vastly greater than that of any known dye-stuff, and the colors they should yield are very brilliant. There is reason then to hope that these facts about metals may some day receive some useful application.

November 7th, 1870.

The President in the chair. Twenty persons present.

MR. A. R. THOMPSON exhibited several specimens of **Minerals,** including fine prisms of Topaz with perfect terminations, from Brazil, and crystals of Quartz and Spinel.

MR. J. HYATT exhibited specimens of **Minerals,** as Serpentine of the kind known as "Noble," from Pennsylvania, Cryolite from Greenland and Blende.

On motion of PROF. C. A. SEELY, it was decided, for the present, to distribute the printed **Proceedings** of the Lyceum, gratuitously to the members.

Hon. E. G. Squier called attention to the advisability of the Society having a course of **Public Lectures**, to be delivered under its auspices during the present winter, and on motion, a Committee, to inquire into this matter, was appointed. Such Committee to report at the next meeting of the Society.

Mr. G. M. Wilber exhibited a specimen of **Green and white mottled Marble,** from near Saratoga, N. Y., which was recognized by Prof. Edwards, as consisting of *Eozöon Canadense.* The specimen was referred to Prof. Edwards for examination and report.

Mr. J. W. Ward exhibited a specimen of a **White Mineral** which, he stated, came from Delaware, and was represented to consist of finely-pulverized Mica agglutinated into a mass. No chemical examination of it had been made and a microscopical examination revealed no traces of organic remains, only irregular granules.

The President remarked that the determining the mode of genesis of such deposits as this one was of great importance geologically, and the specimen was referred to Prof. Edwards for microscopical and chemical analysis if necessary.

Prof. D. S. Martin exhibited a specimen of **Electro-Silicon,** an article found in commerce and used as a polishing powder.

Prof. A. M. Edwards remarked that this was made up of the siliceous skeletons of Diatomaceæ and in the natural state was a rather hard white rock; for use it was crushed. He was strongly of opinion that the specimen exhibited by Mr. Ward was of the same character. But he would examine it and report at a subsequent meeting.

The President, Dr. J. S. Newberry, read the following letter from **Professor C. F. Hartt,** relating to the **Geology of Brazil.**

On Board Steamer "Jurupensem," near Monte Alegre,
Rio Amazonas, Brazil, Oct. 4th, 1870.

My dear Prof. Newberry,—A streak of good luck has happened on the Amazonas. At a place called Itaituba, (place of pebbles,) I have found a series of Limestones, Sandstones and Clayey beds full of Lower Carboniferous fossils, and I have made a collection, of somewhere in the neighborhood of 150 species, the majority of which are represented by very perfect specimens. The most common of the form are *Producti*, of somewhere in the vicinity of six species. There are forms exceedingly like *P. Lyelli* (*Cora*,) *P. semireticulatus*, *P. striatus*, besides these, there are several very small spiny species. Among the other Brachiapods, I find *Chonetes*, *Terebratula*, *Athyris*, *Orthis*, *Rhynchonella*, *Spirifer*, *Strophomena*, &c., &c. From the roof of a grotto in a heavy bed of Limestone, I collected a large number of exquisite specimens of these fossils, showing interior characters. The Sandstones are very rich in large Lamelli branchiates of a large number of species, the most of them in so good a state of preservation as to admit of determination. Among these are some large Aviculopectens, Gasteropods are not numerous, and, excepting a large *Euomphalus*, are all small. I have several species of Polyzoa, two or three Corals, Crinoid stems, a *Trilobite*, apparently a *Phillipsia*, fragments of scales and teeth of Fish, &c. Extending from Itaituba to the falls are heavy beds of green and black Shales with Septaria, furnishing very few fossils. The few I could find appeared to be Carboniferous, but I could not determine the relations these beds bore to the Limestones. The fossils were Fish teeth, and scales, and spines, organisms exactly like what Dawson supposes to be spore cases of Lipidodendron and a single specimen of a Lipidodendron, or some closely allied genus, badly preserved. All these strata are undisturbed and occupy an immense area on the southern side of the Amazona valley. I have become so much interested in this field that I am determined to return and spend a couple of months in studying it more carefully.

I shall give up the little government steamer I have had for the last two months, divide up my party, and go over the ground with a large canoe.

I forgot to say that I found at the falls, very heavy beds of Red Sandstone more or less altered, much disturbed and broken through by numerous dykes of Prophyry and Trap. I have been wondering whether these beds may not turn out to be the equivalents of our Potsdam Limestone.

I have done a large amount of work in the Amazon Clays and Sandstones. They are all marine formations, but I find no fossils. Trap is associated with them, which certainly does not point to a glacial origin for them.

Please pardon this short note, I thought it might interest you to know that my little expedition has not so far turned out a failure.

With kindest regards, &c.

C. Fred. Hartt.

The following paper was read,

Alleged Discovery of the Arch among the Aboriginal Remains of New Mexico.

By E. Geo. Squier, M. A.

On several occasions, I have taken the trouble of calling the attention of the Society to a series of archæological impostures, that have found a place in our newspaper press—chiefly in the newspapers of the West, where there seems to be a morbid tendency in this direction. Most of them are too transparent to deceive any man of ordinary intelligence, but some are rather adroitly conceived, and have led some very clever students into a painful kind of semi-credence. At their instance, I have several times taken the pains to "hunt down" the current story, and to find it "a hoax!" You will remember the "full and particular" account of the vast, subterranean temple in the Palisades; the wonderful excavations under Rock Island, the remarkable tunnel under the Mississippi river, opposite St. Louis, "the great stone jug in Martin County, Indiana, 80 feet high," "the Onondaga giant," "Prof. Scott's discoveries in Utah," etc. *ad nauseum.* I am almost ashamed to refer to these preposterous stories, which fall within the same category with the accounts of the golden plates of Mormon, the "Holy Stones" of Newark, the Grave Creek inscribed stone, and Pontelli's Discoveries in Guatemala. But when we look back to what the exact sciences have had to pass through, in the way of absurdity and extravagance, before they took a positive shape, we cannot wonder that the infancy of American Archæology should be thus beset. The task of fool-killer is not, however, a pleasant one, nor yet that of clearing away the dead wood of falsehood and ignorance. It is far easier to inculcate a truth than to eradicate an error.

Apart from sheer inventions, like those to which I have alluded, there is another class of impostures, made such by extravagance of description, and absence of critical or accurate appreciation on the part of observers. I mean in matters in which there is a basis of truth—a granule around which careless explorers and loose writers contrive to crystalize a mass of startling and utterly erroneous statement, without apparently being fully conscious of what they are doing. Striving after effect—the prevailing vice of Ameri can writers of a certain class—often carries men past the line of simple extravagance, into the region of real, if not intentional falsehood.

I am led to make these remarks, from having just seen in the newspapers, what purports to be a of *resumé* a report of "Gov. Arny, Special Indian Commissioner in New Mexico," in which he describes certain ancient remains in the Cañon of Chelly. There is no reason to suspect the accuracy of the report generally, for the existence of extensive ruins in the region between the Gila and Colorado, has been known for hundreds of years. Nor am I surprised at the popular, uncritical and utterly unsupported hypothesis that ascribes these remains to the "Aztecs." But when I read that among the ruins are found "*handsome arches* and other architectural devices and ornaments," I suspect something more than extravagance of statement.

In all my explorations in the western part of our own country, and in Central and South America, the seats of highest aboriginal civilization, I have only once found the arch proper among remains *prima faciæ* aboriginal, and that was among the ruins of Pachacamac, twenty miles south of Lima, in Peru. The building in which it occurs is of Inca origin, and called the Mamacona—*i.e.* Convent of the Virgins of the Sun. It is one of several of the same origin intruded among the far more ancient structures of the natives of the Coast, subsequently to the Inca conquest. As will be seen from the photographs that I now submit, this is a perfect, well-turned arch, composed of adobes of large size, in all respects equal to any composed of similar material that are raised to-day. It is said that arches are also found among the aboriginal monuments in the vicinity of Tumbez, Northern Peru.

We all know that a kind of bastard arch, formed by overlapping stones, or flat stones set at a certain pitch against each other, like the rafters of a house, was known among all the relatively-civilized nations of the continent; but the true arch is a thing exceptional, and the one to which I have alluded entirely enigmatical, as I can scarcely conceive that the knowledge and skill of which it gives evidence, could have existed even among these wonderful architects, the Ancient Peruvians, without having a wider or more general application.

I do not believe in the existence of arches among the ruins in the Cañon of Chelly, or anywhere else in New Mexico, except among the remains of the old Spanish missionary establishments, which have more than once been confounded with the monuments of the Indians.

But whatever exaggeration or error of statement may have been made about the ruins in the Cañon of Chelly, it is dwarfed by the assertion that was made by Capt. Carmichael, at the late meeting of the British Association in Liverpool, namely, that "he had recently returned from California, where he had heard a Japanese and a Digger Indian of Nevada, then brought together for the first time, *converse intelligibly!*" I heard a similar story about the remnant of the Yunga or Chimu Indians, of the town of Eten in Peru, who preserve their ancient language. These, it was alleged, could converse freely with the newly-arrived Chinese. I hardly need say that I found not the slightest ground for the statements.

November 14th, 1870.

The President in the chair. Thirty-two persons present.

HON. E. G. SQUIER, Chairman of the Committee on **Public Lectures,** reported as to procuring lecturers, which there was found to be no difficulty in doing, and as to rooms in which to hold the lectures; also as to means to be employed in carrying out the wishes of the Society in this respect.

On motion of DR. L. FEUCHTWANGER, the report of the committee was accepted.

On motion of PROF. C. A. SEELY, a Committee consisting of five, including the President and Secretary, be appointed by the chair to carry out the matter of Public Lectures.

The President stated that the names of the gentlemen to act upon this committee, would be announced at a subsequent period.

The President read a letter from Mr. J. C. Brevoort, announcing that **Prof. Poey,** of Havana, a corresponding member of the Society, had prepared a paper for publication in the Annals, to cover about twenty-five pages, on the **Genera of Percoid Fishes of Cuba.**

DR. L. FEUCHTWANGER exhibited and made some remarks on an interesting specimen of **Lignite** or Brown Coal, containing the impression of an Ichthyolite, resembling very much the *Esox Islebiensis* from the Mansfeld Copper-slates of

Prussia. This specimen was from Westphalia, and is reported to contain 72 per cent. of Carbon, and 22 per cent. of Oxygen, with a very little Hydrogen, but it would seem, judging from its light color, that this estimate of the quantity of Carbon present is too high, unless it occurs united with other substances, so as to make up light-tinted compounds. We know that the carboniferous age, and that in which the copper-slates were deposited, are very far apart from each other, particularly the epoch of the Prussian Copper-slates, in which this species of fish, (*Esox Islebiensis*,) and this species only, is so abundant. At the time he (Dr. F.) visited this locality, in 1827, during a very short period of exploration, he had gathered a large number of these Ichthyolites, in fact as many as he could conveniently transport. Almost every specimen of the material examined, contained one or more of these impressions, showing how extremely abundant they are at that point.

The Brown Coal or Lignite is a true Coal, and is very unlike the *Gagates*, our Jet, which is described by Dioscorides, and is thought by some to be a hardened bitumen. In England and elsewhere it is considerably worked up into ornaments and jewelry. The Lignite formation is very abundant in various parts of Europe and in our own country, as Texas and elsewhere in the West, where Tertiary beds of the same material occur covering considerable districts.

The President remarked on the beauty of the specimen exhibited by Dr. Feuchtwanger, and stated that it was evidently from the stratum which is known as the "Paper-Coal" of the Rhine, which belongs to a late part of the Tertiary. This name, in German *Papierkohl*, has been bestowed on certain layers of the Tertiary Lignites, from their papery or leaf-like composition and fracture. On examination it is plainly to be seen that it is made up of masses of compressed leaves. In fact, in the fresh state, the venation of the leaves composing it can be made out.

Lignite, as usually understood, having its name derived from the Latin name for wood, *lignum*, is really fossil wood, and often exhibits woody structure in a very beautiful manner. Lignite beds are found in various deposits up to a very recent date, as in the New Red Sandstone, Upper Cretaceous and Tertiary. The Lignites of Germany and of the continent of Europe generally, are chiefly Tertiary, and from the remains found in them, as leaves, fruit, stems of palms, &c. give evidence of a much warmer climate having existed during that period and in those localities, than occurs at the present time. The same holds good with respect to the Lignites of this continent, which are of very considerable extent, more especially in some of the Western states.

The fish found in the Paper-coal are mostly Cycloid, whilst those of the copper-slates mentioned, which belong to the Permian, are Ganoid.

MR. J. HYATT exhibited several specimens of the **Nutmeg** (*Myristica moschata*), from the West Indies, into which islands it has been introduced from India or the Cape of Good Hope, at both of which places it is native. The specimen showed the fruit as it grows, with the fleshy pericarp upon it, and which constitutes the Mace of commerce, the Nutmegs proper being the seed within.

The following paper was read,

Microscopical Examination of Two Minerals.

BY PROF. A. M. EDWARDS.

There was exhibited, at the last meeting of this Society, two specimens of minerals which, on account of their peculiar characters, seeming to indicate that an examination by means of the microscope, would reveal facts of interest connected with their source and origin, were referred to me for investigation in that manner. I have viewed them by means of the microscope, and now, report upon them as follows:

The first is a specimen of marble reported to come from a spot on the Adirondack and Lake George Railroad, near Thurman Station, Warren County, and about twenty-five miles from Saratoga in this state, New York, and was polished so as to show its texture very well. In color it is white, mottled with light green, and having scattered through its mass large patches of transparent, so-called, Noble Serpentine. Mr. G. M. Wilber, who contributed the specimen, was not acquainted with the exact locality, but Prof. D. S. Martin recognized it to be identical with some in his possession, from that portion of New York State indicated.

Without any special preparation and examination, by means of a simple lens alone, the whole mass was seen to consist of *Eozöon Canadense* in a remarkably-fine state of preservation. Subsequently I cut slices from it and ground them thin enough to permit sufficient light to pass through, so that the microscope with higher power lenses could be employed in studying it. Some specimens I acted upon by means of dilute Hydrogen Chloride, (Muriatic Acid) and compared with very beautiful specimens of the original *Eozöon Canadense*, from Canada, and for which I am indebted to my fellow-member, Dr. L. Feuchtwanger. These specimens from both localities, as well as illustrative plates, I now exhibit, so that all may see and confirm my discovery, which must be considered as one of considerable importance, when viewed from a geological point of view. It will be observed that the New York specimens are very much finer than the Canadian ones, that is to say, they show the structure of this foramenifer in a strikingly-clear manner, and this the more particularly after the action of the acid. At some future time I may take an opportunity of entering into a consideration of some points connected with the structure and affinities of *Eozöon Canadense*, for in this material, thus fortunately brought to light, we have extremely-favorable opportunities of studying its intimate anatomy. This I will have a better opportunity of doing when I receive further supplies of the material, which I am endeavoring to procure, and which is said to occur in large quantities at the point from which this was brought.

It is well known that the presence of this fossil is considered to indicate, that the rocks containing it belong to the Laurentian group or period, and the bringing of them over the border and down thus far into New York State, is of great geological importance. This is the more so, as the members of the Canadian Geological Survey, have only lately traced these rocks down into New England, as far, at least, as Salem, Massachusetts.

The other specimen referred to me for examination by means of the microscope, and chemically if found necessary, is the lump of nearly white material, exhibited by Mr. J. W. Ward, and thought by him to be finely-pulverized mica, and said to come from a bed of clay in the state of Delaware. At the time of its exhibition, I expressed my strong conviction that it consisted of the siliceous skeletons of Diatomaceæ, and my suspicions have been confirmed. In fact, strange to say, it proves to be a mass from the now well-known deposit, existing at Six mile Cañon, near Virginia City, in the state of Nevada, and some of which under the name of "Electro Silicon," was exhibited by another member at the same time. At this locality this remarkable material is reported to occur in the form of a stratum several hundred feet in thickness. It is rather hard and stony, so it is ground down to a fine powder and then comes into commerce as a polishing material, and has been rather fancifully christened, "Electro Silicon." It is an example of the kind of deposit I have had already to allude to before this Society, as Sub-Plutonic, examples of which are so common all through our Pacific States. At some future time I will have something to say concerning the genesis of these deposits.

We have in these two examinations, which I have been enabled to make, further evidence, if it were necessary which fortunately it is not, of the value of a knowledge of the means of employing the microscope to the geologist; for, using it, facts have been thus readily and in a few minutes settled, which no chemical or other analysis, taking perhaps hours to perform, would indicate.

The following paper was read:

Progress of an Investigation of the Structure and Lithology of the Hudson River Palisades.

BY HENRY WURTZ.

This is but a partial report of progress in a work which is to be continued, if permitted to the author indefinitely, as the subject can scarce admit of exhaustion.

1. STRUCTURE AND GEOGONY.

The following notes are chiefly collated very concisely from a paper which was mailed for presentation at the Chicago meeting of the AMERICAN ASSOCIATION, in August, 1868, but which failed to reach its destination.

The two regions of the Connecticut Valley beds and that of New Jersey, (called by DANA the "Palisade Range") appear correlative to each other, the structure of one being repeated in the other inversely; for example, the duplicate ranges of trap through the middle of each, and the convexities of the crescent-shaped trap outcrops facing each other. As yet, there is no reason for supposing that the epoch of commencement of formation of these beds, was later than the close of the Carboniferous. The lithological characters of the Sub-Palisade beds, differ much from those of the overlying beds, arguing different chemical conditions during their deposition. In these the Iron minerals, for example, are usually *Hœmatite* or *Turgite*, instead of *Limonite* as in the beds over the Palisades. It is held, therefore, that if the latter are Triassic, the former may possibly be earlier, say Permian. Dr. DAVID DALE OWEN argued, (*Am. Jour. Science*, iii. 365,) strongly in favor of placing the Permian at the base of the Mesozoic. The author is even inclined to believe that the great movements that are known to have closed the Carboniferous, were simultaneous with the deposition of part of these beds. The author rejects the views held by some, that the beds were originally deposited with their present N. W. dip, or, as this hypothesis is well set forth by Prof. GEO. H. COOK, Geology of New Jersey, 1868, p. 174; "the strata on the S. E. border were first deposited on this N. W. slope; and then that the upper edges were worn off, and the material carried further N. W. to be again deposited and form new strata upon the lower parts of those already deposited. Without any addition of material, there would, in this way, be a multiplication of strata all having the same dip.

And such a process could go on, until the formation had widened out to its present extent. Such a mode of formation, would not require that the whole series of strata should be more than a few hundred, or possibly a thousand feet in thickness. This ingenious notion is upset, by an observation first made by the author of an abundant occurrence in the coarser beds, as for example, under the trap at the Passaic Falls, of fragments of the Green Pond Mountain chain lying to the North West.

President HITCHCOCK's argument of original approximate horizontality, drawn from the "bird-tracks," appears cogent, and, in fact, unanswerable. Moreover, it is hard to see how the above hypothesis necessarily reduces the *length of time* or end of deposition, even if it be fully accepted. Between the Carboniferous and Cretaceous, an immense period is represented in Europe, while RAMSAY makes there at least *three complete breaks in succession*, each of which he believes was greater in duration than the rock-making periods between, whilst here we need not suppose any breaks. The author argues from the general ferric condition of the Iron, that the beds are of fresh-water origin, as the Iron in marine sediments is usually ferrous. Also this ferric condition shows that there might have been a great abundance of organic life, whose remains were chiefly destroyed by the powerful oxidating agencies at work. His theory previously presented to the Lyceum, of the relations of silica in isolated mineral forms, to life, led him at this point in his investigation, to examine the nature of the cement or paste, which concretes these rocks, and which has heretofore been assumed to be, in the granular beds, ferric oxide. Some have also supposed the presence of silicates and Carbonate of Lime and Magnesia, Dolomite, etc. Boiling Muriatic acid, however, removes all these from these rocks, without in the least affecting their concrete consistence, or injuring the cohesion of the mass. The cementing materials are, in fact, as anticipated, largely or chiefly made up of soluble or opaline Silica. This is claimed by the author, as proving that, as in the Eastern Virginia and North Carolina Coal basins, these New Jersey and Connecticut beds were accompanied by abundant vegetation. The angular forms of the granules, is claimed to disprove sea-beach or wind-blown origin. The theory is presented, that the medium of deposition of the New Jersey and Connecticut systems, was an immense elevated fresh-water lagoon or lake, which received in both cases from fluviatile systems corresponding exactly to those now in action, but immensely greater in power and volume, the material eroded from Alpine mountains, corresponding in New Jersey to the present Highlands. The New Jersey beds, were deposited, almost horizontally, on the N. W. slopes, and the Connecticut on the Eastern slopes. As Dana suggests, there must have been continuous, or more probably intermittent subsidences during the whole immense period. In these subsidences the coasts of the basin must have participated.

The trap beds were formed, like the five Coal seams in the Deep River Basin in North Carolina, during epochs of elevation above the water, and were followed by renewed subsidences, at the West End of the New Jersey Railroad cut through the Palisades, the author recognizes sedimentary beds overlying the trap which are mineralogically identical therewith, and which are so regular that they must have been deposited from water flowing S. E. over the previously consolidated trap, and were afterwards themselves metamorphosed, consolidated and crystallized, by permeation of hot solutions exuding from the underlying mass. Close examination has detected bedding and lamination throughout the whole mass of the Palisades, and the author has been forced to the conviction that this whole range is sedimentary and metamorphic. The second range of trap in New Jersey however, (First or Newark Mountain) may be, in places, true eruptive trap. The Hoboken Serpentine has been found also by him, particularly throughout its upper portions, to be bedded and laminated conformably with all the overlying rocks, the planes of lamination being composed of Magnesite. He therefore places this Serpentine at the basis of the Sub-Palisade beds, as an altered sedimentary rock. He connects the formation of this, with that of the Westchester Dolomites. Thus by interaction of water, Silica and Calcareous beds (of Zoic origin) in the metamorphism of the underlying Schists, at a high heat, produced probably by the enormous dynamic tensions in play, Silicates were formed, with concentrated aqueous solutions of Carbonic Acid. Such solutions would necessarily make their way towards the surface, and would meet at lower temperatures Magnesian and Calcareous Silicates. As well known, solutions of Bicarbonate of Magnesia would be formed to the exclusion of the Lime. Still nearer the surface, and at still lower heats, in permeating beds in the one case of Silicious (Opaline or Chalcedonic) materials, the interleaved Serpentine and Dolomite would be formed, and in the other case, Calcitic layers converted into Dolomites. In similar ways the metamorphic traps must have been formed, as well as the heavy beds of highly-laminated rocks which everywhere underlie the Palisades, and which have been designated Trapoid Schists by the author.

The frequent enclosure, in the coarser beds, of pebbles, of the shales and laminated sandstones themselves, as fully consolidated as their present matrix, which must have come from higher levels, shows that during the process of deposition, a tilting must at times have been going on in a direction opposite to that which has since brought up the beds into their present positions, in order to bring up older beds of the Sandstones themselves, towards the N. W., that had been deposited long enough, to have already undergone concretion. Such tilting, however, need have been but comparatively small in amount, and was a necessary consequence of a greater subsidence along the axis of the basin. Such slight inward inclination of the beds on both sides of the basin, explains the crescent form of the edges of the sheets of trap. The flow or the propagation of the metamorphic agent being thus governed.

The concluding epoch of the whole era, was a cessation of subsidence, and the rising again of the whole intervening country, at least fifty miles wide, upon an anticlinal axis, thus draining the Lagoon, tilting the Lacustrine beds which formed the sloping walls of its basin into their present divergent dips, and bringing these slopes up into horizontal planes.

II. Lithology and Mineralogy.

The author expresses his surprise, that notwithstanding the immense use made of the rocks of this range, particularly in New York, for building, paving, etc., there has been so little ascertained with certainty, about their Mineralogical composition and characters. He has himself extensive series of analyses in progress and projected, but pending their completion, finds some most important points determinable by data already on record, with the addition of numerous density determinations he has made, and examinations of Mineralogical characters.

The rock of the Palisades is generally classed as a Diorite, and vaguely described as composed of "Feldspar and Hornblende." Considerable search led to the finding, near the West End of the Erie Tunnel, of a ledge containing bunches of crystals coarsely enough aggregated for mechanical separation. The dark cleavable prisms imbedded in a crystalline milky white paste, are plainly Orthorhombic, and therefore neither Hornblende nor Pyroxene. Their characters are clearly those of a ferrous Bronzite, or the species called by Dana, (5th Edition of Mineralogy,) *Hypersthene*, (a name heretofore obscurely applied to several species, including some Pyroxenes.) The frequent association of this with Labradorite, leads to the suspicion that the Feldspathic constituent is the latter species, and the rock a *Hyperite* instead of a Diorite. 3 grams of it dissected out (of which an analysis will be made) gave density 2·626; that of the whole mass being 2·983; Von Waltershaugen gives for crystals of Labradorite from Etna, a mean of 2·625. An analysis given by Prof. Cook, (Geol. of N. J., p. 215) of rock from the same region, corresponds with this conclusion:

	Erie Tunnel Rock. Geo. H. Cook.	Calculated Labrador,66. Hypersthene,33.	Calculated Labrador,60. Hypersthene,40.	H. Wurtz.
Densities	2·94	2·93	2·98	2·983
Silica,	53·9	53·4	53·5	
Alumina,	17·5	20·2	18·2	
Magnesia,	10·3	8·2	8·7	
Lime,	8·0	8·0	7·4	
Ferrous Oxide,	8·0	7·2	8·7	
Soda and Potash,	2·3	3·0	2·7	

The Feldspar cannot be either Orthoclase or Oligoclase, because there is too little Potash and Soda respectively, nor Albite nor Andesite, because too little Silica. Prof. Cook gives many other analyses of traps from other parts of New Jersey, generally, nearly corresponding to this. A trap from Haverstraw, at the northern end of the Palisades, gave Prof. W. density 2·92.

Many density determinations have also been made of samples of the so-called Sandstones and Shales, preparatory to analyses thereof. All these were taken *upon small fragments*, by the method with a stoppered bottle. One from Haverstraw Quarries, (underlying the above trap,) gave 2·608; one from Newark, 2·589; and so on. These results being lower than expected, led to careful examinations of the materials making up these so-called Sandstones, and with some surprise it was found that the angular granules were almost entirely *Feldspar*, nearly and in some cases, quite free from Crystalline quartz. It is supposed that in analyses of these rocks, (the varieties in use for building purposes are referred to,) the portion insoluble in Muriatic Acid has heretofore been assumed to be Sand, without further examination, and that this fact has thus escaped notice. As before stated, these Feldspathic fragments are chiefly concreted by soluble Silica. Density determinations of the "Shaly" beds gave much higher figures, mean about 2·84. This is much too high for any Kaolinite, of which these Shales have usually been assumed to consist, and correspond to Mica, (Muscovite) 2·80, with a small increase due to the Limonite present. On close examination, accordingly these Shales are found to be composed essentially of disintegrated Mica. It may be added that different layers of the Trapoid Schists that underlie the Palisades, and which appear to have been left in a sort of transition state of incipient conversion, from the sedimentary beds into Crystalline trap, gave densities from 2·63, (that of the compact part of the "Sandstones," or of a Feldspar) to 2·80, (that of the compact Shales or of a Mica.)

November 21, 1870.

The President in the chair. Twenty persons present.

The President announced that the **Lecture Committee** would consist of Messrs. Squier, D. S. Martin, Brevoort, Newberry and Brownne.

Dr. L. Feuchtwanger exhibited a fine specimen of **Greenockite,** Sulphuret of Cadmium, reported to come from Friedensville, Penn. If so, this is a new locality for this mineral. He also called attention to what he said was a **New American Locality for Cobalt and Nickel**; illustrating his remarks by specimens. The recent discovery, and the successful working of a mine of very rich native Silver and Argentiferous Galena in Lake Superior, had caused considerable stir among mineralogists as well as among those commercially interested in the metallurgic resources of our country. The locality was a small Island in Lake Superior, at the mouth of Thunder Bay and just off of Thunder Cape. During last year it was reported that eight tons of Ore has been gotten out, which had yielded a return of five thousand dollars; subsequently ten tons had yielded fully three thousand dollars. The specimens exhibited, coming from this locality, consist of Native Silver in prongs and filaments, as well as distinctly crystalline in structure, all of them imbedded in Calcareous Spar, which has been in some cases removed by means of a dilute acid, and the metal exposed. These resemble very closely, specimens from the Gould and Curry mine, in Nevada, as also the Swedish Ore. And there would seem to be little room for doubt as to this new locality proving a prolific one in other respects than silver, for the reason that a Speiss obtained from the roasted ore contains both Cobalt and Nickel in considerable quantities, and, in nearly every character, resembles very closely a Speiss imported many years since, from Saxony, for the purpose of refining and manufacturing German Silver. This Speiss contained 50 per cent. of Nickel and 10 per cent. of Cobalt, besides Arsenic and Iron. A hasty examination of the Lake Superior specimen, shows it to consist of these metals, besides some Copper. The importance of this discovery will be the more fully appreciated, when it is remembered for how many purposes Nickel is now used in the arts. Not alone is it employed for the manufacture of German Silver, but the newly-introduced process of Nickelizing or plating other metals with Nickel, and which would seem to be destined to a great extent to replace Silver plating calls for a large supply. A company are successfully working this mine, paying to the Canadian Colonial Government, the very moderate royalty of twenty dollars the ton of ore.

The President, DR. J. S. NEWBERRY, made some remarks

On Recent Deep-Sea Dredgings.

He described the *suite* of specimens collected by Count Pourtales, in his two seasons of dredging off the southern coast of the United States, in the service of the Coast Survey. The points of special interest in these explorations were, first, the division of the sediments accumulating off our coast into two distinct belts, the mechanical, and the organic, with a line of junction between the two, where their characteristics are frequently mingled. This, Dr. Newberry said, illustrated the truth of a view held since many years by himself, that the accumulation of sedimentary material to make rocks, was altogether a littoral phenomenon, and ocean currents had no essential agency in its accomplishment. Continental masses were constantly being removed by atmospheric erosion, and the comminuted material carried into the adjacent ocean basins. This sediment was transported only so far as the velocity of the water could carry it, hence all coarse material was precipitated as soon as still water was reached, or immediately upon the shore. But a large part of the material brought down by our rivers was taken into solution, hence this material contributed little to the filling of the ocean basins. The deposit made at a distance of one hundred miles from shore, where the water is five hundred feet or more in depth, is almost entirely organic, derived from the decomposition of the tissues of the animals inhabiting the sea. All our sedimentary rocks are formed under water, and mark encroachments of the sea. The sea, when invading the land, carries forward its beach line, formed by shore waves, as an unbroken sheet as far as the encroachment extends. This gives us a sheet of sand or gravel, if the shore affords materials from which sand and gravel can be formed. Above this, we have the deposit of the more quiet water, a little off shore, fine sand and clay; then a mingling of organic and mechanical sediments; finally, where deep water prevails, of pure organic materials, *i. e.* limestones. Each inundation of the land has given us such a cycle of deposits, and nearly all of the great geological formations consist of such a series, coarse sandstones, and conglomerates below, then argillaceous rocks mixed with lime, then pure limestones. The Potsdam, Calciferous and Trenton, the Medina, Clinton and Niagara, the Oriskany, Schoharie and Corniferous; the Portage, Chemung and Sub-Carboniferous limestone and other strata above form such cycles of this series.

Another interesting fact brought to light by Count Pourtales, was the formation of compact hard limestones in the organic belt, as the immediate product of deposition. He had also discovered many new forms of marine life, among which are numerous new Brachypods, Crinoids and Corals. A number of species dredged up by Count Pourtales are identical with those found by Sars, Carpenter and Thompson, on the European coast, showing a remarkable uniformity in the Atlantic deep-sea fauna.

Referring to the discoveries made by Dr. Carpenter, Prof. Thompson &c., in Europe, Dr. Newberry said, that the conclusion drawn from those discoveries that they overturned geological classification, was simply absurd. These explorations in the depths of the ocean had proved only this: that there had been less change in the fauna of the depths of the ocean, than in that of the shores, and that a few forms characteristic of the *fauna* of the Cretaceous and tertiary periods continued to exist there, while they had disappeared in shallower water, but these were the most insignificant possible fragments of great life-groups, that had almost entirely passed away. The finding of a Crinoid or Foramenifer of the Chalk living in the ocean depths, did not recall the race of the great reptiles, winged, swimming and walking; the huge ammonites and the other infinitely-varied forms of the Cephalopoda, which characterize that period. So with all the other geological ages. They were chapters in the life-history of the globe which were distinct and well-defined, holding each its relative place. Human history may repeat itself, but geological history never can.

November 28, 1870.

Prof. B. N. MARTIN, Vice President, in the chair. Fifteen persons present.

The following paper was read,

On the Formation of Deposits of Fresh-Water Diatomaceæ,

BY PROF. A. M. EDWARDS.

The presentation at a recent meeting of this Society, of a specimen of a material which is commonly known as "Infusorial earth," and the discussion arising therefrom, has persuaded me that a somewhat detailed account of what is known concerning this kind of substance, its mode of formation and geological relations, would prove of interest to my fellow members. I, therefore, propose to give in this paper, a brief resumée of the results of very extended examinations made in this field and extending over the last eighteen or twenty years. At the same time, I shall endeavor to place the subject in such a light, that hereafter the true characters of these deposits, shall be understood and not misrepresented, as is unfortunately almost always the case, in published works treating either of geology, microscopy or general natural history. At the outset, it would seem hardly necessary to describe the characteristics of the Diatomaceæ, the organisms which make up the mass of these deposits, and yet it will be as well to say something on this point so as to assure the understanding of what I have to say hereafter. The Diatomaceæ, then, are extremely minute organisms which are most commonly classed among the algæ or cryptogamous aquatic vegetables, and live in both fresh and salt water submerged and, for the most part, adherent to sticks, stones and other similar substances as well as larger plants. They are considered to be unicellular and have skeletons which consist of usually two sections, which shut together like the upper and lower portions of a box connected by an intervening membrane and constructed of pure Silica, whose siliceous loricæ are beautifully sculptured so that they present some of the most elegant objects which the microscopist has to contemplate. They vary in outline almost indefinitely, but in general those which inhabit the sea are constructed on a different plan from those which grow in fresh water. Hence the observer, who has made these organisms a study, is able to distinguish forms which have lived, grown and reproduced, subject to either of these two conditions. In fact, as I have devoted a very large part of my time for the last fifteen years, at least, to the careful study of the Diatomaceæ under varying circumstances and from many localities, and more particularly as relating to geology, I may say that I am almost prepared to determine by the examination with the microscope alone of a specimen from such a deposit as to whether it has been formed in a lake, a pond, or a river, at what altitude, approximately the size of the lake or the swiftness of the stream, besides other facts connected with its deposition. However, on all of these points, I am not sufficiently certain as yet to warrant any further dwelling upon them here, but hope, as further collections are made and records gathered to obtain more valuable elucidating information in this connection. The circumstances connected with the mode of growth and, in fact, the life-history generally of these minute organisms has been by no means carefully enough studied, but I have been for years gathering data relating to the family which will, I trust, assist very materially in unraveling some complicated and important problems in Biology.

The Diatomaceæ, then, being constituted, as I have said, of essentially two parts, or "valves" as they have been called, united by means of a hoop or membrane likewise siliceous in composition, increase or grow by a process of subdivision, in such a way that between and midway of the two valves, are formed two new ones, so that the original single individual becomes in time two united individuals. This double individual, or really two individuals may, at once, separate into two, or remain united, but, at all events, the process of subdivision appears to continue indefinitely, so that we may have resulting a great number of single and separate individuals, or a chain of united individuals from a single one. Under either circumstances the rate of increase in number is extremely rapid, as can be readily understood if we imagine, for instance, that the subdivision of the first single cell into two, occupied the space of time of fifteen minutes, which certainly is not too rapid for some of the Diatomaceæ. Then in the next fifteen minutes four individuals will have been formed; in the next eight; in the next sixteen, so that at the end of twenty-four hours the number formed would amount to 3,388,608 and a large space of water would in this way, have been peopled from a single individual Diatom. But whilst subdivision, or true growth, has been thus progressing, increase by generation or seeding may have taken place at the same time, and from each individual in turn, several young may have been brought forth, which would multiply the rate of increase very materially, of course. It is true that the mode of seeding of these organisms is not thoroughly understood, but we know enough to say that it does occur, and very frequently, and that the number of new individuals thus formed, is very great. At the same time numerous individuals are dying, and as they do so much of the organic matter of which they are composed is dissipated, but some of it, along with the hard siliceous valves and connecting membranes which constituted the skeletons of the Diatoms, fall to the bottom of the pond, and form a layer of greater or less thickness, according to the time during which it has been accumulating. If it be exposed now by draining such a pond, it may appear as a brown or grey powdery mass, but if it has rested beneath the water sufficiently long, almost all of the organic matter will be removed, and the clean white siliceous skeletons alone remain.

Such are the results, then, of this rapid growth of the Diatomaceæ in ponds, lakes, marshes and rivers, and as the first examples of such deposits which I examined were found beneath layers of Peat, I gave to them the name "Sub-Peat" Deposits, and under that designation they have been generally known up to the present time. After a time, however, specimens came into my hands which were procured from the bottoms of existing ponds, and these, besides consisting for the most part of little else than Silica, and being of an almost pure white color, had no Peat overlying them. Hence, of course, I saw the inapplicability of the term "Sub-Peat" to such deposits, and for them I have coined a new name which I consider more appropriate, and at the same time indicating their usual origin, and including all deposits of fresh-water Diatomaceous remains, with the exception of certain peculiar layers to be hereafter described. This new name is Lacustrine Sedimentary. Of course the Sub-Peat then become a variety of these.

Deposits of this character are extremely common in this country, as well as elsewhere, and it will be at once seen that, although any one of them might be of great thickness, yet it does not necessarily follow that it had been forming for any very great number of years, and geologists or others are not warranted from observance of this one fact of thickness, in supposing that a great length of time has intervened during its deposition. Thus, some years since I examined one of these Lacustrine Sedimentary Deposits, at a spot near the town of East Stoughton, in Massachusetts, which was fully twelve feet thick, but only covered a few feet of surface, which circumstance was due to the occurrence of a dam across the course of a stream which arrested its progress, and formed a small deep pond, into which all of the Diatomaceæ which grew for some considerable distance up-stream drained, and dieing accumulated as a light grey-colored powder. I have received specimens of similar material from many points in this country, so that about one hundred have been examined.

The first recorded discovery of a Lacustrine Sedimentary deposit of Diatomaceæ in this country is found in Silliman's Journal, 1839, Vol. XXV. page 118, in an article "On Fossil Infusoria, discovered in Peat-earth, at West Point, N. Y., with some notices of American species of Diatomæ; by J. W. Bailey." Of this I have a small portion given me by

Prof. Bailey himself and, on examination, it is found to have the general characteristics of these deposits; that is to say, it is of a grey color, light in density and very friable; and is made up of the siliceous skeletons of such species of Diatomaceæ as grow in small fresh-water lakes, ponds and marshes. In fact, Prof. Bailey says, that this deposit, which was "eight or ten inches thick, and probably several hundred square yards in extent," was discovered "about a foot below the surface of a small Peat-bog, immediately at the foot of the southern escarpment of the hill on which the celebrated Fort Putnam stands." He considers the remains present in this stratum to be "in a fossil state." And here, perhaps, it is desirable to say something with regard to the use of this term. Its origin would warrant its being applied to anything dug up out of the earth, and as Mr. Page remarks in his Handbook of Geological terms, "hence the earlier geologists spoke of *native fossils* or minerals, and *extraneous fossils*, or the bodies of plants and animals accidentally buried in the earth." For myself I am disposed to restrict the term fossil to the remains more or less perfect of organized beings dating anterior to the present epoch; if we can conscientiously speak of epochs at all where the progression and rate of change has been so gradual. Considered thus, then, these remains of Diatomaceæ cannot be classed as fossils, and at once the geologist perceives that they are to be taken into account in a very different manner from what they have been hitherto. So much then for Lacustrine Sedimentary Deposits of Diatomaceæ, and I trust that I have made clear as to what they are, and how they are formed and forming. At the time I made his acquaintance, and he presented me with a specimen of the West Point deposit, Prof. Bailey expressed an opinion that similar strata would be found beneath every pond and bog in the country. The clear scientific vision of my late friend, is evidenced in the fact that this prediction has proved almost literally true. I have about one hundred such specimens, and am continually receiving others. Several I have already described, and others remain to be examined, and facts with regard to the geographical distribution and other points, will be elucidated by such investigations; so that I am always anxious to receive contributions from all sources. It is only desirable that all facts connected with their mode of occurrence, as amount in thickness and extent, over- and under-lying material, &c., be noted at the time of making the gathering.

We now come to consider deposits of an entirely different character from those just spoken of, but which yet are also made up almost entirely of the siliceous remains of fresh-water Diatomaceæ. These are the so-called "Infusorial" deposits, found in such enormous quantity in our Pacific States. From time to time, during the last thirty years, specimens of these have come into the hands of Naturalists, from collectors and otherwise, and, also, "in place" they are well known to settlers in the districts where they occur. As their true character has not been understood, they have received various appellations, as "Magnesia," "Porcelain Clay," "White Clay," "Chalk," "Siliceous Marl," "Microphytal Earth," "Tripoli," "Rotten Stone," "Pipe Clay" or simply "Clay," "Trachytic Tufa" and "Phytolitharian Tuff" by Ehrenberg. These specimens are almost always white in color or nearly so, although there are records of some strata occurring of various tints. None of these except the white ones, have come under my observation, so I am not prepared to state that the colored ones are Diatomaceous. Besides this material is of a somewhat hard, stony character, but porous withal and light; as a general thing also it is readily broken, but not easily powdered as are the Lacustrine Sedimentary Deposits. On account of this hardness, there is found to be considerable difficulty in preparing these specimens for microscopical examination. After so preparing by a method I have devised, and viewing with a sufficiently high magnifying lens, this substance is found to be made up entirely of the siliceous remains of fresh-water Diatomaceæ, which have been matted together in the remarkable manner described. The species of Diatomaceæ present however, are found to be very different in character from those to be seen in the other class of recently-formed deposits. Thus, whilst the genera most commonly represented in, and making up the mass of the Lacustrine Sedimentary Deposits are *Navicula*, *Pinnularia*, *Stauroneis*, *Synedra* and similar elongated forms, the hard, white material is in general found to consist of myriads of examples of *Orthosira*, *Cyclotella* and similar discoid forms. Although our knowledge of the forms of these minute organisms, peculiar to different kinds of collections of water is rather imperfect, yet we do know that in moderately-small ponds and lakes, we find the Naviculæform genera spoken of above, whilst in the larger lakes are to be seen growing more particularly the discoid genera like *Cyclotella*. From this fact alone, then, we should be prepared to assume that the waters in which the organisms whose remains make up these deposits, grew at one time, covered large tracts of country. And our surmises on this point, are confirmed by the reports of explorers who have passed over this section of country; that is to say on both sides of the Sierra Nevada Mountains, and extending from Puget's Sound to the southernmost border of California.

I have examined many specimens from this district and on account of the mode of occurrence of this material; being capped by Lava, Basalt or some volcanically-erupted rock, I have designated them Sub-Plutonic. The first specimens of such Sub-Plutonic deposits of Diatomaceæ which were put into the hands of scientists were undoubtedly those brought home by Frémont from his expeditions to the Rocky Mountains in the year 1842, and to Oregon and North California in the years 1843–44. The discovery of these, as detailed in his report, gives a good idea of this portion of a country and is as follows. It must be premised that in that report, what is now known as the Des Chutes River, and which is one of the tributaries of the Columbia, is called "Fall River (*Rivière aux Chutes*,") so, also, he spells Klamath Lake "Tlamatt." Speaking of the tributaries of the Columbia, he says, (page 200,) "These streams are characterized by the narrow and chasm-like valleys in which they run, generally sunk a thousand feet below the plain. At the verge of this plain, they frequently commence in vertical precipices of basaltic rock, and which leave only casual places at which they can be entered by horses. The road across the country, which would otherwise be very good, is rendered impracticable for wagons by these streams. At such places, the gun-carriage was unlimbered, and separately descended by hand. Continuing a few miles up the left bank of the river, we encamped early in an open bottom among the pines, a short distance below a lodge of Indians. Here, along the river bluffs present escarpments seven or eight hundred feet in height, containing strata of a very fine porcelain clay, overlaid, at the height of about five hundred feet, by a massive stratum of compact basalt one hundred feet in thickness, which again is succeeded above by other strata of volcanic rocks. The clay strata are variously colored, some of them very nearly as white as chalk, and very fine grained. Specimens brought from these have been subjected to microscopical examination by Professor Bailey, of West Point, and are considered by him to constitute one of the most remarkable deposits of fluviatile infusoria on record. While they abound in genera and species which are common in fresh water, but which rarely thrive where the water is brackish, not one decidedly marine form is to be found among them; and their fresh-water origin is therefore beyond a doubt. It is equally certain that they lived and died at the situation where they were found, as they could scarcely have been transported by running waters without an admixture of sandy particles; from which, however, they are remarkably free. Fossil infusoria of a fresh-water origin had been previously detached by Mr. Bailey in specimens brought by Mr. James D. Dana from the tertiary formation of Oregon. Most of the species in those specimens differed so much from those now living and known, that he was led to infer that they might belong to extinct species, and considered them also as affording proof of an alternation in the formation from which they were obtained, of fresh and salt water deposits, which, common enough in Europe, had not hitherto been noticed in the United States. Coming evidently from a locality entirely different, our specimens show very few species in common with those brought by Mr.

Dana, but bear a much closer resemblance to those inhabiting the north-eastern states. It is possible that they are from a more recent deposit; but the presence of a few remarkable forms which are common to the two localities renders it more probable that there is no great difference in their age."

I have given, in full, all that Frémont says regarding this locality, as it presents us with the first discovery of strata of the remarkable character of which I am now treating, and is therefore of special interest. Bailey's report, contained in the same volume, merely mentions and figures the principal forms he detected.

The only other description of this locality and these remarkable deposits, fortunately, is a much more complete and scientific one. It is that of Dr. J. S. Newberry, as Geologist of the Expedition, under Lieuts. R. S. Williamson and Henry L. Abbot, which explored the route for a Railroad, from the Sacramento Valley to the Columbia River in 1855, and will be found in Vol. VI. of the Pacific Railroad Survey Reports, At page 44 and subsequent pages of the Geological Report, Dr. Newberry gives a description of the Geology of the Des Chutes Basin, which is essentially as follows. It must be remembered that the Des Chutes and Fall River mentioned above, are one and the same.

The Des Chutes basin consists of a series of plateaus, having varying elevations from 4,000 to 22,000 feet above the level of the sea, separated by subordinate ranges of volcanic mountains. These plateaus are usually covered by a floor of Trap, which extends in a smooth sheet from fifty to a hundred and fifty feet in thickness, unbroken except by and at the cañons of the various streams which, as a general thing, flow from the interior to the ocean at right angles to the coast line. Beneath this bed of Trap, is the whitish or light-colored material consisting of the silicious remains of Diatomaceæ we are considering, sometimes occurring as a single bed only, sometimes as a series of beds locally intercalated with thin beds of Trap. These Infusorial strata, as they have been called, are cut, in many places by the Des

Chutes and its tributaries, to the depth of more than a thousand feet, without exposing the basis on which they rest. They are usually quite horizontal, from a few lines to twenty feet in thickness, and very accurately stratified.

Psuc-see-que creek, one of the tributaries of the Des Chutes River, flows through a valley of a remarkable character, as its sides consist of several alternate strata of Diatomaceous material and Columnar Trap or Concrete. Near the base of this series of layers is a stratum, three feet in thickness, of brilliant white Feldspathic Pumice, so soft as to be easily crumbled in the fingers. Above, and lying upon this, is a line of dark carbonaceous matter, less than a quarter of an inch in thickness, from which up into another layer of pumice projects the remains of the branches of some small plant, which had apparently been killed by the overflow of the Pumice. Lieut. Williamson gives a striking view of this locality, and speaks of it in the following terms: "This river cañon is very remarkable. Its sides vary from 800 to 2000 feet in height. The river has cut down its bed to this immense depth, through successive strata of Basalt, with occasionally a deposit of Infusorial marl and volcanic Tufa, which has sometimes hardened into a kind of Conglomerate Sandstone, ten or twenty feet in thickness, and of a white, grey, or reddish color. We followed down this cañon for about five miles, when a rocky spur cut off all further progress, and compelled us to attempt the ascent. This, with great difficulty, we accomplished, and found ourselves on a plain, thinly dotted with sage bushes and clumps of grass. We continued our course, and, after crossing the bed of a torrent of the rainy season, came to a very small stream called Psuc-see-que by the Indians. It was sunk in a cañon about 500 feet deep, cut through successive strata of Basalt, Infusorial marl, Tufas, and Conglomerate Sandstone, like that found in the Mpto-ly-as cañon." (pp. 84, 85.)

Another locality at which these remarkable deposits occur, is on the Pit River, and Lieut. Williamson's description gives such a good idea of the mode of their occurrence that I transcribe it, also, below.

"The banks of Pit River, both above and below the mouth of Canoe Creek, are partially formed by regularly stratified, sedimentary deposits: the first seen since leaving the valley of the Sacramento. They appear on both sides of Pit River, at intervals, for several miles, being in many places interrupted or covered by beds of trap. They are, perhaps, best exposed in the cañon formed by the passage of the river through 'Stoneman's Ridge,' the most conspicuous of the lines of upheaval, which form what is known as the lower cañon of Pit River. They here exhibit a thickness of about fifty feet, but are considerably tilted up, and are covered by a thick bed of trap, which has been poured out over them. They exhibit narrow and parallel lines of deposition, but are very homogeneous, and can hardly be said to form more than two distinct beds. Of these, the upper is white, resembling very pure Kaolin, derived from the decomposition of crystaline Felspar. The lower bed is light brown, or dirty white in color, and has a slightly gritty feel between the fingers. These strata rest upon a thick bed of rolled and rounded fragments of traps, porphyry and basalt, of all sizes, from masses of two and even three feet in diameter, to pebbles. They are generally as large as one's head, and great numbers are each a foot in diameter. The surface of this bed of bowlders is, perhaps, twenty feet above the present surface of the stream; but it bears indubitable evidence of having, at one time, been covered by it, or, at least, the stones composing it, so large and clear, have been rounded where they lie by a current or waves of water. The appearance presented by this bed of bowlders, is different from that of any of the beds of volcanic conglomerate, which are so common in many parts of California and Oregon, or of the stratified conglomerates of the Sacramento Valley, and it is undoubtedly of local origin. The trap which formed the greater part of the bank above, is evidently of recent date; more recent than the infusorial marls, and the marls more recent than the conglomerate, and the conglomerate an accumulation of rolled stones and pebbles, which belongs to the present epoch. The trap which overlies the infusorial marls, composes a large part of the walls of the cañon at this point, where it has been cut away by the stream, and forms nearly perpendicular faces of several hundred feet in height. The soft nature of the underlying strata has, however, very much assisted in its removal." p. 33.

There are several localities, besides those mentioned, at which this, what I have chosen to designate, "Sub-Plutonic" material is found, as Klamath Lake, on the northern border of California, and elsewhere all through the Pacific states. From these I have received gatherings and have thus been enabled to examine, by means of the microscope, specimens from many points, in what was once this chain of enormous fresh-water inland seas; for such they deserve to be styled. For as the microscope reveals the fact, the organisms whose stony remains constitute the mass of these deposits, were inhabitants of collections of fresh-water which existed at some past period as large lakes, and a careful geographical examination of the country enables us even to indicate the extent, and to a certain extent, situations occupied by these now extinct seas, which at times varied in superficial dimensions, and certainly were, in some cases, drained, overflowed by lava, and renewed and replenished with living organisms as many as seven times.

And this brings me to the description of my ideas and opinions regarding the mode of formation of these deposits. Although it is true that it is the theory of one who has never personally inspected the country treated of, yet I trust that it will be accepted for all that it is worth, and that I shall at least, have accorded to me full credit for the suggestions contained in it. It will be desirable, then, at the outset, to take into consideration the geographical configuration of that portion of our country, constituting what are usually termed the "Pacific States," and which includes Washington Territory, Oregon and California, with the land-locked sections of Idaho, Nevada, Utah and Arizona. Beginning to consider these states at our northernmost boundary in Washington Territory, we find a range of high mountains which extend in a line parallel with and here at about one hundred and thirty miles from the coast. They are here known as the Cascade Mountains, which name they retain as they continue their Southerly course, still parallel with the coast line, through Oregon until they cross the Northern border of, and enter California, where they appear to terminate in the towering peak of Mount Shasta, which at this point lifts its volcanic cone to a height of over 14,000 feet. Throughout this Cascade Range we find several other volcanic cones, as Mount Hood, Mount Rainier, Mount Baker and others; in fact it is essentially a mountain chain lifted to its present attitude by volcanic agency, which has made itself more plainly evident through the openings in the cones mentioned. If we pass Southward from Mount Shasta we find again another chain of mountains, similar to those we have just been considering. These bend at first inwards and away from the coast, and then taking much the direction of the Cascades extend Southward until they would seem to lose themselves in the Southernmost part of the state of California. This range, pierced also by volcanic cones, constitutes the Sierra Nevada Mountains of that state. As they bend forwards towards the coast at both ends of the chain, they present a somewhat bowed shape, and thus form half of the brim of the enormous oval basin of which we are to speak anon. Nearer to, and in fact immediately upon the coast itself, we find another chain of mountains of a much less altitude than the Sierra Nevada, and also of very different characters both physically and geologically. These, receiving various names in different parts of the state, are all to be included very properly under one head, and thus they constitute the Coast Range of Mountains of California. Although this range keeps very much to the coast, yet at both the Northern and Southern parts of the state it bends inwards, as it were to meet the Sierra Nevada, and thus forms the outermost border of the great basin within which lie the beds of the San Joaquin and Sacramento Rivers.

The Coast Range Mountains, are made up almost entirely of sedimentary rocks, but the Sierra Nevadas consist of igneous materials; granites and the like. Although for the most part within the state of California, this distinction of the mountains into two main chains, is evident enough to even a superficial observer; yet north of that district, it is not so well marked, and this is for the reason that the two systems approach each other very closely, and at the same time, the Coast Mountains sink into insignificance when compared with their lofty neighbors. Enclosed, then, between these two chains, we have a vast plain or depression is drained by the San Joaquin and Sacramento Rivers which, uniting, empty through the Golden Gate into the Pacific. Besides, upon the opposite side of the Sierra Nevada, we have another plain which extends much further to the east, until it is bordered upon that side by the Rocky Mountains. With the exception of the Golden Gate, there is no other opening through the Coast Mountains into the ocean within the state of California. Such is not the case, however, to the north of its boundary, for here we find the otherwise opposing chain, broken through by several streams of less or greater dimensions. One only, however, is of any great size, and this is the Columbia River, which, arising far to the north in the British possessions, and on the flanks of the Rocky Mountains, breaks through both the Cascade and Coast Ranges, the latter of which is here pretty markedly represented, before it empties into the ocean. But one fact must be remembered in connection with these streams, that is, that they all, after draining certain valleys to be considered hereafter, break through at right angles to one or both of the mountain chains, forming gates or cañons.

Beginning at the north to consider these rivers and the regions they drain, we find, first, the Columbia, a stream of very considerable dimensions, which arises far to the north in the British Possessions and flows almost directly southward until it reaches the line of the 48th parallel of latitude when it swerves to the west until it strikes the eastern slope of the Cascade Mountains. Here it is again deflected to the south and somewhat east until it reaches the 46th parallel of latitude when it turns a sharp angle towards the west and soon breaks through the Cascades at the Dalles. Its course is now directly west until it arrives at a point about midway between the Cascade and Coast Ranges when, at a point where the Willamette enters it from the south it is deflected to the north, by the Coast Range and, at last, breaks in turn, through that barrier and opens into the ocean about on a level with the 46th parallel of latitude. It will be seen from this description that the river is turned southwards, as it were, by the Cascades, until it finds an opening through them when it escapes into the basin which lies between the Cascades and the Coast Range. From this basin it attempts to escape, turning northwards again for that purpose, until again it finds a weak spot to open through into the ocean. What these weak spots are we shall see anon. Flowing at right angles to the Columbia, that is to say along the lines of the mountains and emptying into that river are several small streams, the most important of which are John Day's River, the Des Chutes and the Willamette. The West Fork of the Des Chutes breaks through the Cascades before it runs *inward* from the coast showing that the Columbia lies in a bed much lower than the head-waters of these tributaries. The next river to the south of any importance is the Klamath with its branch, the Trinity; but this arises outside of the Cascades and cuts through the Coast Range, where it is of insignificant height. Next we came to the Sacramento, which, running almost directly southward, drains the northern half of the great Valley of California, whilst its sister stream, the San Joaquin, runs northward and drains the southern half of the Valley. They unite just before they enter Suisun Bay, and, there becoming the grand harbor of San Francisco, made up of Suisun Bay, the Bay of San Pablo and the Bay of San Francisco, empties at right angles to the coast at the Golden Gate.

South of this point there are no important streams, but it is observable that the tendency of all the streams in this section of country is sometimes slightly northward or southward until an opening is found, not made, through the mountain Ranges, when they escape into the ocean. In fact, on examining the topography of this section of country we find that it is made up of several large basins in which are still found numerous lakes, mostly fresh, but often brackish or saline, which commonly have no outlet, but, on the contrary, have draining into them numerous small streams, which must bring down into these lake beds, the saline materials they have washed down from the surrounding country. But this is evidently not the way in which these saline lakes have been formed, but in my opinion in the following manner.

In former times the Rocky Mountains constituted the coast line of the Pacific Ocean and during the period when its waves beat upon those rocky slopes there were to the east of them large accumulations of fresh water in the form of seas of much greater dimensions than the mighty lakes which now wash our northern borders. In such lakes, of course, lived, increased and died numerous species of fresh-water Diatomaceæ, which as they perished and their remains accumulated on the beds of these seas were stored up as enormous Lacustrine Sedimentary deposits. In time the western coast of the North American continent began to rise still farther up and as this was progressing, islands were thrown up all along and parallel to the coast, mainly by the upheaving action of submarine volcanoes. Perhaps in some cases, these volcanoes broke forth in these islands, but this was evidently not commonly the case, there being no craters formed until some time subsequently. Gradually, however, these islands were pushed farther and farther upwards until, at last, a new coast-line was formed, the space intervening between it and the old coast being raised so gradually that the salt water was all drained off and dry land appeared. Now would seem to have been a period of comparative rest, during which the mountains of the new coast and those which constituted the former coast poured down their drainages into the new basin and rivers and lakes were formed; in which, as before, Diatomaceæ appeared and accumulated. Whilst this was occurring inland, a new coast was again preparing and this state of things was to be repeated at shorter and shorter intervals, and perhaps, and most likely, with more and more violent commotions, new ranges of mountains with basins intervening were formed until we had what we now find; the Rocky Mountains as the first coast line with the remains of vast inland fresh-water seas still remaining, but for the most part dried up; then the next coast line is the Cascades and Sierra Nevada pierced by numerous Volcanic cones, some of them still in action, or, at least, very recently so; and between these two lines again the vast deposits of Diatomaceæ I have mentioned. Subsequently, and at shorter intervals, we have the three or four ridges, which together, are included under the head of the Coast Range; whilst, in turn, we have a new coast, now in progress of formation and making itself evident in the plainly rising islands lying just off and parallel to the coast. In truth, it is a well-known fact, that the whole of our Pacific coast is rising and with a celerity recognisable within the scope of the last one or two generations of man. So, I think I have shown pretty plainly how the parallel ranges of mountains were formed and how the immense deposits of Diatomaceæ accumulated. But why do not these latter appear at the present time as Lacustrine Sedimentary material containing a certain amount of organic matter? For the reason that in every case they are overlaid by and often interstratified with Lava or Trap which has burned out all the originally-existing organic matter and consolidating the siliceous remains has left them in the form of a hard, white, stony mass. The interstratification, in one case at least, as often as seven times, of this material with Lava, shows that this country has been subjected to repeated volcanic convulsions during which Lava has flowed into and obliterated to a great extent, these lakes. Perhaps thereafter, in each case there was sufficient subsidence to permit of the accumulation of water again so as to form a lake. But I think that I have made this point clear and I will leave it here, only calling attention to the fact that besides Sub-Plutonic deposits, which we could have no where else in the world that I am aware of—as no where else do we have precisely the same geographical and geological attendant circumstances—in the

Pacific States we do have true Lacustrine Sedimentary deposits, but they invariably are made up of totally-different forms of Diatomaceæ from those to be seen in the Sub-Plutonic material. In all cases they are such species as live at the present time in small collections of water and are of much more recent formation than the Sub-Plutonic Strata.

Another point requires treating of, and that is the formation of the cañons of the Pacific States. It is generally supposed and, I believe, on all hands accepted, that these have been gradually cut down through the hard Trap and Lava, by the action of the streams themselves. Now there are one or two facts in this connection which it will be necessary to bear in mind, first, to have such a cutting down action the streams should rise from a high section of country, and then flowing in such valleys as were ready formed for them, should follow their direction until they made their way into the ocean. Again the kind of rock through which such a wearing action by water takes place, must be considered. The best studied case of this kind which is undoubtedly due to the wearing action of water, is that of the Niagara River and Falls. We find the facts here stated in the following terms by Dana, (Manual, page 590). "The Niagara has made its gorge by a slow process of excavation, and is still prolonging it towards Lake Erie. Near the fall it is 200 to 250 feet deep, and at the fall itself 160 feet, the lower 80 feet shale, the upper 80 limestone. The distance from Niagara to the Queenstown heights is seven miles. If then the fall has been receding six miles, and we can ascertain the probable rate of progress, we may approximate to the length of time it required. Hall and Lyell estimated the average rate at one foot a year, which is certainly large. Mr. Desor concluded, after his study of the falls, that it was, "more nearly three feet a century, than three feet a year." Taking the rate at one foot a year, the six miles would have required over 31,000 years; if at one inch a year, which is 8½ feet a century, 380,000 years. It must be remembered that the Niagara has had to work its way through only comparatively soft shale and limestone; what time shall we assign to the Pacific coast rivers within which to do the same work, and which run through cañons of hard Granite or Trap hundreds of miles long? The Colorado of the South is 300 miles long, and its cañon 3000 to 6000 feet deep! But as we find on all these rivers innumerable side cañons in which no water flows, and in fact as we find the whole of this country, which is a sterile waste consisting of an almost level sheet of hard lava cracked and fissured in all directions, is it not more reasonable to suppose that all of these cracks, fissures and cañons, have been formed by volcanic agency? That when the volcanic cones were thrust upwards through and carrying with them the mountain chains, that the superincumbent rock, whatever it might be, would be bent, distorted and cracked, until "cañons" and "passes" would be formed, through which, of course, as openings, the streams which were the outpourings of the great inland seas, would naturally find their way. Besides if the cañons had been formed entirely by aqueous action, it seems to me that the Trap would have been worn away so gradually, that they would be much wider than we find them and the Trap strata would be worn in a sloping direction towards the bed of the stream, whilst the Diatomaceous strata, being comparatively soft, would be worn perpendicularly, or even excavated from under the Trap. Exactly the opposite is the case; the Trap invariably presents perpendicular walls whilst the Diatomaceous strata are worn sloping toward the middle of the cañon.

One more point and I must close this long communication. How do I account for the formation of the saline lakes which have no outlet? Simply thus. It is well known that such a thing as absolutely fresh water does not exist in nature. The water of all lakes and, of course, rivers contains more or less salts of various kinds derived from the country over which they and their feeders have flowed. Now I can well understand that if the many millions of gallons of very slightly saline water which is enclosed within the basin of Lake Superior, were to be concentrated by evaporation and condensed into a space equal to many of the small saline lakes of the West, that we would have an extremely large amount of salts of various kinds thrown down and a concentrated solution of others left. And this, in a few words is what I consider has occurred in the localities under consideration.

In conclusion I have only to say that as well persuaded as I am, that I am, in the main, right in my conjectures regarding the mode of formation of these interesting deposits, yet I earnestly and truly court criticism of my views from those who are better versed than myself in the geology and geography of this wonderful section of country.

MR. J. HYATT made some further remarks with regard to the **Aurora**, showing that Aug. 19th, 1870, a brilliant display was observed in this country. Aug. 20th, Auroras observed here and in Europe. This was the great electric storm, continuing for more than twenty-four hours and probably extending over more than 90° of Latitude. Sept. 3d and 4th, Aurora light detected in the day time in England and Scotland. Also seen at night, Sept. 24th and 25th. Another great electric storm, the Auroral light noticed at Montreal and in Europe. Crimson light at Montreal.

Oct. 14th. Records of the Aurora in England and Ireland. The Electric storm of Oct. 24th, 25th, was extensively observed in Europe, from the west and south of which country numerous notices have been communicated to the papers. As to bands reaching across from the eastern to the western horizon, the following indications appear: The Radcliffe observers speak of an arch of light in the vicinity of the equator, extending nearly from the eastern to the western horizon, and of two crimson sheets, one to the east, and the other to the west, with a connecting illuminated cirrus, south of the Zenith.

In Devonshire, on the evening of Sept. 24th, there was observed first a bright band of white light 6° broad across the sky from W. S. W. to E. N. E. Afterwards a broader band of a fiery rose color, from about a degree north of the east point of the horizon, across the sky toward the west, and culminating at an altitude of 54° above the N. horizon.

At Glasgow, A. S. Herschell, of the Andersonian University, noticed at 8.25 P. M., Oct. 25th, a double beam of faint white light, extending from *Altair* in the West, across *gamma Andromedæ* nearly to the E. N. E. horizon; the northern band brightest, 3° wide, and the parallel one 10° or 12° south of it.

From North Shields, Mr. Procter reports that at 8.15 P. M. on the 25th, an arch shot across the sky from N. E. to S. W. "just north of the pole star," certainly a very remarkable position.

From the south of England, are published accounts of great interference with the telegraph lines during this Electric storm, and this interference is supposed to have had a wide extension.

December 5th, 1870.

The President in the chair. Twenty-one persons present.

The following paper was read,

Report on Meteorology for the Month of November, 1870.

By Prof. O. W. Morris.

The Maximum temperature was 64·8°, on the 9th; the Minimum 30°, on the 20th; the range was 34·8°. The mean was 46·55°, which was 5·87° warmer than Nov. of last year, and warmer than any Nov. for the past ten years, except in 1863 and 1864. The month began with the temperature at 44° and ended at 41°. It was below 40° on eleven, and above 50° on fifteen days.

The maximum of the Barometer was 30·277 inches, on the 30th; the minimum was 29·429 in. on the 14th; the range was 0·848 inch. The mean was 29·855 in. The month commenced with the mercury at 29·912 in. and ended at 30·277 in. It was above 30 inches on fifteen days.

The mean Relative Humidity was 49·22°, the maximum being 88·6° on the 22d; and the minimum 11·9° on the 11th; a range of 76·7° for the month.

On the morning of the 3d, a sharp flash of lightning preceded a loud clap, and then a continuous roll of thunder. A strong wind prevailed during the afternoon. On the 23d there was a severe gale from N. E. which caused much damage.

Meteors were observed on the 1st, 9th, 10th, 13th and 27th. Lunar coronas on the 4th and 6th, both very fine. Snow squalls passed over on the 19th, but slight. No Aurora Boreales were observed this month. The London Times mentions one having been seen at Malta, Oct. 24th, the first in sixty years.

PROF. T. EGLESTON remarked that the Aurora mentioned by Prof. Morris as seen at Malta, and which it had been noticed, had been of such a marked and brilliant character wherever seen, and which showed itself over such a large amount of the earth's surface, in Europe at least, was very bright over the Lake of Geneva, where he was at the time. So bright was it, that the fire bells were rung, it being supposed that a conflagration was taking place. So over Germany and France generally, the exhibition was remarkably fine.

PROF. D. S. MARTIN, exhibited specimens of a **Mineral** found occurring in veins in the **Trap Rocks** at **Weehawken, New Jersey,** procured by him during a late visit in company with Prof. Wurtz, for the purpose of viewing some of the points illustrative of the paper read by him, at a late meeting of this society. This mineral occurs associated with Calcite and Pyrites, and is of a black color and has a silky lustre. No chemical examination of it has been made, but he is strongly disposed to consider it to be **Celadonite.** If it should prove to be that mineral, the fact would be one of interest, as it has not been hitherto found in this country.

DR. J. S. NEWBERRY, made some remarks regarding the **Genesis of Sandstones,** in criticism of the theory put forward by Prof. Wurtz, at a late meeting of this society, that the Sandstones of New Jersey contiguous to the Palisade Range are not siliceous, but have been formed from the disintegration of the Trap of which that Range is mainly composed. He called attention to the comparative compositions as evinced by chemical analysis, of a typical Sandstone and Trap rock, as follows:

	Sandstone.	*Trap.*
Silica,	92·40	50·10
Iron,	2·85	12·20
Alumina,	3·00	18·30
Lime,	·36	8·00
Soda,	·50	2·03
Potash,	·35	1·02
Magnesia,	·18	5·00

From such an analysis, he remarked, it was difficult to understand how such a sandstone could have originated from Trap, but, as Prof. Wurtz had promised analyses of both rocks under consideration we must wait for the revelations which such examinations would make. Meantime he was having analyses made of some of the New Jersey Sandstones.

PROF. A. M. EDWARDS called attention to the revelations made by Messrs. Sorby and Forbes in the genesis of crystalline rocks at least, by examining them, in thin section, by means of the microscope and this was the plan he would recommend to be employed in the present case. No chemical examination of a crushed and finely-powdered fraction of a rock which was made up of several associated but chemically different minerals in varying quantities would give the slightest hint as to its true composition or mode of formation, but if a specimen could be so examined by means of a magnifying glass that we had, to all intents and purposes, large masses of the different minerals under examination, then Crystallography, Polarized light or any other assistants could be brought to bear, and any one sufficiently versed in Mineralogy, could at once determine what species were under examination. He had spent some time in investigations of this character, but the more particularly in the examination of fossiliferous rocks, and the results had been of so satisfactory a character that it was his intention to extend his labors to the crystalline rocks, and, as opportunity offered, he would investigate in this way, the Sandstones of our immediate neighborhood.

Prof. B. N. Martin, in continuation of this subject, made some remarks.

He said that he regretted very much the absence of Prof. Wurtz, who would doubtless have offered, had he been present, some important suggestions in support of the views expressed in his paper.

He had recently visited and examined the Palisade ridge, in company with Prof. Wurtz, who had pointed out some very interesting facts. Among these was the occurrence of a bed of truly Felspathic Sandstone, below the whole series of Trapoid Schists, and immediately above the Jasperoid Rock which covers the Serpentine at Hoboken. It is of the variety known as Arkose, and seems to be a disorganized and reconstructed Granite. It is composed of Quartz grains, cemented, apparently by Feldspar, without any Mica. This rock was found at Fox Hill, between the Serpentine outcrop of Hoboken, and the Trap Ridge west of that city, and is to all appearance largely composed of Feldspar.

West of this, and the base of the Trap, the same rock was found in place, underlying the whole series of Trapoid Schists which form the hill.

On examination of the Schists themselves, the lower ones were found to be most obviously stratified, lying in beds of a regular and uniform parallelism and dipping slightly towards the west. This stratified character was beyond all mistake, yet they presented no appearance of Sandstone whatever, but were apparently a compact and fine-grained Trap rock.

These alternated with decomposing beds of the same material, now perfectly soft, and embracing still some undecomposed fragments of the rock.

Toward the upper portion of the Ridge, the stratification was generally less obvious; the rock had all the appearance of Columnar Trap. Yet even here a careful examination of the weathered surfaces showed in many places distinct lines of stratification. These were at some points quite numerous, and in some instances, where the Columnar character was very marked, distinct veins of crystallized material could be seen for long distances preserving the horizontal outcrop and general dip of the series. Even on the very top of the ridge the same features were observed; so that a distinct lamination pervades the mass and seems to indicate the sedimentary character of the whole.

He did not feel willing to pronounce confidently upon the brief examination of a couple of days, but felt sure that the facts were worthy of a very careful study, and hoped that the geologists of the Lyceum would bestow some attention upon this interesting and suggestive locality.

Prof. C. A. Seely called attention to the fact, that in such cases as the present mistakes might arise from the mode in which the chemical analyses had been made. The common custom was to boil the finely-powdered mineral in Nitric or Nitro-muriatic acid, and all which did not dissolve under such circumstances, to set it down as Silica. Now it was well known that many of the Silicates would not be broken up under such circumstances and therefore any such analysis would be totally inaccurate. For his part he did not see why Felspathic Sandstones could not exist as commonly as truly Silicious ones.

The President replied that the question was not as to whether Felspathic Sandstones could occur, as they certainly occasionally did, although they were extremely rare, but as whether in this particular case the Sandstones in question had been derived from the Trap. An examination to determine the hardness of the mineral, would show as to whether the grains composing it, were Siliceous or Felspathic. At any rate ninety-nine out of a hundred of all existing Sandstones examined as yet, were Siliceous, and one of the difficulties which presents itself in the formation of Sandstones in which the grains shall consist of fragments of Felspathic minerals, is, that such minerals are extremely prone to decomposition by the action of moisture, and the atmosphere; the alkalies being dissolved out and alumina deposited in the form of clay.

DR. P. SCHWEITZER remarked that although the error which Prof. Seely pointed out, might appear, if mineral analysis were made by incompetent chemists, yet it was well known that careful observers, when examining Silicates, decomposed them by some means, as by the use of Hydrofluoric acid, in such a way that the Silica was determined directly and not indirectly and by loss.

PROF. T. EGLESTON exhibited a very large crystal of **Magnetite**, from Essex County, New Jersey, which, upon examination, was found to present some features of considerable interest. It is a very composite Octohedron, showing no less than four distinct crystals. It is flattened parallel to two of its diagonally opposite faces, so that the crystal is found to be three inches long, by two inches wide. The appearances thus presented are so deceptive, that this form of crystal has been called "Magnetite pseudomorph after Calcite;" therefore, and to correct this error which some mineralogists have fallen into, this specimen was exhibited.

December 12, 1870.

The President in the chair, twenty-seven persons present.

PROF. C. A. SEELY exhibited a specimen of **Cuttle Fish, (Octopus,)** which had been captured in the East River, near one of the wharves at Williamsburg, L. I. When it came into his possession it was alive and he was enabled to observe some curious facts connected with its dying. During this period it changed several times in color; the tints being various and the changes of a character difficult to describe something like that which takes place in what is known as "changeable silk" when it is moved. The color appeared to come and go at distinct points situated all over the animal's body and this variation continued as long as it lived, until it assumed the pinkish-purple tint which it still had.

In connection with this power of changing their color which several aquatic animals possessed, the President, DR. J. S. NEWBERRY described the way in which the **Stickleback (Gasterosteus)** built its nest. As soon as this nest, which consists of sticks and similar materials welded and woven together and is of a tubular form open at both ends, is finished, the male fish drives its mate into the nest, where she deposits her eggs. As soon as this is done, he enters from behind, driving her out again and begins to deposit his "milt," or spermatic fluid upon the eggs. At the same time and immediately his whole appearance undergoes a great change; the animal appearing to be under considerable nervous stimulation and excitement. The eye brightens and the skin, which hitherto has been of a dull greenish-grey tint, is illuminated with a flush of brilliant scarlet. This same color appears during other circumstances of excitement, as when attacking an enemy, which this fish readily and often does, the Stickleback being an exceedingly pugnacious and courageous little fellow.

PROF. H. WURTZ exhibited specimens of **Cannel Coal** of a very good quality. It is from a new locality situated about sixty miles west of Pittsburg, Pennsylvania, and is said to occur in considerable quantities. In fact, the company working it, state that they consider that it covers a tract of between six and seven hundred miles in extent. The vein is about fourteen feet thick. On examination it is found to be a very "fat" coal and yields a large percentage of good coke, whilst the ash remaining is very white and retains very perfectly the form of the original mass of coal. The ash, also, has disseminated throughout it minute glistening points which apparently are scales of mica. Some of the specimens show distinct traces of organic remains, as rootlets of *Stigmaria* and mineral charcoal.

THE PRESIDENT said that he was well acquainted with the seam from which this coal was obtained as it occurs in the state of Ohio and runs across the border into Pennsylvania, where at one point, it is known as the "Darlington Coal." In many parts the coal is of very good quality but at points it runs out into a bituminous shale which is rich in fossils.

DR. P. SCHWEITZER made some remarks on the subject of the substance known commercially as **Dried Blood,** and presented a table of a series of thirteen examinations, made to ascertain the quantity of Albumen present, as this is the important substance in this material, it being used for clarifying sugar. The Albumen was estimated as insoluble Albumen by coagulating, washing and weighing. The percentage ranged all the way from 52 to 85 per cent. showing a great variation in this substance as it comes into the market.

He also presented the results of an **Analysis of Newark Sandstone**; which was of interest, as he had made it at the request of Dr. Newberry, as bearing upon Prof. Wurtz's paper read at a late meeting of the Society. The analysis was made by first acting upon the mineral with Hydrofluoric-acid, in the manner alluded to at a previous meeting, and the quantities found were as below.

Undissolved Mineral,	1·27
Silica,	67·45
Alumina and Iron,	16·65
Magnesia, Lime and Alkalies,	14·64

The President said that this analysis certainly seemed to agree with Prof. Wurtz's theory, but we would require more extended and fuller examinations to be made of the rocks under consideration, before we could accept it entirely.

The following paper was read,

On Kreosol and Phenol and their Homologues.

BY DR. P. SCHWEITZER.

In the year 1832 a body was discovered by Reichenbach, in the distilled oils of beach-wood tar, which on account of the peculiar property it possessed, of preserving meat and other highly organized substances, was called by him Kreosot. This substance attracted the attention of many chemists who studied its properties and sought to separate it from tar oils in general, and it was with a degree of satisfaction, that two years later F. F. Runge announced his discovery of a Kreosote in coal-tar oil, which he called carbolic acid. Reichenbach, fearing his right of the first discovery, infringed by this carbolic acid, which according to Runge differed slightly from his compound, tried to demonstrate for his own glorification, the identity of both substances, and though Laurent, in the year 1841, proved carbolic acid to be Phenylic hydrate, and pronounced it a different body from Kreosote, Reichenbach did not give up the contest, but conducted it with a pertinacity, which caused a general confusion among chemists, a confusion which became quite lamentable, when in 1855 Cresylic hydrate was discovered in coal-tar by Fairlie, and which on account of the near resemblance to true Kreosote was generally accepted to be identical with the original compound obtained from beach-wood tar.

Many chemists have given their attention since then to the study of those two compounds, but carbolic acid very shortly after its discovery began to be introduced in commerce and sold as Kreosote. It was difficult, and at times impossible to procure the oils made from wood-tar, and it was owing to this, that the publication of some chemists are found to be at variance in their results, as they were in fact working with carbolic acid, while speaking of Kreosote. Hlasiwetz and Gorup Besanez, among many others, have now cleared up the questions, and brought light and intelligence into the many contradictory statements which we find in the literature of Kreosote and carbolic acid. We know to-day that two homologues are contained in that part of the oil of wood-tar which dissolves in caustic potassa, and which bear a certain relationship to the compounds obtained from the same part of the oil obtained from coal-tar. We are justified in saying, that those oils are two distinct and different fluids, for while coal-tar oil contains principally

Phenylic hydrate,	C_6H_6O, and
Cresylic hydrate,	C_8H_8O;

woor-tar oil contains:—

Guajacol,	$C_7H_8O_2$, and
Kreosol or Homo Guajacol,	$C_8H_{10}O_2$.

I intended saying here a few words about the place we have to assign those compounds in organic chemistry and about their constitution, before giving the difference by which one class may be distinguished from the other. Phenylic and Cresylic hydrate belong to a class of compounds, the radicals of which differ by the complex CH'. They are probably very numerous, and of those that are known, I will only mention—

Phenyl,	C_6H_5
Benzyl,	C_7H_7
Xylyl,	C_8H_9

The name of Xylyl is at present somewhat obsolete, and Phloryl is substituted for it. In combination with hydrogen those radicals form—

Phenylic hydride,	C_6H_6 or Benzol,
Cresylic hydride,	C_7H_8 or Toluol,
Phlorylic hydride,	C_8H_{10} or Phloruol (Xylol);

the alcohols of them are—

Phenylic hydrate,	C_6H_6 or Phenol
Cresylic hydrate,	C_7H_8 O or Kresol,
Phlorylic hydrate,	$C_8H_{10}O$ or Phlorol (Wurtz Xenol).

In treating these alcohols with oxidizing substances, we obtain, at least in the case of Phlorol, substances which contain more oxygen and less hydrogen than the alcohols, and which we call—

$C_8H_8O_2$ Phloron, $C_7H_6O_2$ (Kreson), $C_6H_4O_2$ Chinon.

I said in the case of phlorol; for, though we are able to produce the other two compounds, the first by heating chinic acid, which in combination with lime is a constituent of all Peruvian barks, and the second by decomposing kresol, we will no doubt in time arrive at a proper method for obtaining them all directly, by treating the alcohols with nascent oxygen.

In subjecting gum guajac to destructive distillation, we obtain a fluid which in many respects bears a great resemblance to creosote. This distillate has been investigated especially by Völckel and Lobrero and Hlasiwetz, who succeeded in separating it into two fluids, that gave crystallizable compounds with bases, and which they called guajacol and homo-guajacol. A later and closer study of creosote revealed the fact, that it consisted of those two identical compounds in different proportion. Let us compare them with the products, we obtained from the alcohols of the phenylic series:

$C_6H_4O_2$ (Chinon) $C_7H_6O_2$ (Kreson)
$C_6H_6O_2$ (Hydrochinon and Pyrocat.) $C_7H_8O_2$ (Guajacol)
$C_8H_8O_2$ (Phloron.)
$C_8H_{10}O_2$ (Homo-guajacol or Creosote).

But we have also the member corresponding to the chinon in a compound called Pyrocatechin, thereby completing two series of compounds, which differ only by the addition ot two equivalents of hydrogen. If we treat chinon with hydrogen, we obtain directly hydrochinon; the attempt made in this direction with the others, succeeded perfectly, so that we possess another series of homologues—

Hydrochinon,
Hydrocreson,
Hydrophloron,

of exactly the same composition as—

Pyrocatechin,
Guajacol,
Kreosol,

but differs in properties.

Now let us look at the constitution of those compounds.

It is very probable, and almost admitted by Kékulé, that kresol is monomethylated phenol and phlorol bimethylated phenol. In the same way may we feel entitled to consider guajacol monomethylated pyrocatechin and kreosol bimethylated pyrocatechin; in fact, in treating guajacol with hydriodic acid we obtain iodide of methyl and pyrocatechin, which amounts to a proof of this view, and which gives us therefore two links, by which we may connect the series of coal-tar oils with those of wood tar. To render it apparent to the eye I will give the formulæ, as follows:—

$C_6H_6(OH)$ Phenol. $\qquad$ $C_6H_5\ (OH)$ Pyrocatechin.

$C_6H_4\left\{\begin{matrix}OH\\CH_3\end{matrix}\right.$ Kresol, $\qquad$ $C_6H_4O\left\{\begin{matrix}OH\\CH_3\end{matrix}\right.$ Guajacol.

$C_6H_3\left\{\begin{matrix}OH\\CH_3\\CH_3\end{matrix}\right.$ Phlorol. $\qquad$ $C_6H_3O\left\{\begin{matrix}OH\\CH_3\\CH_3\end{matrix}\right.$ Kresol.

It may be stated, as a further proof for the correctness of considering the above compounds as methylated pyrocatechin, that the molecule of methylene, CH_3, may be introduced directly into the constitution of pyrocatechin, by heating it in closed tubes with caustic potassa and methylsulphate of potassa, producing thereby guajacol.

The homologues of the phenylic series are crystallizable compounds, of the respective boiling points of 184°C., 203°C., 220°C., while the two derivatives of pyrocatechin are oily liquids, boiling at a temperature of 200°C. and 219°C.

Phenol,	184°C.	Pyrocatechin,	——
Kresol,	203°C.	Guajacol,	200°C.
Phlorol,	220°C.	Kreosol.	219°C.

It may be seen, therefore, that in cases of working with a mixture of the individuals of both series, we should find it impossible to separate them by fractional distillation. Their products of decomposition, however, may be resorted to as a means of distinguishing between them. For while phenol and its series yields with nitric acid nitrophenol and similar compounds, we obtain with guajacol oxalic acid; chlorine converts phenol into chlorophenic acid and chloranil, while the products obtained in this way from creosote, though similar to them, present differences which stamp them as peculiar and distinct bodies.

The following paper was read,

On the Reduction of Sulphuric Acid by Zinc-Amalgam.

BY DR. I. WALZ.

Although, as is well known, a number of oxidizing agents are capable of oxidizing sulphuretted hydrogen to sulphuric acid, the reverse reaction, viz., the reduction of sulphuric acid to sulphuretted hydrogen, has hitherto been observed only in a few cases, and even then only to a very limited extent. Messrs. Calvert & Johnson published in 1866 some observations upon the action of zinc upon the various hydrates of sulphuric acid, in which they remark that at a high temperature, the mono-, bi-, and ter-hydrates of sulphuric acid, when acting upon zinc, evolve principally sulphurous acid, while the fourth, fifth, and sixth hydrates are acted upon (in the words of the *Jahresbericht*) "with a preponderating evolution of sulphuretted hydrogen," an observation which I can confirm if it is intended to say that more H_2S is formed than SO_2, but less than H, as on repeating the experiment I found that but very little H_2S was formed. According to Messrs. Calvert & Johnson, sulphuric acid which is diluted with more than six equivalents of water, evolves pure hydrogen, an observation which was disproved by Kolbe, who showed that when even chemically pure dilute sulphuric acid acts upon chemically pure zinc, a trace of sulphuretted hydrogen is always formed. In the majority of reactions, however, in which a reduction of sulphuric acid takes place, it stops at sulphurous acid, as when mercury, copper, carbon, etc., act upon the acid. Oppenheim has shown that when concentrated sulphuric acid and phosphorus act upon each other the result is phosphorous and anhydrous sulphurous acid, according to the formula $3SO_4H_2+2P=2PO_3H_3+3SO_2$.

I have lately studied the action of zinc and sodium amalgam on concentrated sulphuric acid, and have made the—in view of the foregoing remarks—somewhat unexpected observation, that in this case a considerable amount of sulphuretted hydrogen is formed. With sodium amalgam the action is almost instantaneous. A small quantity of sodium amalgam is covered in a test tube with an equal amount of chemically pure sulphuric acid, sp. gr. 1·84; the smell of sulphuretted hydrogen is at once perceived, and on pouring water into the test tube the solution appears milky, from the suspension of finely divided sulphur. But the course of the reaction can be better studied by employing zinc instead of sodium amalgam, as the action proceeds slower and more regularly in this case. (In preparing the zinc-amalgam, whether the zinc be used in little sticks or in filings, I find it convenient to cover the mercury and zinc with water, rendered *alkaline* by a drop of soda, potash, or ammonia. The amalgamation takes place very rapidly, and at a lower temperature, and the operator is not exposed to the noxious vapor of mercury. I prefer alkalies to acids in amalgamating zinc.)

Zinc-amalgam is placed in a small H_2S apparatus and covered with about an equal amount of chemically pure sulphuric acid, sp. gr. 1·84, and the gases evolved are passed into a solution of acetate of lead. The first few moments only hydrogen seems to be formed, but presently the reaction becomes intense, and sulphuretted hydrogen is given off in abundance. The liquid in the apparatus becomes white, which is caused partly by the formation of anhydrous sulphate of zinc, and partly by the deposition of sulphur. There appears to be a period at which H_2S and SO_2 are formed simultaneously, and the two, reacting upon each other, give rise to an abundant deposit of sulphur. In the latter stage of the reaction, sulphurous acid alone is formed. At last the generating flask contains only mercury and white, dry sulphate of zinc; that is to say, if too much sulphuric acid is not taken. (An excess of sulphuric acid should be avoided from the beginning, as the reaction toward the end generally becomes very violent in this case, volatilizing mercury and sulphur, and forcing the liquid out of the flask.) If we pour water into the generating flask, the sulphate of zinc is dissolved, and the quantity of sulphur formed becomes then apparent. The mercury, immediately after the reaction is over, generally presents a bright, or but slightly tarnished surface, but on remaining in contact with the liquid is soon covered with a black coating of sulphide. No mercury enters into solution during the reaction.

I believe that the reduction of sulphuric acid in the beginning is not gradual and successive, but is explained by the simple formula,—

$$SO_4H_2 + 4(H_2) = 4H_2O + H_2S.$$

The following paper was read;

On the Role which Chalk plays in Butyric Fermentation.

By O. Loew.

It is a well-known fact, that a solution of sugar, when not protected against the access of air, develops gradually a smell of butyric acid and the formation of micro-organism. Béchamp* found that 1–2 drops of creosote or phenol are sufficient to prevent, in 100 c.c of sugar solution, the development of infusoria and fungi, but that such a small quantity of creosote would not be sufficient to prevent a regular fermentation by yeast. For the latter purpose, much greater quantities of creosote would be necessary.

Béchamp concludes from this observation that small quantities of creosote would kill imperfectly developed micro-organisms, but not the better developed cells of the yeast plant. A series of experiments, however, have shown me that the real cause of the above-named fact, depends simply upon the relative proportions of the antiseptic substance and the quantity of the micro-organisms. The quantity of the spores falling from the air into a sugar solution, is small in comparison with the number of cells in a few cubic centimetres of yeast. That a given quantity of creosote or phenol can only have a definite and limited antiseptic influence is self-evident, but, as regards these limits, few investi-

* Jahresber., 1865.

gations have been made. I instituted a number of experiments, of which I will mention here a few results :—

(*a.*) 300 c.c. of a five per cent. grape-sugar solution were left standing in a glass-stoppered bottle, which was opened from time to time; soon the presence of micro-organisms could be detected under the microscope, and a smell of butyric acid could be recognized; after a lapse of two months, the quantity of decomposed sugar amounted to 9·3 per cent. of the whole.

(*b.*) A similar quantity of the same solution, as in (*a.*), remained entirely unaltered, after the addition of 0·5 grms. phenol.

(*c.*) A mixture of 300 c.c. sugar solution of the same strength and 30 c.c. yeast (2·16 grms. dry substance) underwent a regular and complete fermentation, but after addition of 0·5 grms. phenol, another sample (*d.*) went on much slower, and after two weeks, only 59·5 per cent. of the sugar was decomposed by fermentation; on application of 1 grm. phenol, the fermentation was still more retarded, but 5 grms. stopped it entirely.

An interesting contribution to the understanding of butyric fermentation, seems to have been made by Béchamp, when he announced small fungi appearing like vibrating dots, which are able to produce butyric fermentation in sugar solutions. Béchamp calls these "microsyma cretæ." Simultaneously Béchamp said that the residue of chalk insoluble in acids (0·8 per cent.) consists of a body, containing carbon and nitrogen, the real substance of the "microsyma cretæ." It seemed to me interesting to investigate this residue. 100 grms. of chalk, dissolved in hydrochloric acid, left behind 0·82 grms. residue and this consisted of silica, oxide of iron, alumina, lime, water, and a slight trace of a humus-like substance, the quantity of which was too small to be determined. In order to obtain a clearer insight into the fermenting properties of the chalk, 50 grms. of it were mixed with 300 c.c. of a five per cent. sugar solution and left to itself (*e.*). After a few days, a development of gas bubbles could be observed, and a smell of butyric acid; after two weeks 29·3 per cent. of the sugar was found to be decomposed by fermentation.

In another experiment (*f.*), 0·5 grms. phenol were added, the other circumstances being the same. A fermentation set in very soon and the 0·5 grms. seemed to have but very little influence, which agrees with the fact, described by Béchamp, —but for which an entirely different explanation must be given—after two weeks 22·7 per cent. of the sugar was decomposed. On the addition, however, of 5 grms. phenol, the fermentation was entirely stopped. In a further experiment (*g.*), the chalk was heated with the sugar solution, for a length of time, to 100° C. and set aside in a well-closed flask. No fermentation set in, but after lifting the stopper from time to time, unmistakable evidences of fermentation showed themselves and even an addition of 0·5 grms. phenol could not prevent the process.

In the next experiment (*h.*), the chalk was at first heated to 250° C., then after cooling left in contact with the atmosphere for a short time and then brought into the sugar solution, which had been previously boiled and allowed to cool in a well-closed flask; here the same fermentation made its appearance, as mentioned in (*e.*) and (*f.*).

It seems to me to follow, undoubtedly, from these experiments:—

1. That Béchamp, while powdering his piece of chalk, taken from the interior of a great lump, gave admittance to the spores contained in the atmosphere, which latter produced fermentation.

2. That the effect of the small quantity of phenol which in *absence* of the chalk would have been sufficient to prevent fermentation, was destroyed, the phenol having been absorbed by the pores of the chalk. The phenol, thus absorbed, was no more able to prevent the development of the spores falling from the atmosphere into the sugar solution.

Béchamp maintains that a small quantity of creosote would kill the spores coming from the atmosphere, but would be unable to kill the "microsyma cretæ." Further, he says, that powdered marble could not replace the chalk, the latter only containing the "microsyma." It will be seen very clearly, that a small quantity of phenol is easier absorbed by the porous chalk than by the powdered marble. On the other hand, leaving the creosote or phenol entirely out in both cases, the fermentation proceeds equally well after the chalk as well as the marble had been exposed for a short time to the atmosphere.

3. That in the presence of a lime salt, the fermentation is accelerated, when once initiated by the spores of the air, the development of the cells being much favored by the neutralization of the butyric acid, and by the presence of a lime-salt in solution, as butyrate of lime. Compare (*a.*), (*e.*), and below (*i.*).

4. That the nitrogenized matter necessary for the development of the cells is not originally present in the chalk, but is derived from the sugar, which always contains traces of it.*

In order to furnish a further proof that phenol absorbed by porous bodies has no antiseptic qualities, 50 grms. of powdered charcoal, which, for some time, had been exposed to the air, were brought into 300 c. c. of a 5 per cent. sugar solution, which had been previously boiled, and was allowed to cool in a well-stoppered flask and 0·5 grms. phenol added; after a few days, the development of gas bubbles could be observed, the phenol smell disappeared and butyric acid could be distinctly recognized by the odor; after four weeks, 23·1 per cent of the sugar was decomposed. Doubtless the presence of a small quantity of carbonate of lime would have accelerated the fermentation. In another experiment, 5 grms. phenol were employed, under similar circumstances, but then, not the slightest fermentation could be

* The fungoid growth, observed by every chemist in the solution of tartaric acid, contains in the dried mass 3·5 per cent. nitrogen, besides some sllica, carbon, etc., even when the acid is commonly considered as "pure."

observed; it was clear the absorbing power of the coal was overbalanced.

Béchamp employed 80 grms. sugar, 1,500 c. c. creosote matter, and 140 grms. chalk, and obtained, after two months, 2·6 c.c. alcohol, 4·5 grms. butyric acid, 6·8 grms. acetate of soda, and 9 grms. lactate of lime. This would correspond to 40 per cent. of the decomposed sugar. How is it possible for another than a neutralizing role for the chalk, the common butyric fermentation being over in one to one and a-half weeks, and even, if the "microsyma cretæ" would exist, for which, however, I looked in vain. In all my experiments, I found only the common butyric ferment formed by the spores of the atmosphere.

December 19, 1870.

The President in the chair. Nineteen persons present.

The President read a communication from Prof. J. Henry of the **Smithsonian Institution,** relative to the distribution of **Packages** sent through that Institution for Societies and Individuals in New York and its vicinity, asking if the Lyceum could and would take upon itself the distribution of such packages; thus preventing the delay and extra expense consequent upon their being sent to Washington and back to New York, all expenses to be paid by the Smithsonian Institution.

On motion of Prof. Seely the offer of the Smithsonian Institution was accepted.

PROF. D. S. MARTIN exhibited a specimen of one of the **Zeolites,** from **Bergen Hill, N. J.** It is of a grey color but does not exactly coincide with any distinct mineralogical species as published.

Prof. T. Egleston said the mineral was Pectolite, which occurs sometimes thus altered. Apophylite is often found passing into Pectolite and in fact all of these zeolites are very liable to decomposition.

The President, Prof. J. S. Newberry exhibited a series of beautifully preserved **Fossil Leaves from the Cretaceous Sandstone of Fort Harker.** This sandstone, he said, was the lowest member of the Cretaceous series in the United States, the equivalent of the Raritan sands and clays in New Jersey, of the Upper Green-sand of the Old World. This was the lowest horizon where angiospermous leaves had been found, but here they were quite numerous, and represented, perhaps, a hundred species and, as the specimens on the table demonstrated, formed the foliage of trees of large size and luxuriant growth. Some of these leaves were a foot or more in diameter.

He also exhibited a beautiful series of **Fossil-Plants from the Miocene Tertiary of Oregon,** collected by Rev. Thomas Condon, remarking that the deposit from which they came contained twenty or thirty species which were new, and beautifully preserved. A few others, such as *Sequoia Langsdorfii* connected this deposit with other Miocene tertiary plant beds and determined its age. The collection was made by Mr. Condon at great trouble and risk and reflected great credit upon his scientific enthusiasm.

The rest of the evening was occupied by Mr. J. G. Hochstetter, who has spent some time in the island of Cuba, in charge of Copper mines, the mode of working which and the yield he detailed. The principal fact which he treated of, was the employment of coolie labor in these mines. They there work along with negroes, and so good opportunities were presented for comparing the capabilities of the two races, and it was decidedly in favor of the coolie. In fact the results were, on the whole, very encouraging. Some of these mines are very deep, having been worked for over thirty-five years and the heat of the air down as low as two hundred fathoms was almost unendurable, rising often to 110° F., so that the laborers have to be relieved every three or four hours. This heat is doubtless caused by the decomposition resulting from the air and moisture coming in contact with the exposed ore, which is for the most part Pyrites.

January 9, 1871.

The President in the chair. Twenty-two persons present.

DR. L. FEUCHTWANGER exhibited a specimen of **Galena, from near Salt Lake, Utah.** It is reported to yield one hundred ounces of Silver to the ton and to contain eighty-five per cent. of Lead. He also reported that he had found the Speiss or Matt, from the silver ledge on the island opposite Thunder Bay in Lake Superior, which he had exhibited at a late meeting of the Lyceum, to contain Nickel, Cobalt, Iron, Arsenic, Antimony and Sulphur. The quantities of each substance have not been, as yet, determined.

MR. EMILE GUILLAUDEU sent, for presentation to the collection of the Society, a number of fossils taken from excavations in the Greensand, at Tinton Falls, Monmouth Co., New Jersey. These consisted mostly of the bones of Saurians. There were vertebræ and teeth of the crocodile, and vertebræ of perhaps *Lelaps* or *Hadrosaurus*, besides others.

The President, DR. J. S. NEWBERRY, exhibited a piece of **Red Sandstone, containing Impressions of Leaves,** found in excavating the foundations for the Gas Office in Williamsburgh. This, he said, was a specimen of remarkable interest. In its lithological characters this rock closely resembles the Triassic Sandstone so much used in New York for architectural purposes, but *it contained numbers of very beautifully preserved* *impressions of angiospermous leaves.* No plants of this kind were known to exist during the Trias, or before the Cretaceous; but we know of no such Cretaceous or Tertiary Sandstone on the North American continent. The mass from which this specimen was taken was a bowlder and the associated transported blocks were granite, porphyry, greenstone, dolomite, &c. plainly referable to well-known localities north of New York. But no such Sandstone as this was known and it became a matter of extreme interest to ascertain what was its origin.

PROF. A. M. EDWARDS exhibited a number of specimens of **Sandstones,** procured by himself at the quarries near Newark, N. J. These were various in characters, texture, and more particularly color. Red was the prevalent tint, but a yellow Sandstone had been found which, although not occurring in great quantity, was of interest as associated with it, but also more commonly in a contiguous grey Sandstone was found green Copper Carbonate and the yellow Sandstone was invariably thickly packed with vegetable remains in the form of stems of various sizes made up entirely of a brittle and often pulverulent, charcoal-like, Lignite. These specimens were offered as illustrating the discussion which had lately taken place at the meetings of the Lyceum relative to the genesis of these Sandstones and were collected for the purpose of making microscopical examinations of them; which he was now engaged upon.

PROF. T. EGLESTON exhibited several crystals of Swedish **Euxenite** from his own collections, which were remarkable for size and beauty of termination. They shew the rectangular prism, $i\bar{\imath}$, $i\breve{\imath}$ with the vertical edges replaced by the rhombic prism I and a macrodome $m\bar{\imath}$.

He also remarked that the **Silver Ore from Thunder Bay, Lake Superior,** is said to contain a large amount of Nickel. He was making the examination at the School of Mines to determine whether the Nickel is combined with the Silver or scattered through the ore and has not concluded his analyses so as to report in full.

January 16, 1871.

The President in the chair. Nineteen persons present.

The President, Dr. J. S. NEWBERRY, read a letter from Mr. J. C. BREVOORT, announcing the receipt of **Prof. Poey's paper on the Percoid Fishes of the Island of Cuba** for publication in the Annals of the Lyceum. The paper would occupy the space of a full number of the annals and as it was written in French it was desirable that it should be published as written without translation. Mr. Brevoort wrote that if the Lyceum would consent to such a course he would defray the expenses of publication. Mr. Brevoort's generous offer was unanimously accepted and Prof. Poey's valuable paper ordered to be published in the Annals.

DR. L. FEUCHTWANGER exhibited several fine specimens of **Cuprite**, from Cornwall, England, crystallized in cubes. This mineral is a Red Oxide of Copper, and the specimens exhibited consisted of large crystals of a rich, deep red color and subtransparent. Occasionally isolated crystals of this mineral are found an inch in diameter imbedded in Lithomarge, but they are generally changed upon the outside to Malachite. When found in large quantities it constitutes a valuable ore of Copper.

He also exhibited a number of specimens of **Pearls**, which were of interest on account of their peculiar external structure. Some of them were of the ordinary kind, smooth and exhibiting the brilliant play of colors found in these substances, but most of them were brownish in color, oval in shape or resembling two acorns attached base to base as there was a raised ring around the middle part which was commonly of a dark almost black color.

PROF. A. M. EDWARDS remarked that these pearls were of interest as the genesis of those substances was not thoroughly understood, although considerable had been written on the subject. Dr. Feuchtwanger had presented him with some of them and he would take the opportunity of making sections of them and examining them by means of the microscope; as the mode of formation of such concretions would doubtless throw some light upon the subject of the growth of the shells of Mollusca and the occurrence of what are known as "interglobular spaces" in the dental structures of the higher animals; which he was at present engaged in investigating.

PROF. T. EGLESTON exhibited two large crystals of **Diamond,** belonging to Tiffany & Co. One was a hexoctahedron, very much rounded, in which the lines of outline of the faces of the rhombic-dodecahedron and trigonal tris-octahedron were very prominent. Its weight was two carats, and it was remarkable for its clear color and regularity of shape. The second crystal was octahedral in form and showed the interpenetration of other crystals composed of the rhombic-dodecahedron and octahedron. The weight of this specimen was a little more than two carats and was remarkably clear.

The president, DR. J. S. NEWBERRY, exhibited a series of specimens of **Fossil Fishes from the Devonian Rocks of Ohio.** These embraced eighteen species, representing several new genera, some of which were of remarkable character.

Perhaps the most common of the great ganoids of the coniferous, is *Macropetalichthys*, of which the cranium was composed of a series of polygonal plates covered with a stellate tuberculation, resembling in this and other respects the *Asterolepis* of the Old Red sandstone of Scotland, and attaining about the same size. No teeth had been found with the cranium of this fish, and it was probably soft-mouthed like the sturgeon.

Onychodus, a still larger ganoid, nearly as common in the Corniferous Limestone, was well provided with teeth. This fish had a scaled body, head composed of a great number of bony plates, and both maxillaries and mandibles set with teeth. The most singular feature in this fish was a crest of large teeth, seven in number, forming a single row, set between the extremities of the mandibles, apparently acting as the prow of a ram.

Another bucklered fish he called *Aspidophorus*, or the shield bearer, because the central plate of the thoracic buckler was thirteen by seventeen inches in dimensions, more than an inch in thickness in the centre, and studded all over with enameled tubercles as large as half peas. The affinities of this fish were apparently with *Pterichthys*, but it was a hundred times as large. Its remains were found in the Huron shale, just over the Corniferous at Delaware, Ohio.

The hugest of all these old fishes, he had named *Dinichthys* or terrible fish. In this the head was three feet long by two in width, the under jaws more than two feet in length, an inch and a half thick at the thickest part, and five or six inches in depth. These turned up anteriorly like sled runners, their extremities forming great triangular teeth, which interlocked with equally huge teeth from the upper jaw. The middle dorsal shield of *Dinichthys* was some sixteen inches in diameter.

Rhynchodus was the name proposed for a new genus, represented in the collection by two kinds of teeth. These are semicircular in form, from three to five inches in diameter, very strong and massive. They apparently formed a beak-like rostrum. In one species the teeth of the opposite jaws played on each other like the blades of shears, and the specimens exhibited were so worn as to present sharp cutting edges along the upper margin. The teeth of other species are thicker and more massive and evidently fitted for crushing, rather than cutting.

These teeth Dr. Newberry considered as belonging to *Chimeroid* fishes.

A new species of bucklered fish, now first brought to notice, he called *Acanthaspis* or spiny shield. In this, the buckler terminated laterally in strong defensive spines, like those worn on the backs of sharks.

January 30, 1871.

Prof. T. Egleston, Vice President, in the chair. Twenty persons present.

Dr. L. Feuchtwanger exhibited a specimen of **Crystallyzed Quartz,** which was notable as it had apparently formerly contained within its mass crystals of Arkansite; but that mineral has been removed so as to leave cavities which show the outline of the Arkansite crystals.

Prof. T. Egleston said that specimens of this character were of some interest, but, as he had examined several similar specimens which were supposed to be Quartz crystals penetrated by delicate prisms of Titanium minerals he had found that no such mineral was present; merely cavities more or less colored.

Prof. D. S. Martin mentioned the fact that in Rhode Island Quartz crystals were frequently found penetrated by Actinolite.

Prof. C. A. Seely exhibited a specimen of a material having the appearance of a **Light-colored Clay.** As, however, it took a polish on being rubbed with a hard object, he considered that it could not be clay but was probably something new. It came from Rhode Island and he had made a chemical examination of it and found it to consist of Magnesia 2·8, Silica 28·0, Alumina 70·0. Therefore he considered it to be essentially a Silicate of Magnesia and Alumina. It occurs as a large bed and is of commercial importance. This specimen, as well as that exhibited by Dr. Feuchtwanger, was referred to Prof. Egleston for examination and report.

Mr. S. Smith exhibited a very large **Coleopterous Insect,** from Kentucky, where it, as well as one more, was obtained on splitting open a log, within which it doubtless had been hatched and passed through its larval condition.

PROF. D. S. MARTIN remarked that this was a very fine specimen of a rare insect *Dynastes Tityrus*, and is our only native representative of this genus. It is large, being over two inches in length, but is excelled in dimensions by another species of this genus, *D. Hercules*, which is about six inches long.

PROF. A. M. EDWARDS exhibited a **Cast of a Tree-stem in Sandstone**, procured by him at the Sandstone quarries at Newark, New Jersey, where they are reported by the workmen to be not common. He also detailed the results of a further examination, which he had made of the strata exposed at that locality in continuation of what he had already reported upon this subject before the Lyceum. During his last visit to these quarries he had found the Lignite mentioned before in the grey Sandstone accompanied by Malachite.

PROF. H. WURTZ exhibited a number of specimens of **Iron Nodules** and made some remarks thereon, claiming that they have been formed from Pyrites nodules through the intervention of aerated water. He pointed to the fact that the sand found in their interior was siliceous, sometimes colored by Iron. He also showed Lignite from the same beds from which these nodules were procured.

The following paper was read by title: to be published, in full, in the annals of the Lyceum:

Descriptions of New Species of Birds, from Mexico, Central America and South America, with a note on Rallus longirostus, by G. N. LAWRENCE.

February 6th, 1871.

PROF. T. EGLESTON, Jr., Vice-President in the chair. Eighteen persons present.

MR. R. DINWIDDIE, as chairman of the **Committee appointed to nominate officers** for the ensuing year, reported a ticket which was ordered to be printed; the Vice-President explaining that the printing of such a ticket did not, of course, prevent the presentation of other nominations.

DR. L. FEUCHTWANGER reported that he had completed his examination of the **Mineral** which he had presented at a former meeting, and which came from **Thunder Bay,** on the North shore of **Lake Superior.** He had found in it twenty-five per cent. of Nickel, besides the other metals he had before mentioned; the other prevailing metal besides the Nickel is Silver.

PROF. T. EGLESTON remarked that he had been examining this mineral, or rather ore, with some care, because there were facts of interest connected with it. It had been considered by the discoverer to constitute a good and new mineralogical species; a native alloy of Nickel and Silver. The results he, Prof. E. had arrived at, contradicted this assumption. When the metallic portion alone was examined after careful separation, no traces of Nickel were found in it; in fact it was essentially native Silver. On the contrary, when the whole mass was crushed and the powder thus obtained, analyzed Nickel was found. Such a mechanical mixture of metallic Silver and a Nickel ore was by no means uncommon. Thus at Schneeberg, in Germany, such a mixture occurs where the Silver in fine threads is disseminated through the Nickel ore. In fact, the Silver then becomes the metal of the ore whilst the Nickel is present in the gangue.

He also reported that he had examined the specimen exhibited by Prof. Seely at the last meeting, and which had been referred to him for examination. He found it possessed all of the properties of, and in fact was simply clay.

He also exhibited two remarkable specimens of **Rubellite,** from Siberia, one was seven-eighths of an inch in diameter and one inch long. Its form was the hexagonal and hemi-di-hexagonal prism and basal-pinacoid. The crystal was remarkably transparent. The second specimen was made up of a group of twenty-four crystals, associated with crystallized talc, most of them were one-quarter inch in diameter and three-quarter inches long. They are composed of two varieties, the darker varieties showing invariably the hexagonal prism and pyramid. The lighter and more transparent crystals show the basal-pinacoid associated with the same form.

PROF. A. M. EDWARDS exhibited a specimen of *Helix nemoralis,* which he had captured, alive, upon the pavement of 29th street, between Madison and Fifth avenues, on the 10th of last June, 1870. The day was wet, and the animal was crossing the southern sidewalk at the time. It had evidently come from the grounds of the Church of the Transfiguration, which is situated opposite. The interesting fact connected with this capture is, that *Helix nemoralis* is a common European species, and has not been found native in this country. How this one was introduced could not be ascertained, but if one could thus get loose, many might also, and the species become common here also.

MR. F. A. WOOD remarked, that a short time since he had received a number of specimens of *Bulimus virgulatus* from Central America, from whence they had been imported in Logwood. They had been collected for their shells. They were dried, and had been in that condition for about five months, and were, to all appearances, dead. Notwithstanding, however, he found that they were alive, for they projected their soft parts from their shells, and in fact traveled about a drawer in which they were kept, as was made evident by their traces on the paper lining. But they had not been seen to move, as they would not do so in the light, preferring darkness during their peregrinations. Examples of apparent revival after death, or at least long continued dormancy of Mollusca were not very uncommon, but always of interest and worthy of record.

The following paper was read,

On Preparing and Preserving the Odontophores of Mollusca.

By Prof. A. M. Edwards.

I have at this meeting exhibited the shell of a common European species of *Helix*, which however is not native to this country, and which I found alive upon the pavement of one of our city streets during the last summer. At the same time I showed an Odontophore, or Lingual Ribbon, as these organs are frequently called, of the same creature cleaned, prepared and mounted upon a slip of glass in such a way as to constitute a microscopic object, showing its characteristics in a clear and elegant manner. As this subject is an important one to those who are engaged in studying the Mollusca, and as I have met with such decided success in the preparation of these objects, I have thought it would be well to describe my method, so that others, if they desire, may profit by my experience, and receive as much pleasure as I have from the results.

It is well known, that for a long time the characters which were made use of by naturalists in the classification of the Mollusca, were derived from the shells of these animals alone, and to such a degree was this extremely artificial method carried, that numbers of conchologists existed, who had never set eyes upon the animals, whose dead and dried skeletons they had collected and hoarded in costly cabinets. The natural result was the multiplication almost without end of so-called species; such groups not unfrequently being founded upon single specimens, possessed of some abnormal characters, due it might be to disease or peculiarity of surrounding in its place of growth. Of late years, however, conchologists have given way to naturalists, who have been for the most part Biologists in the true sense of the term; not being satisfied with the examination of the animals whose skeletons were the shells of the older collectors, they have studied the creatures alive, and have watched and noted their life-history from the egg to the adult stage. The consequence has been the discovery of the fact, that the mode of life of many of them as regards their food, is shadowed forth in the organs used for the procuring and mastication of that food. Hence has arisen the plan of classification, or rather, to speak more correctly, determination, by studying the organs of mastication or jaws and odontophores. The importance will then be at once seen of possessing a means of readily and accurately preparing these odontophores, so that their characters may be preserved and conveniently exhibited. The ordinary method pursued, has been to dissect out these organs by means of knives, scizzors or needles, and after washing them, perhaps with the assistance of a camel's-hair pencil, put them up upon microscopic glass slides, either dry or in some preservative. Of these preservatives two types have been in common use; the first is Canada Balsam or some similar resin, which almost totally obliterates the delicate sculpturings of the horny teeth, whilst the second has been the mounting by means of an enclosing cell in some watery fluid, either Glycerine, which also makes these objects altogether too transparent, or a solution of some antiseptic substance like Kreasote or Corrosive Sublimate.

In the first place, although this rough mode of manipulating answers tolerably well with the very largest specimens of Odontophores, it becomes entirely useless when applied to those delicate ones which are by far the commonest, and which, at the same time, possess such great beauty of structure and configuration. And in the second place, the preservative materials commonly made use of, either mask the most important characters or are extremely unreliable. Thus the use of cells containing liquids are notoriously objectionable to microscopists, for they have learned from bitter experience, that it is next to impossible to render such cells perfectly tight. Now the process I am about to describe, I consider does away with both of these difficulties, whilst it is at the same time readily put in practice.

If the animal dealt with be a tolerably large one, or rather if it be one possessing an Odontophore of such a size that it can be readily dissected out by means of knives, such a proceeding is put in practice, and that organ roughly cut away from the surrounding tissues, without any attempt being made at the same time to render it clean. But if the individual be a small one, as for instance our small native *Littorina*, no dissecting by means of knives or other instruments is attempted, but the animal whole, or even with the shell attached, in such cases where the animal has withdrawn deeply into the shell, as is commonly the case with specimens preserved in alcohol, and with which this process works admirably, or, as in the cases first mentioned, the uncleaned odontophore is placed in a test-tube, and there is poured upon it sufficient of Liquor Potassæ to cover it to a depth of at least half an inch. In some cases where the organ is very delicate, it may be necessary to use a weaker solution than the officinal Liquor Potassæ, or the odontophore is merely permitted to soak in the cold solution instead of using any heat. Or there may be, and in fact often are cases where a still stronger solution is required, but this point can only be ascertained by trial. After the odontophore has thus been immersed in the alkaline solution, if time permits, it is allowed to soak therein for some time, varying from a day to several weeks, but if the preparation is to be finished rapidly, it may be heated and boiled for a few minutes. With alcohol-hardened specimens I find it best to boil the liquid, but with fresh material it is not always so safe, as injury is often done by so proceeding. The action of the alkali is to dissolve everything but the shell, odontophore and a few shreds of muscular fibre, converting everything else into a soap. Now the contents of the test-tube are poured into a large vessel of clean water, and what is not dissolved, permitted to settle. The odontophore can then be easily distinguished and taken out by means of a dip-tube or otherwise, and thoroughly washed until all alkali is removed. It can then be transferred to alcohol or glycerine for preservation, if it is not intended to mount it for the microscope immediately. But if it is to be put up permanently, I find nothing answer as well as the material known as Glycerine-Gelatine, and which I have been in the habit of making after a formula of my own, and supplying to the dealers in microscopic materials for some time past. This medium is much more readily used than Canada Balsam, is cleaner to manipulate, requires no alcohol or turpentine to clean off of the slide, and shows the structure of the odontophore in a manner which nothing else that I have tried will. It is also a capital material for nearly every kind of animal and vegetable tissues, and in fact I consider it one of the most valuable media which the practical microscopist possesses. Its mode of use I have more particularly described in a paper lately read before the American Microscopical Society, and which will be shortly published in one of the English Journals, to which I must therefore refer for further particulars..

PROF. A. M. EDWARDS exhibited at the same time a series of specimens illustrating the above paper, and showed them by means of what he has called his **Demonstrating Microscope.** This is a form of instrument which he devised for use in his lecture room, where it was desirable to pass around and exhibit in a satisfactory manner, and to a class of students several microscopic objects in succession. It consists essentially of a microscope of the ordinary form, supported upon uprights and a tripod base. In this form it may be used in the laboratory and upon the table, but when used in the class-room, by means of a simple contrivance it can be unshipped from its upright supports, and can then be held in the left hand by the student, whilst the right is used to manipulate the adjustments. But so that proper illumination of the object under examination may be secured, the mirror, which is upon a tubular arm, and which can be swung from side to side so as to obtain oblique illumination, is removed, and in its place is attached a small lamp fed with Petroleum oil. In this way it can be passed from hand to hand around a class, and the source of illumination be always under the control of the observer. Prof. E. stated that he had two of this form of microscope, besides others, in continual use in his classes, and found them to answer every purpose required.

PROF. EDWARDS said that he desired to place upon record, another example of the introduction of an exotic animal into this section of country. This was an alligator, which he had found alive on the 25th of last June, 1870, in a small stream running through a meadow by the road-side, on the island of New York, near Inwood, which is at the farther end of the island. It was eight or ten inches long, striped transversely black and orange-yellow, and extremely lively, swimming away down stream on being disturbed. The source of this creature had not been ascertained, and on examining those in the collection at the Central Park, they were found to be totally different in color.

February 13, 1871.

PROF. C. A. JOY in the chair. Twenty-six persons present.

PRESIDENT BARNARD presented, in the name of the author, Brevt. Lt. Col. J. J. WOODWARD, twenty-four Photo-micrographs, with accompanying explanatory text, illustrating the use of Magnesium, Electric and Oxy-calcium lights in Photo-micrography, and the Histology of Minute Blood-vessels.

PROF. A. M. EDWARDS made some remarks explanatory of the great beauty and value of these contributions to science, and proposed a vote of thanks to Dr. Woodward for his generous gift; which was passed unanimously.

The chairman, PROF. C. A. JOY, read a letter from Mr. C. M. WHEATLEY, dated Phœnixville, Pennsylvania, February 8, 1871, announcing the discovery by him of a Bone Cave near that place in the Auroral Limestone, the floor of which is covered with the remains of Post-Pliocene Mammalia, Reptiles, Insects and Plants. Prof. E. D. Cope is engaged with Mr. Wheatley in working up the Vertebrates. Mr. Horn will probably study the Insects, and it is proposed to submit the Plants to Prof. Newberry. There have been, so far, found the following genera: *Megalonyx*, 1. *Mylodon*, 1. *Mastodon*, 1. *Tapirus*, 1. *Equus*, 1. ——— ? (*Actinodactyle*), 1. *Ursus*, 2. ——— ? *Bat*, 1. *Lepus*, 1. *Sciurus*, 1. *Hesperonys*, 1. ——— ? *Rodents*, 2. *Coluber*, 2. *Tropidonotus*, 2. *Crotalus*, 1. *Cistudo*, 2. ——— ? *Turkey*, 1. ——— ? *Snipe*, 1. *Coleoptera*, 5. *Plants*, 10 or more. Say 22 Vertebrates, 5 Insects and 10, or more, Plants. The Bear is the full size of the "Grizzly." Prof. Cope says it is entirely distinct in character from all the existing species of North America and the northern regions of the old world, as well as from the Cave Bear.

The following paper was read,

"On some New Derivatives of Albumen."

BY O. LOEW.

The author has succeeded in obtaining several new derivatives of Albumen; among these a Nitro-product, the existence of which was previously unsuspected. A mixture of one vol. of fuming Nitric acid and 3 vols. of concentrated Sulphuric acid was made. 90 C. C. of the Nitric acid was mixed with 270 C. C. of Sulphuric acid and the mixture allowed to cool; then 30 grms. of finely-powdered Albumen was gradually added, shaking well after each addition and taking care that the mixture remained cool. The Albumen was slowly dissolved to a clear solution without any disengagement of Nitrous fumes, and the solution surrounded by cold water, was poured, after a lapse of about 10 hours, into about 15 times its bulk of water. The voluminous flocculent precipitate was immediately filtered, washed, the last time with hot water, and dried with care. The powder thus obtained is of a light yellow color and slightly bitterish taste. It is insoluble in water, dilute acids or alcohol but soluble in dilute alkalies. On heating these solutions a decomposition sets in and new products are formed, which the author has not yet analysed. On heating the powder in a dry test tube it behaves like the original Albumen.

On analysis this new derivative yielded the following figures:

Sulphur Determination: *Balbe's Method employed.
- *I. 0·680 grms. gave 0·144 Barium Sulphate= 2·92% S.
- II. 0·912 grms. gave 0·200 Barium Sulphate= 3·03% S.

Nitrogen Determination:
- I. 17·20% N found.
- II. 17·00% N found.

Oxygen and *Hydrogen* Determination.
- I. 44·26% O and 5·57 H found.
- II. 44·01% O and 5·58 H found.

These figures correspond to an Albumen in which 6 atoms of Hydrogen are replaced by 6 atoms of the Nitro group and 1 further atom of Hydrogen by the Sulphoxyl group.

The Formula of the New Derivative is:

$$O_{72}\left\{\begin{matrix}H_{101}\\(NO_2)_6\\So_3OH\end{matrix}\right\}N_{18}SO_{22}$$

	Theory.		*Experiment.* I.	II.
O_{72}	864	44·13	44·26	44·01
H_{102}	102	5·21	5·57	5·58
S_2	64	3·27	2·92	3·03
N_{24}	336	17·16	17·20	17·00

The rational name of this compound is: "*Hexanitroalbumin sulphonic acid.*"

When this new body is treated with Sulphide of Ammonium, a new amorphous body is obtained, which bears resemblance neither to Albumen nor to Albuminsulphonic acid. This last new body seems to combine with acids as well as with bases. The author intends making further investigations on this point.

The author obtained another derivative by treating Albumen with concentrated Sulphuric acid. In a mortar was mixed

1 part of Albumen gradually with 10 to 15 times its weight of concentrated Sulphuric acid; after cooling for one day the mass was treated with cold water till the free SO_4H_2 was removed. The flocculent mass was placed in a dilute Potash solution, stirred sometimes, and left standing in the cold one day, filtered, precipitated by Acetic acid, the precipitate washed and analyzed. The result showed it to be Albumin-sulphonic acid. It contains twice as much Sulphur as Albumen, is insoluble in water, alcohol, and dilute acids, but soluble in alkalies, which cause it to swell considerably before solution occurs. On boiling these solutions, decomposition ensues. The author intends to still further investigate this subject.

On the Action of Sulphurous Acid on Metals.

BY P. SCHWEITZER, PH. D.

Zinc and Sulphurous Acid.—If we dissolve metallic zinc by means of a mineral acid, and add a few drops of a solution of sulphurous acid, we observe, according to the strength of the sulphurous and hydrochloric acid present, a more or less rapid separation of sulphur and development of the odor of sulphuretted hydrogen gas. This is a reaction we resort to daily in our laboratories for the detection of sulphurous acid in hydrochloric, acetic, and other acids, and is so delicate a test for the presence of this impurity, that the minutest traces of it may be discovered in this way without difficulty.

The reaction according to which this decomposition takes place is exceedingly complicated, and we look in vain to any of our text-books for information. Many false statements too, will be encountered on the subject, which only a close study will reveal as such. In the following will be found the results of some experiments, undertaken with a view of settling this question:—

A strong solution of sulphurous acid was prepared, so as to be perfectly free from sulphuric acid, sulphuretted hydrogen gas, free sulphur, and oxygen, which, by the way, requires a great deal of care. In this acid, care being taken to exclude all atmospheric air, pure zinc was dissolved. No generation of gas could be observed, and the fluid, after deepening gradually in color so as to become at last quite brown like old sulphide of ammonium, commenced to separate sulphur, regaining its original colorless state after some time.*

While brown, and before sulphur had commenced to separate, part of the fluid was saturated with caustic potassa, and tested for sulphur (as sulphide of potassium with nitroprusside of sodium), which was proved to be absent. After repeatedly shaking the fluid, which had become milky from separated sulphur, the solution itself being quite colorless, and allowing it to stand for several hours, a small amount of it was taken and tested in several ways. It contained still an excess of sulphurous acid, which, I may mention here, does not disappear even after standing for several weeks with metallic zinc, owing to the zinc becoming covered with a coating of sulphide of zinc, a trifling amount of which is always formed in this operation; part of it may be seen floating about in the liquid. Upon acidulating a part of the solution in question with hydrochloric acid and heating, sulphur separated in large quantities and of a yellow color, while sulphurous acid was given off; another portion was acidulated with the same acid and left standing; in a few minutes sulphur separated, increasing in quantity while standing, and sulphurous acid being given off again. This established the presence of hyposulphurous acid, as no

* The few bubbles of gas escaping at the beginning are very probably carbonic acid. Zinc, like many other metals, oxidizes in moist air, becoming thereby converted into basic carbonate. A stick of zinc, which had been cleaned beforehand with a file, so as to present a pure metallic surface, did not show the phenomenon of generating gas. Ordinary granulated zinc (which is always coated with a whitish oxy-carbonate) shaken with water imparts to it an alkaline reaction, on account of the carbonate dissolving to a perceptible extent, and which may be easily tested with solution of cochineal. The amount of carbonic acid which all metals absorb, when exposed to the oxidizing influence of moist air, is accounted for by the fact that it dissolves to a much larger extent in moist air than would correspond to 1·25 of a per cent., and that it very likely exists in this solution as carbonic acid and not as anhydride.

other known acid of sulphur is decomposed in the cold by a mineral acid into sulphur and sulphurous acid. Another portion of the fluid was then taken, diluted with water, acidulated with hydrochloric acid and chloride of barium added. No precipitate whatever formed, proving the absence of sulphuric acid. This test has to be done quite rapidly, as after a few seconds sulphur begins to be separated, recognizable when in small quantity by the peculiar opalescent appearance it presents. A third portion of the fluid was acidulated with hydrochloric acid, boiled so as to decompose all polysulphur acids, which in the case of hyposulphurous acid cannot be accomplished in less time than two or three weeks. As the precipitated sulphur does not settle very quickly, the fluid was shaken with a small piece of bright metallic copper which rendered it clear almost immediately, so that it could be filtered and tested for sulphuric acid. A heavy precipitate was obtained with chloride of barium, proving the presence of this acid in large quantity and beyond doubt. This sulphuric acid, though not present in the original fluid, was produced therefore by the decomposition of a sulphur acid, and judging from the synthesis of these acids, this must have been trithionic acid.

$$2\,S_2O_2 + 3SO_2 = 2S_3O_5 + S \quad \text{(Preparation.)}$$
$$S_3O_5 = SO_3 + SO_2 + S \quad \text{(Decomposition.)}$$

We have therefore present in the fluid, after acting with sulphurous acid on metallic zinc, SO_2, S_2O_2, S_3O_5, S, ZnO, ZnS, a trace. I may mention here that a solution of hyposulphite of soda treated with sulphurous acid turns, especially upon heating, first yellow, then brown, sulphur separates, and trithionic acid is formed. The change of color in the original experiments therefore indicates the point when trithionic acid is beginning to be formed. The reaction may be represented in the following way:—

1. $2Zn + 3SO_2 = ZnO{,}SO_2 + ZnO{,}S_2O_2$
2. $2S_2O_2 + 3SO_2 = 2S_3O_5 + S$
3. $(SO_2 + S = S_2O_2)$
4. $(5SO_2 + S = 2S_3O_5)$

The result being $ZnO{,}SO_2$; $ZnO{,}S_2O_2$; $ZnO{,}S_3O_5$; besides sulphur, sulphide of zinc, and the undissolved metal. As regards the reaction under 3, I am perfectly aware that sulphur under ordinary conditions does not unite with sulphurous acid, but if separated in the fluids containing it, its more active state may very likely favor such combination; the reaction under 4 is a fact as it is a method for the preparation of S_3O_5.

This fluid does not contain tetra- or penta-thionic acid, for on saturating it with caustic potassa and dissolving by an excess of alkali the first precipitated oxide of zinc, no sulphur separated to form sulphide of potassium on boiling. Both of these acids are decomposed, by boiling with alkalies, into sulphur and trithionic acid; this latter being decomposed in its turn again, but very much slower, into sulphurous and hyposulphurous acids.

Upon treating now sulphurous acid with metallic zinc in the presence of hydrochloric acid, we obtain a milky liquid, and the odor of sulphuretted hydrogen becomes more or less perceptible. The reaction here is more rapid and complicated. Zinc and hydrochloric acid generate hydrogen, as is well known, and the question may arise whether the hydrogen, being in the nascent state, will directly reduce sulphurous acid to water and sulphuretted hydrogen gas. Many metals decompose water, oxide of the metal being formed, while hydrogen is set free. On filling a little flask with sulphurous acid solution, inverting it and letting its mouth dip under sulphurous acid, contained in a porcelain dish, and introducing into the flask a piece of sodium, a vivid separation of hydrogen took place, while the sulphurous acid remained clear, and no trace of hydrosulphuric acid could be detected in the escaping gas. The same was observed when a piece of aluminium was substituted, in which case the fluid had to be heated to accelerate decomposition. The nascent hydrogen here was therefore without action upon the sulphurous acid, and it is not likely that in the case of zinc and hydrochloric acid the hydrogen should reduce sulphurous acid to water and sulphuretted hydrogen gas.

However, another experiment was tried, the result of which

presents a still stronger reason for not considering hydrogen the reducing agent of sulphurous acid. In treating sulphurous acid with zinc and hydrochloric acid in the cold, until the reaction ceased, freeing the sulphur from the liquid in the way indicated, and adding to it more hydrochloric acid and heating, a precipitate of sulphur was obtained indicative of the presence of a polysulphur acid; but as no sulphuric acid could be found in the fluid, this must have been hyposulphurous acid. In order to succeed in this experiment, much sulphurous and little hydrochloric acid must be taken; the separated sulphur there being also yellow. As therefore nascent hydrogen was without action upon sulphurous acid, but hyposulphurous acid and sulphur were separated, the probability is that sulphuretted hydrogen gas is formed by the direct combination of sulphur with hydrogen. In the moment of separation of both hydrogen as well as sulphur, we obtain all hydrogen and all sulphur as sulphuretted hydrogen; so in the case of treating sulphide of soda with an acid.

$$Fe + HCl = FeCl + H$$
$$FeS + HCl = FeCl + HS$$
$$Fe + HSO_4 = FeSO_4 + H$$
$$FeS + HSO_4 = FeSo_4 + HS$$

But even one of these two elements, while in the nascent state, will combine with the other. We know that nascent hydrogen will combine directly with phosphorus, forming phosphoretted hydrogen; and, though sulphur, presenting so many strange and peculiar anomalies in its different states, may not unite as flowers of sulphur with hydrogen, it is very likely that sulphur, just separated from the decomposing hyposulphurous acid, will form sulphuretted gas, with nascent hydrogen. The sulphur certainly must have retained in this case some active principle, as it will directly combine upon shaking with metallic copper, and, as we shall see hereafter, readily with metallic cadmium. Besides, sulphuretted hydrogen gas is only perceived in this reaction after sulphur has commenced to separate.

Cadmium and Sulphurous Acid.—In treating a piece of

metallic cadmium, which had been rolled out to a very thin and long strip, with the same sulphurous acid, the reaction took place in a similar way to that with zinc. The fluid turned first yellow, but still remained clear, which required, however, a much longer time than with zinc, then darkened, separated a little white sulphur, and precipitated finally a large amount of sulphide of cadmium. This is insoluble in weak sulphurous acid, and therefore precipitated, while sulphide of zinc, being soluble, is consequently prevented from forming. We have a clear case here of separating sulphur combining directly with a metal. But this separating sulphur seems to have even the power of depriving salts like sulphide or hyposulphite of cadmium of its metal, forming thereby sulphide of cadmium and sulphuric acid. For while in the liquid resulting from the action of sulphurous acid upon cadmium, and which has been in contact with the metal for only three or four hours, no sulphuric acid can be detected before boiling, its quantity will be perceptible after standing in contact three or four days, and will increase by standing several weeks. This sulphuric acid derives its origin from the oxidation of the sulphurous acid by the oxigen of the metallic oxide, which is decomposed by the separating sulphur. The experiment can be easily made by adding a solution of either nitrate or sulphate of cadmium to hyposulphite of soda. Upon boiling, a slight opalescence only will be observed, as cadmium salts are generally acid, but no precipitate of either sulphur or sulphide of cadmium. Upon adding, however, a little hydrochloric acid, a heavy precipitate of sulphide of cadmium will be obtained immediately. The sulphur, therefore, from the decomposition of the hyposulphurous acid, was decidedly active.

The original fluid treated in the same way, viz., boiling with a little hydrochloric acid, immediately gave a precipitate of sulphide of cadmium. Before, however, any marked percipitate of CdS was observed, and after the fluid had remained in contact with the cadmium for about four hours, no sulphuric acid was found to be present, as has been already mentioned. Upon acidulating and boiling this solution, filtering out the separated sulphur, and testing the filtrate, much sulphuric acid was found, originating as in the case of zinc from the decomposition of S_3O^5. The total reaction may be thus expressed:—

$$2\,Cd + 3SO_2 = CdO,SO_2 + CdO\,S_2O_2$$
$$2\,S_2O_2 + 3SO_2 = 2S_3O_5 + S$$
$$(SO_2 + S = S_2O_2)$$
$$(5SO_2 + S = 2\,S_3O_5)$$
$$Cd + S = CdS$$
$$CdO.SO_2 + S = CdS + SO_3$$

It is hardly necessary to say that the sulphuric acid will combine with oxide of cadmium, liberating either SO_2 or S_2O_2. The fluid, after a sufficient length of time, will therefore contain CdO,SO_3; CdO,SO_2; CdO,S_2O_5; CdO,S_3O_5; CdS; and the undissolved metal. All sulphur will have disappeared, and entered into combination with cadmium, so that a portion of the fluid, turbid and yellow from suspended sulphide of cadmium, will become clear upon acidulating with hydrochloric acid; no odor of sulphuretted hydrogen will make its appearence, as it is decomposed by the sulphurous acid. After filtering and washing, the precipitate may, however, be readily recognized as CdS.

Nickel and Sulphurous Acid.—Nickel in form of the well-known cubes was treated with sulphurous acid in a bottle; the action proceeded similarly to that of the two former metals, but was very much slower even than that of cadmium. After several hours a darkening and green coloration of the fluid occurred, but a day elapsed before a separation of sulphur took place, and then only small specks of it was seen floating about. In this stage of the operation the fluid contained NiO,SO_2; NiO,S_2O_2; some sulphur, but no S_3O_5 or SO_3. After several weeks' standing all sulphur had disappeared and combined with nickel as NiS, which in this case was certainly formed directly from the metal, as it presented the appearance of a black, heavy, scaly mass; this mass amounted to a considerable quantity, much more than could have formed from the little precipitated sulphur, and as much sulphuric acid was then to be found in the solution, we must conclude that either hyposulphite of nickel is not decomposed by sulphurous acid like the cadmium or zinc salt, but, under the influence and in contact with the metal and sulphurous acid, is converted into sulphuric acid, separating thereby sulphur, which combines with the nickel, thus:—

$$2\,(NiO,S_2O_2) + SO_2 = 2\,(NiO,SO_3) + 3S$$

or we have to admit a secondary reaction of the sulphurous acid upon the metallic nickel, thus:—

$$2\,Ni + 2\,(SO_2) = NiO,SO_3 + NiS$$

I should decidedly favor the former view, which does not appear to be so very strange, if we remember that sulphurous and hyposulphurous acids are decomposed differently when combined with different oxides. I only recall the preparation of trithionic acid either from bisulphite of potassa with flowers of sulphur, or from hyposulphite of potassa by sulphurous acid. We do not get trithionic acid if we take in these cases, soda instead of potassa salts.

However we have in the fluid, after allowing the reaction to proceed for a considerable length of time, NiO,SO_3; NiO,SO_2; $NiO,S_2\,O_2$; NiS.

Aluminium and Magnesium with Sulphurous Acid.—These two metals dissolved readily, the first in cold, the second in hot sulphurous acid. No sulphur is separated in the fluid, and no sulphuretted hydrogen gas is observed, as has been already mentioned. But upon analyzing the clear solution, we find in both cases SO_2; SO_3; S_3O_5; $S_2\,O_2$.

The presence of SO_3 and $S_3\,O_5$, and the non-appearance of S, forces us to admit two or three reactions taking place simultaneously and independently of each other. The first, the solution of the metal by decomposing water, liberating hydrogen, and dissolving as oxide in the sulphurous acid; the second, the action of sulphurous acid upon the metal, by forming a sulphide and hyposulphite, and the third by forming a sulphate, hyposulphite, and trithionate.

1. $Mg + HO + SO_2 = MgO,SO_2 + H$
2. $2\,Mg + 3\,SO_2 = MgO,SO_2 + MgO,S_2O_2$
3. $4\,Mg + 8\,SO_2 = MgO,SO_3 + MgO,S_3O_5 + 2\,(MgO,S_2O_2)$

These reactions seem to take place according to concentration, and depending in general upon conditions, which a future and closer study may reveal, and in the investigation of which, I hope other chemists will participate.

The following paper was read,

"Note on the Absorption Bands of Hæmatin and Cruorin."

By A. H. Gallatin.

The author, after alluding to the attacks of Dr. Forbes Winslow, of Steinmetz, and more especially of Paul Bert, on the reliability of spectral observations generally, and of observations connected with the absorption spectrum in particular, proceeded to defend the use of the spectroscope as an adjunct to the microscope, and to chemical analysis in medico-legal investigations connected with blood stains. The investigations of Hoppe-Scyler, of Valentin, of Stokes and of René Benoît, on the action of oxydizing, reducing and decomposing agents in producing the characteristic bands of Hæmatin, Cruorin and Hæmin, in the absorption spectrum of blood, were briefly described, and it was pointed out how these phenomena enabled us to distinguish solutions of colored organic matter of other origin than blood from blood itself. Moreover it was claimed that by these methods, we could study phenomena, such as the nature of Cruorin, and the question of its solubility and of its transformation by reagents, which we cannot approach by purely chemical means. The author studied the comparative spectra of Cruorin, and of a solution of carmine in ammonia, and discovered that their respective absorption bands were colored and shaded so differently, that by superposing the two spectra by the aid of two prisms near the slit, we could readily distinguish the one from the other. The appearance of these different colors and shades were illustrated by an original colored plate.

February 20th, 1871.

PROF. T. EGLESTON, Vice President, in the chair. Fourteen persons present.

DR. L. FEUCHTWANGER exhibited a **Hemitrope Crystal of Spinel,** from Amity, New York. At this locality, and reaching from Amity, in New York, to Andover, in New Jersey, Dana says, a distance of thirty miles, is a region of granular limestone and Serpentine, in which localities of Spinel abound. At Amity, crystals sixteen inches in diameter have been found, and one has been procured there weighing forty-nine pounds. Talc and Magnetite are also associated with the Spinels at this point. He also made some remarks upon a collection of **Tourmalines** of various colors, one of a fine red tint, and others of a beautiful yellow, which had been brought from the vicinity of Bangor, Maine.

HON. E. G. SQUIER presented some specimens of **Oche,** from Central America, and made some remarks on their mode ot occurrence.

PROF. T. EGLESTON exhibited a large collection of **cut, colored Diamonds,** loaned by G. Tiffany & Co. for the purpose. The stones were thirty in number, several of them weighing 2 and 3 carats each. The colors shown were four shades of honey yellow, four shades of yellowish green, three shades of light green, rose, garnet, brown, white and opalescent. There were three shades of dark colored, nearly black. A blue stone in the collection is doubtful, probably sapphire, though blue diamonds are known. Prof. E. is endeavoring to have a collection of eighteen stones, showing all the colors, presented to the School of Mines.

Mr. G. K. Gilbert presented **some facts in regard to the Surface Geology of the Maumee Valley,** brought to light by his observations while connected with the Geological Survey of Ohio.

I. As there are yet a few scientific men to whom the scoring of the rocks is not proof of the local action of glaciers, and as they have more than once adduced the absence of linear moraines in the western drift, as favoring the theory which ascribes all the phenomena south of the lakes to iceberg agency, the presentation of some facts which have led me to to believe that true terminal moraines exist in the valley of the Maumee river, may not be without interest.

The Maumee occupies the axis of a broad valley of easy slopes, continuous eastward with the trough of Lake Erie, and westward with the Wabash valley. To the northwest it is limited by a divide four or five hundred feet above its median line, and to the south by a flat divide even lower. North of the Maumee the general slope is toward the southeast, and all the small streams flow in that direction. But the St. Joseph river runs to the southwest, and through its whole course skirts the slope. The country on its northwest or right bank, drains into it, and that on its left, away from it. The reason of this is that a ridge runs along its left bank, and restrains it from taking what would otherwise be its natural course. This ridge is six or eight miles broad at base, does not average over fifty feet in height, and presents no superficial peculiarities, by which it can be distinguished from the adjoining country. Everywhere is seen the rolling surface of the undisturbed Erie clay, a drift deposit now admitted by all geologists to have been thrown down by a sea floating icebergs. In this vicinity its average thickness is not less than one hundred feet, and, as it is a deposit from quiet water, we may safely suppose it evenly spread, and aver that the low ridge upon its surface, is but the superficial indication of a more abrupt ridge that underlies it.

The St. Mary's river, which for a distance flows west, and then sweeps with a broad curve to the north, and unites with the St. Joseph, to form the Maumee, at Fort Wayne, Indiana, presents the same peculiar features as the St. Joseph. All its tributaries are from the south and west; north and east of it the drainage is from it, and its right bank is formed by a continuation of the same ridge.

This ridge then runs one hundred and twenty miles across the drainage system of the region, and is cut by a water course in that distance at but one point, and that the lowest in the valley. That it does not consist of rock *in situ* may be affirmed from the fact that it crosses the outcrops of beds of the Waverly, Huron, Hamilton, Corniferous and Waterlime groups. That it is a terminal glacial moraine, is the only explanation I can offer of its existence.

Some other facts appear to support this view.

Lower down, the Maumee receives another pair of tributaries, the Auglaize river and Bean creek. They, too, are determined by a ridge, and present, somewhat less perfectly, all the peculiarities of the first pair. Explaining this ridge in the same manner, we have here two parallel, concentric, crescent-shaped, terminal moraines presenting their convexities toward the south west.

Let us now see in what relation these stand to the glacial striæ. On the islands and mainland in the vicinity of Sandusky City, these striæ bear ten or fifteen degrees south of West; about Toledo, thirty-five degrees; near Defiance, Ohio, due south west; and in the vicinity of Lima and Van Wert, Ohio, from fifteen to thirty-five degrees west of south. We have it thus recorded, that the ice moved west through the west end of Lake Erie, and then curved in the Maumee valley toward the south, a motion entirely in harmony with the position of the moraines, so that I think we may fairly conclude that, as the great ice-sheet retreated, its border was lobed in conformity to the topography of its bed, that one of these lobes occupied the Maumee valley, and that when this margin delayed or reversed its retrograde motion, it marked its outline, at two stages at least, by forming terminal moraines.

II. Some of the members present, may recall that last

winter I endeavored to show that the water of Lake Ontario at Rochester, had been at least seventy feet lower than it now is, since it had been higher. This could have been accomplished only by such upheaval, or subsidence, or tilting of the land, as should make the shore at Rochester, in its relation to the outlet of the lake, seventy feet higher than at present. I have now to offer some facts from the West, that lead to allied conclusions.

The beach lines that record former levels of Lake Erie, are well marked in the Maumee valley. The highest is at 220 feet above the present, and others are at 195 and 170 feet, while from 90 to 65 feet a slow subsidence is recorded. These shore lines run far up the valley, and the higher stretch nearly to Fort Wayne, Indiana, one hundred miles from the present head of the lake. At New Haven, six miles East of that place, the beaches which mark the north and south shores of the old lake at its fullest stage, converge: but, instead of uniting, they become parallel, and are lost in the banks of an old water-course, one and one half miles broad, through which the surplus water of Lake Erie then discharged. This water-course I traced westward past Fort Wayne, twenty-five miles to Huntington, where it receives the Wabash river from the south east. Its sides and bottom are of drift nearly to Huntington, but there it has a bottom of Niagara limestone. No one traversing the ground can question that it is the channel of a former outlet of Lake Erie.

I conceive that this fact has an important bearing on the solution of the question:—what held the water of the Lake more than 200 feet higher than it is now? It precludes the answer that the continent was so submerged that the ocean opposed a watery barrier to the drainage of the lake basin, for there was an outward, descending flow at Fort Wayne. There are now no remnants of a rocky barrier at all adequate. Professor Hall tells us that the rim of rock through which the Niagara river has cut, is but 38 feet higher than the lake at Buffalo; and the rock—likewise Niagara limestone,—over which Lake Michigan once emptied southward to the Mississippi, is but half as high. Professor Andrews, of Chicago, to whom I am indebted for a description of that locality, thinks it possible, though not probable, that the drift has covered the rock there to a depth of one hundred feet; but yet another hundred of feet is needed to complete the dam. So we are not permitted to think that the successive water stages have been caused by the gradual cutting through of a high barrier. There seems to me to remain but one hypothesis, and that the true one; that the warping of the rim of the lake basin has taken place; that there has been local subsidence, or upheaval, or both, so that Fort Wayne is now relatively much higher than formerly; and that it has been by the contortion of the great reservoir, that the point of its outflow has been shifted from point to point, and its capacity has been varied.

February 27, 1871.

ANNUAL MEETING.

The President in the chair. Twenty-nine persons present.

After the Reports of the different Officers were read and accepted, a ballot was taken, and the following gentlemen declared elected for the ensuing year.

President, JOHN S. NEWBERRY, M. D.; Vice Presidents, 1st, THOMAS EGLESTON, 2d, B. N. MARTIN; Corresponding Secretary, ROBERT DINWIDDIE; Recording Secretary, ROBERT H. BROWNNE; Treasurer, TEMPLE PRIME; Librarian, ARTHUR M. EDWARDS; Curators, WM. J. HAYS, LEWIS FEUCHTWANGER, M. D., HENRY WURTZ, WM. H. LEGGETT, A. H. GALLATIN, M. D.; Committee on Nominations, CHARLES A. JOY, ROBERT DINWIDDIE, CHARLES A SEELY, JAS. W. WARD, JOHN H. HINTON, M. D.; Committee on Publications, THOMAS BLAND, JOHN S. NEWBERRY, M. D., GEO. N. LAWRENCE, TEMPLE PRIME, PAUL SCHWEITZER; Finance Committee, COLEMAN T. ROBINSON, J. CARSON

Brevoort, W. R. Sands; Library Committee, Robert H. Brownne, Isidor Walz, O. W. Morris.

Prof. O. W. Morris read a **Meteorological Report for the month of February, 1871,** as follows:

Temperature on the 1st=40° F. On the 27th=40°. Highest on the 25th=60°. Lowest on the 6th=2°. Range=54°. Highest daily mean on the 25th=52°. Lowest daily mean on the 5th=8°. Greatest change in 24 hours from the 4th, to the 5th, at 7 A. M.=34°. Rain or snow has fallen on twelve days, of which four were snow. The quantity of water was 5·78 in. The mean temperature for the 26 days has been 31·45° The maximum of the Barometer was 30·519 in. on the 22d. The minimum 29·407 in. on the 18th, a range of 1·112 in. On the 1st, the temperature at 7 A. M. was 40°, on the 6th=3°, on the 9th=33·8° on the 11th=20°, on the 18th=45°, and on the 22d=12·5° The storm on the 14th, was a severe one both in rain and wind; 1·18 in. rain fell and the snow melted and ran off very rapidly.

March 6th, 1871.

The President in the chair. Thirty-eight persons present.

The following paper was read,

Report of Progress of Work accomplished at the Palæozoic Museum, in the Central Park, New York.

By B. Waterhouse Hawkins.

On the 16th March, 1868, two days after my arrival in this country, I had the pleasure, by invitation, of addressing this Society on popular education connected with science. I then quoted a paper I have now in my hand, namely the printed programme of the Conference on Technical Education, held in England, January, 3d, 4th, 1868, at the Society of Arts in London. The first item of that programme is, "That to establish and maintain a system of Technical Education adequate to the requirements of arts, manufactures and commerce in the United Kingdom, the three following Educational reforms should be effected:

"1st. In the Universities, Grammar Schools, and other Educational Institutions for the upper and middle classes of society, instruction in science and art should be placed on the same favorable footing as other studies. 2d. Efficient means of primary and secondary instruction should be brought within the reach of the working classes everywhere, and encouragement should be given to the study of the elements of science and art in the upper classes of all primary schools which receive aid from government; and 3d, Special Institutions for Technical Instruction, adapted to the wants of the various classes of society, and to the industries of the country, should be established and maintained in the United Kingdom."

Being a member of that Society, I was present at the discussion which then took place between some of our most celebrated men of high capacity. These views of popular education associated with science, were then new to England. I have since found that you had in part anticipated this tardy action of the old country, by your admirable, efficient and popular system for educating the people, but I have also found that the connection of science with education is here, as at home, a barren field awaiting the action of the cultivators. It was my good fortune on my arrival here, to secure the attention of this old-established and most respectable Society, the Lyceum of Natural History in New York, when your President and his Coadjutors were pleased to sanction my then expressed views, by recommending me to bring them before the public of New York, which (as you may remember) I had the honor of doing on the 26th of March, 1868, at the Cooper Union, to one of the largest audiences to which I ever had the pleasure of presenting myself; nearly 3000 persons endorsed your opinion of the views I put before them, by inviting me to deliver a course of lectures on

Natural History, which was eminently successful, and was the introduction to my addressing many thousands of the most intelligent classes in the various cities between New York and Chicago; this successful expression of my opinion on the advantage of combining the Natural Sciences with Education, caused me to be employed by the then Commissioners of Central Park here in your city, where I was to revive the Ancient History of the Earth, by the most suitable and substantial illustrations of its earliest inhabitants. A description of the nature of this engagement is contained in a brief letter in the 12th Report of the Board of Commissioners for Central Park, together with my reply, severally dated the 2d and 9th May. This correspondence is followed by a detailed Report of the work entrusted to my design and execution, up to the 19th Feb., 1869. This first Report was hopeful to me, and apparently satisfactory to the Commissioners and to the public at large. The first six months of my first year's engagement as shown in the Report alluded to, were occupied in comparing the contents of four various Museums and their Collections in reference to the fossil remains of Ancient America, as it had been decided by the Commissioners that my restorations should be confined in the first instance to those forms locally interesting.

I was made aware of the barrenness of the spot on which I had to commence my search for materials, by a little incident that occurred on one of the occasions when I was lecturing at Brooklyn, where a bone was placed in my hand by a gentleman who was under the impression that its concave ends indicated its belonging to a Reptile. I was anxious to compare it with a group of animals to which I supposed it to belong, but neither at Brooklyn nor in New York, was to be found any specimen of Natural History, Ancient or Recent, with the exception of a skeleton of the Irish Elk, (which your President had then recently received at the School of Mines) and some bones of a horse at a celebrated veterinary surgeon's, who happened to be out, and his collection inaccessible when I went to see it the day before I left New York.

As New York was totally destitute of materials for my work, I found it necessary to commence the inspection of the Museums of the other cities. I examined the Natural History collections at Boston, Washington and Chicago, but it was not until I reached Philadelphia that I discovered any materials available for my immediate purpose. There I found some treasures in the way of fossils, and obtained the permission (freely granted) of the Trustees of the Academy of Natural Sciences, to have their fossils moulded, on condition that I should give them duplicate moulds of the principal examples; in this way I was enabled to secure to the Commissioners of Central Park, the complete skeleton (with my restoration of the missing parts made at Philadelphia) of the gigantic Hadrosaurus described by Dr. Leidy. I afterwards had the pleasure of presenting to the Academy of Sciences (at my own expense) an entire restoration of the skeleton, combining the actual fossil remains of the limbs of that extinct giant, which I erected in their Museum, and presented to the trustees on the 21st November, 1868, and I now hand to you the resolutions of the representative council of that scientific body, by which the President and Trustees recognized the accuracy and value of my work and mode of teaching.

I returned to New York to commence my actual work in the Park on the 4th December, and took possession, on 7th December, of the upper floor of the Arsenal building as a temporary studio. My impatient desire to get to work, struggled with the difficulties and apparent unfitness of the place; the upper floor of an old building required some caution where to place a model in wet clay weighing several tons; by the 13th March, 1869, the eighth month of my employment by the Commissioners, I had realized the blocking out of the rehabilitated form of Hadrosaurus in a recumbent position, in submission to the necessities of a low roof under which the Hadrosaurus could not have assumed the walking attitude. The illustration in the 12th Report, contains a true picture of my studio at the Arsenal in the month of June, '69, the large model then nearly completed was afterwards moulded, which was a long operation with only one assistant and a laborer.

As the Commissioners had not decided on the site for the Museum building to protect these models and contain the Geological Illustrations accompanying them, as described in 13th Report, page 29, I was called upon by them, through the Comptroller, to make designs, plans and models, to scale, for the laying out of the then intended Zoological gardens, known as Manhattan Square, on 8th Avenue between 77th and 81st streets—these plans and models to scale, which are now in existence, for Bear-pits, Beaver-runs and so on, occupied me until the end of the year '69, which of course caused my restorations to remain in complete abeyance.

In January, 1870, the site for the Geological Museum was decided upon, and the foundations were commenced. As the Arsenal was required for the Museum of Natural History, it became necessary that my large model and the moulds should be removed, and a small temporary shed was built with a forge, (in reference to the iron frames of my restorations). I now had hopes of the commencement of my real proper work, for the Comptroller promised me that the platform on which alone I could erect my models, might reasonably be expected from week to week.

But sundry administrative changes were then taking place which appeared to postpone the advancement of this platform, and the temporary shelter, under which I could carry on my work through the summer and winter: until in the month of May, the total change of the Commissioners again presented a barrier to the hoped-for commencement of my own legitimate work. Early in June, the Vice-President of the Board of Commissioners informed me, that it was the wish of the Commissioners that I should give my attention to designs for the new Zoological Gardens, and to sundry temporary buildings, for improving the sanitary condition of the animals at the Arsenal. These buildings were to be erected in conjunction with the present Architect-in-chief. It was very distressing to me to find my own occupation was still to be kept in abeyance, with less prospect of continuance than under the former Commissioners, but as I had reason to believe that the great cost of the intended Museum was one of the chief reasons for its delay, I presented a Report to the Commissioners for modifying the design, so as to lessen the expense to a very considerable extent.

This Report, if I may trespass a little longer on your patience, I will now read.

Report on the Geological and Palæozoic Museum, to which it is proposed to add a grand Aquarium, together with a fish-hatching apparatus within the same shelter.

Palæontological Studio, Central Park, 5th Sept., 1870.

HENRY HILTON, Esq., Vice President, Exec. Com. D. P. P.

Sir,

In the 12th Report, page 131, it is stated, "In consideration of the variable climate and the duration of the winter in New York, it has been resolved by the Commissioners that the restoration (of gigantic animals) shall be erected within the shelter of a permanent building." This permanent building was commenced in January of the present year, and with the intention of so quickly preparing the central platform on which the rehabilitated forms of the giant animals of Ancient America were to be placed; that, at the time, I had reason to expect the said platform would have been ready in three or four weeks, when with a temporary protective shed I could have immediately commenced the modelling and casting of those forms for which I had the moulds prepared, while the architectural portions of the building should have been carried on over the temporary shelter of my works. Finding now that not only the required platform, but also the massive foundations of the structure are completed, I believe it to be my duty to renew the requisition for temporary shelter, for the continuance of my work, as accepted and agreed to by the Commissioners of Central Park. If it be a structure for mere shelter, all results might be obtained in a building that was comparatively inexpensive, such for instance as a wooden structure with iron supports, or one of rough hewn stone, of the utmost simplicity of design, suitable to the ponderous characters of the animals sheltered, while the interior should be but a rocky chamber or cavern, wherein the geological specimens of rock composing it, shall be geologically arranged, so as to explain their relationship to the animal forms exhibited. This united with the pictorial representations of the natural condition of the rocks, displaying the connection between the animal and vegetable kingdoms of that time, would convey information in a most complete and consecutive manner; then if to these instructive lessons in Geology, were added a grand aquarium for the display of examples of living fish and other inhabitants of the waters, with the artificial breeding and growth of the fish, the whole would be in such perfect harmony, and would so fitly combine entertainment with instruction, that it would enable the juvenile portion of this vast city to be instructed in Natural History in the easiest form, through the medium of the eye, during the winter; and thus would supply a want long felt by the citizens of New York. This plan of the aquarium has been tried at Hamburg, and has met with such great success that the Directors of the Crystal Palace, England, have now commenced a similar work as an attraction of considerable pecuniary advantage. The Museum in question possesses this great advantage of situation, that the visitors would have entrance and exit at 8th Avenue (where the traffic is already arranged) during the winter, without interfering with the rules respecting the closing of the Park.

Yours faithfully,

B. Waterhouse Hawkins.

On the 22d of December, I received the following notice from the Department of Public Parks:

Sir,

At a meeting of the Department of Public Parks held on the 20th inst., the following resolution was adopted: Resolved, that the existing arrangements for the services of Prof. B. Waterhouse Hawkins, connected with the establishment of a Palæozoic Museum or otherwise, be discontinued until the further action of the Board.

Respectfully, Geo. Van Nort, Clerk, D. P. P.

And thus, at the present critical juncture of Educational Progress, was a very summary ending put to my hopes, of realizing for a second time, the most efficient material for object teaching, in connection with Natural History and Geology.

The reading of Mr. Hawkins' paper was followed by considerable discussion, in which several members took part.

PROF. C. A. JOY made some remarks detailing the condition and doings of these portions of the Central Park, devoted to Natural History, up to the time when Mr. Hawkins took charge of the Museum, and subsequent thereto, with the present status of affairs.

The President, Dr. J. S. NEWBERRY, followed with some remarks illustrative of the great value of Mr. Hawkins' contributions to science, in the restorations of extinct animals which he had put up at Sydenham, England, and the interest which all Naturalists took in the work he had been engaged upon in this city; at the same time expressing the regret which he, in common with all interested, felt in the, it was hoped, temporary suspension of his labors at the Central Park.

Farther remarks were made by HON. E. G. SQUIER and Dr. I. WALZ, when, on motion of DR. L. FEUCHTWANGER, a Committee of three, consisting of Messrs. Joy, Walz and Squier, was appointed to draw up resolutions expressive of the feelings of the Society, as relating to the work accomplished and sketched out to be done by Mr. Hawkins, at the Central Park.

There was laid upon the table, a donation from Brevt. Lt. Col. J. J. WOODWARD, of the Army Medical Museum, Washington, D. C.—four Photomicrographs of Microscopic Test-objects.

PROF. A. M. EDWARDS remarked upon these photographs, and described their peculiarities and what it was intended to show by means of them.

He pointed to the remarkable results obtained by Dr. Woodward, as illustrated in these pictures, which showed the great superiority of the objective with which they were taken; viz.: a $\frac{1}{16}$ immersion lens made by Powell and Lealand, of London. With it the *Surirella gemma*, a Diatom long used as a "test-object" by microscopists, and upon which they had hitherto been only able to see very fine longitudinal striæ or, at best, indistinct elongated hexagons, according to Hartnack, of Paris, was now proved to be covered all over, as these pictures show, with circular, as Dr. Woodward thinks, or perhaps as he, Prof. E. thinks, equilateral hexagonal reticulation. So also *Amphipleura pellucida*, another Diatom and favorite test-object, upon which, up to this time, no markings can truly be said to have been seen at all, Dr. Woodward's pictures show to be marked with transverse striæ, which doubtless further researches will prove to be composed likewise of equilateral hexagons.

On motion of Prof. Edwards, a vote of thanks was unanimously tendered to Dr. Woodward, for his very valuable contribution.

DR. L. FEUCHTWANGER exhibited a fine specimen of *Encrinus liliiformis*, from the Trias of Germany.

The Librarian presented, in the name of Mr. A. J. COTHEAL, thirty-eight volumes of books of Natural History.

On motion of Dr. Feuchtwanger, the thanks of the Society were tendered to Mr. Cotheal, for his valuable contribution. The Committee to draw up resolutions relating to the Palæontological Museum, presented the following resolutions, which on motion were accepted.

Resolved—That the Lyceum of Natural History in the city of New York, has learned with deep regret, of the temporary suspension of the work of restoration of the forms of extinct animals, as hitherto prosecuted in the Central Park, under the able superintendence of Prof. B. Waterhouse Hawkins.

Resolved—That the Lyceum considers the proposed Palæozoic Museum, not only a valuable acquisition to the scientific treasures and resources of the city, but also a most important adjunct and complement to our great system of Public Education.

March 13th, 1871.

The President in the chair. Twenty-four persons present.

MR. J. W. WARD called attention to an error of omission in the minutes of the Lyceum, as published on page 98 of the Proceedings. He wished a correction to be made to the effect that as soon as he heard Prof. Edwards' statement that the white material, said to have come from a bed of clay in Delaware, exhibited by him at the previous meeting of the Lyceum, contained diatomaceous remains, and was in fact the same material as the so-called "Electro-Silicon," or infusorial deposit of Nevada, he had immediately explained that the announcement of Prof. Edwards disclosed to him the fact, that he had inadvertently exhibited the wrong material. Several packages of white earths were lying upon his table, and in the carelessness of haste, he had taken the wrong one; and that although the specimen he had, without due examination, placed on the table of the Lyceum, was truly enough the Nevada Tripoli, with the diatomaceous character of which he was quite familiar, having frequently examined it microscopically, and recorded its contents, it was nevertheless equally true, that the specimen of the Delaware deposit, which he had intended to exhibit, contained, as he had stated, no organic forms, and was largely composed of Mica, though not wholly so, as had by some been supposed. He did not present the specimen, which he now correctly exhibited, for examination for infusorial organisms, for he knew it contained none; but as containing a notable quantity of pulverized mica.

DR. I. WALZ remarked that it was a noticeable fact, that, not uncommonly, material appeared in the market in this city which was represented to be chalk, but, which upon examination proved to be siliceous, doubtless of the same character as the substance alluded to by Mr. Ward. Some, for instance, from Western Virginia, was found to be Kaolin.

The President alluded to the deposits of Kaolin, which are being worked at Brandon, Vermont, and Mystic, Connecticut, and which are washed so as to free them from their coarser particles, and then come into the market under the name of "china clay," to be used in paper making. The material used in China for the manufacture of porcelain is not a natural clay, but is derived from the pulverization of a rock, found in a range of mountains which have given their name to the material.

The following paper was read:

Some Notes on obtaining Photographic Representations of Objects of Natural History by means of the Microscope.

BY PROF. A. M. EDWARDS.

Brief as I shall be compelled to make the remarks I intend here to set down, yet the importance of the subject of which I treat, will, I feel assured, obtain for them a welcome from my fellow microscopists. Although we find our text-books and special treatises truly embellished with beautiful illustrations, colored or uncolored as the subject requires, executed in all kinds of engraving and with all the skill of experienced artists, who are often accomplished naturalists as well, and correctly comprehend the characters and relations of the objects they attempt to delineate, yet in every case the student of Biology finds something wanting, and never completely recognizes in the counterfeit on paper the subject of his study. And this is more particularly and strikingly the case, when we take into consideration the manifold wonders revealed by means of the microscope, and which the artist can rarely move about, turn over and examine from different points. Besides he is compelled to delineate that which he cannot handle, and only sees "in a glass darkly."

Every student of the microscope knows how extremely unsatisfactory are the published engravings, be they the best, of objects as seen by means of lenses. For such required delineations the photograph presents an admirable and always reliable recorder of present appearances, or, in time future changes.

It is not my intention, in these brief notes, to enter very largely into the importance of this mode of recording what is seen by means of the Microscope, as I believe that every student of Natural History is prepared to admit it at once. Nor do I intend to say much of what has already been done by others in this special field of photomicrography, only pointing to the results obtained by Dr. Maddox and others in England, Drs. Woodward, Curtis,—the former at present, the latter late of the Army Medical Museum at Washington—and Dr. Arnold, of this city, as examples of what can be done by perseverance and attention to the requirements of the case. I shall merely, in this short communication, put on record, as possibly of value to intending workers in this same field, some brief notes of my mode of working, and exhibit as the results I have obtained, the accompanying photographs and apparatus.

To begin then—let the intending photographer bear in mind that the first and most important thing he will require, will be what is so rare among portrait operators, that is to say, the power of being cleanly. In this branch of photography more particularly than in any other, is absolute cleanliness imperatively requisite. Clean hands, clothes, plates, bottles, vessels, solutions, camera, lenses, and lastly, but by no means least, clean objects. To begin with anything dirty is to court failure; to begin with everything clean is to ensure the best chances of success. Then have a good dark room into which absolutely no actinic light is permitted to enter. I have the window of my dark room (or more properly working room, for it is by no means dark) made of one large pane of orange colored glass, such as can be now readily purchased at the dealers, and, as it is a very perfect piece, find that it obstructs all or very nearly all the actinic rays, leaving me at the same time, ample light to see what I am doing. But I would advise that all yellow glass which it is intended to use for this purpose, should be tested before setting, as the eye alone is not a reliable test in such cases. There is some light and beautifully colored yellow glass in the market, which is of no use in photography, but that which is darker and of an orange tint I have found to be thoroughly reliable. A small fragment may be readily tested by exposing a piece of paper covered with Silver Chloride under it to the direct rays of the sun for a few minutes.

Perhaps I can best make plain the manner in which I manipulate by describing, first, the room in which I have been in the habit of working and the arrangement of the materials and apparatus therein. I shall begin with the window. It is small, but large enough to illuminate the whole room, which is itself small, as no very great space is required in this kind of work. At the same time the manipulator should not be cramped. A closet of the size that when one is standing in the middle of it, by one step in any direction all of the walls may be reached, will be found to be ample in dimensions; that which I used for a long time, and which I am describing, was somewhat larger, but in it I had space to store much of my photographic apparatus and material, which I now think would have been best left out. On a low table or bench, about two feet six inches high, placed immediately beneath the window, are arranged the vessels, solutions and apparatus I use in such an order that I could always lay my hands on them even in the dark. Thus, on the extreme left against the wall, are shelves with stock bottles of solutions, while on the left end of the table stands a large porcelain bath and dipper encased in a wooden box, with cover made so as to shut when necessary to exclude dust. Porcelain baths I find the cleanest and most reliable, much more so than glass with joints of any kind. Next in order towards the right from the silver bath, comes the pan containing the solution of Sodium Hyposulphite used for fixing. This pan is made of the so-called photographic ware, and I find this answers well, as it is heavy, and so not easily knocked out of place as some others, besides being strong. I should say, let this pan be ample in dimensions, so that the solution may not readily become saturated with Silver Iodide and Bromide, for such a proceeding will be found most economical in the end.

Next to the Hypo. dish comes a common wooden pail to catch the washing from developing, and over it, standing on a higher shelf, is another pail of clean water having a faucet set in one side near the bottom. This is for washing, but when a running stream is obtainable, of course it is preferable, unfortunately in my case such was not readily obtainable. Under the window is placed the plate holder with its Kits, and on the table near the pail the bottle of developer. On the shelf with the pail of clean water, is the bottle of collodion and brush used for dusting the plates. On the table I also have a so-called "manipulator," which I find a very useful contrivance, and since I have used it I can exhibit cleaner hands, clothes and negatives than I had before I bought it. This contrivance is a rod or handle of wood having at one end, and at a right angle to it a "sucker" of caoutchouc which when lightly pressed against the glass plate, holds it sufficiently firm to permit of its being manipulated during development.

The bath I use is one that is not very strong, about 40 grains to the ounce, slightly acid and only partly saturated with Silver Iodide, in fact a bath that is found to give sharp and intense negatives with the collodion I use, for it must be always borne in mind that the bath and collodion must always be suited to each other.

I have used several collodions, but take as a standard one that gives an even structureless film, as thereby I am enabled if I desire to enlarge the pictures I obtain. With care in the selection of collodion and bath, I find no re-developing or intensification of the negative of any kind necessary. But as it may be of value to others to have them distinctly specified, I will here set down the formulæ of a set of preparations which I have found to work well together both summer and winter.

Silver Bath.

Pure crystallized Silver Nitrate,	2 ounces.
Distilled Water,	24 "

Or of the strength of 40 grains to the ounce.

A plate as large as the bath will hold is coated with Collodion, as described below, and left to stand in the bath for about half an hour. By this means it becomes partially saturated with Iodide and Bromide, and is less liable to fog than if used directly without this precaution. Lastly make just acid with Hydrogen Nitrate (Nitric acid.)

Iodo-Bromized Collodion.

Washed Ether, sp. gr. ·720	3 ounces.
Alcohol, sp. gr. ·805	1½ "
Gun Cotton,	16 grains.
Cadmium Iodide, in powder.	18 "
Cadmium Bromide "	6 "

The gun cotton is first placed with the salts in a bottle, and the alcohol introduced and agitated until the salts are dissolved, then the ether is added and the whole allowed to stand until complete solution has taken place. Then the clear collodion poured off and preserved for use.

For development, I have used both Iron solutions and Pyrogallic Developers and found them each to be adapted to special cases. Formulæ for the different Developers, which are very numerous, can be found in the text books on photography The Pyrogallic one which I have found to work well, is made as follows:

Pyrogallic Developer.

Distilled Water,	15 fluid ounces.
Pyrogallic Acid,	15 grains.
Crystallizable Acetic Acid,	1 ounce.

This does not keep as well as the Iron Developer and must be preserved in the dark.

I fix in a saturated solution of Sodium Hyposulphite and wash *very thoroughly* in a copious stream of water.

Printing the positives is done in the usual manner made use of in producing portraits and views.

I have given the preparations I use and it will be seen that they differ in no respects from those used in portrait or view work; in fact Photomicrography, as far as the chemicals and formulæ go, is essentially the same as ordinary photography, only greater care is required in securing accuracy of proportions, and above all things *cleanliness* is absolutely necessary. I am convinced that if more attention were paid to this last injunction by our photographers generally, we should have better pictures than they commonly present us.

With regard to instruments, an ordinary microscope can be used if it be merely made to replace the lens tube on a portrait camera-box but I use a microscope made on purpose, having a flange by means of which it is attached to the front of the camera. Great steadiness is an absolute essential in Photomicography and I find that shutters and slides of all kinds to be used in exposing are detrimental. I withdraw the slide from the plate-holder, after having hung a bent card over the object on the opposite side to the objective; then, when everything has come to a state of rest, carefully remove this card and expose. If the camera be placed upon the earth, not in a building, all the better; and if the operations be carried on away from all streets and roads, still better.

If the lenses used be not specially constructed for photography, so as to bring the chemical and visual foci coincident, the chemical focus can be found either by practice, by using an Ammonio-Copper screen, as described by Dr. Woodward, or by employing a glass prism to illuminate the object. Any or all of these plans are desirable and easy of application.

In short, this brief communication has been more for the purpose of showing that there really are no great difficulties present, in the practice of this extremely beautiful and valuable method of reproducing representations of objects of natural history. Any careful portrait or view manipulator, can easily become a good photomicrographist, by merely attending to the injunctions as laid down in our simplest and best text-books, and being methodical and, above all, cleanly.

In conclusion, it may be of interest in this connection, to know as to who took the first photomicrographs. This question, I think, is answered by the following extract which I have thought of sufficient interest to microscopists to transcribe and register here. In the Journal of the American Institute for 1840, I find some interesting letters from Paris, written by Prof. Morse, detailing the then new and wonderous discovery of Daguerre, by means of which he was enabled to fix the sun-beam, and make it take pictures of still and moving objects. On page 409 he says:

"One of Mr. D.'s plates is an impression of a spider. The spider was no bigger than the head of a large pin; but the image magnified by the solar microscope to the size of the palm of the hand, having been impressed on the plate, and examined through a lens, was further magnified, and showed a minuteness of organization hitherto not seen to exist. You perceive how this discovery is, therefore, about to open a new field of research in the depths of microscopic nature. We are soon to see if the minute has discoverable limits. The naturalist is to have a new kingdom to explore, as much beyond the microscope, as the microscope is beyond the naked eye." This letter is dated March 9, 1839, therefore it seems that Daguerre was the first to take enlarged pictures of objects of natural history, by means of the action of sunlight upon Salts of Silver.

Prof. Edwards' paper was fully illustrated by means of the various apparatus used, and a large series of Photomicrographs taken by Drs. Woodward and Curtis, at Washington, and himself.

At the same time he exhibited a series of specimens of what had been erroneously termed Photolithographs and Photoengravings. These were prints obtained by the action sunlight, but in permanent pigment instead of Silver as in the ordinary Photographs. The best and greater number of these were produced by the process invented, and now being worked to a very considerable extent, and very successfully, by Mr. G. G. Rockwood, of this city. The Woodbury

Relief process was also illustrated. He pointed out the great value of such processes to the naturalist, who would in this way be able to have preserved in permanent pictures, representations true to nature of the objects of his study. Some of Mr. Rockwood's specimens were of a very remarkable character, as, for instance, a complete copy of the London Times reproduced in a page only 4½ by 3½ inches, and Harper's Weekly only 3 by 2 inches, and which latter can yet be easily read by means of a lens.

The President expressed his earnest hope that scientists would have in this or some similar process, the long-looked-for means of representing objects of natural history, in a cheap and truthful manner. It would seem as if we were on the eve of the accomplishment of this great end, and that perhaps we were about to enjoy what those who had gone before us had unsuccessfully longed for. The pictures exhibited certainly held forth great promise for the future.

PROF. H. WURTZ called attention to some **analyses,** made by Dr. P. Schweitzer, **of Sandstones from New Jersey.** They were as follows:

	Schweitzer.			Cook.
	a.	b.	c.	Bergen Hill.
SiO^3	67·4	77·7	73·8	52·6
Al^2O^3	16·63 (Al^2O^3, Fe^2O^3)	11·3	11·3	17·1
Fe^2O^3		1·9	3·8	8·7
CaO	14·6 (CaO, MgO, NaO, KO)	0·6	1·7	7·8
MgO		0·4	1·3	10·6
NaO		6·9	6·9	1·3
KO		——	——	0·9
HO	——	0·8	1·2	——

a. and b. are from Newark, the latter being one of the specimens procured by Prof. Edwards. c. is from Haverstraw, 100 feet beneath the Trap rock. Prof. Cook's analysis is given for comparison. In Dr. Schweitzer's analyses the operations were conducted with great care, and the portions soluble and insoluble in boiling Hydrochloric acid determined.

It is noticeable that the amount of Alumina present corresponds to 58·4 per cent. of Albite or normal Soda Felspar.

March 20th, 1871.

The President in the chair. Twenty-two persons present.

Mr. E. Guillaudeu presented some specimens of **Fossils from the Greensand of New Jersey,** found at Tinton Falls. These were a fragment of *Ammonites placenta*, a scute of an extinct crocodile, a bone probably of a turtle and others. This last mentioned was of special interest, as the bony matter has been replaced by Vivianite.

Dr. L. Feuchtwanger exhibited specimens of **Pumice** in the form of fine glassy threads, and commonly known as **Pele's Hair** from the volcano of Kilauea, in the Sandwich Islands—Pele being the goddess of this volcanic mountain. It is formed by the winds acting upon the liquid lava-jets, and is often thickly strewn over the ground on the leeward side of the mountain. Many of the filaments, when examined by means of a lens, are seen to have little knobs of volcanic glass at one end, precisely like those drawn off from the molten mass of a glass furnace, or formed by heating a filament of ordinary glass in a spirit-lamp flame. He also exhibited specimens of a mineral consisting of Chloride of Silver and Copper, from the White Pine district in Nevada; also fossils from the same locality. These consist of Carboniferous and Silurian mollusks, (*Productus cora*, *Rhynchonella increbescens*, *&c.*, and crinoidal columns,) the last found in a siliceous limestone almost like the Buhrstone of West Virginia.

The President, Dr. J. S. Newberry exhibited a series of **Drawings of Fossil Fishes,** prepared for the State Geological Survey of Ohio, for the most part by Mr. G. K. Gilbert, and described the peculiarities of the species illustrated.

Prof. C. A. Seeley exhibited a specimen of a **White Pulverulent Mineral,** from St. Lawrence county, New York, called chalk. On analysis he had found it to have the following composition.

Lime,	29·57
Magnesia,	6·17
Silica,	39·78
Oxide of Iron,	·75
Water,	·96
Carbonic acid,	22·77
	100·

PROF. H. WURTZ made some remarks relative to the formation of **Vivianite** and **Glauconite** in Greensand, and pointed to the value of studying the chemical phenomena involved in similar points of Geology.

PROF. A. M. EDWARDS alluded to the investigations ot Bailey and Ehrenbergh on the Greensand, whereby it had been shown that casts of Forameniferous shells, similar to those making up the mass of the Greensand, were to be seen in the soundings procured from the bottom of the ocean at the present time.

The following paper was read by title.

Notes on the Genus Pineria and on the Lingual Dentition of Pineria Viequensis Pfr.

BY T. BLAND AND W. G. BINNEY.

The Genus Pineria was established by Poey in 1854, and embraced two species from the Isle of Pines; the shells allied in form to *Macroceramus*, but the animal described as having no "inferior tentacles." Subsequently *Bulimus Viequensis* Pfr. and *Helix Schrammi* Fisch. have been referred doubtfully to *Pineria*, with a suggestion that they belong rather to *Macroceramus.* The authors treat the latter species as synonym of the former, which has, they explain, the lingual dentition of *Cylindrella*, very similar to that of *C. Trinitaria* Pfr. and not of *Macroceramus.*

March 27th, 1871.

PROF. T. EGLESTON, Vice-President in the chair. Twenty-three persons present.

THE CHAIRMAN, PROF. T. EGLESTON, exhibited three large crystals of **Diamond**, weighing about two carats each, loaned by Tiffany & Co., for the purpose. One showed the cube and tetrahexahedron with the cubical faces most prominent, the two others are hexoctahedral crystals. These were remarkable for their size and perfection of form.

He also reported that on examination he had found the mineral from Thunder Bay, Lake Superior, which had been exhibited at former meetings of the Society, to consist, for the most part, of a natural alloy of Nickel and Silver, which is quite malleable. The cobalt present, is in the surrounding mass or gangue.

PROF. C. A. SEELEY exhibited a specimen of a **Fungus**, taken from the faucet of a beer barrel, and made some remarks thereon, calling in question its vegetable character, mainly on account of its growing in the dark.

PROF. A. M. EDWARDS pointed out that there were whole groups of vegetables which normally grew out of the sunshine and that parts of most plants, namely, the roots, grew in the dark. He also remarked that the old mode of distinguishing plants from animals, namely, that plants absorbed Carbonic acid and evolved Oxygen, whilst animals did exactly the opposite, that is to say, absorb Oxygen and evolve Carbonic acid, must be now discarded, as it has been found to be by no means the case universally. In fact, he did not see where the line between the animal and the vegetable was to be drawn. A man could be distinguished from a tree, but when we came to consider the so-called lower forms, no distinction could be found. Dr. Hick's discovery of the vegetable amæboid forms, shows that the commonly-accepted mode of distinguishing these two groups of animated nature, namely, by the supposition that animals took their food into their bodies to digest it, whilst vegetable assimilated theirs from without inwards, could not stand any more than the older hypothesis. In short, he must consider that neither the animal nor the vegetable does exist.

MR. J. HYATT pointed to the fact that the vinous fermentation going on in a fluid, say beer, is not arrested in the human stomach.

MR. E. G. SQUIER described a large natural bed of Truffles existing in Bolivia.

MR. J. HYATT presented a **Scheme for the Indication by Numbers, of Stages in the Flowering and Fruitage of Plants.**

The TIME OF FLOWERING was indicated by Arabic numbers in the following manner.

No. 1. Flower bud visible to unassisted eye.
2. Flower bud fully grown.
3. Some flowers open—one or more.
4. Flowers generally open.
5. Middle of flowering season.
6. Decline begins.
7. Decline very obvious.
8. Flowers scarce.
9. Flowers very scarce.
10. Last flower seen.

STAGE OF FRUIT.

In indicating this Roman numerals are used.

I.	Fruit $\frac{1}{10}$ full size.
II.	" $\frac{2}{10}$ " "
III.	" $\frac{3}{10}$ " "
IV.	" $\frac{4}{10}$ " "
V.	" $\frac{5}{10}$ " "
VI.	" $\frac{6}{10}$ " "
VII.	" $\frac{7}{10}$ " "
VIII.	" $\frac{8}{10}$ " "
IX.	" $\frac{9}{10}$ " "
X.	" full size.
XI.	Ripe fruit.
XII.	Fruit falling.
XIII.	" fallen.

The following are examples of the mode of applying this scheme to practice.

Stellaria media, common chickweed, stages 4, X.

Acer rubrum, swamp maple, stage 4. Locality Newburgh, March 16.

Corylus Americana, hazelnut, stage 5. Locality Central Dutchess Co., March 17.

Alnus serrulata, swamp alder, stage 5. Locality Central Dutchess Co., March 18.

Simplocarpus fœtidus, skunk cabbage, stage 6. Locality Central Dutchess Co., March 18.

Epigœa repens, trailing arbutus, stage 1·7 to 2. Locality Central Dutchess Co., March 26.

He also presented the results of a record kept of the temperature of the Croton water as drawn from a faucet in the city during the month of March, 1871.

In February it had averaged	36° F.
March 2d,	37° F.
8th,	37·5°
14th,	42°
22d,	44°
27th,	44·5°

Mr. E. G. Squier made some remarks relative to a **Copper Axe**, found near Watertown, in this state, and supposed to be made of bronze. It had not, as yet, been shown to contain any Tin and it was not at all likely that it did, as it was plainly cast and not hammered into shape, as was the case with all of those true bronze implements which had been found upon this continent, but as yet only in the West and South West.

April 3d, 1871.

The President in the chair. Thirty-two persons present.

DR. L. FEUCHTWANGER exhibited specimens of **Silicified Wood,** from the White Pine district in Nevada. Also a specimen of light-colored translucent **Blende,** from Spain. Also specimens of **Marble,** from California, Brandon, Vermont, and New York.

PROF. B. N. MARTIN exhibited specimens of **Crystallized Silver,** from Lake Superior and **Crystallized Gold,** in which the form of the crystal was made up of fine metallic filaments, from Oregon.

PROF. T. EGLESTON remarked upon the beauty of the gold specimen, and said that although he was at first disposed to consider the silver crystals to be artificial, on subsequent examination he ascertained them to be natural and, as well as the gold, to present some points of considerable interest.

MR. B. G. AMEND exhibited a specimen of the **White pulverulent mineral,** from Watertown, similar to that shown by Prof. Seeley at a previous meeting. He had found it to contain seventy-five per cent. of material soluble in acid.

The following paper was read,

On a Specimen of Ichthyosaurus.

BY B. WATERHOUSE HAWKINS.

A good fossil specimen of the Ichthyosaurus or Fish-Lizard has arrived in this city, and is deposited in the College of the City of New York, which, in consequence of an invitation from the President, Gen. Webb, I have inspected. I did not measure the specimen, but it appeared to me a little over ten feet in length. It is in an excellent state of preservation, and has been compressed from below upwards, leaving it in a position to exhibit the spinal column. The paddles, and a second specimen, about two feet long, lying outside the abdominal aspect of the larger individual, are also well displayed. The situation of the smaller specimen has, I understand, given rise to various opinions, by naturalists who have seen it, as to whether it be in its present place in relation to Viviparous origin, or to having been swallowed whole, and so taken into the stomach of the larger Ichthyosaurus. I beg to express distinctly my conviction that neither of these causes will account for its position, as the ribs of the larger specimen are covered by the smaller; distinctly proving that the smaller animal was outside the larger one. I do not attempt to define the species, or add a new name to the already overburdened list, on which Palæontologists have amused themselves, by naming more than thirty species, which classification is for the most part based on minute differences in the teeth. The present specimen does not show a sufficient number of them for positive identification. There is the usual break in the line of the caudal vertebræ, in this specimen, which first suggested to Professor Owen his hypothesis as to the necessity for the presence of a caudal fin, to enable this large marine Saurian to move swiftly in the water, the dislocation always occurring in the same relative place, it appeared to him as though there must have been the weight of some appendage at the extreme end of the tail, which when the integuments were decomposed, allowed it to fall and separate from the end of the body. Added to this break, there is the depression on the upper aspect of the terminal vertebræ, which indicates that the fin was vertically placed, as in the shark and other fishes. This reasoning appeared so just, that in each of the large restorations that I made at the Crystal Palace, Sydenham, I adopted the vertical caudal fin for the Ichthyosaurus Platyodon and Communis. The energetic President and the authorities of the College of the City of New York, may be congratulated on the acquisition of so good a specimen of this interesting fossil, which shows in every part the perfection of Creative Power, and which though it lived so many thousands of years ago, yet possesses the most finished perfect organic machinery, as exhibited in the adjustable sclerotic plates of the eye, enabling this ancient animal to adapt the refined mechanism of vision to the varying degrees of light and distance, then in the muddy waters of the Liassic sea of England and other parts of Europe, as now by the eyes of owls, eagles and diving birds.

This animal was contemporary with the Plesiosaurus and Teliosaurus, which make a trio of perfect construction, which certainly exhibits no nearer relation to mere primitive Protoplasm, than the highest expression of animal life in the present day. I trust this instructive fossil may form the nucleus of a collection of fossil remains, that will constitute the basis of the most effective adjuncts to popular education, commensurate with the future grandeur and progress of the City of New York.

The following paper was read,

Notes on the Meteorology of the Month of March, 1871.

BY PROF. O. W. MORRIS.

The temperature of March was in the reverse order of the old proverb, "If March comes in like a lion, it will go out like a lamb," for the lamb came at the beginning, and the lion in the last part.

On the 1st the thermometer was at 40·5°, on the 3d at 59°, on the 4th 38·5°, and on the 5th 35°. The mean on the 3d was 53·83°, the warmest of the month. The thermometer kept above 40° till the 13th, and the mean, above 40° till the 16th, when it was 38·4°, it then went above 40° and kept so till the 28th, when was the lowest mean 36·1°.

The maximum was on the 3d, 59° and the minimum on the 29th, 33°, a range of 26°. The mean for the month was 44·73°, which was warmer than any other March in 10 years, except that of 1865, which was ·89° warmer only.

The mean of the Barometer was 29·857 inches on the 1st. On the 20th, it attained its maximum, 30·211 inches, and its minimum on the 27th, 29·318 inches, both at 7 A. M., giving a range of ·893 inch. The mean on the 31st, was 29·827 inches, ·03 inch lower than on the 1st. The monthly mean was 29·888 inches.

A beautiful Lunar Corona was observed on the 2d. Lunar haloes, on the 5th and 29th. Solar haloes, on the 11th, 20th and 26th. Snow on the 4th, 14th and 26th. Thunder on the 12th, during a long rain; and a brilliant Metéor in the morning of the 25th. Rain fell to the depth of 5·6 inches, which was ·94 inch more than the average for March in 10 years before. On March 3d, 1861, the mean temperature was 8·7° higher than in March 3d, 1871. In 1868 it was 6·26°.

April 10th, 1871.

The President in the chair. Thirteen persons present.

The following paper was read.

Notes on some Microscopic Organisms.

By Prof. A. M. Edwards.

On the morning of the seventeenth of April, 1869, I collected in the water of a spring at Weehawken, New Jersey, some fine filaments of an Alga, which, upon taking home, I, as is always my custom, at once examined by means of my microscope. What I then saw interested me so much, that I spent all the rest of that day and the most of the two succeeding days in studying it. The nineteenth happened to be the day of meeting of the Lyceum of Natural History, and I then took the opportunity of communicating what I had seen; illustrating my remarks by means of carefully made drawings and diagrams. The interest shown in my communication proved to me that my observation was of importance. But, unfortunately, at that time the Lyceum did not publish its

Proceedings, and my remarks were not put into print; therefore what I had seen was only known to the members present. The next evening the Microscopical Society had its meeting, and I again made public my observations, and to all there present they were new and startling. Hence I was induced to repeat my description with more detail at the Salem meeting of the American Association for the Advancement of Science in the following August. My engagements were such, however, that I was prevented from putting my observations upon paper, and I did not endeavor to do so, as I understood that the Association could not provide for the colored plate which I considered necessary for illustration. The consequence has been that they have remained unprinted up to the present time. Now I desire to have them recorded, the more especially as, from all I can learn, my observations are unique, or, at least, have not been seen and published by any one else. At the same time, I wish now to place upon record some further discoveries connected with the life-history of certain animal organisms of minute size which I consider of importance and throwing considerable light upon a rather obscure portion of Biology; namely the so-called subject of "Spontaneous generation." And I must say that I cannot but think that the use of this title, to designate the phenomena considered, is extremely inappropriate and had best be discarded, as it does not properly indicate what is meant and at the same time I am sure, often prejudices persons in advance against even considering the record of experiments or published deductions. A really more correct name to use would be that proposed by Prof. Huxley, of Abiogenesis, until the whole matter has had a fairer hearing than there is a desire to accord it in certain quarters at the present time. Such plain and evidently truthful records as those of Pouchet and Bastian cannot be sneered aside by using the weight of any name, however worthy of honor and respect, and, whatever the deductions to be drawn therefrom, the spirit of fairness, which should always influence the acts and words of truly-scientific observers demands that no aspersions should be cast upon what they, or others working in a similar direction, may have already or should hereafter publish. I speak thus, for I have myself, in a degree, had to encounter much of this very unfairness, and I shall hereafter claim an immunity from it when I publish, as it is my intention to do, some experiments and deductions of my own, tending as I hope, to assist in elucidating this interesting and important subject. In the mean time and even aside from this connection, I desire to call attention to the value of the observations I have been so fortunate as to make and which I now, for the first time, put into print.

It is my intention to make this communication as brief as possible, the more particularly as, although the observations described appear at first sight to be tolerably complete, yet, for my own part, I must consider them as but partial and fragmentary and merely as memoranda of a phase in the hitherto insufficiently studied life-history of a group of plants a more thorough knowledge of which is of the utmost importance and interest. Therefore I thus set down what I have myself seen, intending to follow it up with more extended researches as opportunity offers. At the outset I would remark that the investigation of such phenomena as I now mention require no more special apparatus than a tolerably good microscope furnished with a magnifying power of about four hundred diameters and which is usually and conveniently obtained by employing a one-quarter or one-fifth of an inch objective on the usual ten-inch length of tube or body and a B or No. 2 Ocular. But what is certainly required is a large share of patience and perseverance, as is, perhaps, exemplified by the fact that while studing this subject, as I have mentioned, at one time I remained at the microscope, only at long intervals removing my eye from it, for the greater part of three consecutive days. That is to say certain points were observed about the middle of one day and all the rest of that day and evening, the whole of the next day and evening and nearly all of the succeeding day were spent in these investigations watching the changes and transformations I am about to describe. And this was only at one time, for many hours thereafter were spent in the same way, and I feel sure that it is only by such earnest application that we can acquire any knowledge of the phenomena peculiar to what we know as life which will be of any lasting value.

The plant I examined belonged to the genus *Œdogonium* of Link. The particular species was undetermined and when it is considered upon what slight and evidently artificial characters species have been founded among the Cryptogamia I am sure that I will be excused from venturing upon such delicate ground, especially as by so doing I run no danger of offending those who do not recognize the existence of species at all, or, on the other hand, puzzling those who do recognize the existence of natural species but are not anxious to have them multiplied. The form observed is extremely common, growing in clear springs in various sections of the country, and is especially plentiful around the city of New York. To the unaided eye it appears as a bunch of fine filaments of a light green color and by the unknowing collector of microscopic wonders is usually classed under the inclusive title of "Confervæ." My first investigations were made in the month of April, a season when this peculiar phase of this plant appears to be common. And here I would impress upon students of nature, and more especially those who use the microscope to assist them in their investigations, the great advantage to be derived from making collections early in the spring. At that time the young stage of many organisms may be procured, and, as that season is also the time of rapid change and development, we are placed in the very best condition for watching transformations that may take place and determining the true position of many forms which might be, and in many cases, I am convinced, have been ranked as perfect species. Let the young biologist remember that our knowledge of a species is never complete until we have made ourselves acquainted with the whole cycle of its existence from the germ to the adult, from the parent to the offspring and the early spring in such latitudes as have a severe winter, during which almost all life lies dormant, is the time for such studies.

Up to this time the amount of knowledge bearing the portion of the life-history of the germs Œdogonium of which I desire to treat, is very incomplete; there being gaps which I think it will be found that what I have seen and have to describe, just fit into and fill. The perfect plant itself consists of an extremely fine, green-colored filament, cylindrical in form, and having its frond divided at regular intervals by partition walls so that the individual plant may be represented by a series of tubular cells or boxes, like tall pill-boxes, united end to end. The enclosing wall of these cells is itself colorless, and it would be difficult to see it, did it not possess a different refractive power upon light to the water in which it floats. It probably consists essentially of the same substance, chemically considered, as the enclosing cell-wall of the Desmidiæ, and commonly known as cellulose, (a term, by-the-way, used in an extremely loos eand indefinite manner,) and is possessed of considerable tenacity as will be seen to be the case farther on, and is evident by the fact that we can handle the filament quite roughly without tearing the cells asunder; thus it is common to find this plant growing in running water where it withstands the flow of the stream. The mode of reproduction known to exist is, as far as I can learn, by the shrinking inwards of the inner cell-membrane, commonly known as the "Primordial Utricle" of Mohl, and enclosing the cell-contents away from the tough cellulose coat, while, at the same time, the cell-contents themselves assume a more or less coarsely-granular condition, apparently from the enlargement of the individual particles of which it is made up. It is recorded that thereafter, at a certain period in this change, the outer cell-wall splits across at a point near to one end of the cell, and, while the lid so formed remains attached to one side the other and largest portion, the cell-contents escape from the cavity into the surrounding water, and gradually assume the spherical form. Thereafter there is developed upon one side of the sphere a ring of ciliæ which become more and more active until, at last, they move about with such energy that the little green globe assumes an extremely active motile condition, flying about for some time in such a lively manner that an observer meeting with it and unaware of its origin, would certainly be inclined to rank it within the confines of the animal kingdom. In this state it has been called a "motile spore," but we will see, further on, that it hardly can be ranked as an ovum in the ordinary acceptation of the word.

Up to this period our record, as hitherto published, is complete, but just here is a gap and it has been my good fortune to make such observations as fill it and complete our knowledge of the life history of this plant. It is known, however, that the motile condition just described is but transitory, and perhaps it may have been on account of the velocity of its movement, and the consequent difficulty of keeping it under observation that the next step has not, as yet, been observed. In some unknown way, then, it has been supposed that the active spherical form assumes the static condition, develops rootlets or filaments, which serve to attach it to other objects and then, being fixed, it thereafter by means of the usual well-known method of cell sub-division, developes into a new filament resembling exactly the parent plant from which it sprung. As I have said, I have been enabled to show how the motile form is changed or, more properly speaking, developed into the static form and, at the same time, I think, throw some light upon an important portion of microscopic biology. The changes and transformations which I herein record, I have seen not merely a few times, but perhaps, thirty or forty, so that I am enabled to speak confidently as to the accuracy of my notes, as I have watched the whole process. It is as follows. At first the bright green-colored cell-contents, around and investing which I have not been able to satisfy myself that I have seen a "Primordial utricle," grow gradually coarser in texture by a process of differentiation of the mass in such a way that granules appear which increase in dimensions at the expense of the surrounding and investing substance, until the whole cell is filled with a coarsely granulated mass, differing little in color from the original cell-contents. At the same time the whole green mass recedes somewhat from the enclosing cellulose wall and instead of filling it completely withdraws itself in such a way that its outline, near the ends, becomes rounded. This change is by no means slow, but, when the dimensions of the plant are magnified by the microscope, appears to be rapid. I should say, although I have not timed it, that this stage occupies from fifteen to twenty minutes in its accomplishment. Soon thereafter the cell-contents contract still more, moving towards one end of the cylindrical cell. Then, with a sudden snap, fracture takes place almost entirely across the tough cell-wall at a point about one-twelfth of its length from one end, that is to say a portion measuring about one-twelfth of the length of the whole cell splits across with a perfectly smooth and even fracture, still adhering by a very small portion, and looking like the lid to a box, is thrown back more or less so as to expose the transformed cell-contents to the surrounding fluid. Occasionally but not commonly the fracture extends entirely across the cell-wall, and the two resulting portions become separated. Usually it occurs in the way I have described, so that after a while, and when all the cells of a filament have thus opened, it becomes transformed into a chain of straight portions bent usually in one direction in consequence of the dehiscence occurring for the most part along one side of the filament only. But now the green cell-contents move towards the openings thus formed, and slowly and steadily push themselves outwards, and, being elastic, escape after the manner that a small elastic sac filled with semifluid contents would escape from the hand if pressure were brought steadily to bear upon it. But in this case the emergence is not caused by the closing in of the cell-wall, but by a motile power resident in the elastic sac and its contents. It is not shot forth suddenly from the cell cavity, but squeezes itself out, and as soon as it has escaped assumes the form of a perfect sphere, and, as if exhausted by its previous exertions, comes to a rest. But, although the whole mass is not now in motion, the cell-contents do not remain at rest but go on to another change. The bright green, coarsely-granular sphere being at rest, is seen first to become somewhat clearer upon the surface and evidently a process of differentiation goes on by means of which a very delicate investing membrane is formed, but it is so delicate that it can only with difficulty be seen; and, in fact, can hardly be said to exist as a separate membrane. But upon one side is now seen to appear a bulging outwards of the mass until a nipple-like protuberance is formed which however is not filled with the green matter formed elsewhere, but is clear and colorless. I have noticed that in most cases this protruding portion is formed at the point just opposite to the place in the cellulose cell-wall of the filament from which the spherical body has just escaped. But as this is not invariably the case it can hardly be considered as anything more than accidental. Soon thereafter, there is seen to be a slight agitation going on upon the surface of the sphere, near to, and upon one side of the clear space. This movement then assumes a more definite character, and at last a moving cilia is seen to be formed or differentiated from the outermost portion of the globe. Soon another and another are formed in the same manner, attached by their bases around the clear space, and soon, that is to say in fifteen or twenty minutes, a ring of active ciliæ are seen to surround the nipple-like projection. As soon as they have all made their appearance immediately they all begin to move together and in a violent manner, so that motion is imparted to the whole mass, and it swims about actively through the water. And this motion is so active that it is often difficult to follow the mass, and keep it within the field of the microscope. For several minutes or, more rarely, for half an hour, this motion goes on, and up to this point I find that these changes have been observed and recorded by others. But now comes what I consider the most important part of this history.

It can be readily understood that, on account of its violent action, the further history of the spherical mass could not easily be followed, but fortunately on several occasions I saw specimens entangled in a mass of filaments in such a way that they could not escape from the field of view. Then I saw that the motion became gradually less and less vigorous and at the same time the ciliæ disappeared one by one, melting out of view, being apparently absorbed again into the mass from which they were originally developed. At the same time one of them seems to elongate until it is one to three times as long as the diameter of the spherical mass, and also, its point of attachment changes until we find it springing from the centre of the clear projection. While this is going on, the whole mass, not changing its position, assumes however, a totally different outline. That is to say, the clear nipple-like blunt part remains about the same, but the opposite portion becomes pointed, while the intermediate space is inflate in such a way that the whole creature in outline somewhat resembles a trefoil clover. The inflated part, however, does not remain rigid, but soon subsides, while the clear end becomes more pointed, and now the creature is spindle-shaped in outline. As there is now but one cilium it is by means of it that the creature moves about in an extremely active manner. In some, and in fact in by far the most cases I observed, the swelling of the middle portion is not fixed but moves down the length of the creature towards what may with some propriety be termed the posterior extremity, as it is always projected backwards when it is moving through the water, and there disappears to be soon followed by another swelling and wave-like projection and so on. In fact, an action resembling very closely that seen to take place in the intestines of animals, and known as peristalsis, takes place. Many individuals move directly and straight onwards, preserving their body perfectly rigid, so that after a time the cell-contents are seen to arrange themselves in longitudinal bands. Others, again, revolve on their longest axes, and soon the cell-contents of these are seen to have arranged themselves in spiral lines corresponding to this movement. Some of these retain their straight condition, while others become bent around so as to form almost a complete circle, and then proceed onwards by a rolling motion. There is a regular and determined passage from one of these states to the other, as I was able to ascertain by careful watching; but the most remarkable fact connected with the whole matter, is that all of these forms are precisely similar to creatures which have been ranked by Ehrenberg and others in the animal kingdom, under different names, but most commonly that of *Euglena.* To make the resemblance to the Euglenas still more marked, as soon as the circlet of ciliæ has disappeared, and the mass elongates, a bright red spot appears near the clear end, and usually also, one or more clear seeming vacuoles are seen to arise within the green mass. The red spot has been called an eye, and the vacuoles stomachs; and in this way Ehrenberg was enabled to classify these forms as "Polygastric Animalcules." The spirally twisted forms have been placed in a separate genus and in fact I have seen, in the way mentioned, developed from the cell-contents of a filament of Œdogonium forms identical with several genera of "Polygastric Animalcules." After a little longer time the cell-contents have again changed in appearance so as to be coarsely granular, each granule being so large and distinct that it can readily be distinguished, and now the active motion of the mass ceases, and it takes on the static condition. This it does by increasing in size, elongating and losing its cilium and red "eye" spot, while the clear portion elongates, sub-divides, and branches out and becomes fixed either to a full-grown filament of Œdogonium or some other submerged substance that may serve it as a support. Now the cell-contents become finely granular again, and arrange themselves against the cell-wall which is thickened considerably. Soon a bending in of an inner membrane, or "Primordial Utricle" is seen to take place and cell-division after the well-known method occurs, until a filament is formed exactly like that from which the original green sphere was projected.

The important points, then, recorded in this note are the finding of the means by which the active spherical form is converted into the still state previous to growth into a filament. The most remarkable fact, however, is the identification of this phase with one or more of the forms which have been hitherto classed either in the vegetable or animal kingdom, most commonly the latter, according to the predjudices of the observer.

This note of the transformation of Œdogonium is the only one concerning the life-history of plants that I desire to record at the present time, but I have made so many detached observations very much of the same kind, that I wish to state that I am convinced it will be at some future day shown that all of the green, and some of the red colored forms similar to Euglena, and which have had several names bestowed upon them, are but transition states of fresh water or marine Confervoid Algæ.

The second observation that I have to record is of certain phases in the life of animate organisms which have been commonly considered as belonging to the animal kingdom. But my notes here are more incomplete than in the case of the motile forms of the alga just mentioned, as it has been only within the last few weeks that I have seen what I am about to describe, and then only a few times, so that I wait for more opportunities for observation to confirm my experience. And here let me say, that apparently, the stages of change of these seemingly otherwise simple organisms I here record, are, like the vegetable one just described, confined to the spring time of the year; and even then to a very few days. Of course these changes cannot be supposed to take place, for instance, within the space of one week, and in every individual in a single locality; but the changes are so rapid that it can only be by constant and patient observation that we may hope to see them occur, whilst slight modifying causes may defer or hasten the the stage in different cases.

It was on one of the bright days during this spring that I collected in one of the pieces of fresh water in the Central Park in this city, a mass of matter made up of vegetable and animal material, but containing as I knew, that which would yield material for observation and study by means of the microscope. Observing it, then, in that way, I was pleased to find in it numerous individuals belonging plainly to the group of organisms which have been grouped together under the head of *Amœba.* But remembering the observations of Dr. J. Braxton Hicks on the occurrence of amœboid forms in certain undoubted vegetables, I was of course unprepared to assign them to a position in the chain of life without further study. To decide this question if possible, and ascertain the origin of these wandering masses of protoplasm, I watched them at intervals for the better part of two days, and I saw the following changes take place. From an almost hyaline condition the *Amœba* became gradually more and more granular, the granules increasing in dimensions until the individuals appeared to be packed almost full of dense oil globules. Then they came to a rest, or at least their hitherto lively movements were arrested, and presently near one end appeared evolved, so to speak, from the mass cilia one after the other until a crown of them was seen surrounding what was plainly now a defined locality. At the same time a change was going on all over the *Amœba* by reason of which at last from this simple mass of albuminoid material a true ciliated animalcule, belonging I believe, to either the genus *Kolpoda* or *Paramecium*, which resemble each other very much, was evolved.

The question at once, then, presents itself, is not the amœba, in this case, the young motile condition of the ciliated animalcule? Such is my opinion. But we will require many more observations to decide whether, as I am of opinion is the case, they all pass through this condition and also, at the same time to throw more light upon a field in which I have spent much time in observation, namely, the origin of these simple organisms like the *Amœbæ.* At some future time I may take the opportunity of detailing what I have seen in this direction.

DR. I. WALZ described **a new method of Analyzing Titaniferous Iron Ores,** devised by himself. Under ordinary circumstances, and as described in the books, such ores, after pulverization are fused along with Acid Sulphate of Potassium in a Platinum crucible, and the Titanium Oxide thrown down from the solution of the mass in water by boiling. He had found this mode of procedure to be troublesome to work, and had therefore tried the following, which was found to act in a perfectly satisfactory manner, at least with the particular ore upon the analysis of which he was engaged at the time. · It was his intention to test its applicability to other ores, and report the results at some future time.

The Titaniferous ore is very finely pulverized, and then thoroughly ignited in a Platinum crucible over a Bunsen burner, until it is judged that all of the iron has been peroxidized. Then it is acted upon by means of concentrated Hydrochloric acid, when all of the Iron and a little of the Silicia is brought into solution, the Titanium Oxide and remaining Silica being left as an almost white powder. In the acid solution the Iron can be estimated by the volumetric process, and the analysis completed within an hour from the beginning, a great gain in time over the older process.

The President, DR. J. S. NEWBERRY, exhibited a **Shaving of Wood,** obtained by means of a newly-devised veneer cutting machine. It is of great tenuity, and seven feet long by two feet broad.

DR. L. FEUCHTWANGER exhibited a specimen of **Slag,** from the furnaces in which the **New Jersey** Red Oxide of Zinc is smelted. It is opaque, and of a peculiar yellowish green color, which he considered as due to the presence of Cadmium. He also made some remarks on the Crystallization of Minerals, illustrating what he said by means of specimens of Gold, Pyrites, Columbite and Quartz. He also presented a specimen of **White pulverulent Mineral** from Watertown, Jefferson County, N. Y., which had been under discussion at late meetings of the society. He considered it to be Gurhofian. Analysis of it by Prof. C. F. Chandler, showed it consist of;

Carbonate of Lime,	55·32
Magnesia, 26·28 } Silica, 13·33 }	31·61
Oxide of Iron and Alumina,	1·28
Water and loss,	1·79
	100·

Prof. C. A. Seely exhibited the **Copper Hatchet-head,** found near Auburn, Cayuga County, N. Y., belonging to Mr. Squier and mentioned by him at a late meeting. He had analyzed it and found it to consist of pure Copper with, prehaps, the slightest trace of Silver, but no Tin or other metal. From this analysis and from other facts he considered it to be not of recent manufacture, and hammered, not cast as Mr. Squier had supposed by some of the early inhabitants of that part of the country.

April 17th, 1871.

The President the Chair. Twenty-three persons present.

Prof. D. S Martin exhibited a series of **Sandstones** from the Newark quarries containing the remains of vegetables in the form of Lignite. He described the position of the yellow and grey Sandstones which contain these remains relative to the red sandstone and shale.

Prof. H. Wurtz enquired whether it had been decided if the organisms of which these were remains had grown where they are now found or had been transported there.

The President, Dr. J. S. Newberry, described the mode of formation of these sandstones and stated that they were the remains of ancient sea-shores upon which had drifted and collected the vegetable matter now preserved in the form of Lignite material.

Prof. B. N. Martin exhibited a specimen of a **Fossil Ammonite** named *Ammonites Swallowii*, from the cretaceous of Texas.

Prof. H. Wurtz exhibited a specimen of **Sand** obtained some years since, from hills at that time being cut away, and now entirely removed, from behind Jersey City. It was of interest, as an examination of it showed that it was made up of material derived from the rocks of the immediate vicinity and had a bearing upon the subject of the genesis of our sandstones lately discussed at several meetings of this Society.

The President, PROF. J. S. NEWBERRY, exhibited specimens of **Polypterus Bechii and Calamichthys Calabaricus, Ganoid fishes from Africa.** These he said were of special interest, as they represented, on the African Continent, an ancient group of Ganoid fishes, once doubtless very numerous, but probably leaving no other descendants than these. In the same way the Gar-pike and the Dog-fish *Lepidosteus* and *Amia* are the only remnants of the ichthyic fauna which peopled the rivers, lakes and seas of North America in former geologic periods. These two African fishes are much more alike than the Dog-fish and Gar-pike, and are considered by some Zöologists as species of the same genus. An interesting fact in this connection is the discovery, in the interior of Australia, of what seemed to be a living species, or more than one, of a remarkable genus of fishes known heretofore by some large and strangely-formed teeth found in the Trias and designated by the name of *Ceratodus.* This latter was of much more remarkable structure than either of the fishes before mentioned, so much so that it was perhaps yet an open question whether it was fish or amphibian. *Ceratodus* is allied to *Lepidosyren* and the group to which they belong forms the connecting link between fishes and amphibians and is probably the group through which the transition from fishes to the higher classes of vertebrates took place, if the evolution hypothesis is correct. That the transition was not effected through the highest group of fishes, the *Teleosts,* is certain, as both amphibians and true reptiles existed before the *Teleosts* came into being, unless, as Prof. Huxley suggests, the oldest group of all fishes the *Placoderms*; such as *Cocosteus* and *Pterichthys* were *Teleosts* allied to the modern *Siluroids.*

PROF. H. WURTZ exhibited specimens of **Utensils made of**

fused Cryolite, and constituting what is technically known as "Cast Porcelain." One of these showed a portion to be transparent, whilst all of the rest were opaque. He considered that this was caused by the unequal cooling of the two portions. Such an effect being produced, as he had shown some years back, in blowpipe beads. When these are cooled suddenly they remain transparent, but if cooled slowly, the particles have time to arrange themselves in such a way that the mass becomes opaque.

MR. G. K. GILBERT made some remarks on the occurrence of the **Remains of a Mastodon,** as illustrated by a specimen lately unearthed at St. Johns, Auglais County, Ohio. The question most commonly raised in connection with the remains of this creature was, as to whether they belonged strictly to the peroid of the deposits in which they were found. That is to say, whether they had gone into the bogs, and having become mired therein had died in the places where they were found, or had they expired elsewhere and were their bones transported by water, or otherwise, into the bogs. Unfortunately this question could not be settled by appeal to most of the specimens discovered, as they are commonly separated in such a way as to present no signs of the mode of arrangement during life, or such points are unobserved by those who make the excavation. Fortunately the Ohio specimen presents us with an opportunity of solving this question conclusively. The Mastodon was found in a deep bog erect, just as he had been mired. He was headed for the nearest margin, with feet sprawled out as though struggling. The bones of each foot were in place, with the bones of the lower leg erect above them. Tusks, teeth, ribs and pelvis, all in appropriate positions. All the skeleton above the knees was more or less decayed. The animal probably stuck in the mud when it was but six feet deep, and two feet more have accumulated since. As the whole deposit is post glacial and above lacustrine action, being 450 feet above Lake Erie, the date of the burial of these Mastodon remains is as definitely recorded as is that of the ice period.

The decompositions of the upper part of the skeleton were such as to spoil it for mounting. The lower five feet of the deposit which held the Mastodon bones was marl. The upper three feet peat-earth or black muck.

April 24th, 1871.

The President in the chair, twenty-four persons present.

Dr. L. Feuchtwanger exhibited a specimen of a substance which had been handed to him as perhaps **Ambergris.** t is earthy in appearance, of a light fawn color and burns on the application of a flame. It is plainly not Ambergris, and he presented it to ask if any of the members could tell what it is.

Prof. A. M. Edwards replied that this substance had been presented several years since at a meeting of the Lyceum by a gentleman of the name of Southworth, who owned a large tract of land near Bahia, in Brazil, where it occurred in large quantities. At that time it had been referred to him, Prof. E., for examination and report. He had determined that it was deposited in now extinct lakes beneath whose beds were Bitumen springs, the lighter oils from which substance had infiltrated into and impregnated the mud. Sometimes the roots of plants, the remains of leaves and even wood were found imbedded in it but no Diatoms or other microscopic organisms, by means of which the character of the water beneath which it had been deposited could be determined. The owner proposed, and in fact had to some extent, used it for the production of gas for illuminating purposes, as the town of Bahia had been in this way lighted. If it had not been so light and bulky it had been proposed to ship it abroad for distillation, as the better qualities had been found to yield as much as one hundred gallons of oil to the ton whilst the more inferior qualities gave seventy-five gallons of a similar oil to the ton. If it could be considered to be a true mineralogical species it had been proposed to call it Southworthite. It was well known in Brazil as "Turba" and the locality where it occurs is described by Prof. C. F. Hartt, in his recent book on that country.

Prof. B. N. Martin exhibited the **Humerus** of some large animal, apparently a **Buffalo.** It had been lately found in the drift nine or ten feet below the surface, near Fox Hill, Hoboken, N. J.

The specimen was referred to Mr. W. J. Hays for examination and report.

Prof. D. S. Martin exhibited specimens of **Mica Schist filled with minute crystals of Kyanite,** in such a way as to constitute a variety of the rock, that might be termed a Kyanite Gneiss. These pieces were obtained from the excavation opposite to the néw Union Depot on East 42d Street, where it occurs in considerable quantity, and is quite characteristic. There is also another locality of it, between 45th and 46th Streets, West of Madison Avenue; and the rock is probably continuous from the one point to the other. The mineral Kyanite is not rare on New York Island; but its occurrence in this way, as a constituent of the rock, evenly and closely distributed over large areas, is quite peculiar.

He also showed some specimens of **Crystalline Limestone,** from an excavation in East 124th St., which is indistinguishable from that of the outcrop at Mott Haven, beyond the Harlem River, and similarly filled with minute crystals ot Mica, probably Phlogopite. He expressed his opinion that this bed of Limestone, intersected at a depth of some eight feet at this point, is the prolongation of the same ridge that appears at Mott Haven, and at a number of places in Westchester County, and that it probably comes to view at the summit of an Anticlinal. On the western side of the Limestone bed, he had found the overlying Gneiss dipping very evenly to the West, as it would do if such were the case; and he suspected that there is a similar eastward dip on the other side, though the rock was covered up from observation.

The President, Dr. J. S. Newberry, made some remarks on **Titaniferous Iron Ores**, illustrated by a specimen, from Westport, N. Y. It unfortunately happens that many of the Magnetic Iron ores so characteristic of the Alleghany belt, the Adirondack, and Canada, are so largely contaminated by Titanium that they are practically worthless. The deposit from which this specimen came lies just upon the shore of Lake Champlain and would be of immense value were it not for the quantity of Titanium it contains. In Canada more than half the Magnetic Iron ore is ruined by Titanium. Some of the largest and most accessible of the deposits of Magnetic Iron known come into this category, and any one who will devise a method for working these ores successfully will enrich, not only himself, but whole communities, and confer a great benefit upon the world at large. The percentage of Titanic-Acid in the Canadian Titaniferous ores varies from fifty to a fraction of one per cent. The Kane bed, north of Coburg, contains eighteen per cent. Titanic-Acid. The ore of South Crosby, on the Rideau Canal, about eight. The great bed of the bay of Seven Islands thirty four per cent. That of the bay of St. Paul's, ninety feet in thickness, contains forty-eight per cent. of Titanic-Acid. On the north shore of the lower St. Lawrence, at Moisie, are great deposits of Titaniferous Iron sand from which large quantities of Iron are now made by the bloomery process, probably the only case known where Titaniferous Iron ore is profitable worked alone. The reason why this ore can be successfully treated, seems to be, that it is composed of intermingled grains of Magnetite and Ilmenite. Of these the Magnetite, being much the more fusible, is melted, allowing the Titaniferous Iron to pass up in the slag. In such cases the two varieties of ore may be separated by the magnet, and this is now readily and cheaply done by a machine invented by Dr. Larue, of Quebec. By using a battery of 800 magnets, each capable of lifting five pounds an inexpensive machine and which uses as small amount of power as is able to purify five or six tons per day. The Titaniferous Iron from the Rideau Canal is quite extensively used in the furnaces of Ohio and it is claimed with profitable results. It is, however, here combined with a very largely preponderating percentage of other ores.

Titaniferous ores are also found abundantly in other countries than ours. In Norway vast beds of ore of this character exist, and unceasing efforts have been made for the last half century to smelt both in Norway and England. It must be said, however, that up to the present time all these trials have resulted in failure, except where this ore has been used in connection with a much larger quantity of ore free from Titanium.

The great deposits of Iron ore discovered by Dr. Hayden on the Cling-water, in Wyoming, contain twenty-three and one half per cent. of Titanic Acid, a quantity probably sufficient, without an improvement of our processes, to prevent the use of this ore in the manufacture of iron.

In New Zealand large quantities of Titaniferous ores are said to occur, and there too, efforts to utilize them have been unsuccessful.

Titanium Iron ore not only renders them extremely refractory, but when they are smelted the resulting Iron is very hard. Experiments made by Shoenberger & Blair, of Pittsburgh, showed that puddled Iron containing any considerable quantity of Titanium is so hard as to fly like glass in the shears.

May 1st, 1871.

The President in the chair. Twenty-eight persons present.

HON. E. G. SQUIER exhibited a **Map of the Guanape Guano Islands of Peru,** of which the working has been commenced in consequence of the exhaustion of the Guano deposits of the Chinchas. He also exhibited drawings of a wooden idol found on the North Guanape among the remains of a stone hut, now covered by a few feet of Guano. This discovery was made by Mr. J. P. Davis, government engineer, when making an official survey of the Islands in 1864. Mr. Squier was aware of the alleged discovery of numerous articles, pottery, utensils, and objects of gold and silver in the Guano of all the Islands, but under circumstances requiring authentication. The account of Mr. Davis was about the only one coming from a competent and reliable source. Not that the articles alleged to have been found, were not found, for all the islands were frequented by the aborigines of the coasts, who must have left traces of their visits. But he was not prepared to accept the statements as to the great depth beneath the surface at which the various objects were reported to have been found, nor yet the inference generally made that the superincumbent material had been formed since their deposit—an hypothesis pointing back to an incredibly remote period. Indeed, after a personal inspection of the islands and of the cuttings in the Guano, exhibiting most distinct marks of stratification, he was prepared to listen to the suggestion that had been made, in very competent quarters, that the Guano deposits had been formed beneath the sea, with the exception of the very superficial and relatively modern layers resulting from the excreta of seals and waterfowls. In conclusion he called upon Prof. Edwards, who had already published something on this subject, and Dr. Habel, who had visited and studied the Guano Islands, to make some remarks relative to the origin of this substance, and exhibited photographs showing in a very beautiful manner the parallel stratification of the Guano.

Dr. A. Habel said, that having the intention of publishing, at some future day, something more full and in detail concerning the mode of occurrence of the Whuano on the Chincha Islands, of which he had made a careful examination during a recent visit, he would at the present time confine himself to mentioning some few of the conclusions he has arrived at during a residence of five weeks on the Islands. He must confess that he had made these observations quite unexpectedly and wholly unprepared for the facts ascertained, having up to that time accepted without question the common belief respecting the nature of the Whuano and its mode of formation; it being supposed to consist entirely of the simple accumulation of the excrements, dropped upon the Islands by various species of sea-birds. In fact he had only desired to pay a flying visit to the Chinchas and not leave that part of the world without at least satisfying a natural curiosity to see so remarkable a phenomenon. What he had seen on the first day of his visit had proved so much at variance with what he had expected that he was tempted to prolong his visit, at considerable inconvenience, to the space of time mentioned.

From the very first inspection of the deposit, which was extensively exposed by its removal being carried on continnally, he was forced to admit that the mode of its formation was not as simple as, until then, it had been supposed to be. During this sojourn of five weeks the time was employed in carefully studying and sketching not alone the deposits of Whuano on the different Islands, but also the nature of the various rocks of which the Islands themselves are composed. From these observations he had arrived at conclusions which must eventuate in the adoption of entirely new views regarding the formation of the Whuano.

In the first place the Whuano on these Islands is by no means a homogeneous mass of substance, but, on the contrary, presents itself as made up of two distinct portions, which differ widely the one from the other in the character of their constituents as well as their structure and evident mode of formation. The outer and uppermost portion everywhere overlying the other is the lesser in respect to quantity and does consist of the droppings of various species of sea-birds and mammals mixed with the feathers and eggs of the former and bones of both birds and mammals. This stratum occurs in various conditions of preservation and decomposition, and does not show any signs of stratification whatever but may rather be described as a promiscuous mixture. It is of a reddish-brown color which is more homogeneous and darker than that of the underlying mass. It exhibits very plainly its origin, mode of formation and age. That is to say it is of recent origin as well as dating back to a remote period historically speaking. Its thickness was observed, in different portions, to vary from three to twelve feet, but this fact, must not be considered as proving that it is not or has not been thicker in other parts of the Islands, from whence it might have been removed. Thus from the Northern Island, the Whuano was first removed and, in consequence, at that time it was quite denuded.

Below this covering exists the larger portion of the Whuano proper, which differs from the outer crust by the greater minuteness of its particles, by its homogeneous structure, and by its decided stratification. This stratification is so marked that even a superficial examination must convince every unprejudiced person that it is the product of sedimentary formation. It is made up of alternate white and yellow strata, varying in shade and thickness. All of these strata exhibit distinctly their inclination, or dip, which varies not only on the separate islands but in different parts of the same island. On the middle island, for example, the inclination, or dip of the strata in one part of it, does not amount to more than five degrees, while in another part it is eight degrees, and in a third, close to the first, fifteen degrees.

Of still greater interest are the strata on the South Island, where the Whuano forms an elongated conical hill of over one hundred and twenty feet in height and whose greatest diameter is in a direction north and south. In taking away the Whuano from the South Island the northern extremity of the hill was first removed and thereafter the two lateral were cut off so, that at the time of his visit, the southern extremity of the hill still remained intact, while the main bulk of the Whuano on three sides was exposed to view, as was also the eastern and western portions of the base of the hill. The strata in the middle of this mass were horizontal, while those continuous with it, and running from north to south, showed an inclination, or dip, of six degrees, and those running in the opposite direction, that is to say towards the north, had an inclination or dip, of eight degrees. At the end of the western cut there were exposed several strata of the western base of the hill, which ran in a direction from south-west to north-east, with an inclination, or dip, of twenty degrees, and overlying and resting unconformably upon others which ran from north to south, with an inclination, or dip, of only four degrees.

In all of these strata are imbedded stones of various sizes and weight up to fifteen pounds, as well as eggs and bones. The contents of the eggs has in all cases disappeared and the interior of the shells is filled with crystallized salts. These shells are cracked and more or less compressed and very brittle, as are also the bones found along with them, which crumble readily to a powder on being touched, being more brittle the deeper down they are found.

Another of the proofs which he collected on these islands in favor of the hypothesis that by far the greater portion of the Whuano has become stratified in consequence of deposition, beneath the ocean, is found in the various deposits of sand underlying the Whuano. All these deposits are likewise stratified and the strata dip more or less to one direction or the other. The greatest amount was found to be twenty-five degrees. Many of these beds of sand are already laid bare, but those which are still covered by Whuano present a similar stratification, and an inclination corresponding to that of the overlying Whuano. These beds of sand contain more or less Whuano, but present after different modes. Thus, in one of the beds the mixture of sand and Whuano is perfect; only that the upper portion of the bed is formed of sand and Whuano in equal proportions, while in the lower portion the sand predominates. In another part of the same island the sand contains numerous variously-shaped masses of Whuano, which also vary in size, location, and distance one from the other. The sand is either loose or forms a kind of stone; such sandstone in some places resting upon loose sand. In it are also imbedded eggs, or more correctly speaking egg-shells, and bones. Of these he collected specimens, and he also possesses a skeleton of a bird imbedded in the sandstone.

PROF. A. M. EDWARDS said, I am not prepared at the present time to enter fully into the consideration of this subject of **The Origin of Guano,** but I would merely mention that my views on the subject were first made public at a meeting of the American Microscopical Society, during the winter of 1868. Thereafter on the 4th of January, 1869, I gave the results of my investigations and the deductions I drew therefrom at a meeting of the Essex Institute at Salem, Mass., and an abstract of what I then said was published in the Bulletin of that Association, Vol. I. page 11. The main points then brought forth, and which I desire to dwell upon now, are for the purpose more particularly of calling the attention of scientists to this interesting and important subject. I have spent several years in investigating this subject and have become acquainted with some facts of great moment as bearing upon several branches of science, more particularly Geology, Agriculture, Biology, and Chemistry, as well as Commerce, as connected with the chemistry of Guanos and other fertilizers. I have also been for the last fifteen years or more, studying the so-called 'Infusorial deposits" of marine origin; that is to say, those which are proved, by the character of the remains contained in them, to have been formed beneath salt water. I have been entrusted by Prof. Pumpelly with the investigation of specimens of an Infusorial deposit of this character which he discovered near Netanai, in Japan, and Prof. Whitney has placed in my hands the microscopic material of the State Geological Survey of California; besides I have received many specimens from other quarters and have thus been able to study this matter very thoroughly, but there are still data wanting to make the subject perfect.

Among the specimens thus examined, are some of the

rocks or shales making up the great mass of the mountains of the Coast Range which extend down the Pacific shore, from Washington Territory to the borders of Lower California and even perhaps down as far as the southermost extremity of that peninsular. These shales are usually of a light cream color and mainly consist of the siliceous skeletons of Diatomaceæ and Polycystina; the former being commonly considered as plants, the latter as animals. These are of extremely minute size and often require for their study the use of the highest magnifying powers. Many of them prove to be indistinguishable from forms living at the present day on the Californian coast. Exuding through and often appearing at the upper portion of these rocks, to which situation it has evidently been driven by heat, is found the Petroleum, Bitumen, and Asphalt of California. Hence the Survey has conferred upon these strata the name of Bituminous Shales. Along the Pacific coast and lying generally parallel to it are islands often bearing upon their summits deposits of Guano of more or less commercial value. In many cases the quantity has been small and soon removed, but I am informed that there are deposits of this material in that quarter of the globe still unworked. At the same time it must be remembered that the whole Pacific Coast of both North and South America is in an almost continual state of motion and gradual but constant upheaval, caused, doubtless by the action of internal chemical changes which make themselves markedly evident in the volcanic vents found all along the mountains constituting the Cascades and Sierra Nevadas of North, and the Andes of South America. The Survey has been able to identify at least three former lines of rise or coast and still another is seen presenting its peaks in the islands which will at some future day be united in such a manner as to constitute another Coast Range of mountains.

If now we consider the bearing of these facts on the origin of the substance known as Guano we find the following points worthy of note. Guano may be divided into two great groups, the Ammoniacal and the Phosphatic, but it is of the first mentioned only that I desire to treat at the present time, and to which I wish to apply my deductions. Guano is usually considered as the excrement of the sea-fowl, which has accumulated during a long period of time, so long that attempts have been made to calculate its age from its thickness. Thus Humboldt, who first made this substance known to the Eastern Hemisphere, in 1840, states that on the Chincha Islands it has a depth of 50 to 60 feet and that the accumulation of the preceding 300 years had formed only a few lines of this thickness. The facts brought forward by Mr. Squier show how difficult it is to arrive at any certain knowledge on this point, and in fact show that we have no means of ascertaining the age of the Guano deposits, even if we accept the theory of their origin from the source usually ascribed to them. It is a remarkable fact that in a curious old book entitled, "The First Book of the Art of Metals, written in Spanish by Albano Alonzo Barba, Master of Art, born in the Town of Lepe in Andalusia, Curate of St. Barnard's Parish in the Imperial City of Potosi, in the Kingdom of Peru in the W. I., in the year 1640. Translated into English in the year 1669: London, 1670," we find the following passage. Speaking of the substance we are considering, the author says, "It is called *Guano* (*i. e.* dung;) not because it is the dung of sea-fowls, (as many would have it,) but because of its admirable virtue in making ploughed ground fertile," and both Mr. Squier and Dr. Habel inform me that the name Guano (correctly written and and pronounced *Whuanno*) does not necessarily mean dung, but something that, like dung, causes the plants to grow; being derived from the verb to grow. Then we find that Guano is not confined to islands only, but occurs in large quantities on the contiguous headlands, and many ravines extending into the interior of the country contain Guano in smaller and larger quantities. Thus the ravines of Lobo, Culata, Sacramento, Animas, Morillo, Guajes, Colorado, Chucumata and Pica are reported to contain pure Guano deposits, covered by a thick coating of sand. Neither is it found in rainless districts only, for as I have said it is found on the islands off the California coast, which is by no means rainless, and

Mr. W. H. Dall informs me that it occurs on the Aleutian Islands, where the air is almost always saturated with moisture, and heavy rains fall during a large part of the year. With regard to the upheaval of such coasts, along which Guano occurs it is well known from Darwin's investigations that the whole Pacific coast of South America is in constant motion and upheaval, and that "on the mainland near Lima, and on the adjoining island of San Lorenzo, Mr. Darwin found proofs that the ancient bed of the sea had been raised to the height of more than eighty feet above water, within the human epoch, strata having been discovered at that altitude, containing pieces of cotton thread and plaited rush, together with sea-weed and marine-shells." (Lyell, Principles of Geology, 9th edition, 1853, page 502.) And Darwin says, "I have convincing proofs that this part of the continent of South America has been elevated near the coast at least from 300 to 500, and in some parts from 1000 to 1300 feet, since the epoch of existing shells." Other proofs of this fact are not wanting, but these are sufficient for me to quote at the present time. When the portions of Guano which are insoluble in water and acids, is examined by means of the microscope, it is found to be made up of the skeletons of Diatomaceæ, Polycystina and Sponges, invariably of marine origin, and sometimes identical with those living in the adjoining ocean, and fossilized in the adjacent Infusorial strata. Also we find that some of these forms occur in patches exactly as they grow in nature, and as they would present themselves if they were deposited from water, and not as they would be if they had to pass first through the alimentary canals of mollusca and similar small animals, then through the same organs of fish and birds, in turn, as they would have to do, to get into the Guano in the manner commonly supposed.

I have stated, that in California we have a deposit of "Infusoria" improperly so-called, accompanied by Bitumen, which Bitumen the gentlemen of the State Survey, believe has been derived from those "Infusoria," and that contiguous thereto we have Guano deposits. Now let us see if we have a similar association of facts anywhere else. At Payta in Peru, Dr. C. F. Winslow discovered an "Infusorial" deposit, almost identical in character with the Californian one, near by are Bitumen springs, and lying off the coast are the Guano islands of Lobos, Chincha, Guanape and others; at Natanai, Japan, we have extensive "Infusorial" strata and Bitumen; it is not recorded whether Guano occurs in that quarter. In the island of Barbadoes we have "Infusorial" strata, Bitumen, and near by the Guano islands of the Carribean sea; and I am informed Guano is abundant on the small islands and rocks nearly throughout the West Indian Archipelago. In the island of Trinidad we have "Infusorial" strata and Bitumen, and of course adjacent Guano. At all of these localities volcanic action is evident, but we have some localities of Guano without "Infusorial" strata or Bitumen as yet recorded, while we have the celebrated "Infusorial" strata of Virginia, which by a little stretch of the imagination, may be supposed to be related in some way to the Petroleum of West Virginia and Pennsylvania. In Algeria we have "Infusorial" strata and Bitumen, but I never heard of guano having been found near by. However, now that attention is called to this fact, it is to be hoped that more careful observations will be made connected with the subject, and I hereby call on all scientists and travelers to do all they can to assist in the elucidation of this interesting and important matter. From all of these facts and others that I have collected of no less importance, derived from chemical and microscopical characters, I have come to the conclusion that Guano is not the excreta of birds deposited upon the islands and main land after its upheaval, but that it is the result of the accumulation of the bodies of animals and plants, for the most part minute and belonging to the group which Haeckel has included in a new kingdom, separate from the animal as well as the vegetable under the name of Protista, and subsequently upheaved from the bottom of the ocean. Subsequent chemical changes have transformed it into Guano, or heat and pressure have so acted upon it, that the organic matter has been transformed into Bitumen, while the mineral constituents are preserved in the beautiful atomies that make up the mass of the extensive "Infusorial" strata, found in various parts of the world.

In conclusion, I have to state that the Chincha Islands have been visited by a competent geologist, Mr. Kinahan, of Dublin, and he has pointed out that they have been upheaved by volcanic action within a recent period, geologically considered, and that I have found a remarkable confirmation of my theory, in a paper read before the American Institute some years since by Mr. Alanson Nash, detailing the observations of a Mr. F. Nash, made during a residence on the Chincha islands, while engaged in the Guano trade, for nearly six months. Therein we find it stated, that Mr. Nash was of opinion that Guano was formed in the way I have described; that the anchors of vessels in that locality bring up Guano from the bottom of the ocean; that "the Guano is (much of it) not composed of bird dung, but it is composed of the mud of the ocean." That "the composition taken from the islands called Guano, is stratified and lies in the same form it did before it was lifted up from the ocean; that "the bottom of the ocean on the west coast of Peru, contains vast deposits of Guano. An island, during an earthquake, rose up in the bay of Callao some years since from the sea, containing Guano four feet deep, the formation the same as the Chincha islands." In conclusion he says, "the day will come when the Guano at these islands, will be dredged up with boats like mud from our rivers and harbors." And in this expectation I fully coincide with Mr. Nash. Need I again point to the interest connected with, and the value of further knowledge of this subject, or call on everyone for the contribution of facts, to aid in its thorough elucidation?

The following paper was read.

Notes on the Meteorology of the Month of April, 1871.

By Prof. O. W. Morris.

The month of April, 1871, sustained its reputation, having frequent showers, or sprinkles, but not much water. It commenced with a snow storm, though not very severe, which continued till the morning of the 2d. Rain fell in various quantities on 11 days, only 5 of them, however, in appreciable quantity, amounting in all to 3·45 inches; which is 0·65 inch less than the average for the 10 years preceding, 2·97 inches less than in April, 1868, and 1·88 inch more than in April, 1869.

The mean temperature was 53·33°, which is 3·26° greater than the average mean for April, for the preceding 10 years, and greater than any of them, except in 1865 and 1866. The maximum was 80·5° on the 9th; the minimum was 34·5° on the 2d; a range of 46°, in 7 days.

The mean pressure was 29·778 inches, the maximum was 30·368, on the 24th, and the minimum, 29·397 inches on the 2d; a range of 0·971 inch. It has been above 30 inches only on 5 days.

The mean relative humidity was 50·15°, the maximum was 88·6° on the 28th and the minimum 10·4° on the 24th; a range of 78·2° for the month.

The Aurora Borealis was noticed on the 11th, 13th and 17th. Thunder showers occurred on the 11th and 21st. A Solar Halo on the 14th, and a Lunar Corona on the 29th. The prevailing wind was N. W. although the S. E. came very near being equal.

May 8th, 1871.

The President in the chair. Twenty-four persons present.

Dr. L. Feuchtwanger exhibited the **Tooth of a Mastodon,**

from Warsaw, Missouri, also a photograph of a specimen of *Teleosaurus Tiedmanni* from Wurtemburg.

The President, DR. J. S. NEWBERRY exhibited two **Specimens of Echinoderms,** and made some remarks calling attention to the beauty and complexity of the structure of their skeletons. One was a *Spatangus*, from Nassau, the other *Clypeaster*, from Tortugas.

PROF. O. W. MORRIS exhibited specimens of **Claystones,** from New England, also a supposed **Meteorite,** from Tennessee.

PROF. C. A. JOY said he thought the specimen exhibited was not a meteorite, but a mass of Spiegeleisen.

PROF. A. M. EDWARDS said he was of the same opinion. Spurious meteorites were by no means uncommon.

PROF. D. S. MARTIN exhibited a series of specimens of newly-described lower **Carboniferous Fossils,** discovered by Prof. J. J. Stevenson, of West Virginia University, at Morgantown, in that state. Prof. Stevenson is a most earnest and enthusiastic geologist, and his labors had been rewarded by the discovery of four new species of shells, and one new trilobite, which had been all named and described by Prof. F. B. Meek. The trilobite, of which only one or two fragmentary pieces have as yet been obtained, is described as *Phillipsia Stevensoni.* The shells are the following, all belonging to the family of Arcadæ;—*Nucula* (?) *anodontoides*, *Macrodon obsoletus*, *Yoldia carbonaria*, and *Yoldia Stevensoni*; specimens of all of which, were exhibited to the Lyceum. They were obtained by Prof. Stevenson in his stratum No. 20, Lower Coal Measures, near Morgantown, Monongalia Co., West Virginia. The rock of this stratum is a dark-colored, fragile shale, quite rich in mollusca, which are mainly identical with those of the Chester Group in the Western States.

Prof. Martin also exhibited a number of very small **Sharks' Teeth from the Phosphate beds of Ashley River,** near Charleston, S. C. The large teeth of *Carcharodon* and *Oxyrhina* are abundant in these deposits; but these minute ones have rarely been found. They represent quite a variety of species, and probably several genera; and bear a very close resemblance to the small teeth related to *Galeocerdo*, *Notidanus*, etc., from the Tertiary marls of New Jersey.

DR. A. HABEL exhibited a vial containing a **Red-Colored Liquid** looking like blood. This he obtained at a place in Honduras, known as the **Fuentes de Sangre,** or Spring of Blood. This substance issues from the roof of a cave eight feet high, four feet wide and ten feet deep, occurring in a bed of Trachyte on the bank of a small stream. The mouth of the cave is in the face of the high bank, and the only way of access is by descending the cliff, by means of roots of the trees and shrubs which clothe it. When fresh, this liquid has much of the appearance of blood, and dogs and fowls will lick it from the floor. There is still another locality of this substance in Ecuador. The substance was referred to Prof. Edwards for Microscopic examination and Dr. Schweitzer for Chemical analysis.

May 15th, 1871.

The President in the chair. Twenty-two persons present.

DR. L. FEUCHTWANGER exhibited two specimens of a fossil, showing both sides of an **Archegosaurus medius,** from the coal formation of Germany.

The President, DR. J. S. NEWBERRY, said that this specimen of a rare fossil was of considerable interest, and showed the characters of the creature in a very perfect manner. This literally "primeval lizard," as its name denoted, was a reptile peculiar to the carboniferous era, and has been considered by several Palæontologists, more particularly Owen and Goldfuss, to be nearly allied to the existing *Proteus*, *Lepidosiren* and other Pleurobranchiate reptiles now living. Agassiz, however, considers it a true fish of the Ganoid order. It has been described as having the body of a toad, and the jaws and teeth of a lizard. The skin was covered with long, narrow, tile-like horny scales, arranged in parallel rows, and altogether it was a very remarkable-looking creature, whose position in the animal kingdom entitles it to consideration at the present day.

PROF. A. M. EDWARDS reported on the optical examination of the **Reddish-colored material from the Fuentes de Sangre,** in Honduras, exhibited at the last meeting by Dr. A. Habel. Examination showed that the color was not truly red but rather brownish; and that a considerable amount of sediment had collected at the bottom of the bottle. When this sediment was viewed by means of the microscope, it was seen to be, for the most part, made up of brown grains of no definite form or texture.

Mixed with this material were several Crystalline Plates four-sided and somewhat lozenge-shaped. These depolarize light in some degree. Examination by means of the Spectroscope reveals nothing of interest. It has been turned over to Dr. Schweitzer for chemical examination.

PROF. H. WURTZ said that some years since Prof. S. W. Johnson, of New Haven, examined both chemically and microscopically this material from this same spring, and determined it to be the dung of bats.

The President, DR. J. S. NEWBERRY, said that in some localities such large accumulations of the dung of bats was not uncommon. He had visited a cave in the West in which it existed in enormous quantities, whilst the bats hung in large numbers from the roof.

PROF. H. WURTZ exhibited specimens of a **Greensand Marl,** from Shrewsbury River, New Jersey, which possessed some characters peculiar and of interest. It was not readily acted upon by acids, as he demonstrated. Acetic Acid was without any action even when boiling, but Nitric Acid acted with effervescence, at the same time red fumes were given off, due, doubtless, to the presence of Pyrites. Analysis showed it to consist of

Silica, Soluble	43·10
Ferric Oxide and Alumina	26·07
Ferrous Carbonate	10·41
Iron Pyrites	1·52
Potash	4·41
Lime	1·89
Magnesia	1·79
Water	9·34
	100·

He considered that there had often been a mistake made in reporting the amount of Carbonate of Lime in these Marls. The absence of such a substance was known by the want of action of the Acetic Acid, Nitric Acid however acted upon the Ferrous Carbonate, as was demonstrated. This specimen was from Prof. Cook's "Middle Bed," which runs parallel to the Atlantic coast. The mode of analysis he had used was by grinding it up very finely with hot Oil of Vitriol when the green color disappears and a white, pasty mass results, consisting for the most part of the Silica. Examination with a lens, shows the casts of Foramenifera very perfectly preserved.

Prof. A. M. Edwards said that these casts of the chambers of Foramenifera were not confined to the Greensand marls, as had been shown by the late Prof. Bailey. It was Prof. Ehrenberg who first pointed out the character of these green grains, and that they had been formed by the infiltration of Ferruginous Silicates into the chambers of the Foraminiferous Shells, so that the animal matter which, during life, occupied that space was replaced by the mineral matter. He had found that these green grains were distributed in various strata, from the Silurian to the Tertiary. In 1857, Prof. Bailey showed that the same mode of replacement was taking place within the shells of the Foramenifera of the present day, for when specimens of those brought up from the ocean bottom are acted upon by acid, the calcareous portion outside was dissolved off, and perfect casts, even in some cases showing the more delicate ramifications of animal tissue, were brought to view. Occasionally this solvent action had gone on as the shells lay upon their ocean bed, and he, Prof. E., had specimens of such beautiful green casts from the Gulf of Mexico. The connection of this fact with the still more important discovery of the Canadian geologists of the now well-known *Eozoon Canadense*, was of great interest. Here we have a gigantic Foramenifer, into the chambers and tubes of which a green mineral has been infiltrated, and by the action of acids, as in the case of the greensands and recent specimens, the most delicate organizations of these creatures can be shown to be preserved in durable Serpentine. This was of special interest at the present time, as during the present year a new locality for this fossil had been made known at one of the meetings of this Society, where it occurs in vast quantities, and presenting some new features which will be presented in due time, as soon as they have been properly studied.

The following paper was read.

Notes on the Minerals of the Cornwall Mines, Pennsylvania.

By Prof. D. S. Martin.

This paper was illustrated by a full suite of the minerals mentioned, and will be published in the Annals of the Lyceum.

The President, Dr. J. S. Newberry, exhibited a fine suite of **Fossils from the Phosphatic beds of South Carolina.** These consisted of shark's teeth of several species; the most conspicuous being those of *Corodon Megalodon*; some as large as the hand of an average sized man; vertebræ and teeth of *Zeuglodon;* ribs and vertebræ of *Squalodon Altanticus* and others. With these, and found in the same deposit, were unmistakable fragments of the tooth of an Elephant, apparently, *Elephas Americanus.* Dr. N. remarked that we have had conclusive evidence of the commingling in this remarkable deposit of the fossils representing different geological ages. To account for this, we must suppose that these phosphatic nodules were once deposited in different strata and have been since re-arranged and commingled by river action or shore waves.

May 22d, 1871.

The President in the chair. Twenty persons present.

The President, DR. J. S. NEWBERRY, announced the discovery by Prof. O. C. Marsh, of a species of **Pterodactylus,** which he has named *P. Owenii*, in the upper cretaceous formation of Western Kansas. This fact is of importance, as it is the first occurrence of this genus in America. It has a stretch of twenty feet from the tip of one wing to the tip of the other. He also exhibited a specimen of a substance supposed to be **Asphaltum** of a peculiar character, and found in **Colorado.** The most remarkable fact connected with this substance, is its partial solubility in water. It also possesses a very marked aromatic odor when burned. The specimen was refered to Dr. Schweitzer for Chemical examination. He also exhibited an **Arrowhead and Copper axe-head and Fragments of so-called Aztec Pottery, from Northern Mexico** and beyond the Plains. Also specimens from a mound near Chattanooga, very similar to those from the far West; also modern specimens made by the Moquis, and made some remarks in connection therewith. Also specimens of large **Fossil Oysters,** *Ostrea disparilis*, from Virginia, *O. triton*, from California, and *O. Georgiana*, from Georgia, and made some remarks on the gigantic dimensions of these shells, so much larger than any examples of the genus as it now exists.

Hon. E. G. Squier remarked on one of the pieces of pottery exhibited having a perforation through it. He had seen many similar examples but was at a loss to account for it, or the use to which it could have been applied. He also presented specimens of **Sinter, from the Vents of the Volcano of San Vincente, in San Salvador,** and made some remarks on its mode of occurrence, and the characteristics of this and similar volcanos.

Dr. A. Habel made some remarks on the eruption of water from the volcanos of Central America and Ecuador, several of which he had visited. The water which is now found within the basins of the craters of some of these Volcanos, which have become extinct or inactive, and at an elevation of 6000 feet above the level of the sea, contain living animals, as fish and crustaceæ. He was, however, unable to say whether they were the same species as are to be found in neighboring lakes and rivers.

Mr. Squier said he attributed the eruption of water from volcanos, certainly in some cases, to the breaking away of the sides of the crater; as, when the sides are thick, no great discharge of water has been observed.

Prof. A. M. Edwards said that the subject of the eruption of water from volcanos, had been very thoroughly elucidated by Prof. J. D. Whitney, in a paper he had read a short time since before the California Academy of Sciences, and published in their Proceedings. It was well known that when such eruptions of water took place that there appeared at the same time, along with the water, the siliceous shells of Diatomaceæ, so-called "Infusoria," which were deposited on the surrounding country. Specimens of this kind had come into the hands of Ehrenberg and he had called them "volcanic ash" and had stated that they had come from the bowels of the earth. But it had been shown by Prof.

Whitney that in some cases such so-called "volcanic ash" never came from the volcano at all but was the result of the drying up of lakes, in which the Diatomaceæ had grown and multiplied, by the injection of lava or the draining off of the water by the disturbance of the earth. In other cases where the Diatomaceous remains did come from the volcano, that they got there in the following manner: when the volcano became inactive the crater had gradually become filled with water until a lake was formed, in which appeared, throve and rapidly multiplied the Diatomaceæ and similar organisms. Now if the mountain should break forth again, of course such a lake would be destroyed and its contents be ejected and spread over the surrounding country. In fact, as in every case, with one uncertain exception, that of Mount Erebus, the ejected Diatomaceæ are invariably such forms as live in fresh water only and of a character which have not, as yet, been found in strata below the surface of the earth, so that it was extremely doubtful if we ever have subterranean Diatomaceæ ejected from volcanos.

May 29th, 1871.

The President in the chair. Sixteen persons present.

The following paper was read by title, to be published in the Annals of the Lyceum.

On the Jaws and Lingual Dentition of Helix Turbiniformis and other Terrestrial Molluscs.

By W. G. Binney & T. Bland.

In this paper the authors describe and figure the jaw of *Helix turbiniformis*, of Jamaica, showing a form hitherto unobserved in the genus. It approaches very closely that of *Cylindrella rosea*, of which a photograph was given in the

American Journal of Conchology, Vol. 5, part xi. and also the jaw of *Pineria Viegnensis*, Annals, Vol. x. p. 26.

The President, Dr. J. S. Newberry exhibited a specimen of **Astrophyton Agassizii,** from Nassau, N. P., and a number of **Cretaceous Plants,** from New Jersey and the far West, and made some remarks thereon. He also exhibited a **Skull of the Prong-horned Antelope,** in which the deciduous horns were half grown, covering the tips of the two prongs. This specimen was brought from Colorado by Dr. Hulse.

June 5th, 1871.

The President in the chair. Twenty-four persons present. Prof. C. A. Seely said that he had examined the supposed **Asphaltum,** exhibited by the President at the last meeting, and stated that in some respects it bears a strong resemblance to Asphaltum, but it has not the odor of that substance when burned. It is very soluble in water, to the extent of 56 per cent It contains 36 per cent. of mineral matter. He considered it to be the excrements, somewhat changed, of some animal, but it contained no Phosphoric or Uric acid.

The following paper was read.

Notes on Felsites of the Palisade Range.

By P. Schweitzer, Ph. D.

At one of the late meetings of the Lyceum of Natural History of New York City, Prof. H. Wurtz read a paper on the Lithology of the Palisade range, in which he stated, that the so-called sandstone, underlying the trap, was not a sandstone at all but a felsite, consisting principally of feldspar and quartz, agglutinated by opaline silica. This statement led to a discussion, several of the members dissenting from Prof. Wurtz's view, as not in accordance with any analysis published of these rocks, and the question was finally referred to me, to be decided by analysis and determination of alkalies. I received from Profs. Wurtz and Newberry several specimens, the investigation of which indeed, seems to prove the above statement to be correct.

I communicate my analyses herewith, and the way in which I propose to calculate the results, believing them to be of interest to other parties also. Dana, in his Mineralogy, fifth edition, page 351, cites six analyses of felsites, which correspond in composition very nearly to the samples analysed by me. These samples were all granular, and feldspar could be readily distinguished in them under the microscope; number three contained mica also; this was a coarse variety and is employed largely as a building stone. Number five is shale. The analyses were made by fusing the finely-pulverized rocks with a mixture of carbonate of soda and potassa, and determining in the fused portion SiO_3, Al_2O_3, Fe_2O_3, CaO, MgO. The amount of manganese they all contained was too small to be determined. Water was determined by heating in a closed platinum crucible, and noting the loss; alkalies were determined by heating in a platinum crucible with carbonate of lime and sal-ammoniac, and proceeding in the usual way. The alkali consisted principally of soda, though traces of potassa (and lithia, in number three) could be detected by the spectroscope.

		1.	2.	3.	4.	5.
SiO_3	=	77·70	80·53	73·79	75·95	44·88
Al_2O_3	=	11·81	9·92	11·32	9·52	20·29
Fe_2O_3	=	1·89	1·99	3·75	0·26	16·46
CaO	=	0·55	0·63	1·67	0·03	5·10
MgO	=	0·43	0·63	1·32	0·22	5·20
NaO	=	6·89	5·67	6·90	3·62	2·42
HO	=	0·82	1·14	1·24	3·79	5·55
Mn_2O_3	=	trace	trace	trace	0·28	trace
Cr_2O_3	=				trace	0·62
CuO	=				6·52	none
		100·09	100·51	99·99	100·19	100·12

Part of the finely-ground rock was then treated for nearly one hour, with concentrated boiling hydrochloric acid, diluted with water, filtered, and the residue washed out; this was determined together with what the acid had dissolved, and the following results obtained.

		1.	2.	3.	4.	5.
Insoluble	=	95·79	95·72	89·58	88·69	73·19
Soluble	=	3·39	3·14	9·18	7·52	21·26
Water	=	0·82	1·14	1·24	3·79	5·55
		100·00	100·00	100·00	100·00	100·00
SiO_3	=	0·42	0·30	0·42	0·43	0·19
Al_2O_3	=	0·36	0·12	1·40	trace	trace
Fe_2O_3	=	1·87	2·01	3·75	0·26	16·47
CaO	=	0·37	0·33	1·68	0·03	0·32
MgO	=	0·43	0·31	1·31	0·21	3·66
NaO	=	0·02	0·37	0·82	0·04	0·12
Mn_2O_3	=				0·28	
Cr_2O_3	=					0·62
CuO	=				6·51	
		3·47	3·44	9·38	7·76	21·38

1. From Haverstraw (River Side Quarries) Sp. Gr.=2·608
2. From Newark Quarries, Sp. Gr.=2·589.
3. From Haverstraw (100 feet beneath the Trap rock.)
4. Locality not given. Contained apparently Chrysocolla.
5. Shale from Newark Quarries, Sp. Gr. 2·839.

The specific gravities were determined by Prof. Wurtz.

1. *Of red color, yielding a lighter colored powder and very fine grained.*

95·79 Insoluble in acid.
77·28 SiO_3 (77·70—0·42.)

18·51 Bases combined with Silica.

In subtracting the bases dissolved by hydrochloric acid from the bases found, we obtain;

Al_2O_3 = 11·45.
CaO = 0·18.
NaO = 6·87.

18·50. These two figures agree exactly.

In calculating the amount of alumina, which would be required by soda and lime in the case of feldspar, we obtain ;

NaO	=	6·87	=	Al_2O_3	=	11·41
CaO	=	0·18	=	Al_2O_3	=	0·33
						11·74

which in connection with other facts, entitle us, I believe, in really considering these bases to have belonged to the albite of the rock.

Al_2O_3	=	11·74	=	SiO_3	=	30·79	
NaO	=	6·87	=	SiO_3	=	9.97	
CaO	=	0·18	=	SiO_3	=	0·29	
		18·79				41·05	
						18·79	
						59·84	Albite.

In subtracting the silica of the albite from the total silica found, less the part dissolved in hydrochloric acid, we should obtain the amount of quartz, a figure which will be found also in subtracting the albite from the part undissolved by the acid, making allowance for 0·29 per ct. Al_2O_3, which we counted dissolved ; thus we obtain

95·79 Insoluble in Acid.
59·84 Albite.

35·95	77·28 Silica total.
0·29	41·05 Silica of Albite.
36·24 Quartz.	36·23 Quartz.

The total composition may be then represented in the following way:

59·84—Albite.
36·23—Quartz.
0·42—Silica soluble.
0·82—Water.
2·76—Bases dissolved (3·05 less 0·29.)

100·07

The other three are calculated in the same way.

2. *Of grey color, yielding a light reddish powder and very fine-grained.*

95·72 Insoluble in acid.
80·23 SiO_3 (80·53—0·30)

15·49 Bases combined with silica.

Undissolved bases, and combined with silica.

Al_2O_3=9·80
CaO =0·30
MgO =0·32
NaO =5·30

15·72 These figures agree sufficiently.

In calculating the amount of Alumina again, required by the protoxides we find:

NaO = 5·30 = Al_2O_3 = 8·80
CaO = 0·30 = Al_2O_3 = 0·55
MgO = 0·32 = Al_2O_3 = 0·82

10·17

agreeing closely enough with the amount found, to warrant the supposition of having belonged to feldspar.

Al_2O_3	= 9·80	= SiO_3	=	25·69
NaO	= 5·30	= "	=	8·21
CaO MgO	= 0·30 = 0·32	= "	=	0·84
	15·72			34·74
				15·72
				50·46 Albite.

In determining the quartz in the way indicated, we find it to amount to

95·72 Insoluble in acid.
50·46 Albite.

45·26
0·23

45·49 Quartz.

80.23 Silica total.
34·74 Silica of Albite.

45·49 Quartz.

The composition of the rock is, therefore, as follows :

50·46 Albite.
45·49 Quartz.
0·30 Silica soluble.
1·14 Water.
2·91 Bases dissolved (3·14 less 0·23.)

100.30

3. *Coarse-grained, red, yielding a red powder.*

89·58 Insoluble in acid.
73·37 SiO_3(73·79—0·42)

16·21 Bases combined with Silica.

Undissolved bases and combined with silica.

Al_2O_3 = 9·92
NaO = 6·08

16·00

There is a sufficient correspondence between these two figures. The amount of alumina required by the soda would be 10·10 p. c. instead of 9·92 which agrees almost exactly again, so that we have for albite.

Al_2O_3 =9·92=SiO_3=26·00
NaO =6·08= " = 8·83

16·00 34·83
16·00

50·83 Albite.

The quantity of quartz is found to be

89·58 Insoluble in acid.
50·83 Albite.

38·75
0·21

38·54 Quartz.

73·37 Silica total.
34·83 Silica of Albite.

38·54 Quartz.

The composition of the rock is then as follows:

50·83 Albite.
38·54 Quartz.
0·42 Silica soluble.
1·23 Water.
9·17 Bases dissolved (8·96 plus 0·21.)

100·19

4. *This specimen consisted of white and very light brown grains agglutinated apparently by a light green, and in some places black, compound of copper. The grains of feldspar seemed to have been decomposed and replaced by chrysocolla. It contained no carbonic acid.*

88·69 Insoluble in acid.
75·52 SiO_3(75·95—0·43)

13·17 Bases combined with silica.

Bases undissolved and combined with silica.

Al_2O_3=9·52
NaO =3·58

13·10

The difficulty of calculating the constitution of this rock is much greater than in the preceding samples, as we find more than two minerals. The soda in forming feldspar would require,

Al_2O_3 = 5·95
NaO = 3·58
SiO_3 = 20·80

30·33 Albite.

The rest of the alumina, as a remnant of decomposed feldspar, requires all its silica.

Al_2O_3 = 3·57
SiO_3 = 12·51

16·08 Clay.

The copper, which is not in the form of carbonate, calculated as chrysocolla, which the large amount of water seems to indicate, requires,

CuO	=	6·51	
SiO_3	=	4·92	
HO	=	2·95	(2 Eq.)
		14·38	Chrysocolla.

The total composition being perhaps represented thus:

30·33	Albite.
16·08	Clay.
14·38	Chrysocolla.
37.29	Quartz.
0·43	Silica soluble.
0·84	Water.
0·58	Bases soluble.
99·93	

5. *Shale of a dark brownish red color, yielding a brown red powder.*

The iron of this sample, which according to the views of Prof. Wurtz is in the form of limonite, would require exactly the amount of water found.

Fe_2O_3	=	16·46	(1 Eq.)
HO	=	5·55	(3 Eq.)
		22·01	Limonite.

In subtracting this and the soluble Bases from the total amounts found, we obtain

SiO_3	=	44·81	=	60·51	cont. O	=	32·27
Al_2O_3	=	20·29	=	27·72	"	=	12·92
CaO	=	4·78	=	6·53	"	=	1·87
MgO	=	1·54	=	2·10	"	=	0·84
NaO	=	2·30	=	3·14	"	=	0·81
		73·72		100·00			

In considering this a true compound, we find the oxygen of the bases one half of that of silica, but whether we are entitled to do so, as Prof. Wurtz thinks, he believing it to be disintegrated mica, muscovite, will not attempt to decide.

In conclusion, I may state that I am well aware of the want of positive proof for the existence of the minerals assumed in these rocks, but many facts seem to support such an assumption. The water given is basic water, only dried material having been used for analysis, and may have been contained in the feldspar.

The President, DR. J. S. NEWBERRY made some remarks on the investigations of Dr. Schweitzer, and said he considered them of great importance and value.

PROF. C. A. SEELY made some remarks on **Anthracite**, said to come from New Mexico and the Western Territories. He was not aware that anthracite had been found in those localities.

The President, DR. NEWBERRY, said that anthracites are found in the far West, but they are of later geological age than those of Pennsylvania. They are Triassic Cretaceous, or Tertiary Lignites, changed by local Volcanic action, as eruptions of trap. One deposit of Anthracite near Santa Fe, New Mexico is a Cretaceous Lignite. The Anthracite of Los Bronce, Sonora, is of Triassic age. The most beautiful of all western Anthracite is that of Queen Charlottes Island, off the N. W. Coast. This is a metamorphozed Lignite, probably Cretaceous.

The Coals of Central America were examined years ago by a geologist, Dr. Evans, sent by the United States Government. A Report on them was published by Congress. They are Miocene tertiary Lignites, of medium quality.

MR. E. G. SQUIER said that he had observed Coal in San Salvador resembling Cannel, and in Honduras, Lignite in considerable quantity. In Peru 14,000 feet above the sea, coal is found and is used for reducing the ores of the vicinity.

October 2d, 1871.

Prof. C. A. JOY in the chair. Twenty-four persons present.

The following paper was read, by title,

Notes on North American Crustaceæ in the Museum of the Smithsonian Institute.

BY W. STIMPSON, M. D.

MR. J. HYATT gave an account of the **Aurora of September 7th, 1871,** as seen in Dutchess County, N. Y., and which was characterized by its whiteness.

PROF. T. EGLESTON gave a brief account of the recent **Progress of Metallurgy in Europe.** In the metallurgy of iron the most striking change is the construction of blast furnaces with no exterior of ordinary masonry. The fire brick is supported by iron columns and braces. At Königshutte and Gleiwitz in Silesia, this construction is effected upon old furnaces from the bosh up, but in the vicinity of Borsickswerk the furnace is new and is constructed without any exterior masonry. Another striking improvement is the attempt to turn blast furnace slags to profitable account in the manufacture of paving stones, building blocks and cement, and the utillization of the granulated slag for brick-making and other manufactures.

A very decided change in the machinery for the manufacture of iron is in progress. Most of the new rolling mills doing heavy work use reversible engines. They not only save time but the labor of lifting the material over the rolls. In the middle mills the three high rolls and in the little mill trains one in front of the other are coming into use. Each machine has its own engine, and is independent therefore of any delays or stoppages in any other part of the works. In the blast furnaces upright blast engines which economise space, and which are quite as strong and much more convenient, are taking the place of the expensive beam engine.

In the metallurgy of steel, the Bessemer process makes steady progress often in connection with the Seimen's Martens process. The most noticeable feature, however, in steel manufacture, is the production of ingots of immense size, the weight of a single ingot having reached in Krupp's works, at Essen, to 40 tons. Such ingots as these require powerful machinery to work them, and peculiar furnaces to heat them. Krupp has constructed a 50 ton hammer, and proposes to build one of 100 tons for this purpose. The reheating furnaces have their hearths built on wheels. The ingots give out so much heat that it would be impossible to handle them by the ordinary methods. The great hammer is therefore served by four large steam cranes. The arrangements for moving such immense masses when cold are very perfect. All of the buildings are provided with cranes at right angles to each other, arranged in such a way that a piece of any weight can be transported without apparent effort.

In the metallurgy of the other metals, the most striking changes are the introduction of mechanical Patinsonage, and the almost complete substitution of the Zinc process of desilverization for Patinsonage. The Zinc desilverization has itself undergone some important modifications, and it is expected that even small quantities of gold may be separated by a very slight change in the detail of working. The machines which were first used to produce the mixture of lead and zinc are being given up.

In the metallurgy of lead the most striking change is the introduction of the Piltz furnace, in the place of the rectangular furnaces. The Rachette furnace does not seem likely to have any future. The highest encomium bestowed upon it was, that it was no better than any other.

In the metallurgy of zinc, the introduction of the regenerator system seems to be almost universally determined upon, both in the Belgian and Silesian processes. The Bohetius regenerator furnace is received with general favor. In the Belgian process there are single furnaces near Liege, containing 168 retorts working successfully with both regenerator systems. The introduction of machine-made retorts in the Belgian process is gaining ground. The Silesian process in Silesia, has been modified by the introduction of two rows of muffles in the place of one as formerly.

There is a tendency every where to utilize waste products. In Silesia, furnaces are being constructed for the sole purpose of working over lead slag heaps a century or more old, and in all metallurgical operations the tendency is to make use of poorer ores. Thus in Silesia they work iron ores of 18 per cent. iron, and zinc ores of 9 per cent. These ores of zinc are so poor that it is impossible to use the double tier of muffles, and yet with the regenerator system it is possible to treat them.

He also made some remarks on **False Gems and their Optical Characters,** illustrated by means of specimens. He said that since the study of the optical characters of minerals has become so important there has been a very great demand for sections of minerals. There are certain minerals, such as Ruby and Rutile, which are not easily procured, the one because of its use as a gem, and the other because it is so frequently twinned or fissured, that good sections for optical purposes are not easily obtained. A considerable number of very beautiful specimens have been sold in Europe during the past two or three years which show most of the properties of these minerals. Mr. Stegg, of Hombourg, first doubted them on account of their beauty. He noticed that certain sections of rutile were negative when they should be positive. This induced him to take one of the preparations to pieces, and he found that it consisted of a thin section of Calcite, covered with a plate of gelatine which gave it the proper color. The imitation in Ruby is more deceptive, since Ruby is negative. Mr. Stegg prepared for me, at my request, the three specimens exhibited, for the mineralogical cabinet of the School of Mines. Half of each specimen, artificial Ruby, Rutile and Mellite show the Calcite, the other half shows the Calcite covered with the colored gelatine.

October 9th, 1871.

The President in the chair. Twenty-four persons present.

PROF. A. M. EDWARDS presented, in the name of Lt. Col. J. J. Woodward, three **Photo-Micrographs of Microscopic Test-Objects,** and read the following paper.

Note accompanying three Photographs of Degeeria Domestica as seen with Black Ground Illuminations.

BY LT. COL. J. J. WOODWARD, M. D., Asst. Surg. U. S. Army.

The scale represented in these photographs, was selected from a slide presented to the Army Medical Museum, by Mr. S. J. McIntire of London.

The photograph was made by mono-chromatic sunlight, obtained by passing a parallel pencil of sunlight reflected from a heliostat and plane mirror, through a cell containing a solution of the Ammonio Sulphate of Copper.

The illumination was managed by the parabola of Mr. Wenham, aided by a small truncated lens fixed with oil of cloves to the bottom of the slide, as described in Mr. Wenham's paper in the monthly microscopical journal for July, 1871. The small truncated lens was presented to the museum by Mr. Wenham.

The magnifying power is one thousand diameters, obtained by the immersion $\frac{1}{16}$ in. of Powell & Lealand without an eye-piece.

Photographs No. 1 and 2 are favorable to Mr. Wenham's well-known views of the nature of the markings.

The first is slightly out of focus, but shows the high-light on the knob of each exclamation mark.

The second shows the exclamation marks, with cross bars between as Mr. Wenham describes them.

The third shows double rows of corrugated ribs precisely

as described in my memorandum, on the test Podura, a copy of which was previously sent.

As the time of exposure required to make these pictures, was less than three minutes, I cannot agree with Mr. Wenham's opinion that the object is seen by light reflected from above only. I believe on the contrary, that the scales being semi-transparent they are illumined chiefly by rays passing through them from below, and hence that the surface appearances are complicated by the optical properties of the structures beneath.

The differences between the three pictures result simply from slight variations in the direction of the incident pencil of light, the position of the truncated lens and parabola being the same in all.

MR. P. T. AUSTEN gave an account of some investigations which he had recently made into the **Comparative Merits of the various Methods proposed for the Analysis of Cinchona Bark.** The gravimetric methods he found were almost without exception, tedious and unreliable. Special attention was given therefore to Glenard and Guillermond's method, published by them in 1859, and modified in 1861. After describing the process, the speaker remarked that some modifications were necessary to make it accurate. The standard of the author's solution was incorrect, and an improved filtering cork for drawing off the etherial solution was described. It was found best to use the bark in the condition of a moderately fine powder, and to employ slaked in preference to quick lime. With due regard to these precautions, this method was found to answer very well. It indicates only the amount of Quinine it is true, but this is the principal measure of the value of the bark. It is rapidly executed, and gives results which agree very closley with each other. It can be specially recommended for commercial or technical analysis. The speaker next described a new salt of Quinine, formed by bringing together an Etherial solution of Quinine and an Alcoholic solution of Meconic acid. The salt, which is easily soluble in hot water, separates on cooling, in beautiful acicular crystals, with a silky lustre. Dried over Sulphuric acid and analyzed, the results obtained showed its composition to be

$$\begin{matrix} C_7H_3O_7 \\ C_7H_2O_7 \\ C_7H_3O_7 \end{matrix} \begin{matrix} > C_{20}H_{24}N_2O_2 \\ > C_{20}H_{24}N_2O_2 \end{matrix}$$

Solutions of this salt yield the characteristic reactions of Quinine and Meconic acid.

October 16th, 1871.

The President in the chair. Twenty-seven persons present.

DR. L. FEUCHTWANGER exhibited a specimen of a **Branch of a Tree,** from Long Branch, N. J., which was of interest on account of its conversion into pyrites; also specimens of **Calcareous Incrustations** from a cave near Richfield Springs, N. Y; also a specimen of **Isoliles gigus,** from Trenton Falls, N. Y.

PROF. A. M. EDWARDS exhibited specimens of so-called **Claystones,** from Hanover, N. H. He had had an opportunity of observing the formation of these concretions during the last summer. They were formed in a cliff of fine sand on the shore of the Connecticut river, and when first seen are very friable, but gradually harden so that at last a conglomerate results, in which, in most cases, the grains are very fine, but occasionally the particles united together are coarse, as in one of the specimens shown, where a stone nearly an inch in diameter occurs. Large slabs of the same material are found at Norwich, Vt. A chemical examination reveals the fact that the agglutinating material is for the most part Calcium Carbonate with some Alumina, for Hydrogen Chloride, (muriatic acid) dissolves both Calcium and Aluminum. He thought concretions of this character were of interest in connection with the matter of the genesis of sandstones which had engaged the attention of the Society, for some time past. He also exhibited specimens of crystallized garnets of good color and clear, from Hanover, N. H., where they occur in an irregular vein in syenitic gneiss.

PROF. D. S. MARTIN read a paper on **the Coal of Orange Co., N. Y.**, in which he gave some account of the coal mine recently reported as discovered at Munroe, N. Y.

The Triassic formation is bounded on the north-west by a range of metamorphic hills, which forms part of the great Appalachian system, reaching up from the blue mountains of Pennsylvania, and striking the Hudson river at Peekskill, where it forms the Hudson Highlands. On the opposite, or western side of this ridge, are found successive ranges of Palæozoic beds, of which the age is in dispute. The coal-mine of Munroe, lies upon the western side, near the summit of an isolated hill known as Schunemunk mountain, just beyond this principal range of metamorphic heights, and overlooking the broad Wallkill valley, westward to the hills back of Port Jervis, which run into Catskills. Here an excavation has been made into the rock, which is a dark grey argillaceous sandstone, indistinguishable from the ordinary "Hamilton flags." Much of it is black with carbonaceous matter, but very little coal has yet been found, though the workings have been carried on for some months. The point of greatest interest, however, is the determination of the age of the rock, from its fossils. These are for the most part obscure, being apparently mingled with the debris of a fragmental deposit; but enough has been obtained to fix the age as Devonian, and probably of the Hamilton Group. The forms are *Lepidodendron* (probably *L. Gaspeanum,*) *Calamites*, *Psilophyton*, and Dr. Newberry thinks, *Dadoxylon.*

The prospect of obtaining workable amounts of coal is not by any means flattering; but the scientific results are of much interest. Prof. Cook in his recent report on the Geology of New Jersey, has considered this district to be lower silurian, on the theory that the series ascends regularly, in going westward from the Highland range. But it is now seen that Prof. Mather was nearer the truth, in his conception, that the

Wallkill valley lies in an eroded anticlinal, with an ascending series of rocks toward the hills on either side.

PROF. H. WURTZ inquired of Dr. Newberry, whether any recent information had come to him, in the course of his inquiries into this subject, regarding the present state of the great **Gas Well** at West Bloomfield, New York.

On receiving a negative reply, Prof. Wurtz, made the following remarks:

Nearly two years since, I gave to the Lyceum an account of a visit to the Ontario Co. (West Bloomfield) well, and of a scientific examination thereof. This paper, together with more extended reports and discussions drawn up by me about the same time, was widely circulated, and I am informed that a company was organized to convey the gas to towns throughout that section, but have no special information of their operations. The flame from the five-inch bore-hole, 500 feet deep, was some 30 feet in height; and measurements of the flow of gas have been reported as high as five cubic feet per second, equal to 432,000 feet per day. My analyses showed 82½ vols. per cent. of marsh gas, and 10 per cent. of carbonic acid, with 3 per cent. of illuminating gases, proved by analysis to be probably of the olefine group. The illuminating power was found to be from 5 to 6 candles, and it was inferred that purification from carbonic acid would give a gas equal to that served out to us here in New York city. In heating power, I have calculated this daily flow to be equal to about 14 tons of anthracite, which, at say $6 per ton, amounts to the interest, at 6 per cent., on $511,000. This, up to the time of my visit, four years, and, for aught I know, up to the present time, six years, has run to waste. I would here say that it is not fair towards gaseous fuel to value it according to a comparison of its absolute calorific capacity, with that of coal; for with the latter there are many causes of inevitable waste which can be entirely avoided with gas. Theoretically, one ton of anthracite is equal to about 30,000 feet of marsh gas; but practically, it will be found equal to less than 20,000 feet.

Fearful and wonderful tales were told me of the enormous pressures developed in this well by confinement; for example, that two men with sledges had driven into the upper end of the tube a carefully whittled plug of hard wood, as hard and fast as possible; but that scarce had they ceased driving when the plug was ejected, with a stupendous uproar, and shot up to a height whereto the eye of man reacheth not. This narrative I do not endorse, and it does not seem calculated to command conviction.

I wish to take the opportunity here to add some views of my own, bearing on the important questions of the future development, to the highest attainable degree, by the application of science and art, of these treasures of Nature. The points to be considered are three, the *Geology*, the *Chemistry*, and the *Engineering* of gas wells.

1. Geology.

This subject is one upon which we have already some valuable light, though many obscure questions yet remain, to be cleared away as explorations advance. At the same time the scientific consideration, even of our present developments, cannot fail to be of great service, in guiding our future work.

Upon this subject I had many consultations, some years since, with my friend Dr. R. P. Stevens (now at the Guayana gold fields in South America,) whose familiarity with the geology of the eastern United States is minute. He believed the gas of the Bloomfield well comes from the Marcellus shale, which crops out some miles north of the place, dipping south. This shale is so black as often to have been mistaken for coal, and sometimes will even burn. This he stated to be the lowest or deepest gas-producing horizon he had knowledge of. The facts stated, however, of the Buffalo well, 630 feet deep, which must have been sunk in rocks of the Corniferous period (Upper Helderberg,) below the Marcellus, seem clearly to indicate another productive horizon far below this, and even altogether below the Devonian; and, as at Buffalo, the Lower Helderberg (the upper member of the

Silurian,) as well as the Oriskany (the lower member of the Devonian) are both absent; and the Salina rocks are there many hundred feet thick, it seem probable that this latter group produces the gas there. This consideration points to another belt of gas wells that may be opened across New York, further north than the geological latitude of the Bloomfield well. Without maps it is difficult to make this subject clear, and I can but sum up by stating the probability that across the State of New York, from east to west, at least three belts of gas wells will be obtained, and that special success will be dependent chiefly on the selection of points for boring where the three gas-charged horizons, the Salina, Marcellus and Genesee, lie some 500 feet and upwards in depth. Nearer the outcrops, where the depth is less, the pressure must have been reduced by leakage, in the shape of gas springs, so common in this range of country. Still there is no reason why, in many places where the spontaneous flow is sluggish, great volumes should not be obtained by the application of exhausters to tubed wells, such exhausters being operated, as I have further to propose, by Hugon Gas-engines supplied with a portion of the gas itself. Torpedoes, also, will no doubt find useful application in this connection.

Dr. Stevens believes the Subcarboniferous also to be sometimes gas-producing, and that the Venango county gas wells were from Upper Devonian, or the Chemung and Portage, an opinion, which we have heard also from Dr. Newberry. In Canada, at Petrolia and elsewhere, according to Sterry Hunt, the chief gas and petroleum-bearing rocks belong to the Corniferous.

So that we have here, widely spread over the immense area of the Devonian and Silurian basin of the Great Lakes and the Mississippi Valley, no less than five, probably six, beds of rock indicated, which, wherever lying deep enough, and thick and porous enough, will be found to pour out combustible gas when tapped, in the bountiful and apparently exhaustless way we have seen. I believe, then, that I am fully justified in the editorial dictum indulged by me long since, in the AMERICAN GAS-LIGHT JOURNAL, that:

"It may be accepted with implicit confidence as a fact, that there are vast districts of country throughout the United States within which, by *judicious* exploration, an immense number of such fountains of natural gas may be developed; furnishing a fuel which *raises itself* out of the mine, and which may be made to transport itself, up hill and down dale, to any point required; independently of seasons and circumstances, miners' strikes and railroad monopolists to the contrary notwithstanding."

2. Chemistry.

Two prominent chemical points present themselves, one chiefly of scientific, and the other of practical interest; relating, the one to the mode of origin, and the other to the mode of purification, of the gas. To both I have given much thought, and to the latter much experiment and invention. This latter, however, I shall not now enter upon. As to my views of the mode of formation of the gas that exists now in such enormous compression in these different strata; I ask first, What *is* this gas chemically? Always essentially, from whatever horizon obtained, it is *marsh gas*, that hydrocarbon of all others which contains the most hydrogen, and the least carbon; the compound which naturally and necessarily forms the final residue of the abstraction of carbon from organic matter by a powerful oxidising agent; since in nature we scarce find elementary hydrogen as such a residue. Now what oxidising agents are there, or rather, what have there been in all these rocks, that could effect such a combustion? I reply, *oxides of iron*, now represented in these rocks by iron sulphides, showing the iron oxides to have passed through the forms of sulphates. I again ask; What analogous action have we *now* going on everywhere on the present surface of the earth? The evolution of marsh gas from the black mud of a stagnant pool, loaded with vegetable matter, and blackened by sulphide of iron, which is occupied in conveying the oxygen of the water to the carbon of the mud. Every boy who has thrust a stick into such mud, bringing up a stream of marsh gas bubbles, has opened a gas well on a small scale.

This view of Gas-Genesis is but a corollary of my theory of Coal-Genesis, laid before this Lyceum, Jan. 10, 1870, which makes the oxidating action of ferrous sulphate on carbon the cause of formation of coal, together with its accompanying iron minerals. It will be remembered that coal and marsh gas are usually concomitant, in depth at least.

At the epochs of deposition of these rocks then, the basin of the great North American continental lagoon was filled to varying depths with ferruginous mud, highly charged with organic matter, which after being covered with other beds (of sandy character) during the process of induration into shales (a process without doubt due to the same action) underwent an internal fermentation, such as I have described. The carbonic acid, always formed at the same time, chiefly disappears, from its solubility in water, through which it is transferred to the bases, lime, magnesia and ferrous oxide, always abundant in such rocks.

3. Engineering Points.

In the handling of these gases, ordinary engineering, even ordinary gas-engineering practice, will not furnish rules of much value. The enormous pressures to be dealt with, pressures moreover of a medium which is so subtile, will require special appliances and contrivances. Probably with regard to these it is not becoming to me, belonging to a different profession, to offer anything more than mere suggestion, and I shall therefore be satisfied with pointing out here what appears to me a new and inviting field for the scientific engineer.

After the gas has been controlled and confined, other engineering problems come in; inasmuch as many of these wells will be so situated that it will be highly desirable to convey the gas to long distances through suitable ducts. It will be, in fact is now, a problem to be determined by experiment, as to proper relations of length and diameter of duct, to such heavy pressures. For pressures of a few inches of water, all that is usually dealt with in gas-engineering, an empirical formula has been arrived at, and is in common use, which is regarded as satisfactory, but, when we come to pressures of hundreds of feet of water, such as we must have in some of these well holes, I do not believe it has any reliability. Other problems relate to the best places at which to bore, in view of the varying contour of the surface, to reach the gas horizons with least work. These are problems which must be solved *jointly* by the engineer and the geologist.

It may not be without interest to attempt some calculations as to the amouut of gas that can be relied upon in the future from this source. The gas has been known to expel columns of water more than 700 feet in height. It would be fair then to admit the existence of tensions of compression, of twenty atmospheres. If the porosity of the rock is only five per cent. of its volume, the whole gas would then assume at the surface the volume of the rock itself. Then if the three New York belts are 200 miles long and equal in mass to 10 miles wide of 100 feet thickness (a moderate allowance) they will supply more than 3000 wells like the Bloomfield, for over 100 years. These figures, though stupendous, do not amount to practical inexhaustibility, and I suggest that legislative action ought to be taken in the gas-producing States, to prevent waste of this precious natural product. It may be objected that no man can be prevented from boring any holes he chooses on his own farm, and from leaving them unsealed afterwards; but it appears to me, on the contrary, that the same principle ought to apply here, as in the case of streams of water on the surface, which no man could legally, or with impunity, divert from his neighbor's property, and cause to run to mere waste.

In conclusion, I will venture to enounce, as my own conviction, which (however visionary it may be deemed by many, I claim to be strictly founded on induction from known facts), that throughout large sections of the United States (throughout the middle tier of counties in western New York, for example), every town, nay, every house in the land, ought to be both warmed and lighted by gas drawn from the bountiful bosom of Mother Earth, without money and without price.

The following paper was read:

On the Gas Wells of Ohio and Pennsylvania.

By Dr. J. S. Newberry.

Carburetted Hydrogen escapes from the earth in innumerable localities. It is evolved in the working of coal mines, and constitutes "fire-damp." It is also a constant associate of petroleum, and always issues in greater or less quantity, from oil wells. It is given off too in the decomposition of recent vegetable matter, and may be seen bubbling up through the water of all pools in which plants are decaying. When it escapes from the earth it may be generally traced to beds of bituminous matter from which it is apparently derived, such as coal, lignite, carbonaceous shale, asphalt, oil, &c. From these substances it may be obtained by artificial distillation, and is evolved by the spontaneous decomposition, which all organic tissues suffer on exposure.

As Carburetted Hydrogen produces heat and light in combustion, it is largely manufactured and used for the illumination of cities and residences. So extensively is it employed for this purpose, that it may be regarded as an indispensable element in our modern civilization. It is not strange then, that efforts have been made to utilize the immense quantities of gas which flow from wells and springs in so many different countries. The Chinese have, for hundreds of years, used for lighting and heating, the gas which emanates from the earth, in several provinces of their country. In the United States, the gas which issues from the salt wells of the Kanawha valley, has been for many years employed as a fuel in the evaporation of the brine.

The town of Fredonia, in western New York, has for more than forty years been fully, or partially lighted by gas, which issues from springs at that place. In the borings made for oil in the various oil districts of the western states, the gas which has been produced so abundantly, has been generally regarded as a useless, frequently, an inconvenient and dangerous product. Within a year or two past, however, this gas has been utilized in numerous localities, and already a large number of wells have been bored for the express purpose of obtaining it. In some cases these gas wells have been highly productive, furnishing an abundance of material for heating and lighting in its most convenient and manageable form, so that this now deserves to be reckoned as one of the important elements in the mineral resources of our country. As this method of procuring carburetted hydrogen gas forms in this country a new industry, and one which will probably assume great importance, a few words in reference to its present condition and prospects, may not be without interest to the public. I therefore extract from my notes a few facts in regard to some of the most interesting of our gas producing districts and wells. In the oil district of the Upper Cumberland, in Kentucky, gas accumulates in such quantities beneath the sheets of Lower Silurian limestone, that many hundred tons of rock and earth are sometimes with great violence blown out. These explosions have received the local name of "gas volcanos." In Ohio, gas escapes from nearly all the wells bored for oil in the oil producing districts. Of these, two bored by Peter Neff, Esq., near Kenyon College, in Knox Co., presents some remarkable features. These wells were bored in 1866, at the same geological horizon as that which furnishes the oil on Oil Creek. At the depth of about six hundred feet in each well, a fissure was struck from which gas issued in such volume as to throw out the boring tools, and form a jet of water more than one hundred feet in height. One of these wells has been tubed so as to exclude the water, and gas has continued for five years to escape from it, in such quantity as to produce as it rushes through a two and a half inch pipe, a sound that may be heard at a considerable distance. When ignited, the gas forms a jet of flame three feet in diameter and fifteen feet long. The other well, which has never been tubed, constantly ejects at intervals of one minute, the water that fills it. It thus forms an intermittent fountain one hundred and twenty feet in height. The derrick set over this well has a height of sixty feet. In winter it becomes incased in ice and forms a huge translucent chimney, through which at regular intervals a mingled current of gas and water rushes to twice its height. By cutting through this chimney at its base, and igniting the gas in a paroxysm, it affords a magnificient spectacle—a fountain of water and fire which brilliantly illuminates its ice chimney. No accurate measure has been made of the gas escaping from these wells, but it is estimated to be sufficient to light a large city.

At West Bloomfield, N. Y., is another gas well not unlike these I have described. This is bored to the depth of 500 ft. reaching down to the vicinity of the Marcellus bituminous shales. From some measurements made by Prof. Wurtz, it appears that about five cubic feet of gas escape from this well every second. It is proposed to utilize this large amount of valuable combustible, by conducting it through pipes to Rochester, a distance of twenty miles.

At Erie, Penn., there are now twenty-five gas wells in successful operation, most of which have been bored for the special purpose of obtaining gas. Mr. Henry Newton, my assistant in the School of Mines, has recently made at my request a careful examination of all of these wells, and has given me a detailed description of each. I quote one or two of these for the purpose of giving a clear idea of their general character.

1st. N. Jarecki & Co., (Petroleum Brass Works,) have two wells, the first bored for oil in 1864, 1200 feet deep. No oil was obtained, but brackish water and an abundant supply of gas. This is used to light a few houses. The second well was bored in March, 1871, for gas, is 700 feet deep, and is used to light the shop and heat the boilers. The supply is not at all regular, and has perceptibly failed since the Conrad well was sunk near it. The heating power of the gas, from well No. 2, is roughly estimated at from 8 to 10 tons of coal per month.

2d. Brevillier's well, was sunk for oil in 1864, depth 625 feet, diameter 5 inches. The gas supplies five fires in the soap factory and three in the house of the proprietor, beside lighting both establishments. It has been used in the factory for five years.

3d. Well sunk by Senator Lowrey, for gas, in Oct., 1870, 520 feet deep, passing through 50 feet of sandrock, then through gray shale and flag-stones, terminating in a dark shale. The gas is used for all household purposes, for cooking, heating and lighting. When used in ordinary stoves, the stove is partially filled with furnace cinder or broken brick. In open fires, it is burned in clay boxes made to represent wood.

4th. Conrad's Brewery, sunk in March, 1871, 600 feet deep. No oil was obtained, but salt water and an abundant supply of gas. This gas supplies all household purposes, and heats malt chambers, brew-kettle and steam boiler.

At Conneaut and Painesville, Ohio, wells have been bored for gas with entire success, and others are being bored in these localities, and at many points further West.

Quality of the Gas.

The illuminating power of the gas flowing from the West Bloomfield well, that from Fredonia and several of the Erie wells, has been measured and found to be about one half that of the gas used in most of our cities, or equal to seven to eight candles. It usually has the odor of petroleum, and contains a small percentage of condensable petroleum vapor. It is heavier than common street gas, contains carbonic acid and probably carbonic oxide. Its heating power is greater than that of common gas. Its illuminating power is increased by passing it through a purifier, and removing the carbonic acid. All who use it speak of it in terms of high praise, as being extremely convenient for heating and lighting, and without objectionable qualities. When delivered from the well directly to the burners, if not consumed, the pressure accumulates so as sometimes to burst the pipes. A pressure of fifty pounds to the square inch, has been noticed in some of the Erie wells. A steam gauge applied to one of Mr. Neff's wells, in Knox Co., Ohio, ran rapidly up to 180 pounds, the highest pressure it would indicate. It is certain that the pressure at the bottom of the well, which is not tubed, is much greater, as it lifts a column of water not less than 500 feet in length.

Source of the Gas.

All the gas wells on the Lake shore draw their gas from some point above the Huron Shales. A great mass of bituminous strata, the equivalent of the Genessee and Cashaqua shales of New York. This bituminous formation underlies the oil region of Western Pennsylvania, and all the oil and gas belt of Ohio. Many wells have been carried through this formation, but in no case upon the Lake shore, has gas been obtained below it. For this and other reasons that might be advanced, I think we are justified in concluding that the gas and the oil of the region under consideration are derived by spontaneous distillation from the bituminous shales to which reference has been made.

October 23d, 1871.

The President in the chair. Seventeen persons present.

Mr. R. Dinwiddie announced the **Death of Sir Roderick Impey Murchison,** one of the Honorary Members of the Society, and exhibited a photograph of the deceased.

Mr. R. H. Brownne exhibited a **Necklace of Cut Amethysts,** from Oberstein, Germany.

Prof. T. Egleston made some remarks on the **Artificial Coloration of Agates.**

It is not generally known that most of the Agates which are used for ornament, are artificially colored. This art of coloring natural stones, is carried on on an immense scale at Oberstein in Germany, where the greater part of the Agates of Europe are cut. Most of the Agates which are cut there come from Brazil. Those which are naturally colored are generally different shades of red. If the color is of the desired shade they are immediately cut, but if not, or if the shade of color is not such as desired, they are heated until it is brought to the desired tint. The greater part of them however in their natural state, are of a dirty greyish color, with bands of white of greater or less thickness running through them. By long habit the workman acquires the art of being able to distinguish those bands which will absorb color, and the pieces are cut accordingly with diamond dust. Prepared in the rough they all have the same color. The colors most sought for in commerce are various shades of red, green, yellow and blue. The red color is given by allowing the stone to remain several days in an acid solution of iron, the time depending on the depth of color to be given, and the shade on the absorbent power of the bands. It is then taken out and placed in an oven, where it is kept for some time at a temperature of between 100 and 200° Cent., until no further change takes place. The stone is then red and is cut, according to the depth of the color in the different bands, with a diamond saw, ground on large wheels of sandstone, before which the cutter lies on his breast, and polished on a rapidly rotating wooden wheel with tin.

The black color is given by boiling first in honey and then in sulphuric acid. The bands which absorb the honey, become black from its decomposition. Those which do not, remain white. This is the onyx of commerce. When there are no bands of white the stone is called jet.

The yellow color is produced by Chromic acid. To be certain of a good tint, the stones are first boiled in Hydrochloric acid to clean them and dissolve out anything that may be soluble. They are then placed in Chromic acid and left for several days. It then shows yellow where the acid has penetrated.

To give the beautiful green color which is so much sought for at present, the stone which has been steeped in Chromic acid, is covered with carbonate of ammonia and heated.

The blue color is given by placing the pieces to be treated first in a solution of Ferrocyanide of potassium, then in a salt of iron. All of the artificially prepared stones receive their definite form and polish after they have been colored.

The following paper was read:

Note on Colored Rain.

By Prof. A. M. Edwards.

The subject of colored rain, or the falling, more commonly, of colored matters without water, is one which possesses both a popular and a scientific interest. As a matter of popular wonder we see, from time to time, in the public prints accounts of remarkable showers, sometimes of "blood," sometimes of "sulphur," and similar substances, while at times the particles descending upon the earth, assume more noticeable dimensions, and assume the shape of "frogs" or "fish." Without considering these two last named phenomena, which are of too gigantic size to come within the scope of one who, like myself, uses the microscope largely as an assistant in unraveling difficult problems in Biology, I desire to put upon record a few facts connected with the scientific aspect of this subject.

We find in a late number of Nature (Vol. IV. p. 68) a letter from a Mr. A. Ernst, who, writing from Caracas, Venezuela, states that "in December, 1870, after a heavy rain at Rosaria de Cucuta (New Grenada), a great many small round specks of a yellow clayish substance, were found on the leaves of plants that had been exposed to the rain." On examination of this substance by means of a microscope, Mr. Ernst tells us that "it proved to be composed almost entirely of a species of *Triceratium*, and another of *Cosmarium*, which," he goes on to say, "must have been carried away by a violent storm, from their lacustrine abodes." Here is a possessor of a microscope who evidently is a mere microscopist and not an observer in the true sense of the term. For, if he had been so, he would not so readily have assumed that a Desmid (*Cosmarium*) and a Diatom (*Triceratium*) could be thus readily, even "by a violent storm" carried "from their lacustrine abodes," and deposited, as a yellow clayish substance, on the leaves of plants. Nor would he have expected to find but one species of Diatoms and one of Desmids thus deposited. Nor would he have supposed that a species of a distinctly marine genus of Diatoms (*Triceratium*), for Smith's *Triceratium exignum* found in fresh water, does not belong to this genus, but to the just as well marked fresh water genus *Tabellaria*, would come from the waters of a lake. However, Mr. Ernst's description of the substance deposited as yellow and clayish, will, I think, lead us to define what it really was. But before saying what I wish to on this subject, I would call attention to another letter, published in the same periodical, on this subject. On page 160 of Vol. IV. another gentleman quotes authorities, tending as he thinks, to confirm such showers of solid particles, or, at least, their appearance after rain, and upon the ground or vegetation, and thereby falls into some errors fully as great as those of Mr. Ernst. Thus, after quoting a passage in Pliny, where a rain of "iron" along with "sponges," is spoken of, he goes on to explain that the iron and sponges here mentioned are one and the same thing, namely the now well-known "red snow." And it is a curious fact that in the books of authors who ought to know better, we find it stated that there have been cases in which a red-colored matter has descended from the air, upon the ground and vegetation, and that on examination by means of the microscope it has been ascertained to be made up of individuals of a minute perfect plant, which has been taken up by the wind or otherwise, from its natural habitat, which is in or upon the surface of water, and thereafter rained down upon the earth. Furthermore we find a record as to the occurrence of the so-called "red snow" in Washington Territory, by Mr. George Gibbs, in the American Naturalist, Vol. V. page 116, which presents us with some further information on this point, and will serve as an introduction to what I have to say on this subject.

Mr. Gibbs states that in the summer of 1858, at an altitude of 6500 feet on the Cascade Mountains, he found the "red snow." He disgusted the man who first brought it to him, by eating it, and examination by means of a lens showed it to consist of "tadpole shaped bodies, with rounded head and attenuated tails, perhaps two lines in length." In conclusion he says that he believes "this is the first notice of the occurrence of the 'red snow' within the territories of the United States."

In 1865, when in charge of the Microscopic material of the State Geological Survey of California, I received from Prof. Brewer, a specimen, dried, of "red snow," from Lassen's Peak at about 10,500 to 16,000 feet altitude, collected in September, 1863. And Prof. Brewer informed me that it was found, commonly, on the perpetual snows of the Sierra Nevada. For many years before this I had seen this remarkable appearance, not, however, upon snow, but upon the surface of the water of ditches and marshes all around this city; New York.

A fall of yellow rain is recorded (Nature, Vol. II. page 166) as having fallen on the 14th of February, 1870, at Gêne, Italy, and a chemical analysis of it proved it to consist of

Water	6·490	
Nitrogenous organic substance	6·611	
Sand and clay	65·618	
Oxide of iron	14·692	
Carbonate of lime	8·589	per cent.

Under the microscope it was seen to be made up of blue spherical bodies, and spores of a moss and other vegetable substances along with a few Diatomaceæ. M. Boccardo, who examined it, thinks that if he could have seen it when fresh that "the microscope would have shown the existence of several kinds of infusoria." He thinks it came from Africa, and quotes Maury's suppositions founded on Ehrenberg's loose observations in confirmation of the likelihood of its having traveled so far. More likely it came from near by, as did my New Hampshire specimen, to be mentioned presently.

But, besides these supposed showers of a yellow color, which have been called "Sulphur," and red, which have been termed blood, we have records, which appear periodically most commonly in our rural papers, of showers of "honey" which is white and frothy in appearance, and of a sweet taste. To explain, satisfactorily, all of these phenomena I shall begin with the first—the yellow rain or showers of sulphur. When engaged at Dartmouth College during the last summer, one of my students, Mr. G. F. Stackpole, brought me a quantity of a yellowish powder which he assured me had fallen in great quantity during a heavy shower of rain near Lebanon, N. H., and there covered, not only the corn-fields, but the water of Shaker Pond, a respectably sized sheet of water. On the leeward side of the pond this powder had collected in considerable amount, and from thence that he brought me had been procured. Such showers were not very uncommon in that region, and were usually supposed to be, and were called "sulphur." I assured him it was not sulphur, and showed him under the microscope what it was. Thereafter, on careful inquiry I found, as I had suspected, that the quantity fallen, (for it did descend from the air) was by no means as great as he and his informants had supposed, and was to be found only on one corn field, and on the surface of the water at the side of the pond where he had gathered it. Now what was this substance. Simply the pollen of the Pine tree, which it shed at this season (June—July) in considerable quantity, and I found that on the opposite side of the pond to that where the gathering had been made was a large grove of such trees in blossom. Now I strongly suspect, though, of course I can not speak positively without examining specimens, that the "yellow clayish substance" mentioned by Mr. Ernst was some such pollen, and that his "*Triceratium*" and "*Cosmaarium*" are neither Diatoms nor Desmids, but simply pollen granules, which resemble those organisms very closely in outline and sculpture. I do not see how any force of wind could carry up either Diatoms or Desmids, and certainly, as far as my experience or that of other observers as yet published goes the marine genus *Triceratium* has never been found associated with the fresh water *Cosmarium.* The "Red Snow" has been, and is still very commonly supposed to be a perfect plant, and has been called *Hœmatococcus sanguineus*, but the investigations of Dr. J. Braxton Hicks has shown that many of the forms which have been classed under this and other heads, and some of which are green whilst others are red, are the motile conditions (called *gonidia*) of Lichens. I have shown that some of the green-colored forms, commonly ranked as animals under the name of *Euglena*, are the motile forms of algæ, and the red coating so common in this locality, and which I have found from early spring to late in the fall covering many hundred square feet of the surface of fresh water, is evidently a state of an alga also. This subject is one of great interest, and calls for further patient study. For some time I have been collecting observations thereon, and hope before long to lay them before the Lyceum. We come now to the showers of "honey." These are no showers at all, but merely the juice of plants caused to exude in consequence of the puncture of insects—"plant hoppers" so called—as I had excellent opportunity of proving, as this substance was very common in the fields upon the stalks of grass, around Hanover, N. H., last summer.

PROF. EGLESTON said that he had recently seen some **Chinese Jade,** and asked the question whether any one really knew what Jade was. The specimens he saw had recently been brought from China, and were different from the Chalchihuital, from South America, which Mr. Squier had exhibited at the Lyceum, and from any published description of the mineral.

One of the specimens, cut in the shape of a ball, was transparent, of a yellowish green color, and was not touched by the file. It was set as a gem, and no further observations could be made upon it. The other specimens were of the white variety streaked with apple green, and resembled the Chalchihuital. It appears from such information as can be gathered from those who have been in China, that the real Jade is a gem of great value, and that the Chinese who come in contact with foreigners, are in the habit of selling any white or greenish stone under the name of Jade, if they can get a purchaser, under that name. Hence arises probably the confusion as to what the mineral really is. His informant, who was for a long time collector of customs, in a large Chinese port, told him that as far as he could learn, the real Jade was not a rare stone, but its value was purposely kept up by the dealers, and that in case a large quantity was for any reason, put upon the market at one time, they would combine and refuse to buy it. From his description, he, (Prof. E.,) gathered that there must be at least two stones called the Jade, one brought into China by ships trading at the different ports, brought as near as he could learn from New Zealand; the other, the transparent green stone, resembled some varieties of corundum, though he had never seen any corundum of this peculiar color. He had sent to both China and Japan for some of the minerals, which he intends to have cut and to examine optically, and if he could get enough of them, to analyse.

PROF. B. N. MARTIN stated that he had received from Prof. Schlagintweit the statement that he had, when in Thibet, discovered the locality from which the Chinese had for generations taken the Jadeite which they have been in the habit of carving, and which they regard with a sort of veneration. The mineral when taken from the quarry, was soft, and could be cut and carved readily; and he had put up the specimens without suspecting the probability of any change. On unpacking them, however, a year or two after, he found them very hard. They had evidently undergone a marked change. Prof. S. exhibited several specimens of the mineral in his lectures.

October 30th, 1871.

The President in the chair. Nineteen persons present.

DR. L. FEUCHTWANGER exhibited a **Crystal of Quartz**, from Nova Scotia, with fine hair-like crystals of what seemed to be Pyrolusite traversing it.

Mr. W. H. Leggett exhibited an **Ear of Indian Corn,** of monstrous character, from Chester Co., Pa. It appeared to be made up of four ears united together.

Prof. O. W. Morris exhibited a **Stem of Amaranthus,** distorted in a curious manner, so as to be bent at several right angles.

Prof. B. N. Martin exhibited a series of **Minerals from the Geysers of California.**

Prof. A. M. Edwards exhibited specimens of **Distinctly Stratified Rock,** from beneath the Trap, back of Hoboken, N. J., which was recognized as one of the rocks mentioned by Prof. Wurtz, and called by him, Trappoid Schist.

Prof. H. Wurtz exhibited specimens of **Iron Ochres,** from Mt. Katahdin, Me., and made some remarks on their probable mode of formation. They occur in a bed three to four feet thick, and contain casts of leaves looking like those of the Birch. Analysis shows that there are two varieties, but that they both consist essentially of Ferric Hydrate with water, and a little mineral charcoal, besides traces of Pyrites, Silica and Humic acid.

The following paper was read.

Notes on Meteorology for August and September, 1871, with Remarks on the Spring and Summer of the same year.

By Prof. O. W. Morris.

August commenced with the Barometer at 29·863 inches; it rose for two days, and then fell and was variable during the month; the maximum, 30·288 in. occurred on the 23d, and the minimum, 29·509 in. on the 30th, a difference of ·719 inch. The mean for the month, was 29·855 inches.

The temperature on the 1st, was 67·7°, and kept above that till the 19th, when it fell to 66°. The maximum occurred on the 27th, 86°, the minimum, 65° on the 31st, a range of 21°. The monthly mean was 75·23°. There were six thunder showers, one rainbow and one meteor observed. Rain fell on 12 days, to the depth of 6·41 inches.

September began with the Barometer at 30·108 in. It varied up and down, till on the 22d it attained its maximum, 30·372 in., it then fell, and on the 26th, it marked 29·547 in. a range of ·825. The mean was 30·013 inches.

The temperature on the 1st was 61·6°; it rose to its maximum on the 6th, 79°, the minimum 45·5° was on the 21st, a range of 33·5°, the mean was 62·45°. Only one thunder shower occurred, and one Aurora Borealis, but that was unique and beautiful, no arch, but bright, isolated beams.

Rain fell on 5 days, to the depth of 1·85 inch, an uncommonly dry September.

The warmest spring in a series of ten years, was in 1865, 54·39° which was 6·3° warmer than the average for the ten years. This year, (1871) was also 5·12° warmer.

The coldest spring was in 1869, 43·69°, which was 4·8° colder than the average; and 9·22° colder than this year's spring months.

The warmest summer in the same series was also in 1865, 77·4°; which was 3·82° warmer than the average, and 4·77° warmer than in 1871; and this year was 0·95° cooler than the average.

The coldest summer, was in 1869, 70·15°; which was 3·43° colder than the average; and 2·48° colder than in 1871.

The warmest day in June, was the 26th in 1864, 91·26°.
July, 17th 1866, 90·93°.
August, 1st 1864, 89·60°.
The warmest day in March, was the 3d in 1861, 62·53°.
April, 22d 1866, 73·06°.
May, 30th 1871, 81·83°.

The spring of 1871, had the mean of the barometer 29·843 inches; the maximum was on April 24th, 30·368 inches, the minimum, on March 27th, 29·318 in. The mean of each month was, March 29·888 in., April, 29·778 in. May, 29·863 in. The mean humidity was 51·59°, a little more than half saturation. The quantity of rain was, for March, 5·6 in;

April, 3·45 in.; May, 4·9 in. Total, 13·95 inches, which is a small quantity for the spring months.

The thermometer indicated a mean of 44·45° for March, 53·33° for April, and 61·84° for May; a mean for the spring of 53·21°. The highest was on the 30th of May, 88·5°, the lowest, on the 29th of March, 33°, a range of 55·5° for the spring.

Snow fell on 5 days, rain on 37 days. Solar haloes were observed 5 times; lunar haloes, 3 times; lunar coronas, twice; aurora borealis, 3 times; meteor, once, and thunder showers, 7 times.

The summer season for 1871, was colder than the mean for the ten preceding years, by a difference of 1·15°, and 1·8° colder than the summer of 1870. The mean for the ten years, was 73·78°, for 1871, 72·63°.

The greatest mean maximum for the ten years, was in August, 1863, 79·43°, while in August, 1871, it was 75·23°, a difference of 4·2°; the least mean was in June, 1868, 66·63°, while that of June, 1871 was 69·34°, a difference in favor of 1871, of 2·71°. In 1870, the maximum was 77·92° in July, or 2·69° greater than in 1871; the minimum, was 74·11° in June; in 1871, 69·34° which is 4·77° less.

This summer was only 0·47 warmer than that of 1866, which was the cold year.

The mean of the barometer for the summer, was 29·866 in. The maximum was on the 3d of August, 30·228 in.; the minimum, was on the 12th of June, 29·438 in. a difference of ·790 in.; the mean for each month was, June, 29·821, in., July, 29·924 in., August, 29·855.

Rain fell on 43 days, the quantity amounted to 20·7 in.; for June, 8·02 in. July, 6·27 in. August, 6·41 in. Thunder showers occurred on 18 days; rainbows on 4 days, lightning 1, meteors 2, parhelia 2, lunar corona 1, earthquake 1.

November 6th, 1871.

The President in the chair. Nineteen persons present.

PROF. T. EGLESTON remarked that one of the most interesting, perhaps the most interesting machine in the late Fair of the American Institute, was the **Sand Blast Machine.** He happened accidentally to be present when the judges made their examination of it, and saw all the usual experiments shown, such as etching of fine lace on glass without injuring the lace, cutting letters and ornaments on limestone and drilling a hole through a file, and while admiring the beauty of work and thinking of the numerous commercial applications of which it was capable, a series of experiments suggested themselves, which through the liberality of the managers of the Fair, he was able in part to carry out. By an unfortunate misunderstanding the verbal request that he would commence the experiments did not reach him, until two days before the close of the Fair, though sent a week previously. The experiments were to have been, the examination of the effect of the sand blast, on rocks and mineral aggregates, the substitution of pulverized minerals of different hardness for the sand in the machine, and the examination of the effect of these sands on harder bodies. It was possible only to carry out the last part of the plan, and that too only partially. The sand blast proved to be so much more powerful than could have been imagined, that it was necessary to entirely rearrange the experiments after they had been commenced.

The minerals chosen were Corundum in crystals from Delaware Co., Pa., a piece of Emery, from Chester, Mass., composed of a mixture of Corundum and Magnetite. A pebble of Topaz of the variety known as Goute d'Eau. A large Topaz pebble colorless and transparent, with a large cleavage face, and a black Diamond. The following table gives the results of these experiments.

Minerals.	Time exposed.	Weight in grms. before.	Weight in grms. after.	Loss in weight.
Corundum Crystal,	30 seconds,	1·49	0·22021	1·16979
Emery, Chester, Mass.,	1 minute,	16·65	11·6968	4·9532
Topaz (goute d'eau),	1 minute,	2·097	0·1263	1·9707
Topaz pebble,	1 minute,	9·774	7·6241	2·1499
Black Diamond,	3 minutes,	1·2607	1·2235	0·0372
" "	5 "	1·2235	1·1738	0·0497
" "	8 "	1·2607	1·1738	0·0869

In a former experiment, a hole nearly ¾ of an inch above, and ½ an inch below, was bored through a corundum crystal from Ceylon, one half an inch thick, in 8 minutes. The weight of this crystal previous to the operation was not taken, but the crystal is preserved in the mineral collection of the School of Mines. In the Emery from Chester, a large hole was made, in which pieces of corundum project, showing that the blast acted much faster on the magnetite than on the corundum. A conical hole was made in the Topaz pebble, the point of the cone being quite sharp. The microscopic examination of these specimens, showed that they all presented the same general appearance. The Emery was worn away in a manner very similar to that which is so often seen on the surfaces of rocks near sand beaches, which are exposed to violent winds carrying sand with them, and suggested to me, whether more importance should not be given to this agent as a power of degradation, and as the cause of many phenomena in structural geology not hitherto explained. If such effects can be produced by the fan blast in a very short time, is it not likely that the action of the wind at ordinary velocities continued a very long time, will produce much more powerful effects on a large scale, and may we not expect that a hurricane would produce effects similar to that produced by the injector machine with steam. The peculiar chatoyant lustre of many minerals I was able to produce at will, on any mineral possessing cleavage, by a few moments' exposure to the blast. It seems probable that many of the rounded faces of minerals which have this lustre may have been produced in this way, and that many of those rounded surfaces noticed on minerals which have no cleavage may be traced to this cause. It seems more than likely too, that some of the deep furrows existing in rocks composed of layers of different hardness, may have been produced partly at least by the agency of sand. I greatly regret that though I continued my experiments up to the moment of closing the building the last night of the Fair, that I was not able to carry them out as I first intended. The specimens exhibited, however, show that sand whirled by the wind even at a moderate velocity, is a much more powerful agent than we have generally supposed, and that at the velocity of a whirlwind even the hardest rocks will be worn away with very great rapidity.

PROF. H. WURTZ said he desired to rectify a misunderstanding that had occurred, in connection with his communications to the Lyceum, on the subject of the **Feldspathic composition** that he had observed in the beds of the so-called "**Sandstone,**" used for building-stone, from the Palisade Range in New Jersey. Some analysis, altogether confirmatory of his observations, have been published by Dr. Schweitzer, in the *American Chemist*, for July, 1871, under the title of "*The Felsites of the Palisade Range.*"

The use by Dr. S., of the name *Felsite*, had been due to an incorrect apprehension of the words of Prof. W.; this term applying more usually to compact Feldspathic rocks of porphyritic or porphyroid types. Prof. Wurtz had suggested provisionally the term *Felspathites*.

November 13th, 1871.

The President in the chair. Thirty-three persons present.

PROF. A. M. EDWARDS presented the following resolution:

Resolved,—That the Lyceum of Natural History in the City of New York, has learned, with sincere grief, of the misfortune that has befallen its sister society, The Chicago Academy of Sciences, by the burning of its building, collections and library, and, remembering how it has also passed through a similar trial, tenders its heartfelt sympathy. And desiring to remedy, as far as lies within its power, the loss that has thus fallen upon Science and the City of Chicago, offers to furnish full sets of all the publications of the Lyceum for the new Library, which it hopes to see rapidly acquired by the Academy.

The resolution was unanimously adopted.

DR. H. C. BOLTON moved that the Lyceum appoint a Committee of one to receive contributions of books for the Chicago Academy of Sciences.

The motion was unanimously adopted.

PROF. A. M. EDWARDS was appointed a Committee for the purpose, and proposed that the members of the Lyceum, desiring to assist, forward their contributions to the rooms of the Society, 64 Madison Avenue.

The following paper was read.

On some Chemosmotic Phenomena and a New Theory of Fermentation.

BY O. LOEW.

Electro-capillarity is the name given by Becquerel to certain chemical actions, caused by the reaction of two bodies upon each other through an intervening membrane. Becquerel (Jahresbericht, 1866-68,) has found that under these conditions, the chemical reaction is substantially modified. If a solution of Copper Sulphate is placed upon one side of the membrane, and Potassium Sulphide upon the other, instead of *Copper Sulphide*, metallic Copper will be precipitated. Becquerel ascribes this unexpected result to the action of electric currents, and calls it "Electro-capillarity."

In my opinion this name is not sufficiently definite, since the action of electricity is not required to explain the results obtained. I would propose the name "Chemosmosis," for the cause of these phenomena, because therein we have osmosis accompanied by peculiar chemical decompositions. I have found that without any intervening membrane, similar phenomena can be produced. If a crystal of Copper Sulphate be placed in a test tube or flask, and the vessel be then filled with a solution of Potassium Sulphide of the proper strength, the formation of a black crust of Copper Sulphide, will be first observed upon the surface of the crystal. As soon as this is formed an ascending yellow current may be noticed, doubtless due to the formation of Potassium Bisulphide. If the solution of Sulphide be too dilute, it works too quickly; while on the other hand a concentrated solution works imperfectly, retarding the osmotic action considerably. If after about twelve hours the liquid be removed, and the black lump washed with care and then broken open, we find metallic Copper in the interior, no part of the original crystal being left undecomposed. Here we have a clear case where the deposit of Copper Sulphide takes the place of a membrane. That this deposit must possess a peculiar molecular arrangement to yield the result described, can be demonstrated at once if we repeat the experiment with a crystal of Silver Nitrate. The first step here also, is the turning of the surface of the crystal into a black crust of Sulphide, but we look in vain for the ascending yellow current. Neither do we find a similar result in the interior of the black lump if we cut it open. We find the central portion almost unchanged, only a small amount of metallic Silver being formed. The action of Potassium Sulphhydrate is very different, producing a violent and perfect decomposition of the crystal of Silver Nitrate, the rising bubbles of Sulphuretted Hydrogen gas do not permit of the formation of a crust.

Similar differences we find on pouring Caustic Potash over both salts; the copper salt will yield a loose mixture of black Oxide and blue Hydrate, and the decomposition is complete, while with Silver Nitrate we find under the thin layer of Oxide, the original salt undecomposed.

As regards the molecular structure of the crusts, of metallic Sulphides, it is evident that the crust of the copper salt must be provided with certain molecular interstices, which is not the case with the Silver compound, since the Silver Nitrate does not contain any water of crystallization. If a crystal of Copper Sulphate be placed in the solution of Potassium Sulphide, the Copper Sulphide formed takes the place of the group SO_4Cu whilst the water, having surrounded this group, in a solid condition, becomes liquid, and, escaping, leaves in the precipitated crust of Copper Sulphide interstices through which other particles can move. In the layer following next beneath, the normal decomposition can only proceed when the molecule of Potassium Sulphide can penetrate such interstices to reach the interior, or when the molecule of Copper Sulphate dissolved by the entering water, can penetrate the crust to reach the exterior. But if these interstices are too small to permit such motion to take place, then a "Chem-Osmotic" decomposition will set in, provided the other conditions are favorable. The larger molecules split and give this a partially modified decomposition; the Sulphur of the Potassium Sulphide remains in the exterior liquid, forming Bisulphide, while the Potassium, uniting with the SO_4 group, precipitates metallic Copper. In the case of the Copper salt this movement is soon finished, while in the case of the Silver salt this movement seems to be entirely arrested after a while; the interstices can, in this case be only formed by the difference of the molecular volumes of Silver Nitrate and Silver Sulphide, and are perhaps entirely covered over by several layers; or, at least, contracted.

On the application of Caustic Potash instead of Potassium Sulphide to the Copper salt, metal is not separated, for several reasons, (1.) a body analogous to Potassium Bisulphide cannot be formed under those conditions; (2.) the intermediate formation of voluminous Copper Oxy-Hydrate produces an entire change of the original positions of the molecules of Copper; making the formation of a crust impossible. In the case of the Silver salt an intermediate formation of an Oxy-Hydrate cannot take place and the layer of Oxide protects the remainder of the crystal from further action. When caustic Soda is used it behaves in a different way; that is to say, it penetrates the crystal entirely, and, after a while, Silver Oxide is found occupying the place of, and of the same shape as the original Nitrate. This, however, is not at all surprising if we compare the atomic volume of Sodium, 24·8 with that of Potassium, 45·2.

Osmosis through these molecular interstices, is in many other cases not only physical but chemical, since additional and important duties are performed which may explain many phenomena which have been hitherto imperfectly understood. The obscure chemical actions which we observe taking place in vegetable and animal cells, and which appear to be inexplicable, are always accompanied by Osmotic processes, the contents of the cell being separated by a membrane from the exterior liquid of a different chemical nature; we frequently in such cases find a production and separation of new compounds to occur. As in the crystal, every molecule occupies relatively an unalterable position, so there is a specific arrangement of the molecules composing the substance of the cell-wall, between the molecules of which there are molecular interstices. Where such molecular interstices do not exist, Osmosis cannot take place, and it is possible, if not probable, that these interstices are of various shapes and size, according to the kind of cell. Let us now imagine that the cell-wall possesses molecular interstices smaller than the molecular volume of the external body, then the Osmotic force can only be satisfied and an equilibrium established, by tearing asunder these molecules and the forming of new compounds, provided the power of resistance to such breaking up be not too great. As Nitroglycerine (relatively rich in NO_2 molecules) by motion (as a blow) is broken up into simpler compounds, so, for instance, the Sugar molecule (relatively rich in OH molecules) is, by shifting, pressing and stretching, broken up, and this process of splitting may take a different direction, according to the shape and size of the molecular interstices of the cell wall, in which they are in contact and through which they pass, provided the chemical nature of the Sugar molecule permits of such action. Viewing the subject in this light, furnishes us with a simple explanation of the Alcoholic and Lactic fermentations of Sugar, the cell through the wall of which the action takes place, being different in character in each case. The views of A. Meyers on fermentation, published during the past year in Poggendorff's Annalen, cannot be considered as explaining the matter, as he falls back upon the principle of the existence of a "vital force," and pronounces fermentation to be the consequence of unexplained formation of Cellulose. But he does not explain why Sugar can undergo several quite distinct kinds of fermentation; neither does he show how the fact that under peculiar conditions the yeast may diminish in weight, while the fermentation is still going on, is to be made to accord with his views.

Among all the theories of fermentation put forward, that of Liebig appears, as yet, to be the simplest and most natural; although his otherwise ingenious hypothesis leaves several points unexplained, as, for instance, how it is that Sugar can undergo more than one kind of fermentation. Mitcherlich's contact theory and Pasteur's views, pronouncing fermentation to be the consequence of the vitality of the yeast plant, cannot be considered as fully explaining the process.

Chemosmosis may be recognized as taking an active part in many other changes than those mentioned, as, for example, the action of the Periosteum in animals, and the reduction of Carbonic acid and water in vegetable tissues, under the influence of the sun's rays. Further investigation in this direction may shed more light on many at present obscure phenomena concerned in physiological chemistry.

DR. H. ENDEMANN read a paper **On Meat and the Methods of Preserving it,** in which he described the extract of meat made according to Liebig's process, and stated that its value is overestimated, as experiments have shown that the ashes of the extract are as nutritious as the extract itself. No organic substance has been found that will produce the effects of extract. He then described the process of salting meat and showed that the salts used, as well as any water employed subsequently to freshen the meat, remove a large part of the extractive salts, leaving it difficult of digestion. Smoking depends on the carbolic or cresylic acid contained in the smoke, by which the albumen and fibrin are coagulated, hence the meat is not readily digested. One of the best processes for preserving meat is enclosing it in air-tight cans, but this often fails on account of mechanical difficulties. He proposed to preserve meat by cutting it into slices and drying it in a hot air chamber, at a temperature below 140° F., which may be done within two hours. This dried meat is then ground in a mill. The fibrin and albumen are not coagulated and will take up water. The apparatus used in the preparation of the dried meat, and its applications for soup, solid dishes and for invalids, was also described.

November 20th, 1871.

PROF. B. N. MARTIN, Vice President in the chair. Ten persons present.

PROF. T. EGLESTON exhibited five crystals of **Diamond** and one of red **Spinel**, from South Africa, belonging to Mr. S. L. M. Barlow. Two of the diamond crystals showed the cleavage parallel to the octahedron, two were curved hexoctahedra. The fifth was a cube one quarter of an inch square, weighing 0·906 gms. The cube is a twin by interpenetration, and shows the faces of the rhombic dodecahedron on both crystals. The cube faces are all striated in the direction of the diagonals of the faces of the cube, and show consequently the tendency toward the octahedral form. The Spinel was perfectly transparent, of a beautiful ruby color.. Its form was that of a hemitrope octahedron.

PROF. D. S. MARTIN exhibited specimens of a **Clay containing Recent Shells,** from a deposit which had been the bed of a lagoon within quite a modern period, near the town of

Lewes, Del. The shells are in very perfect preservation, though the epidermis is nearly gone, and the texture is becoming fragile and chalky. The principal species are *Sanguinolaria fusca*, *Nassa obsoleta*, and *Modiola plicatula*, of which the first two are now living on the beaches outside, and probably the last also. These specimens give an excellent illustration of the mode of formation of many of our fossiliferous clays and marls. The deposit may, perhaps, have value as a fertilizer.

He also gave some description of the very remarkable sand-dunes or moving hills at Cape Henlopen, a mile or two east of Lewes. The sand brought down by the Delaware River accumulates at this point, and when thrown up on the beach, is taken in charge by the heavy east winds, and carried inland in a great line of drifting hills, which rises in a very long and gentle slope on the windward side, and falls off abruptly from the crest on the leeward, as is usual in wind-drifts. The whole surface of the windward side is studded with the tops of dead tree trunks,—the remnants of a pine forest, overwhelmed by the advance of the hill. The crest seems steadily approaching the light-house keeper's dwelling, and will, probably, necessitate its removal in the course of some few years.

Prof. A. M. Edwards said the specimens just exhibited are of considerable interest, as they show very nicely the mode in which certain stratified rocks containing fossils are evidently formed. Under certain circumstances, say when formed in a locality like the Tropics, where animal life abounded and the Mollusca especially occurred in large quantities, so that Calcareous matter would accumulate, such a deposit might become, in time, converted into a Limestone in which the forms of the enclosed shells and other organic remains would be preserved in a more or less perfect manner. If, on the other hand, Calcium compounds were not present in abundance, but the particles of the deposit thrown down should consist of coarse and for the most part Siliceous sand, Sandstone, also enclosing fossils, would eventuate. But to me, the material of which the deposit exhibited consists, and which encloses the well-preserved remains of Mollusca, is of more special interest, as this is the third time that such a formation has come under my observation, and I have studied one of these deposits with some care, as it proved to be, for the most part, made up of the Siliceous skeletons of Diatomaceæ, to the consideration of which, both recent and fossil, I have devoted many years. It is well known to Microscopists that the late Prof. W. Gregory had, in the year 1855, described what he had called a "Post-Tertiary Lacustrine Sand," containing Diatomaceous exuvia, from Glenshira, near Inverary, in Scotland. This sand contained the remains of both marine and fresh-water species of Diatomaceæ, which mixture has resulted from the fact that the spot in which it was formed, although a fresh water lake, was at times subject to the incursion of the water of the adjoining Loch Fine; perhaps during the high tides of spring and autumn. Prof. Gregory considered that the land had been raised since the formation of the deposit he examined, and such may have been the case. However this may be, we have in our own country a very similar deposit, which has been forming doubtless for many years. This is the mud brought up from the bottom of Mystic Pond, near Boston, Massachusetts. This has been examined by Messrs. Stodder and Greenleaf, and found to contain the remains of both marine and fresh-water Diatomaceæ. The forms they found are enumerated in the Proceedings of the Boston Society of Natural History. In this case the opening of the pond has a bar across it which prevents the ingress of salt water under ordinary circumstances. During high tides, however, the water of the Bay creeps up the Mystic River and flowing beneath the fresh water ot the stream itself, runs over into the bed of the pond, so thar it is said to carry with it marine forms of life which remain, become acclimated, so to speak, and flourish at the bottom of the excavation. So it is well known that the salt wate creeps up beneath the fresh of the Hudson River, and at West Point certainly a mixture of forms are to be seen. Doubtless it was in this way that *Baccillaria paradoxa*, a brackish Diatom, had made its way up to Fishkill, for there he had gathered it someway out of the Hudson and up Fishkill Creek, in a perfectly healthy condition and lively in its movements.

But the deposit exhibited by Prof. Martin is of a different character from any of those mentioned, and doubtless contains the remains of marine species only. Several years since a friend, residing in South Brooklyn, called my attention to the fact that at a point at Gowanus where the streets had, during the extension of the city, been built of refuse stone across a portion of a former marsh or estuary, that a considerable amount of the heavy superincumbent material had sunk down, crowding up along its side, the ancient bed of the marsh. This inverted material was suspected to contain the remains of Diatomaceæ and examination by means of the microscope revealed the fact that such was the case. But visiting the locality, it was found that a miniature chain of mountains had been raised for many feet along the line of two of the streets and the raised material being split open along its ridge revealed the stratification of the ancient marsh-bed. At top there was the gravel or new material which had lately been brought to the spot. Below this was a kind of peat consisting of the matted roots mainly of *Zostera Marina*, beneath which was a stratum of a light, greyish colored substance consisting almost entirely of Diatomaceous exuvia. Farther down was a layer of littoral shells, oysters, clams and the like, whilst the whole was underlaid by the coarse, sea-shore gravel common along the coast. At some future time the results of the examination of this deposit by means of the microscope will be made public. At the back of the town of Hoboken, N. J., is a brackish marsh which has been for years a favorite hunting-ground for microscopic-object hunters. Ever since the finding of the Gowanus deposit I have expect- to see the same process of inversion of this marsh take place. Within this winter I have observed that streets have been extended from Hoboken across this marsh and in one place a crowding up has taken place and a material very similar in appearance to that found at Gowanus brought to light. All of these cases of marsh inversion are of interest to geologists, and the opportunities they present the microscopist of obtaining specimens for study makes them doubly attractive. The Hoboken and the Cape Henlopen specimens will be examined and reported upon hereafter.

MR. JAS. HYATT made some remarks on the Occurrence of some Plants in the vicinity of New York city. The Cotton Thistle, *Onopordon*, may be found at Fishkill Landing, on the Hudson River, a short distance from the Rail-road Station, at the office of the Iron Works. He was able to secure flowers there for Dr. Torrey's collection. The plant has maintained itself there for several years.

Gentiana Quinqueflora abounds in South-Eastern Dutchess County and, from thence, he was able to furnish, for Dr. Torrey's collection, the only specimens from this State. *Viola rotundifolia* abounds at Weehawken, N. J., at the foot of the Palisades, West of the Ferry dock.

The following paper was read.

How far is Smoke transported by the Wind?

BY F. COLLINGWOOD.

On the morning of Friday, October 6th, I left New York for Elmira on the express train of the Erie road. A severe rain-storm prevailed in the city, but we passed out of it before reaching the summit between the Delaware and Susquehanna rivers, and at Susquehanna station the sun was shining. Soon after passing Binghamton however (the next station west of Susquehanna) I noticed a dense cloud in the west, having the curtain like appearance so common in heavy thunder showers.

To my astonishment, as the cloud approached close to us we met instead of rain, dense masses of smoke which were hurled along by a strong wind until they completely covered the landscape; so that hills a mile distant were absolutely invisible.

We rode in this smoke all the way to Elmira; and it did not leave there until about 8 P. M., when the wind veered to about N. N. W. and soon cleared it entirely away.

I made such inquiries as I could during my short stay; and learned the following additional facts.

A gentleman in the train preceding me, met the smoke about 40 miles west of Binghamton at 3½ P. M. or about one hour previous to its reaching Binghamton. At Elmira it made its appearance about 3 P. M. with a cool, strong, westerly wind.

There were no fires (as far as I could learn) in the woods of the vicinity; and yet the smoke was more dense than I have ever seen it, with the woods burning in plain sight of the valley.

The wind at Elmira was southerly in the morning; and thermometer at 75° to 80°.

The barometer was as follows:

9 A. M. 28·74 inches. 6 P. M. 28·84. 9 P. M. 29 in.

The thermometer at 9 P. M. 55°. These figures are not exact, as the instruments were not first class; and observations were roughly made. The fact is certain, however, that the smoke was traveling eastward at the rapid rate of nearly 40 miles per hour; that it was preceded by a high thermometer and low barometer; that at the time of its appearance there was a rapid change of wind, with a great increase of force; and that as it disappeared the barometer rose, the thermometer fell; and the wind changing still farther, gradually died out.

Now this area of low barometer occupied nearly the entire day (morning till night) in passing over Elmira, and was no doubt central near there about the time of the smoke appearing.

By the "weather report" of that day (Friday at 1 A. M.) I learn as follows:

"The low barometer which was Wednesday night over Wisconsin moved rapidly eastward, and is now central north of Lake Erie, extending probably over a large region. Extensive forest fires still continue in Upper Michigan and Minnesota."

On the morning of Saturday, Oct. 7th, the report says; "The area of lowest pressure has advanced since Thursday afternoon from the lower lakes to the East Atlantic. Smoky and clear weather from Tennessee to Lake Ontario, and extending southeastward. An area of remarkably dense smoke. exists at Washington, with fresh northwest winds."

Taking all these circumstances into account, I think that the conclusion is almost inevitable that the smoke at Washington and Elmira had traveled from the region of the extensive fires in Michigan; and the total distance passed over before dissipation was at least 650 miles; and probably considerably more.

This is greater than any distance I remember to have seen recorded.

I have omitted mention of the prevailing winds west of Elmira as I have not had the leisure to look up the reports.

November 27th, 1871.

PROF. B. N. MARTIN, Vice-President, in the chair Twenty-one persons present.

DR. L. FEUCHTWANGER, presented a specimen of **Infusorial Earth,** said to come from **Nevada,** and reported to occur in immense quantities. The exact locality has not been, as yet, ascertained. It is quite white and much more friable than otherwise similar samples from that region.

PROF. H. WURTZ said the exhibition of the present specimen gave him an opportunity of asking the chemists present whether they had observed that any of the Silica present in these Infusorial Earths was soluble, also whether, as was reported of this specimen, they contained Lime?

It had been remarked that they could be used as fertilizers and if they contained Lime and soluble Silica they could be so used, as both of these substances would be of use for growing crops.

Prof. A. M. Edwards replied that the present specimen was only another example of the extensive Sub-Plutonic deposits spreading over our western country, the mode of formation of which he had fully described a short time since before this society. He had examined the present specimen by means of the microscope, and found it to be made up entirely of the siliceous remains of fresh water Diatomaceæ; as is the case with all of these deposits. With regard to the solubility of the Silica present in these deposits, he would remark that several years since, when investigating the mode of formation of guano and the role that the siliceous organisms therein present played in the act of the fertilization of plants, he had made a series of experiments which he would briefly allude to. First, it must be remembered, that we have no thoroughly reliable chemical analysis of any of these, so-called, "Infusorial Earths," so that we can not say for certain that the skeletons of the Diatomaceæ consist of Silica alone; it may be a Silicate. But he had found that when pure water was made to percolate several times through such an earth, that the earth lost in weight; something was dissolved. At first he thought there might be a soluble Silicate present normally, but this idea was negatived by subsequent investigations and he came to the conclusion that the water on evaporation (for it always evaporates even at a point as low as 32° F.) formed, with the Nitrogen of the air Ammonia or Ammonium, and that a soluble Ammonium Silicate was formed. This was the mode in which he supposed the Silica was dissolved and appropriated by such plants as the Grasses which require Silica for the formation of their tissues. He was subsequently pleased to find that Schönbein had demonstrated that whenever water evaporated in contact with the air that Ammonia is formed. And it had also been shown that Siliceous sand and rock is disintegrated and dissolved by moist organic matters. The existence of an Ammonium Silicate he believes has not hitherto been asserted.

The REV. J. T. GULICK presented a specimen of a **Snake,** from San Jose, California, where they are found during the winter when the fields are converted into sloughs by continuous rains.

PROF. A. M. EDWARDS exhibited two fine specimens of **Crystallized Emeralds,** from the celebrated mines at Muzo, north of Santa Fe de Bogota. They showed the characteristic enclosing Black Limestone. He also exhibited several **Butterflies,** from the same part of the world. Remarking on the brilliant colors of most of these specimens, especially those possessing a metal-like sheen, he said that he had seen in a late number of the Canadian Entomologist that some dishonest dealers in Insects had **dyed specimens** of **Lepidoptera** with the Analine colors. He had experimented on this subject and exhibited specimens of *Danais Archippus* dyed of various colors, and suggested that a knowledge of the fact that they may be thus readily colored might be turned to a useful and honest account, and ornamental objects obtained for the use of florists as it was now the fashion to attach to boquets of natural flowers, and apparently hovering over them dried specimens of butterflies. By the use of the Analine dyes, the tint of the insect might be made to correspond with that of the prevailing flower.

The following paper was read.

Report on Meteorology for the month of November, 1871.

BY PROF. O. W. MORRIS.

Barometer, Mean, 29·882 inches, Max., 30·374 on the 13th, Min., 29·308 on the 15th, Range, 1·066.

Thermometer, Mean, 41·81°, Max., 63·4 on the 1st, Min., 15·0 on the 30th, Range, 48·4.

Rel. Humidity, Max., 96.5° on the 15th, Min., 16·4 on the 5th, Range, 80·1.

Prevailing wind, N. W. 14·3 days mean, Rain, 4·79 inches, 7 days rain, 2 days snow, 1 day sleet.

Aurora Borealis on the 9th, grandly beautiful.

Lunar corona on the 22d, bright.

Lunar halo on the 23d, large, a slight haze.

The mean temperature for Nov., 1871, was higher than during the ten years preceding.

December 4th, 1872.

PROF. T. EGLESTON, Vice-President, in the chair. Twenty persons present.

The Corresponding Secretary announced the death of Sir Roderick I. Murchison, Honorary Member of the Society.

Dr. L. FEUCHTWANGER exhibited a specimen of **Copper Pyrites** and **Plumbago in Gneiss,** from Alabama. The Chairman announced the discovery of **Calomel and Native Mercury in Panama.**

PROF. H. WURTZ made some remarks on the **Streak of Calomel.** The streak of native Calomel is white, whilst that of artificial Calomel is yellow.

DR. I. WALZ made some remarks on the **Supposed existence of Tin Ores** in various parts of **the United States.** He said that he had lately seen specimens which it was claimed established the existence of Tin in Utah; but such was not the case.

THE CHAIRMAN made some remarks on this subject, showing how often the occurrence of Tin in the United States had been falsely reported.

Prof. D. S. Martin exhibited some **Silver Images from Nicaragua**, which Mr. Squier recognized as of modern origin; being very commonly used as votive offerings.

The following paper was read, and the various apparatus mentioned in it, exhibited.

Description of a new form of Achromatic Prism for illuminating Microscopic Objects.

By Prof. A. M. Edwards.

It is my intention, at the present time to merely describe the form of apparatus I have contrived for the purpose of illuminating microscopic objects so as to bring out certain details not otherwise readily made evident, whilst I leave for some future time the consideration of the results arrived at in special cases. For the information of those microscopical observers who are interested in examining the so-called "Test objects," and also as of interest to students of the Diatomaceæ, I must mention that a year or more before Mr. Hartnack published his paper on the structure of the shell of *Surrirella gemma*, wherein he states (and gives figures to prove his assertion) that he resolved the markings on that hitherto considered difficult test, into "elongated hexagons," I had satisfactorily made out for myself, and shown to others, who agreed with me, that the markings consisted of equilateral hexagons, after the manner of those seen on *Tricertium favus*, but which could be made to appear "elongated" by a change of focus or mode of illumination. This result was achieved by using a contrivance similar to that I am about to describe in this paper. To make this paper fully understood it would be desirable to enter somewhat into the consideration of the illumination of transparent, finely-sculptured objects generally on the stage of the microscope, but it is too vast a subject to be treated of properly within the scope of a communication like the present. I must, therefore, confine myself to saying something historical in the form of an introduction, so as to show the steps by means of which I was led to the construction of my achromatic prism.

As a beginner in microscopy, I, like many others, I presume, was not blessed with a superabundance of money or, at least, not sufficient to keep pace with my enthusiasm. The consequence was that I very soon found that I did not see all that I desired to see or that evidently could be seen had I possessed ampler appliances in the shape of lenses or apparatus. Lenses, as magnifiers, were beyond my reach, so that I determined to do the best I could with those I had, and to assist them to the best of my ability by superadding such contrivances for illumination as I could, myself, construct. As the stand I owned had no means of swinging the mirror to one side and thereby making the illuminating beam impinge at an oblique angle upon the lower surface of the slide, I devised a means of converging the almost parallel rays of the sun from all sides upon the object and thus getting oblique light or, in case of need, cutting it off from all but one portion of the field for the same purpose. To do this, I purchased for a few cents and used a simple plano-convex lens of short focus and, to fix and centre it in the middle of my rigid stage, I cemented it by its plane side, and with Canada Balsam, to the lower surface of an ordinary glass microscope slide of the usual dimensions of three inches by one. On the upper surface of such a slide the glass bearing the object rested. A description with illustrating figures, of this simple contrivance I sent to the London Quarterly Journal of Microscopical Science in 1857, and it was published therein, Vol. v, page 110. The idea, however, of such an illuminator did not entirely originate with me, but had been taken from the perusal of a paper by Dr. John Charles Hall, "On an easy method of viewing certain of the Diatomaceæ," in the same periodical Vol. iv, page 205. Dr. Hall employed a hemispherical lens used plane side up and with a dark stop cutting off the central rays. My contrivance was much cheaper, could be made at home, and permitted the use of unilateral illuminating rays. For a long time this simple illuminator answered extremely well, so much so, that by means of it, and

PROCEEDINGS

OF THE

LYCEUM OF NATURAL HISTORY

IN THE

CITY OF NEW YORK.

SECOND SERIES.

January 6th, 1873.

Dr. B. N. Martin in the chair. Sixteen persons present.

This being the monthly meeting, most of the time was occupied with business of the Society.

The following gentlemen, on recommendation of the Committee on Nominations, were proposed, and elected, as resident members: Dr. Adolph Ott, James Gallatin, Jr., Theodore L. Mead, and George M. Wilber.

There was read by title the following paper, published in the Annals, Vol. X, No. 9: "On the lingual dentition of Gæotis," by T. Bland and W. G. Binney.

Mr. Collingwood made some remarks on the recent prevalence of fires, and suggested that under certain circumstances, such as long exposure to a slight degree of heat, in connection perhaps with peculiar atmospheric conditions, wood may acquire great combustibility, so as to ignite even at temperatures lower than 212° F. He illustrated this idea by citing several peculiar instances.

Prof. Seely, in commenting on these remarks, referred to the great combustibility of charcoal prepared at a low temperature, as compared with that made at a greater heat.

January 13th.

The President, Dr. Newberry, in the chair. Thirty persons present.

The following paper was read.

Chemical and Mycological Examination of the Blood and Urine of Diseased Horses during the late Epizootic.

By Herman Endemann, Ph. D.

It will be remembered, that at the end of September, 1872, a disease of an epizoötic character made its appearance in Canada, whence it spread rapidly over the whole Union, and thence to adjoining southern countries. At the beginning of April, 1873, reports were received, that it continued its journey towards Central America, and that many towns of Mexico were infected.

The first cases were found in New York on the 19th of October, 1872; in a few days nine-tenths of all the horses in the city were affected.

The main symptoms were, coughing, discharge of a purulent mucus from the nostrils, and extreme prostration, increasing with the time of affection. The discharge of urine was considerably impaired. Post-mortem examinations showed, that the bronchiæ were also filled with the same purulent mucus which flowed from the nostrils; and in many cases, the lungs and kidneys were found to be considerably affected.

The samples of blood and urine which I examined, were mostly taken from sick animals, which were killed at the dock of the New York Rendering Company. Extreme care was taken in the cleaning and disinfection of the glass jars used for the reception of these samples, as with them not only a chemical but also a mycological examination was to be undertaken.

The blood was in all cases dark colored, even if drawn from the aorta or the carotid arteries. It was uniformly found to contain a large excess of extractive matter and fat, which might have been caused by an inactivity of such organs as the kidneys or lungs, by an excessive decomposition or fermentation of healthy blood-constituents in the blood itself, or by an over-abundant action of the liver.

Venous blood is always richer in extractive and fatty matters; the purification, however, which it undergoes in the above-named organs, removes them again, so that arterial blood contains these substances only in very minute proportions, as compared with the results obtained in this examination.

It is also remarkable that this increase, especially in extractive matter, was more marked in proportion to the time which had elapsed between the first attack and the period when the animal was killed. I assume here, that most of the animals were attacked at about the same time.

The amounts of fat and extractive matter found in 1000 parts of the blood of different animals were, on

Oct. 30th,	23·1
Nov. 2d,	15·1
" 5th,	70·6
" 16th,	98·1

The following tabulated statement gives the results obtained, as compared with the composition of normal horse blood, these figures being the average of a number of well-authenticated analyses. Horse No. 5 had recovered from the epizoötic, but was sick at the time with a secondary stage of the disease (dropsy), which manifested itself during the middle of November in numerous cases throughout the city.

1 Normal blood.
2 Horse killed at the Rendering Dock, Oct. 30th.
3 " " " " " Nov. 2d.
4 " " " " " Nov. 5th.
5 " " " " " Nov. 16th.

1000 pts. of blood contain:

	1	2	3	4	5
	Arterial.	Average samples.		Arterial.	
Fibrin,	6·6	8·4	4·3	15·5	4·1
Blood corpuscles & albumen,	202·0	160·2	214·8	121·3	110·0
Fat,	0·8	5·4	3·2	70·6	3·7
Extractive matter,	2·9	17·7	11·9		94·4
Salts,	7·7	6·8	7·7	7·1	8·6
Total solids,	210·0	177·9	241·9	214·5	220·8
Water,	790·0	822·1	758·1	785·5	779·2

The qualitative examination of the extractive matter showed, that it was largely composed of the constituents of bile and urine.

Urine.—I have unfortunately not been able to secure so many samples of urine as were desirable for a thorough examination.

In many cases the bladders of the killed animals were empty, or their contents were so scanty, that I could not be supplied. The urine obtained was in all cases more or less turbid. That of the horse killed on Nov. 5th, was particularly rich in albumen and oxalate of lime.

The urine of horses during convalescence, loses first the albumen and afterwards the oxalate of lime. According to some authors, oxalate of lime is of common occurrence in the urine of healthy herbivora; but the fact that a decrease was plainly visible during the time of convalescence, shows that even if this be so, its quantity was considerably increased in the period of sickness.

On Nov. 16th, I received the urine of the horse which had been killed on that date, while suffering from the secondary stage of the disease. It contained some oxalate of lime, but no albumen. It was so rich in mucus, that it was of a gelatinous consistence. The short duration of the disease, and the lateness of the date when the investigation commenced, made a more thorough examination impossible; and I only hope, that the points lacking in this investigation will be covered by the researches and observations of others, who

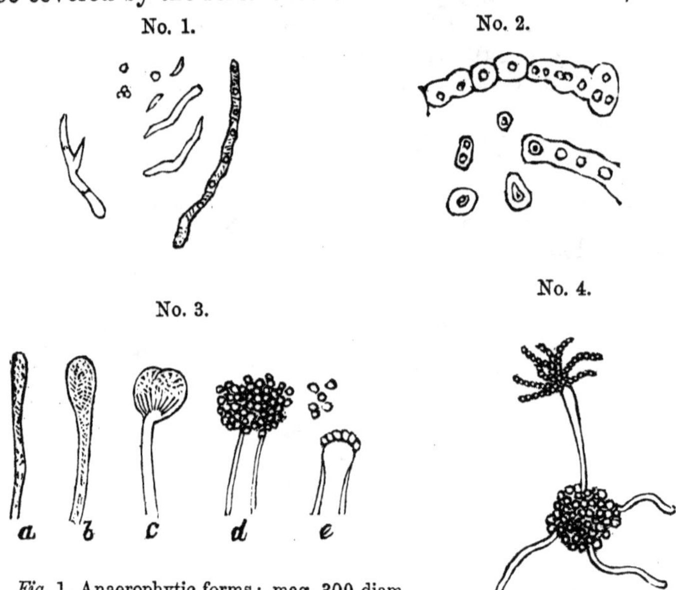

Fig. 1, Anaerophytic forms; mag. 300 diam.
Fig. 2, the same; mag. 2000 diam.
Fig. 3, *a*, *b*, *c*, *d*, *e*. Aerophytic forms, as raised upon lemon-peel, 120 diam
Fig. 4. Development of *Fig.* 3 *d* upon surface of sugar solution: 120 diam.

waiting for the arrival of the disease, have had more time to prepare themselves.

The mycological investigation resulted in the growth of a fungus, the anaerophytic and aerophytic forms of which are given in the accompanying engravings. Experiments to convert this fungus, under changed circumstances, into others representing other families, were unsuccessful, the cells failing to develop.

The only thing accomplished, was a slight variation in growth, the more or less vigorous development corresponding to the richness in nourishing substances, of the objects upon which the fungus was grown.

The same fungus was obtained from the blood and the urine of three different horses; whether its presence, however, was cause or consequence of the disease, I will not venture to decide.

Dr. Charles Am Ende, of Hoboken, N. J., on the invitation of the President, made the following remarks:

After the full and valuable statements of my friend, Dr. Endemann, but little remains for me to say: this, however, bears mainly on the botanical investigations, and on some general physiological deductions.

The material for my examinations was collected, with all necessary precautions, from several sick horses in different stables in and around the city. It consisted of the discharges running from the nostrils of the horses; and these were kept and examined separately.

In addition to more or less decomposed cells of various membranes, all the discharges contained a great abundance of minute globules, finely dotted, varying in size from $\frac{1}{50}$ to $\frac{1}{100}$ of a millimeter. These globules are apparently organized bodies, cells, belonging to the series of forms of some fungus, probably allied to Uredo, growing upon certain grasses or leaves. For some time, I was doubtful as to their nature; but from the results of cultivation in several experiments, and from the process of development as therein observed, I came to this conclusion.

These cells ("spores") are covered, when young, by a cuticle, which becomes nearly or wholly re-absorbed where they grow under certain conditions.

In cultivation, the cuticle remains well distinguishable, and the development of micrococcus within it is less luxuriant. The richness of the food offered to the fungi, on the mucous membranes of affected horses, and by the other fluids of the body, the abundance of moisture, and the high and equal temperature, all lessen the tendency to secrete a thick cuticle; and the whole vital power is thrown instead into reproduction. Micrococcus and sporoids are formed in large quantities, and both will reproduce the fungi spores in a comparatively short time.

Among various observations, I would refer to the fact that one cultivation of micrococcus resulted in a penicillium, and another produced *Tilletia* spores. The particulars of the development in these cases, and the general results of the cultivation, I would prefer to reserve until a fuller account can be presented.

The presence of these spores* in all the discharges, as well as on the mucous membranes, and even in all the fluids of the body, the blood, urine, etc., so far as investigated, revives another question. It has often been asked, whether such organic growths are the consequence of the diseases which they accompany, or their cause. Mycologists, naturally, and many medical gentlemen, incline to the latter belief. A large number of physicians, on the other hand, many of them of very high standing, take the opposite view.

In the case of the potato disease, in Europe, it has been conclusively proved that it is caused by the spores of the *Peronospora infestans;* and for the grape disease, that it is caused by an *Erisyphe.*

I mention these few instances, out of many, to show that in cases of diseases or of epidemics among plants, it has been proved that they are caused by the growth of certain fungi. The same holds good for a large number of epidemics on animals of the lower orders. As examples, the pernicious influence of the micrococcus of *Ascophora elegans*, on bees; of *Fumago salicina*, on the worms of the pine-spinner, and of *Empusa* on flies, may be mentioned.

It appears, then, that for the lower orders of organisms, where the material is abundant and can be gathered without too much expense, the theory has been proved; for the higher orders of animals, where the material is expensive, the acceptance of the theory is refused.

It is certainly a singular coincidence that in the case, for instance, of the Texan cattle disease, so ably investigated by Professors Stiles and Harris, a micrococcus was found in large quantities, which produced a singular fungus, the *Philolobus.*

* Though the term "spores" is not strictly correct, it may serve for the time best to convey the idea.

In the case of pox among sheep, a micrococcus was detected, which produced at last the *Tilletia lolii*, a fungus which occurs on the different species of Lolium in Europe. In cholerine of the human subject, a micrococcus was found in the stools, which gave, when cultivated, the *Tilletia caries;* and the stools in Asiatic cholera contain a micrococcus which produces, under culture the *Urocyotis oryzœ.* I may here point by the way, to the singular relation existing between the *Tilletia caries* and the *Urocystis oryzœ*, and to the conclusions drawn therefrom by Prof. Hallier.*

It is evident that the establishment of this theory would be of the utmost importance. It would furnish a scientific basis for methods both of cure and of prevention, and it would show how it is that epidemics repeat themselves. The general loss by the recent epizoötic, has been large enough to awaken interest; and the facilities for carrying out such researches are perhaps greater in the United States than anywhere else. With Dr. Endemann, I should wish that the investigation may be taken up by others, to correct what little we have found, and to improve upon it.

In the belief that these fungi might prove to be the causes of the epizoötic, a series of experiments was undertaken to ascertain the action of certain well-known chemical agents upon them, with the following results. Carbolic acid, and the sulphates of iron, zinc, and quinine, were found to arrest

---

* The facts alluded to, which are of much interest, and perhaps but little known save to mycologists, may be summed up as follows:—

The spores of Tilletia caries, which grows very abundantly in Germany upon the leaves of wheat, produce under cultivation several sub-generations, which were long regarded as distinct species and genera, especially Penicillium crustaceum, Mucor racemosus, and Achlya,—of course under different conditions of life. These are all open-air (aerophytic) forms. If the spores of these, or of the Tilletia, are placed in liquids, they again produce different forms, as Cryptococcus cerevisiæ, present in all alcoholic fermentations, Oidium lactis, found in the fermentation of milk, etc. The spores of all these reproduce, in our climate, the original Tilletia.

The spores of Urocystis oryzæ, which is a characteristic parasite upon the East India rice-plant, as its name implies, will produce these same subgenerations when cultivated in like manner; but from the spores of these latter, at a temperature in the medium not higher than 85,° the Tilletia is reproduced instead of the parent Urocystis.

The stools of diarrhœa in its milder forms, as cholerine, etc., contain large quantities of micrococcus which will produce Tilletia, but not Urocystis. The latter is developed in the case of true cholera. That is to say, in the lighter forms of diarrhœal diseases, we find the micrococcus of the Northern fungus; while in the deadly Eastern type, we have that of the parasite on Indian rice. Wheat, we know, is indigenous in Asia; formerly the Urocystis may have grown on it, or perhaps a mother-fungus of both this and the Tilletia; but during long cultivation in a Northern climate, the fungus may have changed in the energy of its physiological action.

the vibrating motions of the micrococcus immediately. Sulphate of copper does the same, and also destroys the "spores." Hypermanganate of potassa imparts a straw-like color to the fungi, while its own solution is discolored immediately upon contact with them.

In accordance with these results, I selected, for further experiment, two horses in different stables, both of them strongly affected with the disease, and each standing by the side of another horse in a like condition. A solution of sulphate of copper (one or two grains to four oz. distilled water) was then applied; a teaspoonful was injected into the nostrils, and about the same dose was given on the top of some moist feed. Each horse also received two drachms of sulphate of quinine, in half-drachm doses, morning and night. Within 24 hours a marked change took place; and both animals recovered fully eight days sooner than the others that were not thus treated. Finally, as it might be possible that some of the exhaled micrococcus should attach itself to the stable walls, grow there, and thence respread the complaint, it was ordered that the stables should be thoroughly whitewashed with a strong solution of chloride of lime.

I am well aware that these two cases alone can not be accepted as a sufficient proof for the correctness of the theory, or of its application to the recent horse epidemic; but the facts as here given deserve, perhaps, more attention than they have as yet received.

PROF. LEEDS, of the Stevens Institution of Technology, read a note "on the Volumetric Determination of Chlorine with standard silver solution and potassic chromate."*

DR. I. WALZ made a preliminary notice of the potassium salt of what he judged to be a new acid, which he had obtained by the simultaneous action of picric and pyrogallic acid on potassium cyanate.

The Secretary read a paper by DR. O. W. MORRIS, on the meteorology of the month of December, 1872. The month was remarkable for its changeableness, its general low temperature, and the large amount of snow that fell in a single storm. The range for the whole month was 41°, and the mean 28·86°, a lower average, by a little over five degrees,

* Since published in the American Chemist, for February, 1873.

than that for the Decembers of ten years before, which had been 33·88°, and lower than that of any December during that period, save those of 1867, when the mean was 28°, and 1868, when it was 28·11°. Snows, generally light, fell on eleven days; but on the 26th it fell to the depth of two feet. The quantity of water, from rain and melted snow, was 4·53 inches for the month.

The barometer ranged from 30·436 inches on the 25th, to 29·495 inches on the 26th, a difference of ·941 inch in thirty-eight hours.

The prevailing winds were westerly. Lunar coronas were noted on the nights of the 9th, 11th and 13th, and lunar halos on those of the 11th and 17th.

The total number of deaths in the city during the month was 2243, or an average of 72·35 daily, of these, 906, a daily average of 29·2, were children under five years of age. The chief causes of death were diseases of the lungs.

January 20th.

The President, Dr. Newberry, in the chair. Sixteen persons present.

Prof. Newberry exhibited a series of quartz pebbles and bowlders, obtained by him from bituminous clays associated with the lignite beds of the Cretaceous formation at Keyport, New Jersey. All of these, which had been angular fragments of quartz rock, gave evidence of having been exposed to the action of some chemical solvent, as all their angles were rounded, the surfaces smooth as though artificially polished, or pitted in a peculiar way. This singular appearance was attributed by Dr. Newberry to the solvent power of humus on silica. These pebbles and bowlders occur along certain lines in the clays, and were evidently floated and dropped on what was then a stratum of bituminous mud that formed the bottom of an estuary or lagoon. The clays contain so much carbonaceous matter, as to be almost black, and in certain of the strata we find great quantities of lignite derived from coniferous wood. Numerous cones occur in the lignite beds, and occasionally leaf-bearing twigs are found. The cones belong to the genus *Geinitzia*, and some of the branches apparently represent the genus *Ulmania.*

Enveloped in this vast amount of vegetable matter, the fragments of quartz referred to seem to have been very much corroded by the humic acid generated in its decomposition.

PROF. D. S. MARTIN exhibited a number of Primordial fossils, from Troy, N. Y., some of which are newly described, and made some remarks upon the mode of their occurrence. The recent exploration of these beds, and the discovery of several new species, are due to Mr. S. W. Ford, of Troy (from whom the specimens shown had been received); though the locality had been known for many years, to some extent, and species had been described from it in the State Palæontology. These, however, were supposed to be of Hudson age, and their true horizon has only of late been determined. The rocks occur in a series of ridges, with a slight eastward dip, and a strike about parallel to the Hudson river, on the elevated plateau immediately east of the city of Troy. They consist of sandstones and shales, with intercalated beds of limestone, in which latter the fossils are found. Whether the several parallel ridges, with their similar dip and strike, are due to faults, or to sharp eroded folds, Mr. Ford has not been able to satisfy himself, owing to the drift which occupies the intervening depressions.

The species exhibited comprised Agnostus lobatus and Olenellus asaphoides among trilobites, Obolella desquamata, Metoptoma rugosa, and the following pteropods, Hyolithes (Theca) triangularis, and its operculum, H. impar, Ford, (new), and Hyolithellus micans, Billings, (also new) with opercula. The latter in this species are perfectly circular in outline, and not oval, as they were represented in the figures which accompanied the original description. They are extremely well-defined and characteristic, with their peculiar muscular impression, resembling an eight-pointed star, the four upper rays curving upward, and the four lower ones downward. Prof. Martin gave other particulars of his visit to this locality, which had added nothing, however, to what had previously been described by Mr. Ford, whose labors have revealed one of the best Primordial localities in the eastern states, and given us several new and valuable species from that most interesting horizon.

Dr. R. P. Stevens also made some remarks on this deposit.

The Salina Group.

The President exhibited a series of specimens representing the Salina group of the Upper Silurian in the State of New York, and reported the results of recent observations on the extension of these rocks into Ohio. He said that the Salina group was composed mainly of red and green marls, or calcareous shales, with bands of sandstone and impure limestone, attaining a thickness of several hundred feet in central New York. According to his view, these sediments were deposited in an arm or reach of the sea bordered by the Canadian highlands and the Adirondacks on the north, the Blue Ridge on the east, and the Cincinnati axis on the west; and that in this area the Niagara sea was drained away so as to leave an extensive basin, to which the salt water of the ocean had imperfect access, and where by evaporation its saline constituents were concentrated and finally precipitated, with such earthy sediments as were derived from the wash of the surrounding shores.

On its western margin the Salina group had been traced to a "feather edge" on the flanks of the Cincinnati axis, and in Ohio it diminishes from a thickness of 40 or 50 feet, including several layers of gypsum, about Sandusky, to a thickness of 12 feet at Tiffin, and 1 foot at Moore's Mills. We have here proof that the sea-level in the Salina period was considerably lower than in either the preceding Niagara or the succeeding Helderberg epoch. Prof. Newberry also stated that so far as his observation had extended, the gypsum of the Salina is stratified, and had been precipitated in sheets as a sediment, and not formed by any local change of carbonate of lime. The salt wells of Salina are sunk not in the rocks of the Salina group, but in the gravel and sand which fills a trench cut more than 400 feet deep along the outcrop of the formation. This trench, or buried channel, was evidently an ancient water-course, and one of an extensive series of buried river-channels that were formed when the continent stood much higher above the ocean, than it does now. The salt water which saturates the drift that fills the old river-bed at Salina, flows out of the Salina group; and since it is nearly a saturated solution, it must be formed by the dissolving away of masses of salt which lie somewhere in the formation, either as beds of rock-salt or as disseminated crystals, in all probability the former, and though these have not yet been discovered, we may nevertheless feel almost certain of their existence, as the source of the brines.

He also alluded to Dr. Goessman's theory of the deposition of salts, by which an explanation may be given of the remarkable local differences in the brines, as a result of the different solubility of various contained salts. In the evaporation of a body of water of this kind, there will be a series of precipitations: first, the less soluble gypsum; second, the salt; third, the calcic and magnesic chlorides ("bitters"). It thus becomes possible to trace the deeper and shallower parts of such an ancient sea or lagoon. In a series of connected basins, produced by irregularities of the bottom, those that lay highest would contain only or mainly gypsum; those next below, gypsum mingled with salt, etc., while the last and lowest basins would have an excess of the "bitters," retained as long as possible in the evaporating water. We have a marked instance of such local differences in the salt wells at Goderich, Ontario, which also belong to this formation. The salt here is in some cases so pure as to contain 98 per cent. of sodic chloride, with scarcely any admixture of "bitters," while in the immediate vicinity are other wells in which these latter salts are found in excess.

Dr. R. P. Stevens remarked, in regard to the ancient trough or channel spoken of by Dr. Newberry, that it runs for a long distance through the State of New York, and almost all the salt-borings are made in it, as they are at Lake Onondaga, just now described. It runs along the northern edge of the Salina group, and seems to have been worn in its soft outcrop.

January 27th.

The severity of the storm prevented the meeting from being held.

February 3d, business meeting.

Dr. L. Feuchtwanger in the chair.

Dr. Louis Elsberg read a paper "On the subdivisions of Science, and their classification," illustrated with charts of the distribution of different branches of human knowledge, as related to a comprehensive system. This paper is published in the Annals of the Lyceum, Vol. X., No. 10.

Dr. B. N. Martin and Dr. Walz made remarks on the scheme of classification suggested. Dr. Martin regarded it as the most complete and comprehensive that he had ever met with. The subject is of course one of much interest, and has been treated of by several writers, especially by Whewell & Thomson in England, and by Comte and Ampère in France; but in his judgment, nowhere had so comprehensive a view been combined with so much minuteness and accuracy of detail. The feature which distinguished, in every department, the history and genesis of the objects of study, under the termination *-ogeny*, from the description and arrangement of them, characterized by the ending *-ology*, seemed to him a truly happy and philosophical mode of distinction. While dissenting, in some important points, from the definition of force as given in the paper, he yet regarded the scheme as a very important and interesting contribution to our view of the relations subsisting between the departments of science.

Prof. D. S. MARTIN requested leave to postpone his paper, announced for this evening, "Additional Notes on Mr. Andrew Murray's Theory of the Geographical Distribution of Life." He made some remarks in reference to the great interest which attaches, in connection with questions of this nature, to the life of the Southern Hemisphere, especially in its remoter portions, where it may well be that alone is to be found the key to many problems that are incapable of solution here. The expeditions preparing for the observation of the coming transit of Venus, will furnish unusual opportunities for studying the fauna and flora of the Antarctic Islands; and every such opportunity should be most carefully improved. He urged that Congress should be addressed, perhaps through the Smithsonian Institution, by the scientific societies of the country, to make full and careful preparation for biological collections and observations, in connection with the fitting out of the American expedition. Though the main purpose would be astronomical, yet the occasion is too valuable in its relations to geology and natural history, to be allowed to pass without every facility being furnished for study in these departments.

On motion of Prof. SEELY, it was resolved that Prof. Martin be a committee of one, to conduct any correspondence, or make any suitable memorial to Congress, in the name of the Lyceum, on this subject.

February 10th. Chemical Section.

Dr. B. N. MARTIN in the chair. 30 persons present.

Dr. ENDEMANN read the following note; "On the action of Iodoform on Potassic Sulphydrate, by H. ENDEMANN, and OSCAR LOEW."

The reaction of potassic sulphydrate on iodoform was studied by us with the view of obtaining the proto-sulphide of carbon. This substance, however, we did not succeed in procuring.

The reaction which we anticipated was;

$$CHI_3+3KHS=3KI+CS+2H_2S.$$

After the evolution of sulphuretted hydrogen had ceased, no other gas being mixed with the sulphuretted hydrogen, the residue in the retort was examined and found to contain various substances, the exact nature of which could not, from want of material, be determined. A gray powder containing carbon and sulphur, and insoluble in ether, alcohol, or water, is probably a polymerized protosulphide. Another substance of garlick-like odor, seems to be sulpho-formic acid, in which case it would seem that the reaction had been;

$$CHI_3+3KHS=3KI+CH_2S_2+H_2S.$$

The acid is obtained in combination with potassium, as potassic sulphydrate ($CHKS_2$), which would indicate as the probable reaction;

$$CHI_3+4KHS=3KI+CHKS_2+2H_2S.$$

One of us having left the city for some time, we have not thus far, been able to repeat the experiments on a scale sufficiently large, to obtain more light on this reaction.

DR. LOEW gave an account of his chemical examination of the peculiar red liquid obtained by Dr. Habel from the cave of the Fuente de Sangre, or blood-spring, of Honduras.* Reviewing all its chemical reactions, he concluded that it could not arise from any excrementitious matter of bats, as had been suggested; but it corresponds almost perfectly with the behavior of the aqueous extract of rhatany (*Krameria triandra*, DeC.). This plant is a native of Peru, and is used as an astringent in pharmacy. *K. Ixina* is a closely related West Indian species; and the presumption seems quite strong that this red liquid arises simply from the drainage of water through the roots of some species of rhatany growing above the cavern.

* This communication has appeared in full in the Scientific American.

The subject was further discussed by Mr. E. GEORGE SQUIER, who referred to another similar spring in San Salvador, in which he was strongly convinced that the liquid does arise from the excrement of bats.

DR. ENDEMANN remarked that Dr. Habel had made no reference to bats as having been seen at the Honduras spring.

MR. F. COLLINGWOOD read a paper on Combustion in Compressed Air.*

The paper was announced rather as a series of notes, than as a statement of positive results. The caissons of the East River bridge gave remarkable facilities for experiment; but the observations obtained have been rather incidental, than the result of systematic tests. The disengagement of large amounts of unconsumed carbon, in the form of smoke, etc., was early found to cause so much inconvenience, that experiments were set on foot for the purpose of obviating it. Col. Paine, of the engineering staff, was the first to engage in this work, using different kinds of oil, ordinary candles, and adamantine "coach" candles, 1¼ inch diameter. In all cases, increased consumption resulted from increased pressure; the most careful tests, however, were with the adamantine candles, and may be tabulated thus, in their results:

No. of Experiment.	Temperature.	Absolute pressure per sq. in.	Time of consuming 1 lb. of candles.	Relative consumption.	Square root of pressure.	Ratios of sq. roots of pressure.
1	80°	Open air 15 lbs.	32 hours.	1·	3·873	1·
2	80°	23 "	27 "	1·185+	4·796	1·239
3	80°	25 "	25½ "	1·255—	5·000	1·291
4	88°	Open air 15 lbs.	28 hours.	1·	3·873	1·
5	88°	46 "	16 "	1·75	6·782	1·751

The two sets of experiments, Nos. 1 and 4, made at different temperatures, show an increased rate of consumption, as might have been anticipated in a warmer atmosphere,

* Subsequently published in full in the Journal of the Franklin Institute, Philadelphia, for May, 1873.

irrespective of pressure. Experiments 4 and 5 show an increased consumption of 75 per cent. under an increased pressure of three atmospheres.

The chief point of interest brought to view, is the close correspondence between the relative consumption and the square roots of the pressures. The series of tests was not really extensive enough to establish a definite law, but the results thus far are of much interest, as pointing to this principle.

Much may depend, however, on the capillary attraction of the wick, and therefore upon its structure. It is probably due to this cause that, in one set of experiments, conducted by Prof. Chas. A. Seely, standard candles, with small wicks, increased only 5 per cent. in consumption under a pressure of 46 lbs. On the other hand, alcohol, far lighter than the melted hydrocarbon fats, and supplied through a very open wick, gave an increase of consumption at the same pressure, of 200 per cent., or directly in proportion to the pressure. The alcohol flame under such circumstances, changes its aspect completely, becoming white and luminous, so as to give three-fourths the light of a "coach" candle.

Gas from the street-pipes was finally introduced, and employed for lighting the caisson. Here again, increased energy of combustion was noticed speedily, and much trouble was also found from smoking of the gas under advancing pressures. Six-foot "fish-tail" burners had to be abandoned for two-foot "bat-wing" ones, at 20 lbs. pressure; and at 28 lbs. these latter had to be replaced by one-foot burners of the same pattern. These were used until the close of the work, with fair results.

The paper concludes with a discussion of the theoretical conditions of this increased combustion. Conceiving a flame as the oxidation of a distilled hydrocarbon, its volume will be determined as follows:—the vapor or gas will expand until combustion goes on over its surface at precisely the same rate as the supply goes on from below. In the case of a candle, the supply depends on the heat of the flame, i. e. on the energy of combustion. Compressed air allows a greater number of oxygen atoms to combine at the surface of the flame, that is to say, gives greater energy of combustion, in proportion to the pressure; and hence will result a more rapid distillation, and a greater consumption of material.

The fact that the size of the flame is reduced by compression, does not alter this result at all, though it may modify it somewhat. The mere fact of condensation of volume would tend to increase the temperature of the flame, apart from energy of combustion. Moreover, the surface does not diminish under such condensation in proportion to the volume. If four flames have diameters as 1, 2, 3, 4, their surfaces will vary as the squares of those numbers, and their volumes as the cubes. The comparative volume of the last flame would be 4^3,=64, and its surface 4^2,=16; half that volume would be 32, but the surface of this latter flame would be much more than 8. Applying these principles to the experiments described, we may construct another table, as follows:

Absolute Pressures.	Volume of gases, by Marriotte's law.	Surfaces; obtained by taking the $\frac{2}{3}$ power of volumes.	Ratio of surfaces to corresponding volumes.
15 lbs.	1 = 1·	1·	1· : 1
23	$\frac{15}{23}$ = 0·652	0·752	1·153 : 1
25	$\frac{15}{25}$ = 0·6	0·711	1·185 : 1
46	$\frac{15}{46}$ = 0·326	0·474	1·453 : 1

Of course it is assumed in this table, that the temperature of the air does not vary, and that no other accidental circumstances affect the result.

Mr. Collingwood regretted that his observations had been necessarily so limited, on so interesting a topic, but desired to place them on record.

Prof. Seely remarked upon the paper as follows:—

The effect of varying pressure on combustion, was first investigated by Sir Humphrey Davy; and his conclusion, that increased pressure favors combustion, has been accepted without dissent, until the present time. Frankland, Deville, and others have reinvestigated the subject, but it is doubtful whether anything has been developed by them, which was not plainly foreshadowed by Davy. An interesting presentation of some of the most important facts may be found in an article by Prof. Le Conte, published about 20 years since in the American Journal of Science.

The tests with standard candles, which are alluded to by Mr. Collingwood, were made with all convenient care. Four trials were made, four burnings in the caisson and four at my laboratory. The apparent discrepancy with the coach candle trials is satisfactorily explained, if we consider that the carrying capacities of the wicks did not vary with the other conditions of the experiments.

PROF. JOY read a paper by Dr. O. W. MORRIS, on the meteorology of the month of January, 1873. The month exhibited unusual variations of temperature, the total range having been 50°; while the mean was 28·5°, a lower average than has been recorded for this month during ten years past, with the exception of 1865, 1867, and 1868, and 1·96° lower than the total average for the ten years.

The most rapid change of temperature took place between 2 P. M. of the 28th, 32°, and 7 A. M. of the 29th, 2°, a fall of 30° in fifteen hours. The highest mean for any one day was 44·33°, on the 16th, and the lowest was 7·56°, on the 29th.

The barometer ranged from 30·467 to 29·437, a difference of 1·03 inch. The mean for the month was 29·946.

The prevailing winds have been north and north-east. Snow fell on eight days. The quantity of water from rain and melted snow was 6·82 inches, an amount greater than that in any January for the past ten years. The mean relative humidity has been 67·71, full two-thirds of saturation. The air was actually saturated on the mornings of the 3d and 16th, and nearly so on those of the 24th and 27th; while on only four mornings, the 6th, 12th, 23d, & 31st, has it been less than half.

During the first fifteen days of the month the total number of deaths in the city was 1163, giving an average of 77·5 daily. 190 of these were caused by consumption, and 95 by whooping-cough, croup and diphtheria. The number of children under five years, included in the above total, was 493, a daily average of 32·8. 63 were over seventy years of age. In comparing these statistics with those for the previous month, a considerable increase is observable.

February 17th.

Dr. B. N. Martin in the chair. Fifteen persons present.

Prof. J. J. Stevenson read a paper, "On the Coals of the Kanawha Valley," published in the Annals, Vol. X, No. 10.

The subject of the Kanawha coals, and their relations to those of Pennsylvania and Ohio, was further discussed by Dr. R. P. Stevens and Prof. Stevenson.

Prof. Seely referred to some remarkably fine specimens of African copal which had lately come to his notice in the hands of importers.

Prof. D. S. Martin said that the whole subject of the copals is one of great interest. These resins seem to occur very widely and in large quantities, throughout many parts, not only of Africa, but of the Southern Hemisphere generally. They have as yet, however, received little or none of the study which they deserve. The only good account that he had ever met with, was that of Dr. Kirk, British consul at Zanzibar, from whose interesting statements in the Journal of the Linnæan Society of London, it appears that these copals are to a great extent true fossil resins, of middle post-tertiary age, what in this country we should call Champlain. Dr. Kirk finds three qualities of copal known in the trade at Zanzibar: first, the fresh resin of Trachylobium Mossambicense, a tree which grows only upon the immediate sea-coast, from 3° to 15° S. lat. This is a very inferior article, hardly exported at all. Second, the harder and better resin that is dug up in a partially fossilized state, in the same littoral regions in which the tree now flourishes. Third, the true fossil copal, forming most of that which is exported; this is found on the ancient beaches, 20 to 40 miles inland, and far from the modern habitat of this strictly shore-loving tree. There seems no question that the three varieties are all from the Trachylobium, but represent different stages of alteration. The true commercial copal, produced when the littoral tree grew at these points now so far from the sea, belongs of course to the "era of elevated beaches," corresponding to our Champlain epoch. The included insects, therefore, have a peculiar interest, as giving us remnants of the post-tertiary entomology of Eastern Africa. Prof. Martin stated that he had been giving a good deal of attention to this copal fauna, since reading Dr. Kirk's account, and hoped to lay some material in regard to it before the Lyceum at no very distant day.

With reference to the peculiar "pitted" or "goose-skin" surface which is found upon most of the pieces of copal, he stated that there had been much discussion, and but little clear result. Consul Kirk finds it occurring on the second and third of the varieties, that is to say, upon those that have lain long in the ground; but he had attributed it to the impression of grains of sand upon the buried resin, while the latter was yet soft. That such is not the cause, may be seen from the most superficial examination: the marking is perfectly regular over the whole surface, and it consists not of depressions, but of elevations. This Dr. Kirk had more recently referred to, abandoning his previous view. Prof. Martin claimed that it is due to an alteration in the structure of the resinous mass in the course of fossilization, perhaps merely a long-continued contraction, at length covering the surface with regularly intersecting systems of cracks. He had sets of specimens illustrating almost every stage of this process. A very similar, though slightly different, structure of the surface is seen in the early amber from the Cretaceous.

February 24th, 1873.

Annual Meeting.

The President in the chair. Nineteen members present.

After the organization of the meeting, and the reading of the minutes, the annual reports of the several officers and committees of the Lyceum, of which abstracts are here given, were presented and accepted.

The following appropriations were made for the year 1873–4:—

Rent of rooms,	$200.00
Insurance,	50.00
Committee on Publications,	550.00
Miscellaneous expenses,	106.00

After various discussion on minor matters of business, the society proceeded to the election of officers for the year, with the following result:

President:

John S. Newberry.

Vice-Presidents:

1st, Thomas Egleston,
2d, Henry Morton.

Corresponding Secretary:

Robert Dinwiddie.

Recording Secretary:

Robert H. Brownne.

Treasurer:

John H. Hinton.

Librarian:

BERNARD G. AMEND.

Curators:

WILLIAM J. HAYS, HENRY WURTZ,
LEWIS FEUCHTWANGER, WILLIAM H. LEGGETT,
JOHN J. STEVENSON.

Committee on Nominations:

CHARLES A. JOY, *Chairman;*
ROBERT DINWIDDIE, CHARLES A. SEELY,
BENJAMIN N. MARTIN, ALBERT H. GALLATIN.

Committee on Publications:

THOMAS BLAND, *Chairman;*
JOHN S. NEWBERRY, GEORGE N. LAWRENCE,
DANIEL S. MARTIN, H. CARRINGTON BOLTON.

Finance Committee:

BENJAMIN N. MARTIN, *Chairman;*
J. CARSON BREVOORT, D. JACKSON STEWARD.

Library Committee:

ROBERT H. BROWNNE, *Chairman;*
LOUIS ELSBERG, ORAN W. MORRIS.

Abstract of the Report of the Publication Committee.

New York, February, 1873.

The Publication Committee report that during the year commencing with March, 1872, three numbers of the Annals have been published, Nos. 6, 7, and 8 of Vol. X. Numbers 6 and 7, embracing six papers, consisted of 50 pages, with three plates, and number 8, of 32 pages, also with six papers and three plates.

The papers so published were by the following authors: viz:—Thomas Bland, Thomas Bland and W. G. Binney, Dr. P. Fischer, W. J. Hays, George N. Lawrence, Prof. Benj. N. Martin, Prof Edward S. Morse, Dr. Felipe Poey, and

Temple Prime; the subjects treated by these authors being as follows;—

By Thomas Bland;

Description of a new species of Mollusc of the genus *Helicina.*

By Thomas Bland and W. G. Binney;

On the Systematic Arrangement of North American Terrestrial Molluscs.

On the Relations of certain genera of Terrestrial Mollusca of, or related to, the Subfamily *Succinineæ*, with notes on the Lingual Dentition of *Succinea appendiculata*, Pf., with plate IX.

Description of *Hemphillia*, a new genus of Terrestrial Mollusca.

On the Lingual Dentition of certain Terrestrial Pulmonata, foreign to the United States.

By Dr. P. Fischer;

Note sur l'Anatomie des Cyrènes Americaines, with plate VIII.

By William J. Hays;

Description of a species of Cervus, with plate X.

By George N. Lawrence;

Description of New Species of Birds of the Genera *Icterus* and *Synallaxis.*

By Prof. Benj. N. Martin;

Essay upon a Necessary Limitation of the Doctrine of the Unity of the General Forces of Nature.

By Prof. Edward S. Morse;

On the Tarsus and Carpus of Birds, with plates IV. and V.

By Dr. Felipe Poey;

Monographie des Poissons de Cuba compris dans la sous-famille des Sparini, with plates VI. and VII.

By Temple Prime;

Notes on Specimens of Corbiculadæ in the cabinet of the Jardin des Plantes at Paris, and on the authorship of the Encyclopèdie Méthodique, with plate VIII.

The Committee, while referring to the unusual extent of the plates thus published, desire to record the facts that the Society has incurred no other cost than that of paper and printing for the necessary number of copies of plates IV., V., VIII. and IX.; being indebted for the drawings on stone of plates IV and V, to Prof. Edward S. Morse, and of plate IX to Mr. W. G. Binney; for the engraving on copper of plate VIII, to Mr. Temple Prime; for the entire cost of plates VI and VII, to Mr. James Carson Brevoort, and of plate X to Mr. W. J. Hays.

An additional number of the Annals, making up the quantity of matter promised to subscribers, for the year 1872, is now in press, and will shortly be issued. It will contain papers by Messrs. Bland and Binney, Prof. John J. Stevenson, and Dr. A. S. Packard.

The Committee recommended that an appropriation of $500 be made for the ensuing year.

THOMAS BLAND,
GEORGE N. LAWRENCE.

Abstract of the Report of the Library Committee.

The Library Committee report, that during the year ending February 17th, 1873, there have been added the following books and periodicals:—

From societies, 8 quarto volumes, 26 octavo volumes, 52 parts of quarto volumes, 240 parts of octavo volumes, and 15 pamphlets.

From members, 8 parts of octavo volumes, and 7 pamphlets

From others, 3 octavo volumes and 17 pamphlets.

Making a total of 37 volumes, 300 parts of volumes, and 39 pamphlets.

There have been bound during the year 450 octavo volumes; and there still remain more than 800 volumes that should be bound.*

ROBERT H. BROWNNE,
BERNARD G. AMEND.

---

* These volumes represent a large amount of valuable scientific material, consisting of the transactions of learned societies, mainly European.

Abstract of the Report of the Corresponding Secretary,

For the year 1872-3.

The Corresponding Secretary reports that the correspondence for the year ending on the 24th of February, 1873, has, as in former years, chiefly arisen from the exchange of publications with kindred societies.

Acknowledgments for publications received have been made to the following societies and individuals:

United States.

Smithsonian Institution, Washington, D. C;
Academy of Natural Sciences, Philadelphia;
American Philosophical Society, Philadelphia;
Prof. Edward D. Cope, Philadelphia;
Boston Society of Natural History;
American Academy of Arts and Sciences, Boston;
Trustees of the Museum of Comparative Zoölogy, Cambridge, Mass.;
Trustees of the Peabody Museum of American Archæology and Ethnology, Cambridge;
The Essex Institute, Salem, Mass.;
Trustees of the Peabody Academy of Science, Salem;
Editors of the American Naturalist, Salem;
Editors of the American Journal of Science and Arts, New Haven, Conn.
Trustees of the New York State Library, Albany, N. Y.;
New York State Agricultural Society, Albany;
Prof. J. A. Lintner, Albany;
Editors of the American Chemist, New York;
The State Microscopical Society of Illinois, Chicago, Ill.;
Wisconsin Academy of Science, Arts, and Letters, Madison, Wis.;
California Academy of Sciences, San Francisco, Cal.
Editors of the "California Farmer," San Francisco, Cal.;
Prof. James Hall, Albany;
Indianapolis Academy of Sciences.

British North America.

Nova Scotia Institute of Natural Science, Halifax;
The Director of the Geological Survey of Canada, Ottawa;
Literary and Historical Society of Quebec;
Natural History Society of Montreal;
The Canadian Institute, Toronto;
Entomological Society of Ontario, London, Ont.

West Indies.

The Scientific Association of Trinidad:

Great Britain.

The Royal Society of London;
The Geological Society of London;
The Zoological Society of London;
The Society of Arts, London;
Francis Walker, F. L. S., London;
Royal Cornwall Polytechnic Society, Falmouth;
Royal Geological Society of Ireland, Dublin;
Belfast Naturalists' Field Club, Belfast;
The Edinburgh Geological Society,
The Botanical Society of Edinburgh;
The Linnean Society of London.

France.

Musée d' Histoire Naturelle de Paris;
Dr. F. G. Lemercier, Paris;
Société des Sciences Physiques et Naturelles de Bordeaux;
Société Nationale des Sciences Naturelles de Cherbourg;
Société des Sciences Historiques et Naturelles de L'Yonne, Auxerre;
Société Academique de Maine et Loire, Augers.

Switzerland.

Société Vaudoise des Sciences Naturelles, Lausanne;
Naturwissenschaftlische Gesellschaft, St. Galen;
Société des Sciences Naturelles de Neufchatel;
Naturforschende Gesellschaft, Zurich;
Naturforschende Gesellschaft zu Bern.

Germany and Austria.

K.K. Akademie der Wissenschaften, Wien;
" Geologischen Reichs Anstalt, Wien;
" Zoologisch-botanische Gesellschaft, Wien;
" Gesellschaft der Arts, Wien;
Deutsche Geologische Gesellschaft, Berlin;
Kon. Preus. Akademie der Wissenschaften, Berlin;
Kon. Akademie der Wissenschaften, Berlin;
Naturwissenschaftlischen Verein, Bremen;
Verein zur Beforderung des Gartenbaues in dem Kon. Preus. Staaten, Berlin;
Naturforschende Gesellschaft, Bamburg;
Naturhistorischen Verein der Preus. Rheinland und Westphalen, Bonn;
Verein fur Erdkunde, Darmstadt;

Naturforschenden Verein, Brunn;
Zoölogische Gesellschaft, Frankfurt, a. M.;
Senkenbergische Naturforschende Gesellschaft, Frankfurt;
Entomologischen Verein, Stettin;
Naturforschende Gesellschaft, Halle;
Naturwissenschaftlische Gesellschaft Isis in Dresden;
Kon. Phys. Okon. Gesellschaft, Konigsberg;
Wurtemburgische Naturwissenschaftlische Ges., Stuttgart;
Naturhistorischen Verein, Augsburg;
Naturforschende Gesellschaft, Freiburg;
K. Sachsische Gesellschaft der Wissenschaften, Leipzig;
Offenbachen Verein fur Naturkunde, Offenbach;
L'Institut Royal Grand Ducal de Luxembourg;
Verein der Freunde der Naturgeschichte in Mecklenburg, Neubrandenburg;
Naturwissenschaftlischen Verein, Hamburg;
Naturhistorische Gesellschaft, Nurnberg.

ITALY.

R. Comitato Geologico d'Italia, Florence;
R. Academica della Scienze, Turin.

HUNGARY.

Société Royale Hongroise des Sciences Naturelles, Pesth.

BELGIUM.

Société Entomologique de Belgique, Brussels.

HOLLAND.

Société Hollandaise des Sciences, Harlem.

DENMARK.

Kon. Danske Videnskabernes Salskab, Copenhagen.

SWEDEN.

Kon. Svenska Vatenskaps Akedemiens, Stockholm;
Bureau de la Recherche Geologique de la Suede, Stockholm;
Mr. C. Stabb, Upsala.

RUSSIA.

Société Imperiale des Naturalistes, Moscow;
L'Academie Imperiale des Sciences, St. Petersburg;
Gelehrten Estnische Gesellschaft, Dorpat.

Respectfully submitted,
ROBT. DINWIDDIE,
Corresponding Secretary.

New York, 24th February, 1873.

Publications have also been received from the following additional sources, too late for insertion in the preceding report:—

Naturforschende Gesellschaft in Danzig;

Kon. Bayerische Akademie der Wissenschaften, Munchen;

Nassauischen Vereins fur Naturkunde, Wiesbaden;

Société de Physique et d' Histoire Naturelle de Geneve.

Société d' Agriculture, d' Histoire Naturelle, et des Arts Utiles, de Lyon;

Academie des Sciences, Belles-Lettres, et Arts, de Lyon,—Classe des Sciences;

Société Linnéenne de Lyon;

Dr. Charles Girard, Paris;

Academie Royale des Sciences, Lisbon;

The Canadian Entomologist.

Report of the Treasurer.

See third page of cover.

March 3d, Business Meeting.

PROF. B. N. MARTIN in the chair. Fourteen persons present

On the recommendation of the Committee on Nominations, the following gentlemen were elected to membership in the Lyceum:—as Resident Members, Rev. Wm. Hayes Ward; Prof. Albert S. Bickmore, and Dr. Isaac Adler; and as Corresponding Members, Mr. R. P. Whitfield, of Albany, and Mr. S. W. Ford, of Troy.

After the routine business had been completed, Mr THEODORE L. MEAD exhibited a suite of specimens of fossil insects obtained by him in the South Park, Colorado. The species are probably all undescribed: they occur in a beautiful state of preservation, in fine dove-colored shale, undoubtedly of Tertiary age. The forms principally represented are Diptera, of genera closely related to, if not identical with, *Culex* and *Tipula*, some small Hymenoptera, and several beetles, one species closely resembling our modern *Chauliognathus*.

THE CHAIRMAN made some remarks on the beauty of the

specimens, and on the little knowledge that we have thus far had regarding the fossil insects of America.

Prof. D. S. Martin said that he considered this series of specimens one of the most interesting that had been brought before the Lyceum for a long time. It is to be hoped, and expected, that with the great number and extent of our Tertiary lake-deposits in the far West, from which we are obtaining such wonderful richness of both mammalian and vegetable fossils, there will be found, by suitable care and search, a correspondingly ample harvest in fossil entomology. This beautiful set, which Mr. Mead has exhibited, seems a foretaste of what lies in store for us, when these Miocene lake-beds shall have been thoroughly explored by geologists familiar with insects.

He also called attention to the article in the last number of the Geological Magazine, on fossil Lepidoptera, in which several new species are described, and some interesting suggestions presented as to their geographical relations as compared with existing types.

Mr. James Hyatt called attention to some peculiar barometric phenomena observed by him, in connection with the action of wind in mountainous districts. He had been wont to carry with him, while traveling up and down on the Hudson River railroad, a very reliable aneroid barometer, and had been led to notice its curious variations in passing from station to station. These variations at first seemed wholly inexplicable; but they were soon found to follow a very simple law, in relation to the ranges of hights traversed by the railroad. With a north wind the barometer stood highest on the northern side of the Highlands, and with a south wind, on the southern side. This result seems, therefore, to be due to a condensation or compression of the air, when strong currents strike against ranges of mountains or hills.

With a north-east wind, again, the barometer stands higher at Newburgh, at the base of the hights, on the western side of the river, than it does at Fishkill, on the eastern side. Mr. Hyatt also gave the details of several other observations.

Mr. Collingwood made some remarks on the effect of forests on the pressure of the air, and on the amount of rain, and on the dangerous results arising, in this latter respect, from the removal of woods.

The Chairman observed that in regard to the effect of denuding a country of wood, a serious error prevails. The belief that it produces a diminution in the amount of the rain-fall, is by no means well established. There seems to be a conflict of opinion, and even of evidence on the subject. While in some instances such a reduction is very positively alleged to have taken place, in many others this result has not been observed.

Some very important effects of a different kind, however, are quite unquestionable. When the mountain summits have been robbed of their wood, the soil upon the upper slopes, deprived of the support furnished it by the roots of the trees, is no longer able to maintain its place, and is washed down into the valleys below. These are then sometimes overwhelmed by a deluge of sand and gravel, which covers up completely the fertile plains of the lower districts, and renders them unfit for cultivation. Mr. George P. Marsh, in his valuable work upon "Man and Nature," recounts some very destructive instances of this effect among the Alpine valleys of South-eastern France. The mountain summits, thus stripped of their soil, become barren slopes of rock, down which the water rushes with rapidity and violence.

In the next place, the smaller rivers undergo a change of the most serious kind. They lose their sustained and equal flow, and become altogether irregular. The rain of a summer's shower drains rapidly from the precipitous and rocky heights which are no longer covered by a soil. It fills the bed of the stream, overflows it, and passes off in a torrent to the sea, leaving the stream shrunken and insignificant, till another storm of rain creates another inundation. Thus brooks that formerly were wont to turn mill-wheels, and do much valuable work, are changed into irregular mountain torrents, and not only lose their character of usefulness, but become dangerous and destructive.

These effects have grown so marked, that the European governments have been forced to recognise them. They have even undertaken some measures of protection against an evil so serious, and have attempted to restore the wood of those summits, which still retain a sufficient amount of soil. In some instances the effort has proved successful; and streams that had become so capricious as to be worthless, are found to regain their former constancy and fulness, with the restoration of the forests which had been ruthlessly cut down.

Few subjects are of more importance to us, than a right understanding of the disastrous effects of the constant and rapid destruction of our native forests. Every year the country is more and more denuded; and at length, the high price of lumber drives the wood-cutters farther and further up into the mountains. Regions so precipitous as to have been hitherto secure from intrusion, are now reached by the axe. From the windows of the rail-car, the traveler sees upon the distant summits great gaps in the forest, where some adventurer, more enterprising than the rest, has found means of bringing down in a season the growths of a century; and soon we shall find it too late to protect our rural districts from the dangers which already threaten them.

Prof. J. J. Stevenson referred to the changes just described, as illustrated in Ohio, where the rivers, from being full during the whole year, are now very low for months together. The actual quantity of rain is not less than it was; but the surface of the country being cleared, the water runs off or evaporates, instead of remaining in the soil, and draining away gradually, as it did before the removal of the forests.

Prof. Seely also made some remarks, confirming the views expressed by Dr. Stevenson.

PROCEEDINGS

OF THE

LYCEUM OF NATURAL HISTORY

IN THE

CITY OF NEW YORK.

SECOND SERIES.

March 10th, 1873. Chemical Section.

President Newberry in the chair. Forty persons present.

Dr. Feuchtwanger exhibited specimens of metallic silver-leaf, formed, by electro-chemical action, from a solution of sulphate of copper and silver. The liquid was allowed to stand at rest for twenty-four hours, in a large tank lined with lead, and in which some metallic copper had also been placed. The silver, becoming detached, was then found floating on the top of the solution, as a lace-like sheet of aggregated crystalline scales, so thin as to be translucent, and of very elegant aspect. The upper surface of the film, exposed to the air, has a brilliant metallic luster; while the lower surface, resting on the liquid, is dark.

He suggested the inquiry whether any such action could explain the peculiar association of metallic silver with copper, in the Lake Superior region.

Mr. W. Goold Levison read the following

Note on the Production of Ammonia in Nitric Acid Batteries.*

I first noticed the production of ammonia in a nitric acid battery, in the month of January, 1869; and on the 23d of that month I showed the phenomenon to Mr. Charles Pearce, at Cambridge. It was, however, observed under circumstances that led me for a long time to consider it due to a mere local action of the dissolving zinc upon nitric acid which had diffused through the porous cup; but recent experiments show, to my mind, that this ammonia results from a reaction between the electrolytically-liberated hydrogen and the nitrogen of the nitric acid in the inner cup.

As no discussion of the theory of the battery, to the best of my knowledge, takes cognizance of this reaction, I thought it might be new and worthy of attention. I must, however, confine this note to a mere statement of the fact.

January 14*th*, 1873. I put up two small Grove cells, constructed of zinc and platinum. The inner cups were filled with a mixture of

Saturated solution of potassic bichromate, .	5 parts,
Commercial oil of vitriol, ...	2½ "
Nitric acid, C. P., ...	1 "

The zincs, newly amalgamated, were put in dilute sulphuric acid. Distilled water only was used. One cup was set in operation, the other left. After 24 hours the liquids in these two batteries were examined for ammonia; the cup set in operation being called Battery A, the other Battery B. In testing the liquids from the inner and outer cells of both batteries, ten cubic centimeters of each were separately concentrated, by evaporation in a platinum dish, to about one-fifth, treated with an excess of caustic soda, and the dish covered with a watch-glass having a piece of red litmus paper adherent to its under side.

Battery A. Liquid from inner cup. Paper immediately turned blue. Odor of ammonia strongly perceptible.

Battery A. Liquid from outer cup. Paper became blue in a short time. Odor of ammonia very faint. Only a trace present.

Battery B. Liquid from inner cup. Paper faintly changed in ten minutes. No odor of ammonia perceptible.

---

* This note has been published in the Journal of the Franklin Institute for May, 1873. It now appears with some corrections by the author.

Battery B. Liquid from outside cup. Same result precisely.

Local action does not produce ammonia in important quantity.

January 26th, 1873. Set up a single cell, Grove form, with dilute sulphuric acid in the outside cup, and a mixture of equal parts of saturated solution of potassic nitrate and Kalbfleisch's commercial oil of vitriol in the inside cup. Proved in advance that each liquid was free from ammonia.

After 24 hours, tested both liquids for ammonia. That from the inner cup contained great quantities; but that from the outer one gave no indication of it.

February 1st, 1873. Set up a single Grove cell, with nitric and dilute sulphuric acids. Immediately after setting up, and before closing circuit, tested both liquids for ammonia. The nitric acid gave no trace; the sulphuric acid gave a faint ammonia reaction, and yielded a trace of nitric acid, which probably got into it by diffusion through the porous cup. Ten minutes after putting the battery in operation, ammonia in large quantity was found in the inner cell.

The conversion of nitric acid into ammonia must be taken into consideration in preparing the nitro-chromic battery fluid, as proposed by me in the Journal of the Franklin Institute, vol. LIX, page 376; inasmuch as enough nitric acid must be used to provide an excess over and above the quantity converted into ammonia during the time which elapses before the last molecule of chromic acid is reduced to chromic oxide.

Mr. Levison's paper was discussed by Professors Leeds and Seely.

Mr. James Gallatin, Jr., exhibited and explained an improved adjustment, by which the carbon points of a battery can be kept steadily in the focus of the lens. The instrument is automatic, giving notice if at any time the points are not in the proper position.

Dr. A. H. Gallatin mentioned that a constant and steady light had been maintained for two hours, by means of this instrument.

A more detailed account of the adjustment is reserved until some contemplated improvements shall have been finished.

Prof. A. R. Leeds read a paper "On the Spectroscopic Examination of Silicates," published in the Annals, vol. x, No. 11, pages 324–330.

Dr. I. Walz commenced the reading of an extended paper entitled "Contributions to a General Theory of Solubility." The hour of adjournment having arrived, Dr. Walz was requested to finish the reading of the paper at a future meeting; as the discussion was one of such interest that more time, and the opportunity of a full exchange of views upon the subject, would be highly desirable.

March 17th. Geological Section.

President Newberry in the chair. Twenty persons present.

Dr. Feuchtwanger announced the death of Professor John Torrey, of Columbia College, the last of the original incorporators of the Lyceum. On motion, it was resolved that a committee be appointed to prepare a series of resolutions expressive of the esteem felt by the members of the Lyceum for the deceased, and also to suggest some suitable mode in which to commemorate the life and services of their late associate.

The President appointed Prof. B. N. Martin, Dr. Feuchtwanger, and Mr. Dinwiddie, as such committee. By request, the President was added as a fourth member.

Dr. Feuchtwanger exhibited a specimen of lazulite from Africa, of a deep green color upon one axis, and pale green upon another, and differing from the North Carolina specimens in possessing a vitreous luster. He made some accompanying remarks upon the characters and distribution of lazulite.

Dr. B. N. Martin exhibited a specimen of the sword of *Cœlorhyncus ornatus*, Leidy, the fossil sword-fish, from the "Upper Marl Bed" (Eocene) of Farmingdale, N. J.

The President made some remarks on the occurrence of this species.

The following paper was read :—

On the Fossils found in the "Flag-stones" used in the Cities of New York and Brooklyn.

By Dr. R. P. Stevens.

The "blue-stone" flaggings of our streets may be regarded as the perfection of sidewalk stones. For evenness of wear, as well as durability, they surpass all other materials used, unless perhaps the sandstones of the Highlands and of northern New York.

These flags appear to consist of somewhat varying layers of sediments, chiefly fine-grained sands, with silicious, calcareous, or silico-calcareous cements. The marks of ripples, rain-drops, and cross-wave action, which they exhibit, show them to have been littoral or mud-bank deposits.

When closely examined, the evidence on this point is conclusive. We find all the phenomena of sea-shore action which we see on the beach of the modern ocean. Where thin films of deposition, which form the surface of the best class of flags, are worn away, there may be seen little ridges of coarse sand and pebbles, such as are familiarly produced by the sorting action of tidal waves.

Some of these ridges consist of pebbles of black flint, suggesting their source to have been among the cherty limestones of the Upper Helderberg group.

All the fossil remains of these flags appear, moreover, to have been stranded waifs upon a shore.

According to Prof. Dana, the rocks lying back of Kingston, N. Y., where these flags are quarried, belong to the Hamilton group. Similar flags in the south-western counties of the state, and along the Delaware River, I have been disposed to refer to the Chemung and Portage epochs. The slabs are of great beauty and durability; I have seen them full forty feet square, and have obtained specimens of good strength not a quarter of an inch thick, and literally filled with impressions of organic remains, chiefly cavities once occupied by joints of encrinal columns.

Here I am brought to the subject of the Organic Remains found in the flag-stones used in New York and vicinity.

It may be worth while to remark, that specimens are most readily found either by inspecting the flags of newly-opened and out-of-the-way streets, where the rougher and poorer qualities of stone are employed, or by examining the reverse sides of slabs in the "blue-stone" yards.

Flora.

I have seen one species resembling a *Carpolithes*, of oval shape, three quarters of an inch long by half an inch wide.

Two other species of fossil fruits have been observed, one oblong, and of the size of a common Madeira nut, the other smaller and more rounded. These are often encrusted with a thin coating of peroxide of iron, and may readily be overlooked, as mere concretions. Their markings, also, are frequently obscured by thin layers of sediment. They are not rare, however, as slabs are often covered with them.

I have noticed one species of *Psilophyton.* Fragments of this plant often appear as bits of carbonaceous matter covering the under surface of slabs. These carbonized surfaces have led the hopeful sons of speculation to engage in the hopeless task of searching in these rocks for coal.

Fucoids are quite common. To this group I refer those flags which have bulging elevations, with fragments of leaves appearing through the worn surface, as if a tuft of bunch grass had been covered with sand, its leaves pressed down, and the whole then petrified.

Impressions of a plant with triangular, ensiform, reed-like leaves are often seen on slabs in Williamsburg. They seldom appear singly, but usually in groups, lying more or less parallel to one another. I have never seen the upper slab, only the lower. These show one angular edge of the leaf, in the bottom of the cast. The impressions are generally ten to twelve inches long, smooth, triangular, dagger-shaped, coming to a point at both ends, usually straight, or slightly curved.

A slab at the corner of Division Avenue and Second St., Brooklyn, E. D., has six of these plants, of large size; two of them are fifteen inches long; one that is a foot in length, is, in the widest portion, half an inch broad and a quarter of an inch deep. Another slab, on the same avenue, at the crossing of Third St., has sixteen casts in two groups.

Fauna.

Crinoids. A large crinoid resembling *Caryocrinus*—the size of a black-walnut—is sometimes seen. A slab in one of the streets of New York, which I vainly endeavored to purchase for the State Cabinet, was quite filled with this species, well preserved, showing ornamental markings, plates, and portions of the stems.

Plates, arms, and parts of columns of other species, are often seen dissociated. In one instance, a slab three feet by five, on Gates Avenue, near Washington Avenue, Brooklyn, has its whole surface covered with fragments of a once most magnificent crinoid.

Of fish remains there seem to be several species. In a slab now lying in a yard in Brooklyn, are what I judge to be large dermal plates of an immense fish.

A slab, at one time in front of the Astor House, bore the impression of a fish well preserved. The scales were dissociated, but the form and outline of a fish some sixteen inches long could be readily seen when the slab was clean and a little wet.

Scales, bones, teeth, and rays are often well preserved in sulphuret of iron, and present quite an ornamental aspect when the stone is wet by showers.

I have frequently seen clusters of pebbles, resembling, and suggesting, the spawning-beds of fish.

Casts and impressions of worm-burrows often cover the reverse sides of slabs. The burrows are sometimes filled with fine sand, and then appear in *alto relievo.* They are of various sizes and shapes, and would indicate several species, if methods of progression are evidences of specific relations.

Of course, under the circumstances, it is impossible to study these remains carefully; we cannot remove them to our cabinets and examine them at our leisure; we can only glance at them as we pass along after summer showers. Enough is seen, however, to reveal to us some of the stranded denizens of Devonian seas, and some fragmentary remains of ancient forests; enough to make us wish for time and opportunity to study them fully at the Kingston quarries.

Dr. Adolph Ott read a paper upon Recent Improvements in the manufacture of Artificial Stone. He described in particular, the Portland, the Ransome, and the Sorell processes, detailing the composition in each, and the respective advantages and disadvantages.

Mr. Collingwood referred to the remarkable account given by Gen. Theodore G. Ellis, in No. 54 of the papers published by the American Society of Civil Engineers, concerning the great durability of the floors used in some parts of Mexico, composed of two parts of sand and one of lime, and repeatedly beaten and worked over.

The subject was further discussed by the President, Prof. Seely, and Dr. Feuchtwanger.

Dr. O. W. Morris read the following paper:

Summary of Meteorological Observations at the Cooper Union, for the month of February, 1873.

The month has been unusually cold and boisterous, more so than any February in the last ten years, with the exception of 1868, which was nearly 8° colder. The mean temperature was 29.79°.

The maximum was 48° on the 8th, and the minimum 0.5. —a range of 47.5°. There were only three days when the mean temperature was above 40°; on thirteen days it was between 30° and 40°; on eight days between 20° and 30°, and on four, below 20° The weather was quite changeable, during the whole month.

The consequence of this, was an unusual number of deaths, not only from affections of the lungs, but from those incident to exposure, foul air, and insufficient food and clothing, as well as want of attention.

354 persons died from phthisis pulmonalis; 228 from pneumonia, and 123 from bronchitis.

Of the 2175 deaths from all causes and of all ages, 971 were children under 5 years of age, an average of 34.7 each day; and the whole number shows 74.1 deaths in every 24 hours.

Could all these cases be traced to their dwellings, and the privations made known, sanitary measures might doubtless be adopted, that would at least alleviate the misery, especially among the children, of whom the fearful number of 971, under five years of age, died in this city in 28 days!

The mean of the barometer was 29.848 inches; the maximum was 30.416 inches on the 15th, and the minimum 29.044 inches on the 21st, a range of 1.372 inches in six days.

The greatest monthly mean during the ten years referred to, was 36.76° in 1864; the least 22.97° in 1868: the greatest daily mean was 53.3° on the 24th of February, 1866; the least, 6.3° on the 3d of February, 1868.

The mean of February for the whole ten years was 32.11°, or 2.262 higher than in 1873.

The quantity of water from rain and melted snow was 4·75 inches, which is about the average for the ten years.

Snow fell on 5 days, though it was not deep. Lunar haloes were observed on two evenings, and one lunar corona.

March 24th.

President Newberry in the chair. Sixteen persons present.

PROF. C. A. SEELY made some remarks upon an improved form of spectroscope invented by Prof. A. K. Eaton.

The PRESIDENT gave a discussion of the "Coals and Lignites of the Western States and Territories,"* illustrated by a large suite of specimens from many localities, and with numerous analyses.

Looking for a moment at the coals of the eastern states, it is familiarly known that in going eastward from the great mining centre of Pennsylvania, the coal becomes less bituminous, changing first to the hard anthracite of the Rhode Island mines, then into graphitic anthracite, and finally at Worcester, Mass., into an incombustible graphite. On the other hand, in going westward, the coal becomes increasingly bituminous, and maintains the latter character through out the great coal areas of the Mississippi basin.

In the Far West, however, the coals are of different geological age from those of the eastern and central states, which are true Carboniferous. In the West are found only Triassic, Cretaceous, and Tertiary lignites, varying much in character and value, but in some cases becoming true hard coals.

The Triassic formation, as a whole, contains little carbonaceous material; but to this general rule, there are some notable exceptions. Such are the valuable coal mines of Richmond and of North Carolina, and in the far West, those of Los Bronces in Sonora. In China, Prof. Pumpelly has shown that these Mesozoic coals are extensively developed, as they are also known to be on Vancouver's and Queen Charlotte's Islands. At all these points, the palæontological evidence as to the age of the deposits is unquestionable.

Cretaceous coals and lignites have an important developement at many points in the far West. One of the most interesting is that near Santa Fé, in which a trap-dyke has cut through a bed of Cretaceous lignite, and altered it locally to a true anthracite. Many coals which have been thought by some observers to be Eocene, are in reality of Cretaceous age, as shown by unmistakeable animal remains.

* The leading points of this paper are fully presented in the Annals, Vol. XI.

Our Tertiary lignites are almost entirely Miocene, and of these there are large deposits at the far North—in Alaska, Greenland, etc.

PROF. SEELY made some remarks on the various sources of error in the ordinary methods of analyzing coals, both as regards the amount of carbon and that of ash.

DR. H. C. BOLTON presented some notes on the fluorescence of uranium compounds, in regard to which Dr. Henry Morton and himself had been continuing their observations. Some sixty different salts containing this metal had lately been prepared and examined, chemically by himself, and physically by Dr. Morton. Of these, several are new to chemistry; they will be more fully reported upon hereafter.

March 31st.

President Newberry in the chair. Twenty persons present.

DR. FEUCHTWANGER made some remarks on the present state of the diamond market.

The diamond cutters and polishers of Amsterdam and London are now under the control of a League; and it has lately been resolved to advance the price for cutting rough diamonds, from forty to a hundred per cent., particularly on small stones; 24 shillings per carat will now be charged, instead of from 12 to 14 shillings, as before. This state of affairs has seriously depressed the market for rough stones, both in London and at Cape Town. The cleavage of the large African diamonds is a matter of great importance. The original size of the stone often has to be greatly reduced, in order to remove flaws, etc.; and the pieces removed by cleavage are much used, if of good quality, for cutting into small brilliants or rose diamonds. A skillful cleaver, therefor, commands far higher wages than a mere cutter or polisher; as on him depends the form and size of the stones.

Mr. Collingwood mentioned a peculiar circumstance in regard to the apparent alteration of iron water-pipes in certain localities, and presented the subject for inquiry. At a point in New Jersey, near this city, where pipes of this description are carried through a marsh, a part of the pipe is found to be seemingly decayed, and altered into a substance resembling graphite. Of course no satisfactory conclusion could be reached without an examination of the changed material.

The President gave some account of the explorations of Mr. Gilbert in the Western Territories, under Lieut. Wheeler, and illustrated his remarks by diagrams on the board. He referred particularly to the change of level of the Great Salt Lake, which formerly had an area equal to Lake Michigan.

Prof. Seely made allusion to the views of Mr. Herbert Spencer on the origin of instinct, advocating his theory that animal instincts are to be regarded as inherited habits.

Prof. Stevenson claimed that these opinions had been set forth long before, by Dr. Darwin, in his Zoönomia.

Dr. B. N. Martin argued that all instincts are not merely inherited habits. There may be such, indeed; but by far the most important and universal animal instincts have a physiological basis, and stand in the closest relation to the structure and functions of the organism. Mr. Spencer's view is wholly defective and inadequate. The instinct of food-taking, for instance, is not an inherited habit, but a physiological necessity.

April 7th. Business Meeting.

President Newberry in the chair. Fifteen persons present.

Communications from the Publication Committee, and from the Corresponding Secretary, were received and discussed, together with various other items of business.

The PRESIDENT referred to an article which had lately been published in various papers, concerning the discovery of ancient human remains, of large size, in Ohio, and expressed his incredulity in reference to the whole account. He proceeded to mention the mammalian remains of the Ohio drift, and to assign to them their exact horizon. The mastodon and elephant occur in the peat marshes, and reach from a very remote period, down almost to the present time. Their first appearance was in the "Forest Bed," as he had termed it, which is overlaid by the iceberg drift, and underlaid first by the Erie (or Champlain) clays, and then, lower down, by the true glacial drift. After the great ice-sheet of the glacial era had passed away, there was a depression of nearly a thousand feet, and a vast submergence of much of the northern interior beneath an expanse of cold, fresh waters, which laid down the Erie clays. The land seems then to have risen, and for some time to have sustained quite a wide-spread vegetation, of boreal character, consisting largely of coniferæ. In this cool-climate period, the great mammals above referred to appear; they are never found in any of the underlying glacial deposits. Then there came another northern depression, and a second submergence, even greater than the former. The forests were destroyed, and covered up with the deposits of this new inland sea, which are largely sand, gravel, and boulders borne by floating ice from the farther North. The animals retreated now to the heights of Southern Ohio, and to the Alleghanies, whence they again descended when the land rose, and the iceberg sea gradually dwindled into our present chain of the Great Lakes; and they would seem then to have followed the retreating cold climate to the shores of the Arctic sea, where their numerous remains indicate their last abiding-place. The great extinct beaver, *Castoroides Ohioensis*, also appeared in the old Forest Bed; but it has never been found in the more modern bogs, and would seem to have died out during the second submergence.

April 14th.

President Newberry in the chair. Twelve persons present.

The PRESIDENT made some remarks on the explorations of Major Powell in Utah and Arizona, referring to his important scientific determinations in regard to the possibility of navigating the Colorado River, to his descent of that stream from Grand River down through the Great Cañon, and to his researches among the aboriginal tribes. The Utes, Pah-Utes, Moquis, Shoshonees, and Comanches, who occupy the region over which his travels extended, are probably all branches of one great family of Indians. Major Powell is projecting a work on these tribes, when he returns to the States.

DR. H. C. BOLTON made some remarks which may be entitled "Preliminary Notes on New Salts of Uranium." He exhibited specimens of thallium uranate, thallio-uranic sulphate, thallio-uranic acetate, rubidio-uranic sulphate, and rubidio-uranic acetate, and compared them with specimens of other compounds analogous and already known.

He stated that he had sought to form the basic ammonio-uranic sulphate described by M. Becquerel, in the *Comptes Rendues*, and the preparation of which he thought erroneously given. He had obtained a sub-sulphate of uranium and ammonium, and in conjunction with his friend, Prof. Henry Morton, had examined its fluorescent spectrum. This spectrum is not continuous, as was claimed by M. Becquerel for his compound. Dr. Bolton had determined the exact composition to be:

$$2\,(U_2\,SO_6) + (NH_4)_2SO_4,$$

and proposed the name ammonio-di-uranic sulphate. It was obtained by the action of heat on the normal ammonio-uranic sulphate.

PROF. SEELY announced that the bichloride of tin is a solvent for all the petroleum oils, and that hence this substance might be found highly useful in purifying the hydrocarbons of the marsh-gas series.

April 21st. Geological Section.

President Newberry in the chair. Twelve persons present.

The Corresponding Secretary read by title the following papers, which are published in the Annals, Vol. X, Nos. 10 and 11.

On *Prophysaon*, a new Pulmonate Mollusc, on *Ariolimax*, on *Helix lychnuchus*, and other species. By Thomas Bland and W. G. Binney. (With two plates.)

On the Physical Geography of the Bahama Islands, and the Distribution of Terrestrial Mollusca therein. By Thomas Bland.

Prof. D. S. Martin exhibited some recently-described fossils from the Cretaceous of northern Texas, among which were *Ostrea quadriplicata* and *belliplicata*, *Baculites Navarroensis*, and *Ammonites Swallowii*, (all named by Shumard,) from various localities in Grayson, Lamar, and Navarro counties.

Prof. C. F. Hartt, of Cornell University, made some remarks on the geological results of his recent visit to Brazil. The field which he had examined was chiefly the eastern part of the basin of the Amazonas, particularly along the Rio Tapajos, one of the principal southern affluents of the Amazon, into which it falls in about long. 22° E. from Washington. This stream cuts through a considerable area of the Carboniferous rocks of Brazil; though the several sections obtained were so disconnected that they were not at all satisfactory, in a stratigraphical point of view.

Far up the Tapajos, the river falls over ledges of sandstone, of pre-carboniferous age, greatly displaced and broken by dikes of porphyry and trap.

Below these falls, the Carboniferous series begins; appearing first as heavy sandstones, poor in fossils. To the north of these, are bluffs of fine black shales, also with few fossils, though containing some specimens related to *Lepidostrobus*, and also large septaria, with occasional ichthyodorulites and fish-teeth. These shales are followed by limestone, with layers of cherty nodules; and lower down, these limestones become highly fossiliferous, yielding very perfect and beautiful specimens of *Productus*, *Strophalosia*, etc., all of which are generally silicified, and may be obtained in great perfection, where the water has worn away their calcareous matrix. The lower layers of these limestone beds are quite soft, and the upper ones much harder. At many points along the bank, the floods have eroded these lower layers, leaving the upper ones over-hanging, sometimes so as to form perfect grottoes, from the roofs of which project beautiful specimens of *Productus*, with their long spines unbroken, and delicate *Strophalosias*, hanging almost by a thread of rock, and ready to drop at a touch into the delighted collector's hand.

All the species obtained,—brachiopods, lamellibranchs, gasteropods, and cephalopods (of which there is only an *Orthoceras*, no *Nautili* or *Goniatites*)—bear a singularly close resemblance to the familiar Carboniferous species of the northern hemisphere. Further down, these rocks become covered up by the Tertiary beds of the Amazon valley; but they appear again, with the same fossils, in corresponding positions on the northern side of the great stream, on the Rio Trombetas.

An extended area of Carboniferous deposits, for the most part undisturbed, is thus traceable through this portion of the basin of the Amazonas; while eastward of the Tapajos no indication thereof has been found. On the southern side, however, of the great Brazilian plateau, rocks of the same age have been recognized.

In the more eastern portion of the Amazon valley, a considerable Devonian area has been proved to exist. These rocks contain many species of characteristic Devonian brachiopods, *Chonetes*, *Spirifer*, *Vitulina*, etc. Two fine trilobites have been obtained here, a *Lichas* and a *Homalonotus*.*

Prof. Hartt also gave an account of his researches among the antiquities of the country, and discussed their relations

* Most of these are to be described in the Annals, Vol. XI.

to those of Peru and Central America. Pottery and utensils are extremely abundant at many points, and would indicate the former existence of a large population, in parts of the Amazonas region now very sparsely inhabited.

Among the most interesting and peculiar indications of this kind, are the great fresh-water shell-heaps, true *kjokken moeddings*, which he had found on the banks at Taperinha, near Santaren, in the province of Pará. Here is presented the evidence that the aborigines used for food the species of *Hyria*, *Castalia*, etc., which still inhabit the waters of the Amazonas.

The PRESIDENT gave a brief account of the several expeditions which are preparing to carry on explorations during the summer of 1873, in the western states and territories.

April 28th.

President Newberry in the chair. Twelve persons present.

DR. FEUCHTWANGER exhibited a large series of specimens from the Yellowstone geysers, comprising silicified wood, geyserite, sulphur, etc., and made remarks on their occurrence.

PROF. D. S. MARTIN showed specimens of octahedral and dodecahedral crystals of cuprite, coated with malachite, and with edges variously replaced, from Texas. He remarked upon their singular resemblance to those from Chessy, France, specimens of which, almost indistinguishable from them, were exhibited for comparison.

THE PRESIDENT, remarking upon the copper ores discovered in Texas by Prof. Roessler and others, said that though this occurrence of copper in the Triassic is especially marked in Texas, it is well nigh universal in the South-west.

The sulphides of the farther West are in true descending veins; but in the Triassic the copper ores never occur thus, but are found constantly present over vast areas of "red beds" in Texas and New Mexico. No trace of copper is found in the Carboniferous rocks below, or the Cretaceous rocks above; and the great abundance of it in the undisturbed Trias is a most singular problem.

All around the Llano Estacado is found this prevalence of copper; and in New Mexico are many abandoned mines. On visiting those on the Chama River, north-west of Santa Fé, the locality was found to be an amphitheatre of hills, 400 to 500 feet high, situated on the northern side of the stream, and composed of sandstones and shales, of the most brilliant tints, crimson, orange, yellow, etc., (like the true Poikilitic of Europe,) and richly covered with verdure. Into the faces of these hills ran old adits, 200 to 300 feet long, the inner extremities of which were occupied by myriads of bats. These adits follow no veins or beds, but were simply worked in the undisturbed sandstones; the copper was everywhere, chiefly as bornite, occurring in concretions, and as replacements of fragments of wood, etc. Tradition makes these mines very ancient, but they are Spanish.

The same character appears in the Trias of the Atlantic coast, both in New England and in the Middle States,—a wide but scanty distribution of copper. This circumstance has led to many mining ventures, which have been uniformly unsuccessful. All the copper thus occurring must have been indigenous, deposited from solution in the water that laid down the vast mass of fragmental sediments. The Triassic sea must have been charged with copper. What the causes or conditions were, which gave rise to such a state, it baffles our present knowledge to say.

The subject was further discussed by several members.

May 5th, 1873. Business Meeting.

President Newerry in the chair. Fourteen persons present.

On the recommendation of the Committee on Nominations, Mr. E. R. Straznicky, of the Astor Library, was elected a resident member of the Lyceum.

On motion, it was resolved that a committee of five members be appointed by the President, to devise measures for the more effective carrying out of the objects of the society, such measures to be reported at the next business meeting.

After the transaction of routine business,

MR. JAMES HYATT gave an account of the recent labors of Dr. J. W. Doughty, of Newburgh, Orange Co., in obtaining accurate measurements of the heights of the principal mountains in the vicinity of that city. Dr. Doughty employed a line of 10,000 feet, measured on the ice of the Hudson, as the base of his triangulations, carefully testing and verifying his work. In one or two cases, heights were also determined, in addition, by levelling. The results obtained in regard to the principal peaks of the Highlands, by triangulation, are as follows:

North Beacon, 1519 feet, (by levelling, 1518 feet.)
South Beacon, 1502 feet.
Butter Hill, 1363·5 feet. (Prof. Gillespie, in his report, gives it as 1365 feet.)
Black Rock, 1344 feet.

Passing west from the Highlands, Dr. Doughty determined the height of Skunnemunk Mountain, as 1656 feet; the distance of this ridge from his river stations is about 45,000 feet.

The extreme height of Polopel's Island was approximately determined to be 112 feet.

It may therefore be safely assumed that the elevations of these points are now accurately known.

Dr. O. W. Morris read the following paper:—

Summary of Meteorological Observations at Cooper Union, for the months of March and April, 1873.

March, 1873.

The temperature at the beginning of the month was 29.5°; at its close, 45°. The maximum, 52°, occurred on the 30th, at 2 P. M.; the minimum, 11°, on the 5th, at 7 A. M., a range of 41°. The lowest mean for any single day was 17.33°, on the 4th; the highest mean, 47.66°, on the 30th,—a difference in mean temperature of 30.33°. The mean for the month was 36.49°; warmer than March 1872, by 6.25°, but colder than 1871, by 8.28°, and 1.08° colder than the average for the ten years preceding. The greatest daily range was 21°, on the 6th, and the least, 1.5°, on the 20th.

The amount of rain and melted snow was 3.25 inches.

The prevailing winds were N. W. and W.

On the 17th, the mean humidity was 31°, and on the 29th, 95°, a range of 64° in twelve days. The mean for the whole month was 61.44°.

The barometer indicated 30.564 inches on the 6th, and 29.024 inches on the 29th, a range of 1.54 inches. The mean for the month was 29.809 inches; less than that of March 1872, by .06 inch.

One solar halo, one lunar halo, and one parhelion, were observed.

The mortality of children under one year old was 583, and under five years, 991. The total number of deaths for the month, from all causes and of all ages, in this city, was 2394.

April, 1873.

The temperature on the morning of the 1st was 42°; and the maximum was attained on the 2d, 62.5°. It was at 40° or above, at 7 A. M., on every day except the 13th, when it had fallen to 37°. On the evening of the 12th, also, it reached the same point: this was the minimum, the range for the month being 25.5°. The highest mean was 55.06°, on the 28th; and the lowest 40.93°, on the 21st; a difference of 14.13°. The mean for the month, was 47.35°, which was lower than that of any April for ten years past, except 1868, which was 3.91° colder.

The prevailing wind was N. E.

The quantity of water from rain and melted snow, was 5·1 inches.

The mean humidity was 64.25°. On the 17th and 18th complete saturation (100°) prevailed, while the minimum was reached on the 25th, when it was only 27.6, giving a range of 72.4 for the month.

The maximum of the barometer was 30.132 inches, on the 5th, and the minimum, 29.384 inches on the 12th, a range of .748 inch. The mean for the month was 29.779 inches.

The casual phenomena observed, were lightning on the 1st, thunder showers on the 2d, 5th, and 6th, one lunar halo, and one lunar corona.

May 12th, 1873. Chemical Section.

President Newberry in the chair.. Thirty-two persons present.

DR. H. ENDEMANN read the following paper:

The Air we Breathe.

During the month of February, 1873, I commenced an investigation, which from want of time, could not be so thoroughly treated as the importance of the subject requires. This is an investigation regarding the composition of air in school-rooms, factories, theatres, halls, tenements, and cellar lodgings.

The impurities generally found in the air of inhabited places, are carbonic acid, vapors of various organic substances, and dust.

The latter is seldom found in much larger quantity inside of structures than outside, with the exception of certain places, where peculiar manufactures may contribute largely to its quantity. In the manufactories of curled horse-hair, for instance, the room in which the horse-hair is spun is filled with a dense cloud of dust, which, when collected and examined, appears to be a mixture of inorganic substances with those of organic origin. Of the latter, fine, sharp-edged pieces of horse-hair form evidently the most dangerous part, inasmuch as they irritate the mucous membranes of the air-passages, and therefore become the cause of the various affections of those organs which are frequently found in persons thus engaged. To remove this dust by ventilation, is certainly impracticable, on account of the vast volume of air required to pass through such rooms. It has been tried, however, but, as might have been expected, with only insignificant effect.

Respirators, constructed of wire gauze, filled in with cotton, and which must cover both the mouth and nose, are the only means of effectually protecting the workman. These have lately been again recommended and introduced in England, and are said to accomplish all that could be expected.

Against the other impurities found in the air of inhabited places, as mentioned above, we have but one remedy, and that is ventilation, or speedy renewal of the air.

A certain amount of ventilation is always going on through the walls, if they be dry and not constructed of impenetrable material, and also through cracks in doors and windows.

For ordinary purposes, this ventilation might suffice to keep the air in a room about at the proper standard; but this is not the case in rooms which are uncommonly crowded. Here recourse must be had to artificial means for promoting the renewal of the air. I cannot go into the details of the various modes of ventilation in use; but can only mention, that the main object is, not only a desirable activity in the flues used for supplying good air and removing that which is waste, but also a system insuring a good distribution of the supply of air. The latter can be obtained, either by causing an adequate circulation of the air in a room, or by supplying the air through numerous openings in the floor. The first method was found to be in use in some of our public schools, the latter in two of our New York theatres.

The bad influence of damp walls is found not only in the fact that they do not admit any outside air, but that they also condense the dangerous portions of exhaled air. The air in under-ground tenements is for this reason always richer in organic substances than might be anticipated from the amount of carbonic acid found therein.

As I have used Pettenkofer's method of the examination of air, which consists merely in a determination of the carbonic acid present, it was necessary to calculate on certain occasions the amount of carbonic acid formed by the combustion of gas. It was thus ascertained, that in theatres the amount of carbonic acid thus produced exceeds that due to respiration from 3 to 7 times, according to the more or less crowded state of the place.

The following tabular statement gives the results obtained.

	CO_2 in 10,000 parts of air.
E. S. Higgins, Carpet Factory,	14·7
Johnson & Falkner, Hair Cloth,	16·7
Tombs, prison, male dept., average of 2 experiments,	14·7
" female " "	8·45
Elm Street school, average of 3 experiments,	14·6
Roosevelt Street school, " 2 "	19·5
School, 13th St., near 7th Av., " 2 "	21·3
" 6th " " 2 "	28·1
Greenwich Street school, " 2 "	17·6
Vandewater " " 2 "	14·7
Madison " " 4 "	24·2
Tenement, 45 Baxter Street, 2d floor; 7 persons,	15·4
Cellar tenements, 223 Division Street; 4 persons,	12·6
" 26 James Street; 16 persons,	21·9
" 64 Cherry Street; 8 persons,	13·4
" 64 " 11 persons,	18·8
" 58 " 12 persons,	15·1

Theatres and Halls.

Tony Pastor's, Gallery, full house,	37·1
" Parterre, "	29·8
Atlantic Garden, Parterre, full house,	18·75
Stadt Theatre, Gallery, slim attendance,	19·1
" Parterre, "	27·7
Bowery Theatre, Gallery, crowded,	36·5
" Parterre, "	23·2
Union Square Theatre, Gallery, moderately full,	28·9
Cooper Institute, large hall, "	27·0
Germania Theatre, Parterre, full house,	26·0
Niblo's Garden, Balcony, "	33·9
Wallack's Theatre, Gallery, "	36·5
Booth's Theatre, Balcony, moderately full,	10·6
Olympic " " full house,	20·0
Fifth Avenue Theatre, Gallery, full house,	40·6
" " Parterre, "	14·2
Atheneum, " "	13·0
Bryant's " "	17·0
Grand Opera House, " slim attendance,	11·8
" " Balcony, "	23·7

PROF. C. A. SEELY presented a discussion on the Reduction of Iron, in which he described some methods that had never come into use upon a large scale in manufacture, though possessing much theoretical interest.

He made particular reference to the production of the so-called "iron sponge," and to the process which Mr. Siemens has lately brought forward in England. In regard to this subject he remarked, as a matter of some interest, that the first experiments in this process had been made by Mr. Siemens, at Trenton, N. J., while residing temporarily in this country.

DR. H. C. BOLTON described some points in chemical manipulation, lately introduced into the laboratories of the School of Mines. He exhibited a knife of Wootz steel, for cutting glass tubing, in every way superior to a file. He described the battery of water-baths, as used at the School of Mines, exhibiting drawings and portions of the apparatus itself. He also mentioned a simple apparatus for hastening filtration.

May 19th. Geological Section.

President Newberry in the chair. Sixteen persons present.

The PRESIDENT exhibited a specimen of chrysolite, (called also peridot) from Arizona, which he had had cut and polished into a very clear and beautiful gem. These chrysolites occur, with pyropes (Bohemian garnets), quite widely distributed through portions of Arizona and New Mexico, as rolled specimens, probably derived from the conglomerate which forms the lowest member of the Trias of that region; and thence washed out and scattered along the beds of streams, in old gravels, etc.

He also showed a series of plates now preparing for the forthcoming volume on fossil plants, in the series of reports of the U. S. Geological Survey of the Territories. Those exhibited were illustrations of the Miocene flora of North America. He remarked upon the great development of angiospermous plants and trees in the vast Miocene lake regions of what are now the Great Basin and the Plains, and especially upon its far northern extension. This rich and abundant vegetation, presenting the clear evidence of a climate not colder than warm-temperate, spread northward over Alaska, Greenland, Spitzbergen, and Northern Europe; between all which points it is plain that a land connection must at that time have existed. The whole flora was so similar to that of the United States to-day, that it is hardly necessary, or possible, to draw a sharp line of distinction between the two. The approach of the glacial period drove all this vegetation gradually southward, upon both continents; but the great geographical differences of Europe and America are strikingly shown in the subsequent results. In this country, the Miocene plants, which had retreated before the ice to lower latitudes, and had there lived during the cold period, returned again at its close, and gradually overspread, once more, much of their old home. But abroad, the retreating flora was driven up against the impassable barriers formed by the great East and West mountain ranges of Southern Europe and the Mediterranean: thus it died out; and, the old land connection with America having never been restored, the Miocene flora is scarcely represented in Europe now, its place being taken by a different vegetation, which came in from Western Asia, after the glacial era had passed.

PROF. D. S. MARTIN exhibited a series of specimens from northern New York, consisting of crystallized quartz and apatite, with the edges and angles rounded, associated in some cases with calcite, and in others with loxoclase feldspar, having the angles sharply defined. Remarking upon the idea that has been current, that this rounding of angles is an evidence of the action of heat, he pointed out that the loxoclase specimen alone would show the error of this view, as in it the feldspar crystals are unaffected, while the far more infusible quartz is so rounded as to resemble rock-salt that has been wet.

In all these cases, the evidence is clearly, as Prof. Hunt has pointed out, in his paper on the Laurentian limestones, that chemical agents, and not heat, have been concerned in producing these effects; that solution, and not fusion, is the cause. Dr. Hunt has shown that certain alkaline solutions, which have no action on feldspar or pyroxene, attack both quartz and phosphate of lime, and that this is the only explanation of the phenomena presented in such specimens as these.

He also remarked that, so far as he had seen, this re-solution of the surface of apatite crystals, which is common, and almost universal, in specimens from the Eozoic regions of northern New York, is not found in those from the crystalline belt that flanks the sea-coast region, from the vicinity of New York City southward. In some cases, Pennsylvania apatites exhibit a surface with longitudinal striation, very different from the aspect of the northern New York crystals. He had not enough material to make a generalization of this kind, but called attention to it, as an interesting point for inquiry.

DR. B. N. MARTIN showed specimens of stibnite (with cervantite) from Battle Mountain, Nevada, where it is reported as occurring in large quantities. The metallic antimony, reduced from the sulphide, was also exhibited.

THE PRESIDENT made some remarks reviewing the history of the class of fishes, as traced in the older rocks of North America. The earliest appearance of fishes would seem to be a point not capable of precise determination. The first definite traces of the group found in American rocks are, up to the present time, clearly in the Devonian age; but in Europe, the existence of quite a number of genera and species in the Upper Silurian period, is well established. In regard to the presence of fishes in the Lower Silurian seas, the case is very doubtful. Prof. Pander, many years since, announced the discovery in Russia, in rocks of Lower Silurian age, of small and peculiar tooth-like organs, which he regarded as the teeth of fishes, and designated as *Conodonts.* The opinion of Pander has not found general acceptance, however, and these bodies have been regarded by different writers as the teeth of gasteropodous mollusca, the spines of crustaceans, &c. It is perhaps, not impossible, nevertheless, that they may yet prove to be dermal ossicles of a tribe of small cartilaginous fishes.

The discovery of fish-remains in the Upper Silurian of this country, has been repeatedly announced, but never as yet confirmed. In the Palæontology of New York, (Vol. II, page 320 and plate 71,) Prof. Hall has described and figured what he regarded as the fin-spine of a fish from the Clinton group, giving it the name of *Onchus Deweyi*. *Onchus* is a genus of sharks from the Ludlow rocks of Great Britain, (the equivalent of our Lower Helderberg series), described in like manner from spines; but this fossil has not been accepted as a fish relic, but is by general consent regarded as the spine of a crustacean.

Hugh Miller, (Footprints of the Creator, p. 143) has figured a fin-spine, "from the Onondaga Salt-group." He was here misled by a confusion of names; the specimen having come from the Onondaga Limestone, a local New York division of the Corniferous, and being in fact a spine of the Devonian genus *Machæracanthus*.

All the evidence bearing on the first appearance of fishes is, however, but negative; and as the upper part of the Upper Silurian series abroad has been proved to contain quite an ichthyic fauna, it is possible, at least, that something similar may at any time be discovered here. It is worth while to observe that the Silurian crustacea seem to have been provided with means of defence against enemies of some kind. Although they were highly ornamented, yet there is more than ornamentation implied in the spiny and bristling character of quite a number of Lower Silurian trilobites, as well as in their power of rolling themselves into a ball. *Acidaspis*, for instance, was a perfect hedgehog in its armament. It is probable, however, that the defences of the Silurian crustaceans were to protect them against the cephalopods, such as *Orthoceras*, which was abundant and attained great size. Fishes, if they existed at all on this continent, in that age, were few and small.

When we pass to the Devonian rocks, however, all is changed. Then appears a rich development of ichthyic life, in many varied and remarkable forms. Especially noticeable is the elaborate armament, offensive and defensive, of the ancient sharks. In the Corniferous limestone, we find the fossils described under the name of *Machœracanthus.* These were fin-spines of fishes, but were unlike anything known among modern sharks, being "double bayonets" in structure, of great size, and constituting most formidable side-arms. At present, but few sharks, and those of small size, have spined fins. In the Huron shale, equivalent to a part of the Portage group, the fossils known as *Ctenacanthus* appear; these were dorsal spines a foot long. As the complement of all this system of weapons among the sharks, the ganoid fishes of the same period had an amount of bony encasement that was well adapted to the necessities of their circumstances. It would seem, however, as though there must have have been numerous less protected fishes, probably of smaller size, which have left but few traces in the rocks, but which served as food to these mail-clad and sword-spined monsters of the period.

In coming down to latter ages, we find a general disarmament among the sharks, and a consequent, or at least a corresponding, disappearance of the heavy armor worn as a defence by the ganoids. Our living fishes certainly have nothing of spiny side-arms, or bony encasements.

An interesting question arises in reviewing the history of these remarkable forms of fish-life in the Devonian age. When and how was all this offensive and defensive armament acquired? Are we to look to direct endowment, or to inheritance, as the source whence it was derived? Of the latter, the evidence as yet is wanting; and the inquiry remains, as one of no slight interest. A similar problem is presented by much of the ornamentation of the lower animals. The minute and elegant chasing upon so many ganoid scales, the ornamental shields of so many trilobites, the evident beauty that must have belonged to much of the Palæozoic shell-fauna, all suggest this query; and it becomes still more marked in considering the exquisite sculpturing of the Upper Silurian crinoids and cystideans, and the beauty of color and form in modern polyps and both modern and ancient echinoids; in all of which groups the explanation of sexual selection, advanced in regard to higher animals, has no possible application. This prevalence of beauty, seemingly without any relation to utility or advantage, suggests a view of intelligent design quite foreign to Mr. Darwin's principle of mere natural selection.

May 26th.

President Newberry in the chair. Nine members present.

Among a number of specimens brought in for exhibition and discussion by those present,

Mr. WILBUR showed a large moth which he had lately raised from a cocoon.

Prof. D. S. MARTIN said that this insect was the newly introduced Japanese silk-moth, *Saturnia Cynthia*, and spoke of the persevering efforts of an associate of the Society, Mr. John Akhurst, of Brooklyn, carried on through several years past, to naturalize this species, and to ascertain how far its cocoons are capable of being made the basis of silk production. Mr. Akhurst had proved abundantly that the insect thrives in our climate; and indeed it has already escaped from cultivation on his premises, and is spreading spontaneously into the streets and gardens of Brooklyn.* Its food-

* Mr. Akhurst has ascertained that two broods are produced each year; the first hatching in the early summer, and after reaching maturity, laying their eggs, which hatch very soon, and produce the late summer brood in time to pass through all their changes, and lay their eggs for the following year, before the close of the season. This last fact is one of much importance; as any failure of the second brood to lay their eggs in due time, would prove a serious bar to their successful propagation.

In the early part of the summer, Mr. Akhurst placed a hundred young larvæ upon a cluster of small ailanthus trees in the outskirts of Brooklyn. After a long and cold storm, he visited the place and searched for the worms. None of them had been beaten off or injured, but all were found securely lodged underneath the leaves of the trees. This experiment was a pretty thorough test of the hardy constitution of the insect, and its adaptation to our climate.

plant is our commonest city tree, the Ailanthus, and the culture of the insect is easy; the silk is strong, lustrous, and, in the raw state, of a pale grey tint. Mr. Akhurst had carried his experiments as far as energy and enthusiasm could avail; and all that is wanting now to the full solution of the problem is capital. If some persons possessed of means would enter into the investigation, the question as to whether the silk can be profitably used for manufacture could be speedily decided.

The PRESIDENT laid before the Lyceum, for the inspection of the members, the new geological map of the entire territory of the United States, compiled by Prof. C. H. Hitchcock; and spoke of it as an improvement upon anything of the kind previously issued, and as meeting a long-felt want.

Prof. D. S. MARTIN exhibited the closing part of the first volume of Prof. Wm. H. Edwards' work on the Butterflies of North America. He called attention particularly to the very interesting and suggestive discoveries of Prof. Edwards in reducing, in several instances, two or three so-called species which had been regarded as distinct, to seasonal, or other, modifications of a single species. This fact was proved in part IX of the present volume, with regard to several familiar butterflies. *Grapta interrogationis*, Fabr., for instance, and *G. umbrosa*, Lintner, are but well-marked varieties; as Mr. Edwards has raised them both in abundance from eggs laid by individuals of *G. umbrosa*. He therefore proposes the name *Fabricii* to denote the lighter-colored form, originally described by that eminent entomologist, while the name *umbrosa*, given to the dark individuals by our corresponding member, Mr. Lintner, remains, both being but varieties of the species *interrogationis*.

In the same way, *Papilio Ajax* presents three distinct seasonal types, two of which, at least, have been regarded as separate species, *P. Marcellus*, *P. Telamonides*, and *P. Walshii*. The two last named appear in the spring, from pupæ that have lived over the winter, *Walshii* coming out earlier than *Telamonides.* The former produces broods of both types by the early summer, and of *Marcellus* in the later summer and fall. *Telamonides* produces *Marcellus* in the later summer, and its own type in the spring, (some chrysalids hatching out promptly, and some living over till the next year). *Marcellus* develops its own type the same season, while the chrysalids that go over till spring, appear as the early brood of *Walshii* and the somewhat later brood of *Telamonides.* A large series of careful observations has placed these facts beyond further question, seemingly; and American entomology is under much obligation to Mr. Edwards for thus unravelling some of the most perplexed relations of our species and varieties, and giving us a clear insight into their interesting circles of change. It is to be hoped that he will be able to carry on his observations, and yet further elucidate our nomenclature, not only, but our ideas.

The PRESIDENT exhibited specimens of *Cœlacanthus elegans*, Newb., from the coal-measures of Linton, Ohio, and made some remarks upon the structure and history of the small and peculiar group of fishes represented by this genus. It is customary to meet with the statement, that all the ancient fishes possessed the so-called heterocercal tail, in which the vertebral column is prolonged into the upper lobe of the caudal fin. In the Carboniferous age, however, this group of Cœlacanth ganoids appears, having a tail-structure quite different from the heterocercal, and to some extent resembling that found in our modern fishes, in which the tail-fin is equally developed above and below the end of the spinal column. There is, however, a marked difference from the modern type, in that the Cœlacanths have the vertebral column not terminating abruptly, but prolonged through the caudal fin, and carrying a smaller secondary fin at its absolute tip.

The genus *Cœlacanthus*, represented by several species from the Carboniferous and later rocks of England and the Continent, originally described by Agassiz, is now found to have had three species in the coal-measure rocks of Ohio, *C. elegans*, *C. ornatus*, and *C. robustus*. It is interesting and curious to note the very marked resemblance existing between this genus, and *Undina* in the Jurassic, and *Macropoma* in the Cretaceous, amounting to something almost like generic identity, as pointed out lately by Prof. Huxley. The hollow fin-spines, whence the name of the type-genus was formed, the ornamented bony head-plates, the ossified air-bladder, and the peculiar tail, equally lobed on both sides of the prolonged vertebral column, (for which structure the name *diphycercal* has been proposed by McCoy), and supplemented by a small additional or terminal lobe, all make up an assemblage of characters which, more or less fully exhibited by these several genera, link them very closely together as a well-marked natural group. This peculiar type extends from the Mountain Limestone of Europe to the Cretaceous, preserving its characteristic and unusual features with remarkable persistence, through a series of ages, and a succession of changes, which our minds strive in vain to grasp.

The same persistence of type is seen at many points in the history of life. It is exceedingly marked in *Nautilus*, which began in the Lower Silurian, and has lived on till the present time, while sending out offshoots into *Clymenia*, *Goniatites*, and through *Ceratites*, etc., into the *Ammonitidæ*, all of which forms speedily became extinct. The Ammonites, in particular, sported into every conceivable variety of form, and frittered themselves away in excessive ornamentation; and after a brief, though brilliant, reign in the Mesozoic age, they passed utterly away.

In reference, yet further, to fossil ganoids, it is a matter of much interest that species of the genera *Amia* and *Lepidosteus* have recently been brought to light from the Tertiary lake-beds of the Great Basin. The plated ganoids are all long extinct; while of the scaled ganoids, but seven genera have living representatives, five of these being American and two African. The scaled-ganoids have been traced from the Devonian to the Cretaceous, and they again appear in the present period: but this recent discovery of them in the

Tertiary, supplies an interesting link in their chain of succession. The living genera are as follows:

AMIADÆ. *Amia*; North America.

LEPIDOSTEIDÆ. *Lepidosteus*; North America.

CROSSOPTERYGIDÆ. *Polypterus*; Nile.
Calamichthys; Senegal.

CHONDROSTEIDÆ. *Accipenser*; N. America and Europe.
Spatularia; North America.
Scaphirhynchus; North America.

June 2. Business Meeting.

President Newberry in the chair. Thirteen persons present.

On the recommendation of the Committee on Nominations, the following gentlemen were admitted to the Lyceum:

As Resident Members,—Mr. G. W. McNulty, Martin E. Waldstein, Esq., and Gen. Egbert L. Viele.

As Corresponding Member,—Mr. A. M. Tryon, of Philadelphia.

The Publication Committee announced that the Proceedings of the Society for the months of January and February had been issued, and were ready for distribution. This first number begins the New Series of Proceedings, which is to be issued by the Committee henceforth, officially.

THE PRESIDENT remarked upon the memorial of the late Dr. Torrey, and suggested that, as Prof. Gray was preparing a full notice for the American Journal of Science, which would soon appear, it might be best to defer the Lyceum memorial until that paper had appeared.

On motion, the Lyceum adjourned until the first Monday of October, as usual.

[By an oversight, the second number of these Proceedings was paged like the first, 1–32, instead of 33–64, as it should have been.]

PROCEEDINGS

OF THE

LYCEUM OF NATURAL HISTORY

IN THE

CITY OF NEW YORK.

SECOND SERIES.

October 6th, 1873. Business Meeting.

Dr. B. N. Martin in the chair. Eleven persons present.

The evening was chiefly occupied with a variety of routine business, in regard to the publications and exchanges of the society.

The Secretary read by title a paper, "On the Lingual Dentition and Anatomy of Achatinella and other Pulmonata," by T. Bland and W. G. Binney, with two plates, published in the Annals, Vol. X, No. 12.

A number of minerals were exhibited and remarked upon by Dr. Feuchtwanger.

October 13th, 1873.

President Newberry in the chair. Thirteen persons present.

Dr. Feuchtwanger showed a deposit of silver-leaf on glass, prepared in the same way as that described in the Proceedings of March 10th, from a solution of sulphate of copper and silver, but with the film deposited upon a glass plate, which was first immersed in the liquid, and then carefully lifted to the surface.

He also announced the discovery of rare ores, orpiment, native bismuth, and pitchblende, in the Western Territories.

The President and other members discussed these discoveries at length, Dr. Bolton dwelling especially on the very rich pitchblende from Georgetown, Colorado. A large amount of this ore had been brought to New York and Hoboken, and had been employed by Dr. Morton of the Stevens Institute, and by himself, for the manufacture of oxide of uranium, to use in preparing the many uranic salts upon which they were experimenting as to fluorescence.

The occurrence and yield of chromic iron were likewise discussed. The President described its mode of association with the serpentine which is found among the upheavals of the Coast Range of California and Oregon. Parts of this range, which is of Cretaceous and Tertiary age, are quite unaltered, and rich in fossils; others are much changed, sometimes even to a jasperoid rock, such as the gangue of the cinnabar at New Almaden and New Idria. The serpentine is plainly an altered rock, not an eruptive one; but whether it forms part of the late strata of the Coast and Cascade Ranges, or is an old core, is yet uncertain. The Golden Gate is cut through this ridge of serpentine, which shows conspicuously at its entrance.

Prof. D. S. Martin remarked upon the striking differences between the serpentines of what he termed the Atlantic belt, and those of the Blue Ridge and the Eozoic mountains, as shown both in their aspect and in their associated minerals. The serpentines of the eastern belt are massive and opaque, and are marked by a minute, but very constant, percentage of nickel and of chromium, occasionally rising to amounts that become of economic importance. They also abound in hydrated magnesian minerals of many species, but do not contain chrysotile, are rarely associated with calcite, and manifest no traces of *Eozoön.* The Blue Ridge and Adirondac serpentines, on the other hand, are frequently precious, or noble, in character, seamed with chrysotile, and associated with calcite so as to form ophites and Eozoön rock; while they are destitute of nickel or chrome, and likewise of the various hydrated magnesian minerals which are so exceedingly characteristic of the other series. The difference is most remarkable, and may be traced for hundreds of miles along the two ranges. In his view, it was indicative of important differences in the mode of formation; the Eozoic serpentines having been probably chemically deposited, as we know them to have been when they fill the chambers of rhizopods or other organic structures, (as glauconite at later periods, and even now); while the eastern serpentines, which Dr. T. Sterry Hunt regards as Huronian, have probably resulted from alteration. He was himself engaged upon this subject, and hoped to present it more fully hereafter.

The President said, in response to an inquiry, that he was not aware that the mineralogy of the Coast Range serpentine had received any attention.

Dr. H. C. Bolton gave some accounts of his observations in Europe during the summer, in regard to the progress and present state of chemical science, as shown in the arrangements of the best and newest laboratories of Germany, and the libraries of Berlin, Vienna, Paris, and London.

Dr. B. N. Martin described a remarkable and unknown fossil, apparently fucoidal, but very difficult of reference, discovered by Dr. R. P. Stevens at the very base of the Potsdam sandstone, at Palmer's Falls on the upper Hudson. He had himself visited the spot during the summer, but the river had risen, and access to the locality was cut off. He trusted that Dr. Stevens would describe it more fully to the Lyceum.

October 20th, 1873.

President Newberry in the chair. Nine persons present.

Dr. Feutchwanger exhibited a large series of specimens of the zinc ores and franklinite from Sterling, New Jersey, representing many peculiar varieties and modes of occurrence.

Prof. D. S. Martin showed specimens of muscovite lately brought to view in blasting gneiss rock at Rye, Westchester Co. The crystals were remarkable for their elegant cleavages, especially for a set parallel to $i\check{3}$.

He also exhibited a series of magnesian minerals lately procured from the old serpentine locality at New Rochelle, comprising marmolite, deweylite, magnesite, and chromite in serpentine; and remarked upon them in connection with the facts referred to at the last meeting, as illustrating still further the points then presented. He had visited the locality for the purpose of examining its mineralogy; and his expectations in regard to its character were abundantly verified. The general features that mark the eastern, or Huronian, serpentines, in distinction from those of the Blue Ridge and Eozoic districts, were plainly to be seen.

Mr. W. P. Jenny gave an account of his recent explorations in the geology of Western Texas. His principal line of travel had been across the Llano Estacado, near the 32d parallel, to the Pecos River, and on to the Rio Grande near El Paso.

The first important formation encountered was, of course, the Cretaceous of the Llano Estacado, (Jurassic of Marcou). A section from the base, near the Pecos, gives:

(A.) Red sandstone, 50 feet, like the Trias of the Eastern States, underlaid by, and probably resting on, a gneiss.

(B.) Soft, brown sandstone (Cretaceous?) passing upward into limestone, 50 feet.

(C.) Great limestone, 450 feet, rich in typical Cretaceous fossils, *Exogyra Texana*, *Gryphœa Pitcheri*, *Ammonites pedernalis*, *etc.*

(D.) On the mesas, here and there, are found some 40 feet of a limestone full of *Caprina*, but usually worn away by denudation.

The sharp edges of the Llano are very remarkable, generally much sea-worn. No drift action was visible; though occasionally on these edges there occur local beds of small jasper and chalcedony pebbles.

The next important point noted, was the great developement of Carboniferous limestone in the Guadaloupe mountains, the most eastern of three main ranges that lie between the Llano and the Rio Grande. The rocks here dip eastward, and the Carboniferous limestone at some points attains a thickness of 1,200 or 1,500 feet, full of crinoids, etc. In some places this limestone has all the aspect of a great shore-reef, its edges almost vertical cliffs, hundreds of feet high, and full of caverns and wave-lines worn by the ancient sea.

Beneath the limestone is a brown or yellow sandstone, 600 or 700 feet thick, non-fossiliferous, and of undetermined age.

Passing westward to the Hueco mountains, a like section is again found, the dip also being eastward. Here the Carboniferous forms the crest, and is underlaid by Lower Silurian, which in turn rests upon gneiss.

The most interesting and important series, however, was found thirty miles farther west, in the Organ mountains, close to the city of El Paso. Here the base is a coarse feldspathic granite, very similar to much of the eastern gneiss, and upon it rests:

I. Quartzite, passing upward into

II. Sandstone (Potsdam), filled with *Scolithus linearis.*

III. Crystalline limestone (Calciferous), containing several species of fossils resembling *Archæocyathus*, and rarely a gasteropod, like *Pleurotomaria.*

IV. Magnesian limestone, (Chazy), with flints, and containing some straight cephalopods and a *Receptaculites.*

V. Black limestone (Trenton), with *Maclurea* abundant, *Orthis*, *Orthoceras*, and a "chain coral."

VI. Lower Hudson, very rich in corals.

VII. Upper Hudson, with *Orthis*, etc., and many characteristic fossils of the period.

The dip of all these beds is about 30° west, facing the eastward dipping rocks of the Hueco range. Their total thickness exceeds 1,200 feet.

Upon them rests a great limestone reef, some 400 feet thick, unconformable, dipping west about 10°, and passing upward into what appears to be Carboniferous, judging from the position of rocks of that age on the ranges lying to the north and east. Its lower portion, however, contains some imperfect fossils resembling *Pentamerus*, and suggesting an Upper Silurian age; while at the base is a conglomerate, made up of pebbles of beds V, VI, and VII, which seems to hold the position of the Oneida.

No Devonian can be recognized at any point.

The President remarked that this account has peculiar interest. Among many important points, it shows the great age of the Rocky Mountains, or at least, of their core. Farther north, at Santa Fé, the Carboniferous is the oldest rock on the flanks of the range; and above are found the later formations, dipping away from the line of the mountains on either side, and appearing in succession as the explorer travels either east or west. At Los Cornudos, also, in western Texas, there is a large mass of crystalline rock, which rose as an island from the Carboniferous sea. The deposits of that age rest against and surround it, and have filled a multitude of crevices in and around its flanks. But farther away to the west, down on the great Colorado cañon, where the rocks have been cut down thousands of feet, the older formations are revealed, in order, with the Potsdam beds at the base.

Now, it appears, there are found in the Rio Grande valley, the crystalline base-rocks overlaid in succession by the Potsdam and Primordial, the Trenton, Hudson, Upper Silurian (?), and Carboniferous, just as they occur in the northern and eastern states. The absence of the Devonian is a remarkable feature, but it may be locally paralleled at many points in the east. The great invasions of the sea, that laid down the several Palæozoic series, varied somewhat in extent, generally lessening as time passed on, until the vast submergence of the Carboniferous age. The Devonian sea did not reach as far as some of the others, at points; and did not carry its deposits far enough to cover this region.

It would seem as though the Organ mountains had formed one border, and the New York and Canadian highlands the other, of the great Palæozoic invasions of the sea. The sections on the Ohio anticlinal, and many other facts, give evidence that these old formations extend continuously over the whole vast area of the continent, though largely covered and concealed by deposits of later age.

October 27th, 1873.

President Newberry in the chair; nine persons present.

DR. FEUCHTWANGER showed a large series of fossils obtained by him during the summer, from the "Upper Marl Bed" (Eocene), at Deal, N. J., five miles below Long Branch.

DR. R. P. STEVENS described, and drew, a remarkable silicified skull of some marine animal, which he had lately seen in Accomac Co., Virginia.

THE PRESIDENT identified it as the skull of a walrus (*Trichecus rosmarus*). Several simular walrus skulls have been found on the coast within some years past, and likewise in the old shell-heaps. They are of glacial age, and possess much interest; as the species does not now occur south of Nova Scotia.

PROF. D. S. MARTIN exhibited a set of specimens of coral, of several species, altered to chalcedony, from Tampa Bay, Florida. Prof. Dana, in his Mineralogy, (Ed. 1868, page 196) refers to such a coral-pseudomorph, from Devonshire, as having been described as a separate variety of chalcedony, under the name of Beckite.

THE PRESIDENT referred to the vast amounts of chalcedony in the far West, amounting, at some points in southern California, to thousands of tons. There, as doubtless also locally at Tampa, it is the product of thermal waters which have taken up silica, and which, in the far West, are connected with the great volcanic disturbances that have taken place.

DR. R. P. STEVENS read the following paper:

Recent Observations on Drift.

In some late geological excursions in the south and southwest, I have observed indications which carry the limit of glacial action further south than I had previously supposed.

In the Potomac valley, drift deposits are apparent: at Cumberland, Md., they rival those of any northern river valley. Some years ago, I found glacial indications at the sources of the Potomac; among them a true Canadian boulder of red felspathic gneiss. Lately, in the same region, I found on the summit of the West Front of the Alleghany mountains, a series of drift deposits, mainly derived from Carboniferous rocks, and including fragments of coal, resting upon the upturned and shaved-off edges of Devonian (?) sandstone.

In the valley of the Greenbriar river, west of these mountains, heavy deposits of drift appear at various points; and especially at the junction of the Greenbriar with New river, at Hinton, Va. In digging the foundations of depot buildings for the Chesapeake and Ohio Rail-Road, large surfaces of the Sub-Carboniferous limestone were laid bare, They are smoothed, polished, striated, and broken down on the edges, and covered with a mantle of drift twelve to fifteen feet thick.

On a branch of the James river, at Covington, Va., I found the upturned edges of the slates of the Blue Ridge cut off by glaciers, and bearing their load of drift. Like indications are visible along the Chesapeake and Ohio road, as far as the tunnel opening into the Greenbriar valley. This branch of James river rises on the east flank of the same range of mountains, and also southward from the head waters of the Potomac.

These facts lead to very interesting inquiries. Did the glacier of the Greenbriar, after reaching New river, move on southward into the great valley of Virginia, and meet the glacier of James river moving along the same valley? Or did it turn westward, follow the valley of New river into the Kanawha, and then pass down this latter valley to join the great glacier of the Ohio? Possibly it divided and did both.

These observations carry the southern limit of glaciers as far down as Lat. 37°30′ N. At and near Richmond, Va., I have seen long trains of boulders (small, white, and gravelly) streaming away in a north and south direction. I found, also, that the northern out-crop of the lower coal of the James river (Triassic) coal-field, had been torn up and carried over and deposited upon the upper and higher coal measures.

Although signs of ancient glaciers are not so frequent and palpable south of the Potomac as north of it, yet I am persuaded that by due inspection they can be found in places little imagined.

Dr. Stevens also made a communication, entitled "Irregularities in the Floor of the Coal Measures of Eastern

Kentucky," in which he described a number of observations which he had recently made in the vicinity of Mount Vernon and Livingstone. This account will be found in the Annals, Vol. xi. No. 1.

November 3d, 1873. Business Meeting.

Dr. B. N. Martin in the chair; thirteen persons present.

After the transaction of ordinary routine business, Prof. D. S. Martin reported progress in the matter of preparing a memorial to the Secretary of the Navy, recommending the appointment of one or more naturalists to accompany the Transit Expedition to the stations in the Southern Hemisphere.

DR. R. P. STEVENS described some observations made by himself, upon the so-called "carbonite," or "natural coke," of Richmond, Virginia, which is associated with the Triassic coal, in some portions of the field that lie north of the James river. The theory generally held in regard to the genesis of this singular material, and which originated with Prof. Wm. D. Rogers, ascribes it to an alteration of the coal by a trap-dyke, stretching over and across it, at or near this point. No such dyke, however, can be detected in any section or shaft. No rock in the series is changed; the fossiliferous roof-shale, between the coal-seam and the supposed overlying trap, shows no signs of alteration, even when resting on the coke. Moreover, the seam in which the coke occurs, which is some eight feet thick, is full of alternations; sometimes it is coke all through, sometimes coke and coal interlaminated, sometimes coke above and coal below, or *vice versâ*, and sometimes the seam runs out, the shale coming down and cutting it out.

It seems hardly possible, especially in the absence of any observable dyke, to retain this hypothesis longer. Some other explanation of the change must be sought. It may possibly be found in the decomposition of sulphides in the vein itself.

Dr. Stevens also described some features of the geology of the cañon of New river, in West Virginia, referring particularly to the existence of three seams of coal, the upper one quite good, exposed on the south side of the river, above the red Umbral shales, which occupy the base of the cañon, and the true conglomerate, (No. xii).

These he thought, could scarcely be the same as the Subcarboniferous coals found in Rockingham Co., Virginia, and near the head-waters of the Potomac.

Above the conglomerate (No. xii.), there are four regular coal seams exposed, at the same locality, between White Oak and Big Sewall mountains; these are traceable on both sides of the river. The general dip of the beds is here some 12° west.

November 10th, 1873. Chemical Section.

Dr. B. N. Martin in the chair; eleven persons present.

Dr. H. C. Bolton exhibited specimens of the pitchblende from Georgetown, Nevada, whence it has been obtained in large quantities, and gave some account of the mode of its occurrence. He also showed a number of other uranium minerals, among them autunite from Limoges, France, torbernite, and artificial specimens of the new compounds Zeunerite, $CuO.2U_2O_3.As_2O_5+8H_2O$, and uranospinite, $CaO.2U_2O_3.As_2O_5+8H_2O$ both of which were originally described and prepared by Dr. Winkler.

Prof. D. S. Martin remarked upon the occurrence of the uranium phosphates in the gneiss of the Atlantic border, especially at the celebrated autunite locality opposite Fairmount, in West Philadelphia.

Prof. C. A. Joy gave an account, by request of the members, of the leading features in the chemical department of the Vienna Exhibition. He referred to the contrast presented between the German and French portions of the chemical division. The richness of the latter was mainly, and almost wholly, in articles of taste and elegance, as perfumery, etc., of which there was an endless variety; while the German department was much more remarkable for strictly scientific products, and for such as have high economic importance. Particularly interesting was the great and varied display of the alkaloids, which were very finely prepared and arranged. Grape sugar was exhibited in immense quantities, and formed a conspicuous feature. The anthracine colors were also well represented. Perhaps the most important feature, economically, was the new process for the manufacture of soda-ash by ammonia, which attracted a great deal of attention. The iron industry also was very largely displayed, by varied products and models of furnaces.

The collections of minerals were extremely rich and interesting, particularly the sets of coal from the United States. In the department of photography, also, the American division was especially rich, the specimens furnished from this country being the finest in the Exhibition. A ceaseless throng surrounded the large cases that contained sets of photographic views from the Yosemite valley and from the Yellowstone, and the portraits by Wm. Kurtz.

The greatest importance, however, probably attaches to the Educational Department, in which almost every object relating to instruction might be found.

As a whole, the Vienna Exhibition must be considered a great success, despite all that has been said and written to the contrary. In its presentation of the industries of the civilized world, in its stimulus to labor, thought, and invention, and in its liberalizing and elevating influences,—many of them peculiar and not readily observed,—it marks an auspicious era in the development of regenerated Austria, where a wonderful contrast is presented to the condition of ten years ago.

November 17th, 1873. Geological Section.

President Newberry in the chair. Eight persons present.

Among the books received, was the Journal of the Linnean Society of London, Botany, vol. xiii, Nos. 68 to 72 inclusive, in regard to which the President called particular attention to the importance and interest of Mr. Bentham's paper on the Compositæ.

He also exhibited a suite of specimens of *Cœlacanthus elegans*, Newb., from the coal measures at Linton, Ohio, and after briefly referring to their structure and geological position,* read portions of the paper of Mr. Cope, in the Proceedings of the Academy of Natural Sciences of Philadelphia, part 2, March to September, 1873, in which that gentleman describes the new genera *Conchiopsis and Peplorhina.* Of these, the former, at least, is founded simply upon some imperfect specimens of *Cœlacanthus elegans.* He had engaged Mr. Cope to describe, for the final report of the Ohio Survey, the new amphibians discovered in the Linton coal-bed ; for which work his skill and familiarity in that department of zoölogy render him eminently fit. On the slabs containing the amphibian remains, occurred some specimens of the *Cœlacanthus ;* and upon these Mr. Cope founds his new genera, although he had been notified that the fossil fishes of Ohio, were all either already described, or now in his (the speaker's) hands for determination. He could speak with certainty upon these points, as over five hundred specimens of this fish had passed under his examination, exhibiting every variety and all the parts ; and there is no question that Mr. Cope's *Conchiopsis* is the same genus as *Cœlacanthus* of Agassiz ; that two of his species, *C. filiferus* and *C. anguliferus*, are founded on *Cœl. elegans* (described in Proc. Acad. Nat. Sci., Phil., April, 1856, and in the final report of the Ohio Survey, vol. I, part 2, Palæontology; page 337, plate 40) ; and that his third species, *C. exanthematicus*, is identical with his *Peplorhina anthracina*,

* Cf. these Proceedings, May 26th, 1873.

which may be a fish, but is so fragmentary as to be practicably undeterminable.*

PROF. D. S. MARTIN exhibited specimens of *Palæotrochis minor*, Emmons, from Troy, North Carolina, and also of the rock which they form when aggregated. The interest which attaches to these much-disputed and oft-ridiculed fossils (?) from the Taconic, is certainly very considerable, and no prejudice or authority should be suffered to warp the judgment of geologists regarding them. When seen in a mass, aggregated and partially crushed, they have a strongly concretionary aspect, it is true; but when good specimens are examined singly, their regularity of form and of apparent structure becomes very striking. They are evidently worthy of most careful study.

THE PRESIDENT said that in Oregon, 150 miles south of the Dalles, there occurs a tufaceous rock filled with peculiar small concretions, the product of hot waters charged with silica, which strongly resemble the *Palæotrochis*; he had been wont to suspect that such was the real nature of the latter.

PROF. MARTIN also showed large specimens of *Ostrea borealis*, from the great shell-heaps on the Damariscotta River, Maine, procured by Miss Helen C. Kingsley of this city. The largest of these kjokken-moeddings are described as extending along the river-bank for a full half-mile, with a height of some thirty feet, and bearing a growth of large and ancient trees. So immense is the deposit of shells, that it is now extensively worked for the purpose of procuring lime as a fertilizer. Many of the oyster-shells are a foot and a half long, and with them have been found many stone implements, and some human skulls. The oyster is now scarcely found on that portion of our coast, and when it is, the individuals are few and small.

THE PRESIDENT exhibited a set of skulls of the large post-tertiary peccary, *Dicotyles compressus*, Leconte, lately dis-

* Cf. Note on the genus *Conchiopsis*, Cope. Proc. Acad. Nat. Sci., Phil., 1873, part 2, page 425.

covered near Columbus, Ohio, and also of the two living species of peccary, *D. torquatus* of Mexico, and *D. labiatus* of South America, for comparison, as likewise of the common hog, *Sus scrofa.* He described the mode of occurrence of these highly interesting fossils. They were found in two groups of six specimens each, about a rod apart, buried in the valley drift of a small stream tributary to the Scioto; and from the fact that all the heads were turned in the same direction, it would seem as though the animals had been sleeping under the edge of the steep bank, which had caved in and buried them.

The size of this extinct species was a little larger than that of the living *D. labiatus.* The circumstances of their occurrence hardly allow us to assign them any more definite date than Post-tertiary. They probably belong to the same period with the elephant and mastodon, which, appearing shortly after the glacial epoch, continued down for some time into the present geological age.

November 24th, 1873.

President Newberry in the chair. Ten persons present.

THE PRESIDENT made some statements respecting the article of Prof. Lesquereaux upon the lignite-flora of the far west, in the Report of the U. S. Geological Survey of the Territories for 1872. In this extended paper, Mr. Lesquereaux takes the ground that nearly all the lignites of our far West are Eocene, whereas the evidence is conclusive that much of what he so regards is Cretaceous, and much is Miocene. The lignites of Nebraska, Kansas, and the Indian Territory, at first held to be Tertiary by Profs. Heer and Lesquereaux, are now conceded to be Cretaceous, as the speaker had originally pronounced them. As to those of Arizona and New Mexico, he had become familiar with them during a two years' residence, and the evidence of their Cretaceous age, from overlying marine fossils, is unquestionable. The same is the case, according to Profs. Cope, Marsh, Meek, and Stevenson, with the lignites of Colorado and Utah. These facts are even more strongly marked in the case of Vancouver's Island, where the overlying fossils are of the most typical Cretaceous character.

The Upper Missouri lignite beds, on the other hand, which Mr. Lesquereaux calls Lower Eocene, are doubtless of Miocene age. The flora of the Miocene period was very characteristic and wide-spread, covering our continent far into what is now the frozen north, and stretching over, by way of Iceland and the Hebrides, where there was doubtless an old land-connection, to and through Northern and Central Europe. The Eocene flora of Europe is altogether different in its character, and there is no evidence yet furnished that its analogue exists upon this continent at all. It was distinctively Oriental and tropical, and widely removed from the succeeding Miocene flora, which is substantially identical with the Americo-Japanese flora of the present day.

Of course, if stratigraphical evidence could be brought forward, to counteract the lack of botanical proof, the claim of Mr. Lesquereaux would be established. All that could then be said would be, that the Eocene flora of the Western countinent was unlike that of the Eastern; but when, as in Vancouver's Island, and, according to Profs. Meek and Stevenson, in Colorado, the so-called Eocene lignites are overlaid by hundreds of feet of marine strata containing such universally recognized Cretaceous forms as *Inoceramus*, *Baculites*, *Ammonites*, etc., the evidence of their age can hardly be a matter open to question.

Dr. Habel described a peculiar form of sensibility to sunlight, observed by him in a *Wistaria* growing in his garden. In the morning, the leaflets occupied a position inclined upward from the rachis; in the sunshine, they gradually expanded to a horizontal extension; and as the day declined, they drooped.

The President suggested that such a phenomenon is probably best explicable on the view that the leaf is composed of an "erectile tissue," which, under the activity induced by the sun's rays, becomes distended and congested, as it were; so that a temporary rigidity is assumed, which passes off again when the cause ceases to act.

Dr. Hinton described a remarkable natural grafting which he had lately seen in a young black walnut tree (*Juglans nigra*) in the grounds of St. Stephen's College, at Annandale, Dutchess Co., N. Y. The grafting has occurred some three feet above the first bifurcation of the trunk, between the primitive easterly branch, and a branch crossing over to it, and passing it, from the primitive westerly one. The fusion in the bark is perfect; and the grafting is shown to be complete, by the fact that the limb is one-third larger upon leaving the easterly branch, than where it meets and joins it; it thus appears that nourishment is received from the main easterly branch.

December 1st, 1873. Business Meeting.

The President in the chair; eight persons present.

After the transaction of routine business;—Dr. H. C. Bolton read a paper entitled:

"Contribution to the History of Sulphur Matches."*

After alluding to the general opinion that sulphur matches, in their primitive form, are quite a modern invention, he showed that such an impression was in accordance with the scanty information on the subject found in our great dictionaries and encyclopedias, as most scientific works are content with the statement that "friction matches came into general use about the year 1832." By casually lighting on a passage referring to matches in a work published in 1604, Dr. Bolton was prompted to trace back their history, and obtained the following results. Hoefer, the French historian of chemistry, mentions that George Agricola make allusion

* This article has appeared in full in the *American Chemist*, for December, 1873.

to matches in his "De Natura Fossilium." On examining the original work of Agricola (edition of 1558), the passage alluded to was found, commencing thus: "Plinius scribit: sulphuratis quoque ellychnijs, * * * * arida ligna et candelas accendimus * * * *."

Hoefer, apparently, has not examined the original work of Agricola, for he quotes the passage erroneously, and omits the important words "*Plinius scribit.*" This takes the use of matches back to the first century A. D. A search in the Natural History of Pliny the Elder was rewarded by finding the following passage (Lib. xxxv, 15.)

"In terrae autem reliquis generibus, vel maxime mira natura est sulfuris * * * *. Quarto autem ad ellychnia maxime conficienda."

Dr. Bolton also quoted passages from the Epigrams of Martial, and from the Satires of Juvenal, containing plain allusions to sulphur-tipped slips of wood, or matches in their earliest form.

December 8th, 1873. Chemical Section.

President Newberry in the chair. Thirty persons present.

PROF. A. R. LEEDS read a paper "On the Compounds of Tungsten," in which he described the several modes of preparing tungstic acid, and gave an account of a new class of salts which he had succeeded in forming, for which he proposed the name of tungsto-molybdates.*

MR. WILLIAM FALK read a paper upon Renal and Urinary Calculi, illustrated by an extended suite of specimens of almost every known variety of calculus, from various parts of the body both of man and of animals.

DR. H. C. BOLTON read by title a paper giving the "Outlines of a Bibliography of a History of Chemistry," published in the Annals, vol. x, No. 12, pp 352 to 361.

MR. PIERRE DE P. RICKETTS read a paper upon "Assays

* The full discussion of this whole subject is reserved by the author until a further series of investigations is finished.

of Iron Ores," giving full descriptions and results of the mode of testing such ores, as practiced in the Assay Laboratory of the School of Mines of Columbia College. The ores employed were mainly magnetite, hematite, and limonite; also siderite, ilmenite, and franklinite. The furnace had a cross section of 18 inches square, and a depth to the grate bars of 21 inches. The fuel employed was anthracite.

Specimens of the crucibles used, (Hessian) were first shown, and the mode of preparing them described. They are filled with a brasque composed of pulverized charcoal, 4 parts, and molasses, 1 part, carefully kneaded and packed. A conical hollow is then cut out, and its interior well polished, to render the button obtained smooth. With such a lining, the slag neither adheres, nor takes up any foreign matter; and hence it may be weighed in verification of the assay.

Into this smooth cavity the ore and fluxes are charged, after thorough mixing: a thin charcoal cover is then laid on, and the whole luted up. The charge of ore is ten grammes. As the object is to learn not the absolute percentage of metal so much as the probable yield on a large scale, the usual blast furnace fluxes are used. These of course vary much with the ore. If the composition of the latter is known, it is easy to compute the flux needful, to give a slag of the ordinary blast furnace type,—

$$R_2O_3,SiO_3,+2(3RO,SiO3)$$

according to Percy; where the sesquioxide is alumina, and the protoxides mainly lime and magnesia.

If the composition of the ore is not known, three trial-fluxes are prepared,—an acid one, a neutral, and a basic,—one of which usually gives a good result.

Eight crucibles are introduced at once, resting upon fire-bricks in the midst of the glowing coal. The furnace is filled with fuel above the tops of the crucibles; and the fire is kept up in force from 2½ to 3½ hours, according to the ore. With two furnaces, therefore, one man can make, in a single day, 16 assays in duplicate: these should not differ by more than $\frac{4}{10}$ of one per cent; and with proper care they will show very nearly the real percentage of metal in the ore. But if the fire is too hot, the result will be somewhat above the true yield, owing to combined carbon.

Besides the percentage of iron, it is readily possible to judge of the quality produced and of the nature of the impurities present, by the physical characters of the button and slag. [Of these, many specimens were shown from iron ores of various kinds, and the indications which they give pointed out.]

As the general result of many experiments, it is found practicable to determine by this mode of assay, (1) the quality of the ore, by the slag; (2) the yield of the ore; and (3) the quality of metal produced. The process recommends itself as a quick and easy way for the superintendent of a furnace to test his ores.

DR. H. C. BOLTON exhibited about eighty engraved portraits of chemists, many of them of considerable interest and rarity, which he had collected in Europe and in this country during the two years previous. He also exhibited an album containing over 100 carte-de-visite photographs of deceased and living chemists of France, Germany, England, and America.

December 15th, 1873.

President Newberry in the chair. Sixteen persons present.

DR. FEUCHTWANGER announced the the death of Prof. Louis Agassiz, an Honorary Member of the Lyceum.

On motion, it was resolved that a committee be appointed, to consist of the President and two others, to draft resolutions expressive of the feelings of the members of the society in view of the death of Prof. Agassiz, and of the loss therein sustained by science.

The PRESIDENT appointed Dr. B. N. Martin and Mr. Dinwiddie as the other members of the committee.

MR. WILLIAM FALK exhibited several specimens of fishes from a new locality in the Trias of Connecticut. They occur in a bed of black shale, cut through by a small stream which feeds the reservoir, five miles north-east of Middletown: both the stream and the shale-bed lie between two of the feldspar ridges which run in a north-east and south-west course toward the Connecticut river.

The President said that the locality is probably new. The specimens belonged to the genus *Ischypterus*, which, with *Catopterus*, is found at Durham, and at various points in the Triassic of the Connecticut valley.

Prof. D. S. Martin exhibited several specimens of *Dictyophyton tuberosum*, Hall, from a (probably) new locality, at Alfred, Alleghany Co. N. Y., where they had been found in some abundance and great perfection, by Rev. Dr. J. Allen, President of Alfred University, at a horizon just below the very top of the Chemung group.

The President gave a discussion of the relations of the whole group of supposed algæ to which these forms belong. The tribe was quite peculiar, and apparently has no living representative of any kind. It belongs to the Chemung and Waverly groups, mainly, though found quite low in the Devonian; and during certain periods it attained quite a marked development, so as to form a characteristic feature in some of the beds. One of the first species noticed was that described by Vanuxem under the name of *Uphantenia chemungensis*, a wide-spread reticulated frond, of which we have but imperfect specimens. (Geol. N. Y., vol. 3, p. 183.) *Dictyophyton* is generally cyathiform, or cup-like, varying in different species from cylindrical to widely funnel-shaped. In both the earlier and later Devonian, the genus *Spirophyton*, one species of which is so characteristic of the lowest member of the Corniferous period in New York and Pennsylvania, under the name of *Fucoides Cauda-galli*, doubtless belongs to the same group. Its form was spiral funnel-shaped, much like that of the *Archimedes;* and the familiar "cock's-tail" outline is given by looking down on the crushed and flattened top of the fossil.

PROF. A. M. MAYER read by request a letter lately received from Prof. Agassiz, and probably one of the last that he wrote, expressing his interest in the researches of Prof. Mayer in regard to the physiology of audition.

MR. COLLINGWOOD made some remarks as a tribute to the character of Prof Agassiz, after which

THE PRESIDENT gave an address, in which was comprised a summary of the life, labors, and scientific services of Prof. Agassiz, dwelling especially upon the impetus which science has received in this country through his great and magnetic influence. Whatever else he has done, this was his greatest work. His development of the glacial theory, and his researches in ichthyology, however enduring their fame, cannot equal the power with which he stimulated, trained, and directed the younger minds that came under his influence, and at the same time gave science a prestige and a popularity among our people, that it had never gained before. Cambridge Museum and Penikese are his memorial; and a host of young and ardent students of science, taught by Agassiz, are fast pressing into various fields of new research, to which, with something like prophetic intuition, he had directed their course.

December 22d, 1873.

Dr B. N. Martin in the chair. Twelve persons present.

DR. O. W. MORRIS read a paper on the Meteorology of the months of September, October, and November, 1873, as observed at the Cooper Union. The principal data may be summed up as follows:

September.	Thermometer.	Barometer.
Morning of the 1st	75°	29.735
Evening of the 30th	58°	29.923
Maximum	87.5°, on the 1st	30.279, on the 9th
Minimum	47.°, on the 15th	29.453, on the 13th
Range	40.5°	.826
Mean	66.85°	29.929

Total rainfall, 3.47 inches. Rain occurred on 13 days.

Lunar corona on the 3d; lunar halo on the 8th; thunder storm on the 4th; lightning on the 5th.

The relative humidity ranged from 33.1° to saturation (100°); the force of vapor, from .217° to .863°.

The mean temperature of the month was not far from the average for the past twenty years.

October.	Thermometer.	Barometer.
Morning of the 1st	51°	30.055
Evening of the 31st	49°	29.834
Maximum	72°, on the 5th	30.391, on the 15th
Minimum	40.5°, on the 29th	29.223, on the 20th
Range	31.5°,	1.168
Mean	57.11°	29.950

Total rainfall, 2.05 inches. Rain occurred on eight days; snow and rain, on one.

Lunar haloes on the 2d and 30th; solar halo on the 24th; thunder shower, on the 6th; rainbow, on the 24th.

The relative humidity ranged from 21.1° to saturation; the month as a whole was rather dry.

November.	Thermometer.	Barometer.
Morning of the 1st	40°	30.069
Evening of the 30th	29°	30.389
Maximum	56° on the 3d	30.389, 29th & 30th
Minimum	24°, on 21st and 26th	28.764
Range	32°	1.625
Mean	38.25°	29.799

Total of rain and melted snow, 4.73 inches, much more than usual in November. Rain fell on seven days, rain and snow on five, and snow on two.

Lunar haloes appeared on the nights of the 4th and 5th; and a beautiful magnetic cloud, like a bright narrow band, spanned the heavens from the north to south, on the evening of the 15th.

The mean temperature at New York was 6.14° below the average, in this month, for the last 53 years. Prof. Loomis of Yale College, reports this November as the coldest at New Haven, for 85 years; but this is not the case here, 1823 having been slightly colder.

These records have now been kept for twenty years; and it may be a matter of interest to present in a tabular form the results for the autumn months, as obtained during that time.

Temperatures in Autumn, 1854 to 1873, inclusive.

Year.	September.	October.	November.	Mean.	Days of Snow.
1854	66·256	56·071	43·633	55·32	1
1855	66·183	53·309	46·424	55·30	3*
1856	67·269	54·561	44·860	55·56	2
1857	67·466	55·120	44·970	55·85	1
1858	67·214	57·781	40·921	55·30	5
1859	64·375	51·850	47·007	54·41	3†
1860	65·699	56·484	45·574	55·92	2
1861	67·60	59·86	45·04	58·88	3
1862	68·951	58·226	46·773	57·88	6
1863	65·688	56·477	47·755	56·64	4
1864	65·70	54·41	46·94	55·35	2
1865	72·714	53·976	45·716	61·35	1
1866	65·34	54·05	45·18	54·86	3
1867	64·20	54·27	44·09	54·19	2
1868	64·362	50·01	42·098	52·16	1
1869	67·643	52·014	40·675	53·44	6
1870	68·91	58·42	46·55	57·96	2
1871	62·45	60·05	40·81	54·44	2
1872	67·11	54·80	41·86	54·59	3
1873	66·85	57·11	38·25	54·07	8*

The average autumn temperature for the past twenty years is 55·67°. Seven years were above this average, 1865 being the warmest; and thirteen fell below it, 1868 being the coolest.

The Chairman spoke of the remarkable features of the recent report by Prof. Daniel Draper, of the Central Park Meteorological Observatory; referring particularly to his determinations, and charts, of the course of our great storms, from their origin in the Rocky Mountains, south-eastwardly across the continent to the Atlantic. He called special attention to the views of Prof. Draper respecting the passage of the same storms across the ocean, and to his comparative tables of their predicted and observed arrivals on the English coast. It is plain that these facts possess a degree of practical importance, not less high than their scientific interest.

---

* One of these in October, slight.
Two of these in October.

A discussion arose in regard to the apparent changes in the dryness of the climate, and the causes which had led thereto, between Messrs. Collingwood, Morris, Stevenson, and the Chairman. Particular reference was made to the removal of timber, as causing, not indeed an actual lessening of annual rainfall, but an effect similar in its results, viz.; the loss of all the spring rain and snow-water, in freshets, etc., and a resulting summer drouth. The Chairman stated that one important agency in this injury, is the clearing out of the streams on hills and mountain-sides, to serve as timber-shutes. In a state of nature, the flow of water in the streams is greatly slackened and checked by the accumulations of fallen logs, and other forest debris; and thus the spring freshets of a river are largely reduced, by these impediments to a free and rapid flow in all the little tributaries. But when these small streams are used to float down timber, the lumbermen clear away every such obstacle; and the consequence is that with each spring rain, the water rushes down unchecked, creates a flood for a day or two in the country below, and is then lost to further use. All along the Alleghanies of Pennsylvania this ruinous process has been, and still is, going on, as he had lately learned from gentlemen of intelligence living in those regions; and here is seen another danger growing out of our reckless tampering with nature.

Prof. Oscar Loew gave a brief account of his observations, while travelling during the past summer with the War Department survey, in portions of New Mexico and Arizona, and referred particularly to the richness of the latter territory, in its south-western part, in copper mines.

Prof. J. J. Stevenson gave an outline of the course pursued by Col. Wheeler's party, to which he was attached, in southern Colorado.

PROCEEDINGS

OF THE

LYCEUM OF NATURAL HISTORY

IN THE

CITY OF NEW YORK.

SECOND SERIES.

January 5th, 1874. Business Meeting.

DR. B. N. MARTIN in the chair. Ten persons present.

On the recommendation of the Committee on Nominations, Henry A. Mott, Jr., E. M., was elected a resident member of the Lyceum.

The Secretary read by title a paper containing a "Description of a New Species of North American *Helix*, and note on *H. Mobiliana*, Lea," by THOMAS BLAND, published in the Annals, vol. X, No. 12.

The matter of addressing a memorial to the Navy Department, in behalf of the Lyceum, recommending the appointment of naturalists to accompany the Transit Expedition, was taken up; and on motion, it was resolved that a letter be prepared by Prof. D. S. Martin, special committee, and after approval by the Society, that it be signed by the committee and the President, and transmitted to Washington.

MR. COLLINGWOOD spoke of the physiological effects produced by condensed air on the animal system, and particularly the human. Several deaths have taken place among workmen engaged in the caissons of the New York and

Brooklyn bridge; and it becomes a matter of much importance to ascertain with some precision what is the nature of the injury thus caused. As yet, no satisfactory explanation has been given.

Dr. Theo. Hilgard was disposed, from his observations during the building of the St. Louis bridge, to attribute death under such circumstances to inability to expire the air from the lungs, against so great an external pressure.

The subject was further discussed by Prof. Seeley, Dr. Stevenson, Mr. Wm. Falke, and the two previous speakers.

Prof. D. S. Martin remarked upon the high importance of two papers contained in periodicals laid on the table of the Lyceum this evening; that of Prof Morse, in the Proceedings of the Boston Society of Natural History, on the "Affinities of the Brachiopoda and Worms," and Prof. Owen's account, in the Quarterly Journal of the Geological Society, November, 1873, of the remarkable new fossil bird, *Odontopteryx*, from the Eocene beds of the Isle of Sheppey.

January 12th, 1874. Chemical Section.

Pres. Newberry in the chair. Twenty-three persons present.

The President referred to several of the geological articles in the January number of the American Journal of Science, particularly that on the Geology of Western Texas, by Mr. W. P. Jenny, who had laid his facts and his specimens before the Lyceum in October last, [these Proc., pp. 68 to 70]; also that of Mr. Lesquereaux on Land Plants from the Lower Silurian. He dissented entirely from the view that there is yet any proof of the existence of land vegetation in this country before the Devonian age. The specimens described by Mr. Lesquereaux are too obscure and uncertain to found any such argument upon, and are probably simply roots or stems of large fucoids.

He remarked also upon the article on the geology of Vancouver's and Queen Charlotte's Islands, as affording further proof of the views that he had presented, [these Proc., p. 79], of the Cretaceous age of the lignites found in those islands, and in much of our Western territory.

DR. H. C. BOLTON read the following paper :*

Notes on the Early Literature of Chemistry, (Abstract.)

The first mention of Chemistry. The word chemistry first occurs in an astrological manuscript of the 4th century, A. D., by Julius Maternus Firmicus, and usually known under the title *Mathesis.* Writing of the position of the moon in the heavens, and of its influence on the nativity of individuals, Firmicus says; "If the moon stands in the house of Saturn, the newly-born will be devoted to the science of chemistry (or alchemy)." Of the meaning attached to the word chemistry at this early date, we have no definite knowledge.

The earliest Chemical Manuscript. The most ancient MS. treating of chemical operations, is supposed to be a Greek papyrus of the 3d century, preserved in the library of the University of Leyden. It is described in Kopp's Beiträge.

The first Dictionary of Chemical Terms. Several "vocabularies of the sacred art," are preserved in the National Library at Paris. They are probably of the 15th century, and their definitions are very obscure.

The first Text-book of Chemistry. Libavius' "Alchymia," published at Frankfort, in 1595, is generally regarded as the first work on chemistry worthy of being called a text-book. It forms a medium-sized folio, handsomely printed, and abounds in curious woodcuts and enigmatical plates.

The first Chemical Periodical. If we exclude journals in which chemical memoirs are only incidentally contained, the "Journal de Physique," by the Abbé Rozier, is perhaps the first periodical devoted to physics, chemistry, and kindred sciences. This journal was begun in 1771, and continued by various editors until 1822.

The first History of Chemistry, was written by Olaus Borrichius, and is entitled, "De ortu et progressu Chemiae," published at Copenhagen in 1668. The author accepts the fables of the Alchemists.

* Published in full in the American Chemist, Vol. IV, p. 241.

The first Professor of Chemistry. In 1609, Johann Hartmann was appointed Professor of "Chymiatrie," at the University of Marburg. Previous to this date, chemistry had been taught in universities by instructors in medical science.

The first Public Chemical Laboratory, for instruction in chemistry proper, was opened at Altorf, near Nuremberg, Bavaria, in 1683, under the charge of Johann Moritz Hoffmann. A public address was delivered on this occasion, and afterwards published under the title, "Laboratorium novum chemicum, etc.," Altorf, 1683.

In this same year, 1683, the first laboratory connected with a state establishment was opened in Stockholm, under the patronage of Charles XI. The first director of this laboratory was Urban Hiärne.

The paper of Dr. Bolton was discussed by Professors Seeley and Joy, the former urging that in the opinion of many, chemistry proper dates from the time of Lavoisier, and cannot be said to have existed before; and the latter regretting that Dr. Bolton had not continued his history down to more recent times, and adding a brief sketch of the progress of chemical science, nearly to the present day.

JANUARY 19th. Geological Section.

PRESIDENT NEWBERRY in the chair. Twenty persons present.

THE PRESIDENT exhibited drawings and specimens of the remains of the great extinct beaver, *Castoroides Ohioensis,* an animal closely allied to the beaver of modern times, but of giant size, being about five or six feet in length, and weighing probably from 200 to 400 pounds.

The first description of this animal was given by the late Col. Foster, in the report of the first geological survey of Ohio, 1838, and was based on two specimens of the right ramus of the lower jaw. It was subsequently found that the generic characters, as then given, were somewhat imperfect; but the genus still holds, the great size of the bones and the structure of the teeth being quite adequate to distinguish it from the modern *Castor.* More recently, nearly an entire head was discovered in a peat-bed near Rochester, and this has been fully described by Prof. Jeffries Wyman, in the proceedings of the Boston Society of Natural History.

The specimen now exhibited was one of those described by Col. Foster. It is half of a lower jaw, nine inches in length, having the general form of the corresponding bone in the living beaver, but more than twice as long. The most striking peculiarities of this specimen, apart from its size, are the strong striation of the exterior surface of the great incisor, and the figure formed by the enamel-folds of the molars. These are distinctive of the genus.

This specimen was found at Nashport, on the Ohio Canal, in a bed of peat, which was buried under strata of clay and sand, and apparently belonged to the same age with the Forest bed found in the middle portion of the drift deposits of Ohio. The teeth of *Castoroides* have also been met with in a similar peat-bed in Montgomery County, Ohio. The Rochester specimen was taken from a deposit of peat lying behind one of the old beaches which mark the ancient shore lines of Lake Ontario, when the water stood at a higher level than now.

In Europe, the remains of an extinct beaver have likewise been found in Post Tertiary deposits; and this has been called *Trogontherium Cuvieri*. It was intermediate in size between *Castoroides* and *Castor*, and the teeth and bones show differences from both, and such as have been considered of generic value.

PROF. J. J. STEVENSON presented an account of the Lignites of Colorado, as observed and studied by him—with particular reference to the question of their age—during the summer of 1873, while accompanying the expedition of Lieut. Wheeler.

The age of the lignites of Colorado is still disputed; but the evidence, both stratigraphical and palæontological, seems to show altogether that they belong to the later Cretaceous. At Cañon City we find the Lower Cretaceous, consisting of massive sandstones with some dark shales. Above these are the shales and limestones of the Middle Cretaceous, containing the characteristic fossils of that period. These pass imperceptibly through a mass of clay into a loose-grained reddish sandstone containing impressions of *Halymenites major*, Lesqx., and very indistinct impressions of mollusca. This sandstone includes thin beds of lignite, and is regarded by Hayden and Lesquereux as Eocene. On it rests the lignite series proper, containing many fragments of leaves, but no marine fossil other than the fucoid already referred to. The whole series, beginning with the loose-grained sandstone, is evidently one, and is called Eocene. No fossil of marine origin is found here, which can in any way assist in determining the age, for the rock is of such a character as not to preserve shells. But followed northward, the sandstone at some points shows calcareous bands containing occasional mollusks; and when we reach St. Vrain's Creek, nearly fifty miles north from Denver, where the general section is the same as at Cañon City, these bands are very numerous and rich in fossils. Some of the beds contain *Halymenites major*, in such profusion as to be fairly matted with it; while interstratified with these are other layers containing *Ammonites lobatus*, *Mactra alta*, *Anchura*, *Nucula cancellata*, and many other species very characteristic of the Upper Cretaceous. These fossils overlie the lignite beds of Platteville. As to *Halymenites major*, it needs only to be said that in New Mexico, all the geologists have used it as a very characteristic fossil of the Upper Cretaceous. In this connection it may be said that the Cretaceous is pre-eminently a lignite-bearing group. In New Mexico and Western Colorado, as well as in Southern Utah, enormous beds of lignite occur in the Lower Cretaceous, and even in the lower portion of the Middle Cretaceous. There seems to be no indication of the Eocene age of the lignites of Eastern Colorado, save a few fragmentary leaves; while all other evidence shows strongly that they are of the Upper Cretaceous.

Mr. Henry Newton read a paper on American Iron Ores suitable for the Manufacture of Steel.*

After describing the great changes which the introduction of the Bessemer process has led to, involving almost a new era in the metallurgy of iron, and calling for a purity and uniformity in the pig-metal employed, and a scientific skill and exactness in the process of its production, that were before unnecessary and unknown, Mr. Newton proceeded to give the best results attained touching the maximum amounts of the three chief contaminating ingredients, phosphorus, sulphur, and silicon, in ores that are used for the production of Bessemer steel. The silicon should not exceed 2.5, the sulphur .05, nor the phosphorus .10, as average maxima.

Passing then to the main question of the paper, whether the United States can furnish, out of its vast and numerous

* This paper will probably appear in the Annals, Vol. XI, No. 3.

iron deposits, any ores that are fitted for steel manufacture on an extensive scale, the ores used for this purpose abroad were first reviewed. The rich and pure hematites of Lancashire and Cumberland, the great magnetic ore-beds of Sweden, and the spathic irons of Germany and Austria, were described as furnishing almost the exclusive basis of the steel industry in the respective countries in which they occur. The two former, and the recently-developed hematites of Bilbao, Spain, and Mocta, Algeria, are largely exported for steel-working in other parts of Europe, and also here. The black band and clay-iron stone of the Carboniferous, and the Oölitic ores of England, France, Belgium, etc., are too impure for the Bessemer process.

In our own country, we have, first, the enormous magnetic deposits of the older crystalline rocks of the Alleghanies, extending from the St. Lawrence to Georgia, and largely developed also in the Laurentian hills of Canada. These were discussed and described at many points, with analyses, etc. In some cases they are pure enough for producing Bessemer pig; but they vary much, and often are hopelessly injured, even for common use, by containing titanium. Only in North Carolina is there much promise. There, among the vast deposits lately brought into notice, some are very pure, as that in Mitchell County, and especially the "Cranberry ore." This has not yet been tried; but the analysis is most hopeful.

Equally important are the rich and remarkable hematite regions of Marquette, Mich., and eastern Missouri. Excellent descriptions of both these iron districts have lately been given, by Major Brooks, in the Geological Survey of Michigan, and Prof. Pumpelly, in the Missouri Report for 1873. The importance of these deposits, and the excellence of the iron that they yield, can hardly be overestimated; though they also vary, that of Marquette sometimes being very silicious, and when smelted with the sulphurous coals and cokes of the Western States, instead of with charcoal, the iron is apt to be too impure. Both of them, however, and no others, are used in the Bessemer process in the furnaces of the West.

The great and valuable ore beds of the Clinton group, sweeping in a belt from Wisconsin through New York and East Tennessee to Alabama, have nevertheless too much phosphorus for steel-working, like the oölitic ores abroad. Our limonites, spathic irons, and coal measure ores are all either too impure or too limited, or both, to enter into the question of the American manufacture of steel.

PROF. T. EGLESTON said that, in his judgment, the reason why America cannot compete with Europe in the manufacture of Bessemer steel, is the absence of iron ores containing manganese, a metal abundant in some of the most highly-prized ores of Germany and Sweden. The great success which attends the use of these ores in steel production, is usually attributed to their great purity. His own observations abroad, however, had shown him that it is due less to this cause, than to the presence of manganese. If we can discover manganiferous iron ores in this country, the obstacles can probably be surpassed much more readily than is supposed.

THE PRESIDENT remarked that in East Tennessee, ores are to be found which contain manganese and are free from phosphorus; and that on Lake Superior a black manganiferous ore, with but little phosphorus, would yield a good spiegeleisen: these two localities might furnish ore suitable for the Bessemer steel manufacture. Most of our manganiferous iron ores have too much phosphorus to allow of their advantageous use; but these two are exceptions. The Lake Superior deposit has as yet scarcely been described or noticed.

PROF. T. STERRY HUNT, of Boston, stated that in the hands of Mr. Blair, of Pittsburg, the phosphatic iron ore of the Moriah bed, in the Adirondack region (magnetite with apatite), has lately been successfully worked, by first obtaining from it a spongy iron, with the phosphate of lime distributed through it in grains, and then throwing this into a furnace of molten iron, which takes hold of the spongy iron, while the phosphate floats and is drawn off unaltered, without interfering with the subsequent process.

Dr. Hunt also spoke of having examined, during the previous summer, the iron deposits of North Carolina, which had been described in Mr. Newton's paper, and corroborated the account of the great purity of the Cranberry ore.

The subject was further discussed by Dr. Feuchtwanger, Prof. Seeley, and Mr. Newton.

January 26th, 1874.

PRESIDENT NEWBERRY in the chair. Twelve persons present.

A number of specimens were exhibited and discussed by members.

PROF. D. S. MARTIN remarked upon Prof. Owen's new Eocene bird from the Isle of Sheppey, *Odontopteryx toliapicus*, and pointed out its peculiar relation, or non-relation, to certain other forms. The so-called dentirostral birds of the present age have merely one or more serrations or denticulations on the edge of the horny sheath or casing of the beak, and not on the bony beak itself. This fact Prof. Owen refers to in his description. If now we go back to the Cretaceous period, we find in Prof. Marsh's *Icthyornis*, discovered last year in Kansas, a bird with numerous true teeth, inserted in well-defined sockets. Prof. Owen's bird belongs to an intermediate age, and presents at first sight an intermediate character, between *Icthyornis* and the modern Dentirostres; that is, it has a series of tooth-like processes extending from the jaw-bones proper, and which in Prof. Owen's view, were originally sheathed all over with horn, like the bill in living birds. But this intermediate character is, after all, only apparent, and has no structural relation, although it seems to simulate a connection. The bony projections on the bill of *Odontopteryx* have no homology with true teeth, such as those of *Icthyornis*. A really intervening form, between the last-named type and the toothless birds of our own day, would possess only rudimentary teeth imbedded in the jaws, somewhat as in young whales; and the "gradual change," were such to be found, would appear in a progressive diminution in the number of teeth, and in the efficiency of their character, until all became rudimentary, and even these finally obsolete. Instead of this, we have in *Odontopteryx* a marked and peculiar form, well-developed, and seemingly out of relation to anything else, either earlier or later; though affording a curious semblance of relationship. A careless Darwinist might readily seize upon such a type among birds, as an example of a missing link restored; but he would be misled by an aspect without a reality. In like manner, Prof. Owen's claim of "the transitional character which it manifests to the Pterosaurian order," rests upon a foundation, striking indeed to our minds, but hardly sustained by a close study of homologies. A genetic connection between the life of successive ages, must have been influenced by other laws than those of gradual modification alone; and evolution is a process far more elaborate and far less understood than pure Darwinism would allow.

MR. WILLIAM FALKE made the following communication:

Experiments with Poisons on Limulus.

During a sojourn in Connecticut last summer, I caught a number of horse-shoe crabs, (*Limulus polyphemus*).

Being struck with the idea of trying the effect of poisons on them, I procured a hypodermic syringe, and injected two grains of morphia sulphate, about half an inch below the cephalic shield, on the under side, into the soft parts. About fifteen minutes after the injection, the crab showed slight signs of being under the hypnotic influence of opium, but only for a short time. After this, five grains were injected, and with more effect, as the crab ceased crawling about, and rested on the floor of the laboratory. On turning him on his back, he appeared quite in a state of unconsciousness, interrupted only at long intervals by a slow aud peculiar contraction and expansion of the *chelæ*.

When struck with a stick, the crab became conscious again for a few seconds, trying to turn over and regain his normal position; but he was unable to do so, and would soon fall back into his narcotic slumber. I left him over-night in a corner of the laboratory, but by morning, he had, to my great surprise, turned over and crawled to the other side of the room, being again quite active.

I then injected one drachm of hydrocyanic acid, (2 per ct.,) which only acted as a powerful sedative, the crab being unwilling to move about. Another drachm was introduced, but this time into the soft parts where the telson is articulated to the dorsal shield; the crab then became quite sluggish, but lived nevertheless for two days. Then, on cutting into the soft parts, the crab still moved, and a strong odor of hydrocyanic acid was perceptible, but no particular *lesion* could be detected.

Into another very large Limulus I injected two grains of strychnia sulphate, which produced a powerful contraction of the *chelæ* and appendages (tetanus), very unlike the easy movements noticed in the other crab under the influence of morphine. Next day, this specimen was still alive, when I injected two drachms of chloroform, which first stimulated, but afterwards tranquilized him. It did not kill him, however, as he still showed signs of life on dissecting him three days afterwards.

A third specimen was taken, and half a grain of woorari (curare) was injected; the crab soon became motionless and paralyzed, and remained so for two days, when signs of life were still manifested on cutting into the body.

A number of other poisons were employed, but without killing the crabs, when I came to the conclusion that it is very difficult to destroy these curious crustaceans with any of the poisons tried.

February 2d. Business Meeting.

The severity of the weather prevented any meeting.

February 9th. Chemical Section.

Dr. B. N. Martin in the chair. Twenty-two persons present.

The Chairman read by title a paper by Mr. George N. Lawrence, giving "Descriptions of six supposed New Species of American Birds," published in the Annals, vol. X, No. 13.

PROF. A. R. LEEDS read a paper on "Alizarin as a Test."*

He proposed the employment of alizarin in place of litmus in volumetric analysis, its extreme sensitiveness rendering it capable of detecting infinitesimal amounts of acid or alkali. By digesting alizarin with alcohol of 95%, a solution was obtained containing 0.00425 grms. of alizarin in one c.c. By means of this solution, $\frac{1}{300000}$ part of potash is capable of changing $\frac{1}{200000}$ part of alizarine from a brilliant yellow to a dark red. The delicacy of the reaction is so great that one part of soda in three million parts of water, and one part of sulphuric or hydrochloric acid in one million parts of water, may be recognized with facility. Compared with litmus, three times as much litmus and three times as much acid are required to produce a corresponding change of color.

Some experiments were made for the purpose of arriving at an approximate quantitative determination of the alkalinity of calcic and magnesic carbonates, and the acidity of various salts, as compared with the alkaline and acid reactions of standard solutions of potash and sulphuric acid. A number of samples of drinking water gave a strongly alkaline reaction. It was found that distilled water, condensed in a worm of block tin, was invariably alkaline when collected in stone-ware jugs, but neutral when collected in bottles of white glass.

For making a test-paper, fine white Swedish filtering paper is recommended. Alizarin test-paper is strongly reddened by the saliva. Many other examples of the exceeding delicacy of the reaction were likewise noted.

MR. WM. FALKE read an extended paper "On Adipocere." He gave some account of Fourcroy's comprehensive investigation and memoir upon this substance, presented to the Academy of Sciences in 1789, and occasioned by the discovery of immense quantities of adipocere in the burying ground connected with the Church of the Innocents, in Paris.

* Published in full in the American Chemist, vol. IV, p. 333.

Adipocere consists of a mixture of palmitic and stearic acids, with more or less ammonia derived from the decomposing bodies. These two acids remain and are present in the bodies, while the glycerine and oleic acids are removed during decay.

Adipocere exhibits the following reactions:—heated to 100° C., it melts, and by slowly raising the temperature it gives out about $\frac{1}{16}$ its weight of water. With water it behaves like soap. It forms with lime a soap, which on being treated with hydrochloric acid, deposits the fatty acids as a waxy, lustrous, crystalline mass, soluble in hot alcohol, and yielding feathery crystals on cooling.

Mr. Falke alluded to deposits of adipocere in England and America; and among other specimens, exhibited a remarkable cross section of a thigh, from Potter's Field, New York City, in which the whole mass of the limb appeared changed into adipocere.

PROF. HENRY WURTZ read an extended paper "On the Water Supply of Jersey City and Newark."*

This paper contained the results of a careful and laborious examination of the waters of the Morris Canal, the Passaic River, Lake Hopatcong, the Jersey City Water Works, and the Newark Water Works, with several other waters; these being investigated from a chemical and sanitary point of view, with special reference to the availability of the Morris Canal as a source of pure water-supply for the cities of Newark and Jersey City.

The results of the analyses cannot be here reproduced, but a comparison of these results developed the interesting fact that the water of Lake Hopatcong is one of the purest in the world, containing only 1.79 grains total solids per gallon; —the waters of Bala Lake, in Wales, and of Loch Katrine, Scotland, but slightly exceeding it in purity, (1.63 grains per gallon).

Some remarkable facts were stated relative to the powerful

* Published in full in the American Chemist for March, 1874.

agencies in the purification of water, residing in the vegetable and animal life inhabiting it, which co-operate in consuming effete matter with surprising rapidity.

Prof. Wurtz concluded by recommending in high terms the proposition to convert the Morris canal from an unprofitable channel of navigation into a source of pure water-supply for the two cities above named.

PROF. A. R. LEEDS read a paper "On the Dissociation of certain Compounds at very low Temperatures."*

Fittig, Debbits, and others, have shown that salts of ammonia, especially the nitrate, sulphate, chloride, oxalate, and acetate, liberate ammonia when their solutions are boiled, and also when a current of an inert gas is passed through their saturated solutions at ordinary temperatures, or even at 0°C. Prof. Leeds then showed :—

1st. That it is not necessary to change the atmosphere in contact with the particles of the salt held in solution, by passing a current of an inert gas, in order to induce dissociation at temperatures below the boiling point.

2d. That there is a certain fixed temperature, which is different in the various salts, at which the dissociated constituent can be detected and recognized by sufficiently delicate tests.

3d. That it is highly probable that the dissociation of these salts in solution is analogous to the evaporation of the solvent, and that while it arrives at a maximum (under ordinary atmospheric pressures) at the boiling points of their saturated solutions, yet it takes place in a diminishing proportion at much lower temperatures, and in some cases even below their freezing points.

The reagent employed in these experiments was alizarin, which will readily detect 1 part of soda in 3,000,000 of water. Prof. Leeds gave a table containing the results of about twenty determinations, the dissociation of ammonic oxalate being that observed at the lowest temperature.

---

* Published in full in the American Journal of Science, March, 1874.

February 16th, 1874.

Vice-President Egleston in the chair. Twenty persons present.

Prof. Henry Wurtz read a paper "On the Subaerial Oxygenation of Waters, with Experimental Illlustrations," of which the following is a brief abstract.

Over two years since—in 1872—I was charged with the examination of a highly-important question of water-supply, that of the cities of north-eastern New Jersey from the river Passaic. Seeing the necessity, and the benefit, of some new and accurate micro-chemical method for determining oxygen in solution, I began during that summer, and have continued at intervals, to experiment with a new chromo-volumetric method, founded upon the use of alkaline *pyrogalline* added directly to the water.

In the subsequent fall of the same year (1872), Schutzenberger and Girardin made and published, in France, their proposed method with "hydrosulphite of soda." This latter method was afterwards found, by its authors, to give but a moiety of the oxygen, and has required many modifications. My own new method, first published with my official report, in March, 1873, (see *American Chemist*, Sept. and Oct., 1873, pp. 102 and 135) I believe preferable.

A solution of pyrogalline in alcohol, to which a drop of muriatic acid has been added, may be kept, for some time, in a state suitable for use. The water tested is first rendered feebly alkaline by carbonate of soda or ammonia.

It has thus been found, in confirmation of the results of Bunsen (Gasometry, pp. 142–3), that the attempt to free water absolutely from air by boiling in the open air alone, is uncertain and impracticable; and water has even been boiled down to dryness without freeing it from a faint oxygen reaction. To obtain water without oxygen, oxidable agents added were found generally useless. Sulphide of ammonium was effective; but an excess interfered with further use of the water. Many experiments were made with saline substances. Common salt is capable of expelling all oxygen from water, this being the first demonstration of the cause of its preservative functions. On agitation, oxygen is not again taken up; and such a brine is useful in many cases in applying this test. For preservation of liquids under test from the air, use was made of petroleum (previously freed from oxygen by sodium), and of different hydrocarbons, including in case of hot liquids, paraffine, which, on cooling, forms for a time a solid seal: fixed oils were also used from the first. Such liquid seals were found but transiently to protect against the 3 lbs. per square inch pressure of aerial oxygen. All the oils in time admitted it, either chemically or mechanically.

To collect and transport samples of natural waters, I draw down small at points a tolerably heavy glass tube, fill with hydrogen or nitrogen (first washed with alkaline pyrogalline), and seal at these points. One of the elongated bulbs thus made is introduced into the bottle of natural water to be preserved, one point broken off under the water, the bottle then hermetically stoppered or sealed when completely full. Expansion will not then break it. It must be opened only under quicksilver (previously wetted with alcohol to detach air), and portions of the water passed into a eudiometer for analysis. Carbonic acid gas upon the surface, was found preferable to liquid hydrocarbons, in protecting from air. Causing, for this purpose, the CO^2 to be evolved from the liquid itself, a most important discovery was made, viz.: that free oxygen cannot coëxist in water with an excess of CO^2, within ordinary atmospheric pressures and temperatures. This new principle has numerous applications in almost every science.

All effervescent waters, natural and artificial, are found free from oxygen. "Plain soda water," is a very convenient menstruum for these experiments. Beer and champagne also contain no oxygen, proving the principle to hold also at higher pressures. Quantitatively, I have so far generally used, for comparison, a solution of permanganate whose coloring power with pyrogalline and ammonia has been normalized to some standard. The value of the color and shade must of course be referred at the start, and as often as practicable, to that given by actual aerated water whose oxygen has been measured directly, as usual, by boiling and exhaustion. Beside permanganate, other oxygen solutions have been tried, with more or less success.

I apply pyrogalline also in another way altogether new—to determine the *rates of absorption* of aerial oxygen by different waters and other liquids. Like columns of different natural waters, *ceteris paribus*, exhibit progressive penetrations of air to greatly varying depths in like times.

PROF. C. FRED. HARTT, (of Cornell University,) presented an account of the "Aboriginal Manufacture of Pottery," among the South American tribes, particularly in Brazil. The methods employed vary in different parts of the country; but the most frequent process, as observed by him, was as follows:—the clay is first tempered, and then blackened by means of the ashes of certain particular woods. It is next rolled out into long thin strips, and the vessel is constructed by coiling up these strips one above another, and pressing the whole together. When the vessel is baked, a glazing is applied, which really consists of a layer of varnish, made from the South American copals. The resin is pulverized, and sprinkled over the surface to be glazed; and then the application of heat melts the powder into an even coating.

In southern Brazil quite a different process exists; the articles are molded in pieces, and then luted together.

With regard to the ornamentation of pottery, Prof. Hartt said that this whole branch of manufacture is in the hands of the women; and he was strongly disposed, from what he had observed, to attribute the constant effort at ornamenting the articles produced, to the natural taste and genius possessed by the female mind for beauty, which leads to an endeavor to develope something of elegance and attractiveness in their humble handiwork.

There are some exceedingly interesting principles apparent in regard to the devices on Indian pottery, which he had set forth in his lecture on "Evolution in Ornament."* Among these the most important are two, viz.: (1) That no rude people ever commence by the imitation of natural objects, as leaves, flowers, etc., however familiar these may be; but that all this is an after-thought, the process beginning with the simplest formation of straight lines. These are then variously repeated and combined, curves take the place of angles, etc.; and finally accidental resemblances suggest the

---

* Cf. also Proceedings of the University Convocation of the State of New York, 1873,—"The Beginnings of Art."

imitation of natural objects, but only after this long process of simpler training.

The other principle is that, (2) in this way, similar and even identical devices grow up spontaneously and independently, in tribes and nations wholly separate from one another. This is notably the case with the beautiful "Grecian fret," so called, which is represented in every stage of its 'evolution,' in the pottery of Brazil.

PROF. EGLESTON said that when Prof. Hartt described the mode of making pottery among the Amazonas tribes, by coiling up long strips, he should have supposed, had he not known otherwise, that the account referred to the manufacture of retorts as used in some of the Belgian zinc-works. The process is precisely identical; and it would now seem as though it were the survival of a very ancient custom, rather than an exceptional and local peculiarity, as he had before supposed.

PROF. D. S. MARTIN referred to the presence of Dr. Charles E. West, of Brooklyn, and hoped that he would give the Lyceum some account of the very active and valuable work lately done by the Long Island Historical Society in forming collections illustrating the geology and natural history of Long Island.

At the request of the Chairman,—

DR. WEST spoke, and after referring to his strong interest in the Lyceum, when formerly residing in New York, described the recent organization and growth of the Long Island Society, its building, library, cabinets, etc. He mentioned among other recent additions, that the entire series of specimens collected in the work of blasting out the reefs under the river at Hallett's Point, had been deposited with the Society by the engineer in charge. It forms a valuable illustration of both the rocks and the drift material there obtained.

February 23d. Annual Meeting.

President Newberry in the chair. Twenty persons present.

After the reading of the minutes, the annual reports of the several officers and committees of the Lyceum were read, discussed, and accepted. Abstracts of the more important of these are here given.

On proceeding to the annual election, the existing officers of the Lyceum were unanimously re-elected for the year 1874–5.*

Abstract of the Report of the Committee on Publications.

New York, February, 1874.

During the year commencing March, 1873, two numbers of the Annals have been published, numbers 10 and 11 of Volume X.

Subsequently to the date of the last Annual Report, but as part of the Annals for 1872, No. 9 was issued, containing the following papers:—

Additional Note on the Genus *Amphibulima.* By Thomas Bland and W. G. Binney.

The Upper Coal Measures West of the Alleghany Mountains. By Prof. John J. Stevenson, with Map, (plate XII).

On the Lingual Dentition of *Gæotis.* By T. Bland and W. G. Binney, (with plate XI).

Note on a Curious Form of Lingual Dentition in *Physa.* By the same.

Catalogue of the *Pyralidæ* of California, with the description of New California *Pterophoridæ.* By A. S. Packard, Jr.

Notes on some *Pyralidæ,* from New England, with remarks on the Labrador species of this Family. By A. S. Packard, Jr.

The papers in Nos. 10 and 11, 1873, are as follows:—

Note on the Coals of the Kanawha Valley, West Virginia. By Prof. John J. Stevenson.

On the Subdivisions of Science and their Classification. By Dr. Louis Elsberg, (with a table).

On *Prophysaon,* a new Pulmonate Mollusk, on *Ariolimax,* on *Helix lychnuchus,* and other species. By Thomas Bland and W. G. Binney, (with plates XIII and XIV).

* See list on 3d page of cover, or these Proceedings, pp. 22 and 23.

On the Physical Geography of, and the Distribution of Terrestrial Mollusca in, the Bahama Islands. By Thomas Bland.

Spectroscopic Examination of Silicates. By Prof. Albert R. Leeds.

The committee have to acknowledge the obligation of the Society to Prof. Stevenson, for the cost of Plate XII, and to Mr. W. G. Binney for that of drawing on stone, plates XI, XII, and XIV, and also plates XV and XVI.

An additional number of the Annals, making up the usual amount of matter for the year 1873, and concluding Vol. X, is now in press, and will speedily be issued.

It will contain the following papers :—

On the Lingual Dentition and Anatomy of *Achatinella* and other Pulmonata. By Thomas Bland and W. G. Binney, (with plates XV and XVI).

Outlines of a Bibliography of the History of Chemistry. By Dr. H. Carrington Bolton.

Description of a new Species of *Helix*, and note on *H. Mobiliana*, Lea. By Thomas Bland.

Catalogue of the Birds ascertained to occur in Illinois. By Robert Ridgway.

Description of six supposed New Species of American Birds. By George N. Lawrence.

(The remainder of the report was occupied wholly with matters of detail regarding the issue of the New Series of Proceedings, and certain delays in the appearance of the second number.)

THOMAS BLAND, *Chairman.*

Abstract of the Report of the Librarian.

The Librarian respectfully reports that during the year ending February 16th, 1874, there have been received the following books and periodicals :—

From societies, 3 folio volumes, 14 quartos, and 54 octavos; 25 parts of quarto volumes, 265 parts of octavos, and 6 pamphlets.

From the State of California, 5 imperial octavo volumes.

From the Department of the Interior, 5 octavo volumes.

From resident member, 2 octavo volumes.

From corresponding members and others, 1 12mo. volume and 33 pamphlets.

Total, 84 volumes, 290 parts of volumes, and 39 pamphlets.

BERNARD G. AMEND, *Librarian.*

Abstract of the Report of the Corresponding Secretary.

The Corresponding Secretary reports that the correspondence for the year ending on the 23d of February, 1874, has mainly arisen, as in previous years, from the exchange of publications with kindred scientific bodies.

Acknowledgments for publications received have been sent to the following societies and individuals:—

UNITED STATES.

Smithsonian Institution, Washington, D. C.;
Department of the Interior, Washington, D. C.;
Academy of Natural Sciences, Philadelphia;
American Philosophical Society, Philadelphia;
Prof. Edward D. Cope, Philadelphia;
Mr. William M. Gabb, Philadelphia;
Col. R. L. Maury, Lexington, Va.;
Boston Society of Natural History, Boston, Mass.;
American Academy of Arts and Sciences, Boston;
Trustees of the Museum of Comparative Zoölogy, Cambridge, Mass.;
Trustees of the Peabody Academy of Science, Salem, Mass.;
The Essex Institute, Salem;
Editors of the American Naturalist, Salem;
Prof. A. S. Packard, Jr., Salem;
Editors of the American Journal of Science and Arts, New Haven, Ct.;
Prof. J. D. Dana, New Haven, Conn.;
Mr. Horace T. Carpenter, Pawtucket, R. I.;
New York State Library, Albany, N. Y.;
New York State Agricultural Society, Albany, N. Y.;
Prof. C. F. Hartt, Ithaca, N. Y.;
Buffalo Society of Natural Science, Buffalo, N. Y.;
Department of Public Parks, New York City;
Editors of the American Chemist, New York City;
The Torrey Botanical Club, New York City;
Ezra C. Seaman, Esq., New York City;
Prof. A. M. Mayer, Hoboken, N. J.;
Minnesota Academy of Natural Science, Minneapolis, Minn.;

Academy of Sciences, St. Louis, Missouri;
State of California;
California Academy of Sciences, San Francisco, Cal.;
Editor of the "California Farmer," San Francisco.

British North America.

Director of the Geological Survey of Canada, Ottawa;
Entomological Society of Ontario, London;
The Canadian Institute, Toronto;
Editor of the Canadian Ornithologist, Toronto;
Natural History Society of Montreal;
Literary and Historical Society of Quebec;
Nova Scotia Institute of Natural Science, Halifax.

Brazil.

The Imperial Government.

Great Britain.

The Royal Society of London;
The Zoölogical Society of London;
The Geological Society of London;
British Association for the Advancement of Science, London;
The Society of Arts, London;
W. A. Mansell & Co., London;
The Literary and Philosophical Society of Liverpool;
The Royal Cornwall Polytechnic Society, Falmouth;
The Edinburgh Geological Society, Edinburgh.
The Botanical Society of Edinburgh;
The Philosophical Society, Glasgow;
The Royal Geological Society of Ireland, Dublin;
Naturalist's Field Club, Belfast.

Belgium.

Société Entomologique de Belgique, Brussels;
M. Ad. Quetelet, Brussels;
L'Académie Royale de Sciences, de Lettres, et de Beaux Arts de Belgique, Brussels;
Société Royale de Sciences, Liége;
Prof. Edouard Morren, Liége.

France.

Dr. Ch. Girard, Paris;
Société Nationale des Sciences Naturelles, Cherbourg;
L'Académie Nationale de Sciences, Arts, et Belles Lettres, Caen;
Société d'Agriculture, Histoire Naturelle, et Arts Utiles, Lyon;
Académie de Sciences, Belles Lettres, et Arts, Lyon;
Société Linnéenne, Lyon;

Société des Sciences Historiques et Naturelles, Auxerre;
Société des Sciences Physiques et Naturelles, Bordeaux.

SWITZERLAND.

Société Vaudoise des Sciences Naturelles, Lausanne;
Naturwissenschaftliche Gesellschaft, St. Galen;
Société de Physique et d'Histoire Naturelle, Geneve;
Naturforschende Gesellschaft, Basel;
Société Helvétique des Sciences Naturelles, Fribourg;
Schweizerische Naturforschende Gesellschaft, Frauenfeld;
Schweizerische Naturforschende Gesellschaft, Bern;
Naturforschende Gesellschaft, Bern;
Société des Sciences Naturelles, Neufchâtel.

ITALY.

R. Comitato Geologico d'Italia, Florence;
Accademia delle Scienze dell' Instituto, Bologna;
Instituto Lombardo delle Scienze e Lettere, Milan;
Frères Villa, Milan;
R. Instituto Veneto delle Scienze, Lettere, ed Arti, Venice.

HUNGARY.

Société Royale Hongroise des Sciences Naturelles, Pesth.

PORTUGAL.

Académie Royale des Sciences, Lisbon.

DENMARK.

Kon. Danske Videnskabernes Salskab, Copenhagen.

SWEDEN.

Société Royale des Sciences, Upsal.

NORWAY.

Kon. Norske Universitet, Christiania.

RUSSIA.

L'Académie Impériale de Sciences, St. Pétersburg;
Société Impériale des Naturalistes, Moscow;
Gelehrte Estnische Gesellschaft, Dorpat;
Naturforscher Verein, Riga.

GERMANY & AUSTRIA.

K.K. Akademie der Wissenschaften, Vienna;
" Geographische Gesellschaft, Vienna;
" Geologische Reichs Anstalt, Vienna;
" Zoologisch-botanische Gesellschaft, Vienna;
" Gesellschaft der Arts, Vienna;
Verein fur Erdkunde, Darmstadt;

Naturforschender Verein, Brunn ;
Zoologische Gesellschaft, Frankfurt, a. M. ;
Senckenbergische Naturforschende Gesellschaft, Frankfurt, a. M. ;
Deutsche Geologische Gesellschaft, Berlin ;
K. Preus. Academie der Wissenschaften, Berlin ;
Verein zur Beforderung des Gartenbaues in den Preus. Staaten, Berlin ;
K. Akademie der Wissenschaften, Berlin ;
Naturwissenschaftlicher Verein, Bremen ;
Naturforschende Gesellschaft, Halle ;
Naturwissenschaftlicher Verein fur Sachsen und Thuringen, Halle;
Naturwissenschaftliche Gesellschaft Isis in Dresden.
Kon. Phys. Okon. Gesellschaft, Konigsberg ;
Naturforschende Gesellschaft, Freiburg;
K. Sachsische Gesellschaft der Wissenschaften, Leipzig ;
L'Institut Royal Grand Ducal de Luxembourg ;
Verein der Freunde der Naturgeschichte in Mecklenburg, Neubrandenburg;
Naturwissenschaftlicher Verein, Hamburg;
Naturhistorische Gesellschaft, Nurnberg;
Naturforschende Gesellschaft, Danzig;
Kon. Bayerische Akademie der Wissenschaften, Munich ;
Nassauischer Verein fur Naturkunde, Wiesbaden ;
Naturforschende Gesellschaft, Emden ;
Zoologisch-Mineralogischer Verein, Regensburg;
K. Bohmische Gesellschaft der Wissenschaften, Prag ;
Oberheissische Gesellschaft, fur Naturkunde und Heilkunde, Giessen;
Naturwissenschaftliche Gesellschaft, Chemnitz ;
Verein fur Vaterlandische Naturkunde in Wurttemberg, Stuttgart;
Entomologischer Verein, Stettin ;
Naturhistorischer Verein der Preus. Rheinlande und Westphalen, Bonn.

EAST INDIES.

Bataviaasch Genootschap von Kunsten en Wettenschappen, Batavia.

The number of correspondents for 1873, as will be observed by the above list, was 123, of whom a largely-increased number, as compared with any previous year, acknowledged the receipt of the Annals of the Lyceum.

Respectfully submitted,

ROBERT DINWIDDIE,

Corresponding Secretary.

New York, 23d February, 1874.

Abstract of the Report of the Special Committee on the Transit Expedition.

At the meeting of the Lyceum, held February 3d, 1873, the opportunities which the expedition for the observation of the transit of Venus would afford, for natural history researches in the remoter parts of the Southern Hemisphere, were discussed, and the undersigned was appointed a Committee to conduct correspondence in behalf of the Lyceum, with the proper authorities of the Government.* Advice was first sought from Professor Spencer F. Baird, of the Smithsonian Institution, who most cordially responded.

In accordance with his suggestion, a memorial was drawn up by the Committee, and, after approval by the Lyceum, forwarded to the Hon. Geo. M. Robeson, Secretary of the Navy.

In furtherance of the important object sought, letters, containing copies of the memorial, were addressed by the committee to the Boston Society of Natural History, the Chicago Academy of Science, the Philadelphia Academy of Sciences, and the Maryland Academy of Science (Baltimore), requesting their coöperation. Most satisfactory action was taken by the Philadelphia and Baltimore societies, both of which sent letters to the Secretary of the Navy, urging a favorable consideration of the plan, and informed the Lyceum officially to that effect.

Copies of the memorial and of the letter to the above mentioned societies, together with a copy of the reply received from Washington, are hereto annexed.†

Respectfully submitted,

D. S. Martin,

Special Committee.

---

* These Proceedings, page 14.

† This action of the Lyceum and other scientific societies, was followed at a later day, by the appointment, as Assistant Surgeon to the Expedition, of Dr. J. H. Kidder, a highly-scientific gentleman, with ample facilities and instructions for carrying out the objects sought in the Memorial. See these Proceedings, meeting of June 1st, 1874.

MEMORIAL.

Lyceum of Natural History, in the City of New York,
No. 64 Madison Avenue,
New York, January 15th, 1874.

To the Hon. George M. Robeson, Secretary of the Navy.

Sir;—It is with great interest that this Society, together with all similar scientific bodies in the country, has observed the provision made by appropriation from Congress, for the equipment of several astronomical parties, who are to represent American science in connection with the observation of the coming transit of Venus. We rejoice that our country is preparing to take a worthy part, among other and older nations, in this great work of common interest for all civilized communities.

While, however, this fact is a matter of much gratification and pride, there is yet another aspect of the subject, to which the undersigned beg leave to call your attention, and in regard to which we would desire, without any wish to complicate the arrangements of the Expedition, to present a few suggestions.

Among the places to be occupied by the Transit parties, are several which are rarely visited by civilized man, lying far in the southern seas. These are points of great, and now of increasing, interest in connection with geology and natural history. Enough is already known, to show with much clearness the fact that vast areas of land have, at periods not very distant in the course of geological ages, gone beneath the southern waters, leaving only a few scattered and outlying points of land, to represent, by their surviving remnants of life, the fauna and flora that occupied the submerged Antarctic areas. Under these unfavorable conditions, and in such contracted limits, these relics of ancient life must almost of necessity be constantly passing away; and it therefore becomes of the greatest interest to science, to seize every possible opportunity of exploring and observing these distant regions, if we would preserve or decipher the record of those geological and geographical changes which constitute the physical history of our globe.

The Lyceum of Natural History would, therefore, inquire whether any arrangements have been made, and if not, how far it would be possible to provide them, for the prosecution of zoölogical, botanical, and geological studies in the course of the Expedition. We are well aware that the primary purpose of the Expedition is astronomical, and that the appropriation voted by Congress is specifically designed for such objects. But while this is the case, the opportunities for biological and geological studies, afforded in visiting such places as the

Falkland Islands, Kerguelen's Land, and other localities suggested as points of observation, are so unusual and so valuable, that it would seem a great loss to science if no provision were made for employing them. We would, therefore, earnestly suggest the propriety and importance, if it can be done without actually interfering with the work of the Transit Expedition, of associating with each of the station parties one or more gentlemen, competent to make observations and collections in these departments of science.

In default of appropriations available for this end, a valuable purpose might be served by authorizing collections and reports on these subjects to be made by those members of the corps, whose tastes and attainments may enable them to make use of any favorable opportunities of scientific observation which their more specific duties may allow.

(Signed.) J. S. NEWBERRY, *President.*

D. S. MARTIN, *Special Committee.*

LETTER.

LYCEUM OF NATURAL HISTORY, IN THE CITY OF NEW YORK,
No. 64 Madison Avenue,
New York, January 19th, 1874.

TO THE PRESIDENT OF THE ———

Dear Sir;—The approaching departure of the astronomical parties sent out under the authority of the Navy Department, for the observation of the transit of Venus, is an event of so much interest in many respects to all scientific bodies in our country, that we beg leave to address you in regard to it. It has seemed to us that there are great opportunities presented in the course of these expeditions, for collections and observations in the departments of natural history and geology, and that the occasion thus presented should not be suffered to pass without some provision for its use. The questions of geographical distribution are assuming so much importance in modern biology, that the visit of parties like these, to such remote and interesting points in the Southern Hemisphere as Kerguelen's Land, the Falklands, etc., becomes in our judgment an opportunity not to be lost.

Acting upon these views, this Society has addressed to the Secretary of the Navy, a formal memorial, of which we enclose you a copy. We have been encouraged to take this course by Prof. Baird, of the Smithsonian Institute, of whom our first enquiries in regard to the matter were made, and who is fully in sympathy with the object proposed.

It has seemed to us both desirable in the interests of science, and fitting as a matter of courtesy, to inform your society, and some few others, of our action in this respect, and to ask whether you would not be disposed to coöperate with us in seeking to secure from the Department facilities for the prosecution of biological and geological studies, in addition to the specific work of the Transit parties.

If this recommendation should be presented to the Navy Department with the combined influence of several leading scientific societies at different points, it would assume almost a national character. We should be highly gratified to have the coöperation of your Society in this movement, and therefore beg leave to lay the subject before you for consideration. We venture no suggestion as to the manner or form of your action, if taken, but only observe that the time that remains is now brief, and that whatever is done at all should be done at the earliest moment.

With much respect, I remain, Sir,

Yours very truly,

(Signed.) D. S. Martin,

Special Committee on Memorial.

Response of the Secretary of the Navy.

Navy Department, *Washington*, *January* 26*th*, 1874.

Sir;—Your communication of the 15th inst. has been received and referred to Rear Admiral B. F. Sands, President of the Commission on the Transit of Venus, who replies as follows;—

"The Commission has had under consideration the question of the practicability of affording facilities for investigating the geology and natural history of the stations occupied by the parties of observation,—all the collections made to be deposited in the National Museum, Washington; but the difficulty of finding room on board the ship for any besides the regular observers, has deterred them from taking any decisive steps towards this end. The only point mentioned in Prof. Newberry's communication, which will be actually visited, is Kerguelen Land; and if it is possible for any of the party there to make the necessary collections, the Commission would be glad to receive full suggestions respecting what is to be done, from any competent scientific authority."

Very respectifully, etc.,

(Signed.) Geo. M. Robeson,

Secretary of the Navy.

Professor J. S. Newberry,

President of the Lyceum of Natural History,

New York City.

March 2d. Business Meeting.

PRESIDENT NEWBERRY in the chair. Sixteen persons present.

On the recommendation of the Committee on Nominations, Messrs. John O. Robinson and William Falke were elected Resident Members.

DR. B. N. MARTIN announced the death of the Rev. John Bachman, D. D., of Charleston, S. C., and gave a review of his life and labors.

Dr. Bachman was one of that older body of American naturalists to whose devoted exertions our Natural History is so largely indebted; and among those assiduous cultivators of American science, none was more assiduous or successful.

Born in Northern New York in the year 1790, he early acquired a strong taste for scientific pursuits, and gained a personal acquaintance with the fauna and flora of his native state. Subsequently, when he had entered the ministry of the Lutheran Church, and was compelled by pulmonary weakness to seek a sphere of labor at the South, he experienced fresh delight in the novel and ample field there thrown open to his researches. He devoted his leisure to his favorite pursuits, and acquired a very large fund of accurate knowledge upon the botany, the ornithology, and the mammalogy of our entire country. For this purpose, he traveled much, and visited, among other interesting objects of inquiry, our Indian tribes; till he could say, as perhaps no other anthropologist could, that he had personally examined many individuals of every Indian tribe existing within the last fifty years in the Atlantic states, from Maine to Florida.

His observations upon the birds of America were very numerous and exact. He was perhaps the first to determine the power of distinguishing species by their note. Audubon, to whom he imparted this skill, was at first unwilling to believe it trustworthy; but the readiness with which he saw Dr. Bachman himself employ it, soon convinced him of its great practical value.

Dr. Bachman also gave extended study to the mammalia of this continent. He was at great pains not only to distinguish species, but also to ascertain their peculiar habits and characteristics. The question, for instance, of the way in which the young of the opossum are transferred from the womb to the external pouch of the mother, required very numerous observations before it could be determined. He was obliged to procure, with much trouble, specimens approaching this precise stage of gestation, and to watch them almost incessantly; and if any circumstance interrupted his sustained attention, the young would be sure, upon his renewal of his watch, to be found duly attached in place: he would then be obliged to commence the same research with another specimen, procured with similar difficulty.

When Sir John Richardson reported the occurrence of the common eastern mole beyond the Rocky Mountains, he took great pains to obtain specimens from that then remote region, and successfully proved that the two species are distinct.

All these extended observations he subsequently gave to the world in his work on "The Quadrupeds of North America," the text of which was exclusively his own, while the elegant plates which accompanied it were the work of his two sons-in-law, the younger Audubons.

His treatise on the "Unity of the Human Race," contains the conclusions upon this subject derived from his extended study of the organic world, and is a volume of high interest. He was the first to give any general and trustworthy account of the origin of animal varieties; and his work, though subsequently thrown into the shade by the more elaborate treatises of Darwin, is yet a most valuable repository of accurately-observed facts, and illustrates some important laws nowhere else so distinctly stated.

This publication, in which he controverted the views which had recently been set forth by Agassiz, was entirely successful in its aim, and compelled a complete change of ground by his distinguished antagonist in regard to the definition of a species.

Of the Christian earnestness of his life and character, as well as of his religious labors, which were very assiduous and important, this is not the place to speak; we can only refer to his scientific attainments. In this respect we must regard him as an observer of great research and accuracy, and at the same time of great candor and fairness, who has enlarged our knowledge and extended our views, and to whom the scientists of the future will owe a permanent debt of obligation.

Some further tributes of respect to Dr. Bachman were given by members present; after which,—

The President called attention to the interest and importance of the recent researches of Dr. Schliemann among the ruins of Troy.

Dr. Feuchtwanger, Prof. Egleston, and Dr. B. N. Martin exhibited several specimens of minerals, which were examined and discussed.

March 9th. Chemical Section.

Dr. H. Endemann in the chair. Twenty-five persons present.

Dr. Feuchtwanger exhibited a number of interesting minerals, American and foreign.

Prof. H. Wurtz presented an outline report on the "Greenland coal," or lignite, brought from the mines at Disco Island, by the U. S. steamer Juniata, in 1873.* He described minutely the structure of the material, its treatment in analysis, and its behavior in the various stages of the process. It yielded,

Water,		14.00	
Volatile matter,		35.38	
Coke, containing	Carbon,	41.79	
	Ash,	8.83	100.00

Sulphur was present in minute amount.

Should the above proportion of volatile matter be found to hold good when the water is expelled, which can be done at the low heat of a sand-bath, this lignite would rank as an excellent gas-coal. This interesting and perhaps important point, he had not had opportunity to investigate.

The dehydrated lignite, when in powder, becomes somewhat pyrophoric, igniting very readily. The coke would appear to yield a powerful and valuable fuel.

This lignite is remarkable as having the highest density recorded, 1.46 (mean). The coke also, which shrinks greatly in forming, has the unequaled density of 1.836, higher even than any anthracite known, apparently. It contains, however, a large proportion of ash.

The analysis is remarkably close in its results, to that of the lignites of Mt. Diablo, California, as given by Prof. Whitney (Geol. Cal., 1865, p. 30), especially when the variable ash, in the two cases, is left out. The Mt. Diablo lignite

* Published in the *American Chemist*, Vol. IV., p. 401.

is Cretaceous, while that of Greenland is regarded as Miocene; but the close correspondence is curious.

PROF. D. S. MARTIN remarked upon the geological position of this Disco lignite, and its association with Miocene plant remains, as described by Prof. Heer (Brit. Assoc., Exeter, 1869), such as *Magnolia*, *Liquidambar*, *Sequoia*, etc., very closely related to our own existing species. This is, doubtless, one of the many localities where the great Miocene flora, so close to that of North America at the present day, has left the record of its wide extension over what are now the frozen wastes of the Arctic zone, indicating the prevalence of a mild climate and a rich vegetation, throughout the whole of the far North, and the probable existence of a land-connection by way of Greenland, Iceland, etc., between our own continent and Europe.

PROF. A. K. EATON read a paper on the "Construction of the Spectroscope," reviewing the history of the instrument in its several forms, and also presenting some important improvements and simplifications devised by himself. For a direct-vision spectroscope, he uses a single bisulphide of carbon prism, right-angled, and with a thick glass plate fastened upon its hypothenuse side in such a position that the rays shall be refracted into or out of the prism, by total reflection from the inner surface of the glass plate, entering or leaving through one of its ends, which are beveled so as to form a right angle with that face of the prism to which the plate is attached. There are thus two modes of transmitting light through this instrument; and the resulting dispersion is very different in the two cases. When the rays enter one of the opposite sides of the prism, and pass out through the edge of the plate, a dispersion is obtained four times as great as when they take the reverse course, entering on the end of the plate, and emerging on the opposite side of the prism.

The power of this simple spectroscope is very great indeed. On a screen ten feet distant, it projects a spectrum of eight feet long, in which a hundred lines may be counted. Used for direct vision, a number of lines are discernible even by the unaided eye; while with proper appliances, it resolves the sodium line, D, and reveals that of nickel between the two. This is regarded as an excellent result with some of the best four-prism instruments. The lines are made visible without a slit, which at first sight seems impossible, by the fact that the beam of light is refracted at such an angle that it is reduced to an extremely narrow band, like that which passes through an ordinary slit. The value of this instrument for many uses, especially in the lecture-room, will doubtless become very great.

Prof. Eaton illustrated his paper by numerous drawings on the blackboard, and also exhibited several of his instruments, with slight modifications of construction and results.

Prof. C. A. Seeley presented illustrations of a "New System of Filtration." The ordinary mode of filtration is defective, in that one-half of the paper employed is not utilized, and that the process is somewhat obstructed by contact of the paper with the funnel. These and other objections are obviated by the devices proposed. For the funnel, a tube is used, an inch or more in diameter, and about ten inches long. The lower end of the tube is covered with filtering paper, held in place by a piece of Swiss muslin fastened by a rubber ring or stout twine. The upper end of the filter-tube has a rubber cork, carrying a small rubber tube which leads to a simple pressure apparatus. To support the tube, a rubber ring, fitting it, is stretched over an upright rod or peg set into the table or shelf. The rapidity of filtration may be changed at will by varying the diameter of the tube and the pressure.

Prof. Albert R. Leeds described a method which he had recently devised for the rapid and complete "Purification of Mercury." It consists in the filtration of the mercury under atmospheric pressure, through acidulated water and plugs of cotton wool, so as to remove entirely all the dust, dirt, and foreign metals, as well as the water or other liquids, and to render large quantities of mercury perfectly dry and clean in a very short time.

March 16th. Geological Section.

PRES. NEWBERRY in the chair. Twenty-six persons present.

DR. FEUCHTWANGER made some remarks on the recent low prices of diamonds, and read from lately published price-lists in illustration.

THE PRESIDENT presented an extended discussion, accompanied with a series of charts, "On Circles of Deposition in Secondary Sedimentary Rocks, American and Foreign."

In this account Dr. Newberry described the application to these later formations, of the views presented by him at the Portland meeting of the American Association for the Advancement of Science, 1873, and published in the proceedings thereof; and also set forth, with especial reference to the Palæozoic rocks, in Vol. I of the Final Report of the Ohio Geological Survey.

The first conception of this theory had been derived by him from the succession of Cretaceous beds, as studied in their great developement in the far South-West, between the Colorado River and the eastern part of Kansas and Texas. Everywhere he had found the lowest member to be a heavy sandstone and conglomerate, full of fossil wood and angiospermous leaves, so abundant and well preserved as to prove that they had not been carried far from their original place of growth. Over this series (equivalent to No. 1 of Meek and Hayden) comes a great limestone, rich in marine fossils (Nos. 2 and 3, M. and H.); and this in turn is overlaid by a double series, first of limestones, and then of clays, shales and mixed sediments, together corresponding to Nos. 4 and 5 of the Upper Missouri rocks. The record is simple and clear,—a great submergence of the Triassic land beneath the waves of a gradually-encroaching sea. Such a sea lays down, of necessity, first, a great sheet of fragmental beds, formed from the wear of the land, and containing the remains of the vegetation that clothed that land; then, if the sea continues to advance, this formation of beach-deposits will be carried farther and farther inland, while, as the water grows deeper, they will be followed, over what was previously the shore region, by the lime-deposits of clear, open seas, with the shells, etc., that there occur. The third series, shales and mixed sediments, represents the gradual withdrawal of the sea, and the concluding stage of the great cycle of deposits.

More recent studies, in connection with the Ohio Survey, had revealed to him a like series of conditions in the rocks of the Mississippi valley.

This peculiar and suggestive succession he had shown to exist in each of the great Palæozoic ages (Ohio Final Report, Vol. I, part 1, chap. iii.), as clearly as it is seen in the Cretaceous of the West and South-West. It can likewise be recognized, though less perfectly, in the Cretaceous of the Atlantic coast. The Trias of the far South-West also shows a like succession, though with certain peculiarities of difference. In New Mexico it is beautifully displayed at many points, affording sections in some cases of over 2000 feet. At the base there is always a mass of sandstone and conglomerate (the source of the pyrope garnets and peridots, which are found washed out and distributed in the gravel of stream-beds, etc.). Then follow shales, marls, and occasionally magnesian limestones. The succession is so precisely similar to that of the Triassic rocks of Europe, that Marcou recognized and named the group before he had procured from it a single fossil. (These several series were all discussed and tabulated at length.)

The distribution of Mesozoic rocks abroad was then taken up and treated of in like manner. The facts of this kind of succession have for some time been familiar to geologists, but their origin has never been fully understood or presented, as the simple and inevitable consequence of great periodic invasions of the ocean. Eaton, years ago, had remarked the succession of three types of formations, calling them, in their order, "silicious, calcareous, and carbonaceous series." Profs. Dawson, Hall, and Hunt have recognized the same facts distinctly; while in Europe, Murchison and his colaborers in Russia have described the Permian as having a trinal character, similar to that of the Trias, which, as every student of the science knows, derives its name from this three-fold division—sandstone, limestone and shale. More recently, Mr. Edward Hull has given extended tables of both the Palæozoic and later rocks of England and the Continent, based on this system of grouping.*

Of course, the operations of nature are everywhere complicated by countless minor circumstances, which tend to break the regularity and simplicity of such outlines. We find smaller cycles sometimes within the greater ones (as notably

---

* Jour. Geol. Soc., London, Vol. XXVIII, p. 132. Geol. Mag., Vol. V, p. 143. Quart. Jour. Science, Vol. VI, p. 353.

in the coal-measures), periods of rest or of regression in the course of these movements. But the great outlines are there, and may be clearly read by the observant eye and mind.

The lowest member of each series is always a fragmental deposit, made by the wash of the ocean on the shore, and containing as fossils the remains of land-plants. The middle member is a limestone, with marine fossils, plainly the product of deeper and clearer waters. The series is closed by the deposits of a retreating and shallowing ocean, clays, shales, and mixed material, in which neither the coarse deposits formed by the wear of an invading sea, nor the calcareous organic sediments laid down by the clear ocean, could prevail.

PROF. WURTZ suggested for the three types of formation, the names of Silicious, Calcareous, and Aluminous. He dwelt upon the importance of recognizing chemical action as one great agency in determining the character of deposits, and referred to his use of the terms "ferric" and "ferrous," to denote certain alternate and oft-recurring periods in geology. The lowest members of each of these great cycles of deposition are generally ferric, i. e. contain iron in the state of sesquioxide, having been exposed, during their formation, to atmospheric oxidation. To this fact, as is well-known, is due their prevailing red color. In like manner, the upper members of the series are usually ferrous, having their iron in the protoxide state, from the deoxidizing agency of organic matter present in the sediment when laid down.

THE PRESIDENT observed that Prof. Wurtz's generalization as to the state of the iron is usually correct. He preferred, however, to designate the three types of deposits as Mechanical, Organic, and Mixed.

PROF. E. H. DAY made some further remarks on the President's paper, comparing its principles with the facts as illustrated in the Jurassic rocks of Europe; and referring to Prof. Huxley as having, in 1862, dwelt upon the similarity frequently observed in rocks of the same age, in different countries, and having proposed the term "homotaxis" to designate such phenomena.

Prof. D. S. Martin read, in the absence of its author, a paper entitled, "Notes on the Coal-Measures of Beaver County, Penn." By I. C. White; published in the Annals, Vol. XI, No. 1.

Mr. White finds along the steep banks of the Beaver River, which flows southward into the Ohio, near the western line of Pennsylvania, a very complete and interesting section of the Lower Coal Measures, from the Tionesta to the Mahoning sandstones inclusive. He gives a concise description of the entire series as there developed.

The President remarked on the paper of Mr. White, with much interest, and drew sections of the adjacent and closely corresponding series, as developed by the Ohio survey, in Columbiana Co., Ohio, just across the Pennsylvania line.

Prof. Wurtz presented some facts and illustrations concerning the use of the streak or trace left upon paper, as a means of distinguishing between various carbonaceous materials, as cannels, asphalts, etc. The differences of color and aspect in these streaks are very remarkable, though little known; and the whole subject deserves attention, as a ready means of field determination. The blackest trace obtained is that of Albertite; it is intense and velvety. Grahamite, on the other hand, gives a deep reddish or maroon-colored streak. Other like substances differ in various ways. In one instance, he had already applied this test with much advantage, to distinguish a valuable slaty cannel from a closely-associated carbonaceous shale. The two are indistinguishable to the eye, even by the workmen in the mine, save after long familiarity; but the streak serves to indicate in a moment. This was at one of the mines of the so-called Darlington Cannel, in Ohio.

March 23d.

Pres. Newberry in the chair. Fourteen persons present.

Prof. D. S. Martin read by title, in the absence of the author, the following paper:—

Catalogue of Plants observed in Monongalia County, West Virginia; by I. C. White.

This list enumerates 312 species of phænogams and ferns. The author states, at the outset, that it by no means includes the entire flora of the county, but only those plants identified by himself; and that as his observations have been very imperfect during some important parts of the year, he estimates that it could be increased by at least 200 species.

Among the notes to this paper, are several facts of much interest. *Pastinaca sativa* (feral) is reported as completely overrunning some meadows. *Ambrosia artemisiæfolia*, generally regarded as worse than useless to farmers, is by some mown down and used as fodder for sheep, which are said by their owners to eat it eagerly, and to winter very well upon it. *Asimina triloba* (papaw), abundant east of the Monongahela River, is rare west of it.

The President made some observations in reference to the paper of Mr. White, and to the flora of the Western States. The last circumstance, respecting the distribution of the papaw tree, can only be a local peculiarity.

Prof. D. S. Martin brought forward some views concerning the distribution of the Mesozoic rocks in the Middle States, particularly of the Cretaceous formation and its old shore-line, as compared with that of the Triassic. He discussed the relative distribution of these two series, at a number of points, from New York southward to North Carolina;

but said that he had not yet obtained all the data that he wished, in order to set forth his views fully. This he hoped to do at a later day, in a more formal and extended manner.

With regard to the occurrence of the Cretaceous on Long Island, concerning which some discussion has been caused by recent criticisms on Prof. Hitchcock's new map, Prof. Martin claimed that the evidence is exceedingly strong, that beds of that age do occupy the north-western part of Long Island, and probably underlie much of it. Prof. Hitchcock is right in so representing it; and the criticism made against him in that respect cannot stand. Reference was then made to the positive identification of the Cretaceous on Long Island, by Prof. Mather years ago in his report (Geol. N. Y., vol. 1, chap. iv), and to a number of facts mentioned by recent observers. Especially important is the sandstone with angiospermous leaves, a mass of which was found in digging the foundations of the Williamsburg Gas House, some three years ago.

Prof. Stevenson expressed his concurrence with the views of the last speaker on these points, and recalled the the fact of the finding of *Gryphœa* in a well-excavation, many years since, in the northern part of Long Island.

The President described a sandstone containing angiospermous leaves, very similar in aspect to those of the Raritan and of the Lower Cretaceous in the far West, which occurs in boulders at Lloyd's Neck, L. I. This is undoubtedly the same rock with that of the Williamsburg Gas House, as he was satisfied from comparison. It is totally unlike anything known in this vicinity, and, unfortunately, has not yet been found *in situ*. Whenever it is, some interesting light will be thrown on this whole question. But its presence under these circumstances, points to its existence in place, at some locality not far away.

March 30th.

PRESIDENT NEWBERRY in the chair. Fourteen persons present.

DR. HABEL gave a description of his observations on humming-birds in Central America, particularly as to their insectivorous character, as shown both by noting the habits of the birds, and by frequent dissections.

DR. B. N. MARTIN remarked further upon the subject, and stated that the fact that many Trochilidæ are, to some extent at least, insectivorous, has been long familiar to ornithologists.

The remainder of the evening was occupied by MR. BOYLE, in the presentation of some views concerning astronomical agencies as producing changes of climate in past geological periods, and a discussion thereon by the President.

April 6th. Business Meeting.

PRESIDENT NEWBERRY in the chair. Twelve persons present.

On the recommendation of the Committee on Nominations, the following gentlemen were elected as Resident Members; Mr. L. E. Chittenden, Prof. Clarence King, and Dr. H. Le Baron Hartt.

The evening was almost entirely occupied with matters of business, mainly with the nomination of a large number of new members, for election at the May meeting, and with some questions as to the manner of issuing the Proceedings.

The meteorology of the three winter months, as reported by DR. O. W. MORRIS, may be summed up as follows:—

DECEMBER, 1873.	Temperature.	Pressure.	Humidity.
Maximum	65·5°	30·512	*Saturation.*
Minimum	22·°	29·254	25·°
Range	43·5°	1·258	75·°
Mean	37·49°	29·985	70·29°

Snow fell on three days, rain and snow on three, and rain on seven. Total amount 3·4 inches.

Lunar coronas were noted on the 6th and 28th. In the sun the thermometer reached 79° on the 12th and 15th.

JANUARY, 1874.	Temperature.	Pressure.	Humidity.
Maximum	44·33°	30·467	*Saturation.*
Minimum	2·°	29·437	31·6°
Range	42·33°	1·03	68·4°
Mean	28·94°	29·946	67·69°

Snow fell on five days, snow and rain on four, and rain on seven. Total amount, 6·82 inches.

One aurora was observed, and one lunar halo. On the 14th, the thermometer reached 79° in the sun.

FEBRUARY, 1874.	Temperature.	Pressure.	Humidity.
Maximum	66·°	30·582	*Saturation.*
Minimum	9·°	29·516	10·6°
Range	57·°	1·066	89·4°
Mean	31·92°	30·428	64·46°

Snow fell on five days, snow and rain on three, and rain on three. Total amount, 4·44 inches.

Lunar haloes were noticed on the 24th and 26th. In the sun, the thermometer attained the hight of 98° on the 23d.

On comparing the death-rates of the city with the temperature, pressure, and humidity of the three months, and of the entire winter, we have the following results:—

	December.	January.	February.	Winter.
Mean temperature	37·49°	28·94°	31·92°	32·78°
Mean pressure	29·985	29·946	30·428	29·968
Mean humidity	70·29°	67·69°	64·46°	67·48°
Deaths under one year	481	510	482	1473
Deaths of all ages	2179	2172	2065	6416

April 13th. Chemical Section.

PRES. NEWBERRY in the chair. Thirty-eight persons present.

The Publication Committee reported the issue of Nos. 12 and 13, closing Vol. X of the Annals. After this and some other communications had been heard,—

DR. FEUCHTWANGER exhibited a number of minerals from North Carolina, and a specimen of *Scutella interlineata* from the Tertiary sandstone of California.

Mr. Pierre de P. Ricketts read a paper giving the "Results of some Experiments upon Cremation," lately conducted by him at the laboratory of the School of Mines of Columbia College. The public interest recently manifested upon this subject, and its possible, if not actual, importance, had led him to make these investigations.

Mr. Ricketts described the muffles which he had used in his experiments, and exhibited the smaller one to the members. These were such as are ordinarily used in the Assay Laboratory for the scorification of gold and silver ores, and were simply inserted in the usual assay furnace. He had commenced with the body of a mouse, and had then successively incinerated those of a rat, a cat, and a dog. (The ashes of these animals, beautifully white and clean, were exhibited in glass jars). The results obtained are set forth in the following table, together with the estimated proportionate results in the case of a human body weighing 150 lbs.

	Weight of body.	Weight of ash.	Time required.	Estimated ash of a human body.
Mouse,	5·317 grms.	·29 grms.	20 min.	8⅕ lbs.
Rat,	181·25 "	5·57 "	30 "	4⅗ "
Cat,	5·48 lbs.	3·6 oz.	1½ hours.	7 "
Dog,	54· "	2·0 lbs. 2·3 oz.	7½ "	6 "

The last example, that of the dog, is probably the most reliable; it was also much the most troublesome, since the body had to be cut in pieces, there being no muffle at hand large enough to contain it whole. These experiments show what may be done by means of proper furnaces. There were no odors or unpleasant accompaniments of any kind, all the gases passing off by the tall chimney. Were cremation to come into use, suitable furnaces should be erected at various points in or around the city, and the process could be carried on with perfect neatness and readiness, the only residuum being a clean white ash. Cremation would have many advantages over interment, in a sanitary point of view; but popular feeling will doubtless long oppose its adoption, although with little real ground. If the idea of consuming our friends' remains in a furnace, is unpleasant and painful, that of their slow decay in the ground is certainly no less so; while so far as religious feeling is concerned, Almighty power can raise our ashes as well as our dust.

PROF. WURTZ remarked that in his view, this whole question of cremation was much less a scientific than a social one. He could not believe that such a practice was to be revived in this day. After mentioning that some individuals had willed their bodies to gas companies to be converted into gas, he stated that he had made calculations as to the possibility of such a disposal. In a human body, some seventy per cent. of the weight is water; there would, therefore, be about twelve gallons of water in a body weighing 140 lbs. A gas-retort would be so much cooled by the conversion of such a mass of water into vapor, that the production of gas would be rendered impossible.

DR. A. N. BELL, of Brooklyn, strongly urged the sanitary importance of cremation, and dwelt especially on the danger arising from graveyards. Even at such a distance as three-quarters of a mile, fatal cases of disease have been traced to the deleterious influence of a burying-ground. Typhoid fevers, in particular, are apt thus to arise. Nor is it only during the period of use, that graveyards are thus dangerous; they remain so for a long time after any interments have been made. The grass is green and the vegetation rank and luxuriant, to a most notable degree, even in very old burial-grounds; and farmers know that this fertility lasts for twenty or thirty years. The organic matter is at a considerable depth in the soil, and hence is not acted upon rapidly by the sun's heat; but the evolution of gases, etc., is slow and long-continued; and for that very reason, the vicinity of such places is highly perilous to health.

Dr. Bell dwelt upon this subject quite fully, citing various illustrations; in conclusion he argued that there is no possible objection to cremation from a Christian point of view, and that it presents a truly-scientific question of much moment.

DR. H. C. BOLTON and PROF. EGLESTON both observed that in some regions the modes of burial are attended with circumstances far more repulsive than the idea of cremation could be. The former gentleman described scenes that he had witnessed in Spain, and the method pursued in New Orleans; and the latter referred to the celebrated horrors of the Campo Santo, at Naples.

The debate was continued for some time, by PROF. WURTZ, DR. AM ENDE, of Hoboken, and the PRESIDENT, who, in summing up the discussion, vindicated its introduction as a matter of high scientific interest.

PROF. T. EGLESTON read an extended paper on "The Analysis of Furnace Gases,"* describing particularly the Orsat apparatus, both as to its mode of working, and its great prospective value.

It has long been very desirable to have an apparatus for the industrial analysis of gases; as none of those that are familiarly known fulfil the necessary requisites of simple construction and rapid operation. Such analyses must be executed quickly, in order to give the key to what is going on; so that operations in course of execution may be modified or not, according to the indications furnished.

The Bunsen, Doyere, and Regnault methods cannot, save in rare cases, be introduced into industrial establishments; and hence the practice of making gas-analyses, in such quarters, has been confined to certain special manufactures, mainly of recent date, wherein the necessity of analyzing the gases has been from the outset assumed.

M. Orsat, of Paris, however, has invented an apparatus evidently destined to work an important change in this whole matter, since it meets all the requirements of industrial use. It is not costly, it is solidly built, and is easily put together; so that any workman of fair intelligence can manipulate it quickly, and obtain results even more than sufficient in accuracy for commercial purposes.

Prof. Egleston here proceeded to give a detailed description of the construction and working of the Orsat apparatus, accompanied with drawings on the blackboard. He also noticed certain possible sources of error in the results obtained. These, however, are of no account in industrial operations; and even in scientific experiments, they are more

* Published in full in the *American Chemist* for April, 1874, with engravings, tables, etc.

apparent than real. They were described, however, and also the methods of guarding against them. In closing, Prof. Egleston discussed the general importance of this subject.

There is no chemical or metallurgical industry wherein the constant analysis of the gas, rendered possible by this apparatus, will not very soon furnish the key to effecting an important saving, and where the theory and working of the process may not be studied in minute detail. Moreover, in order to adapt the apparatus to the study of any gases given off in any operation, it suffices simply to vary a little the character of the absorbent liquids used. Experiments and modifications are now in process, to adjust and perfect this apparatus for the analysis of hydrocarbons and complex gases, or for any operation which can be performed by the Regnault or Doyere methods.

Mr. W. Goold Levison read the following paper:—

On a Simple Connective for Battery Carbons.

To follow the interesting papers we have heard, with so simple a thing as a means of attaching a connecting wire to a battery-carbon, would seem to me too great a transition for your attention, were I not aware that just such simple matters often give great aid in difficult and laborious work. The connecting wire is usually fastened to battery-carbons by means of a clamp, costing from 25 cents to $1.00, which needs, especially when nitric acid is used, to be often renewed (except in case of the more expensive forms), and always requires a large portion of the carbon plate or rod to project above the liquid. Not only is the projecting carbon a considerable item of expense, as well as of weight, in batteries of the Bunsen form, when true gas-carbon is used, but the liquid, creeping over it, evaporates rapidly, and it soon becomes covered with an efflorescent crystallization of salts. In such batteries, all these inconveniences may be obviated by the simple means which a glance at the carbon I hold in my hand, will explain to you. It is drilled to a depth of two centimeters, with a seven millimeter drill, and to a greater depth by a three millimeter drill. In the inner hole is then driven a brass pin, to which the connecting wire is soldered; and a glass tube slipped over the wire is then cemented in the larger tube by means of melted shellac or other suitable cement. The carbon may be so short as to be wholly immersed in the acid; and although the acid certainly does penetrate to the wire, and ultimately corrode it, yet it lasts a long time and is easily renewed. The whole adjustment costs but a few cents, and may be constructed by any one. The carbon here exhibited has been under acid for more than two months. This device may have been already in use, for aught I know; but I have found it so convenient, that I have thought it not amiss to present it.

April 20th. Geological Section.

PRESIDENT NEWBERRY in the chair. Twenty persons present.

Among the books received at this meeting, was the "Catalogue of Air-breathing Vertebrates from the Coal-measures of Linton, Ohio;" by Prof. E. D. Cope, in reference to which,—

THE PRESIDENT gave a description of the Linton coal-bed, and of its remarkable fauna. The locality had evidently been a lagoon or sheltered bay on the shore, quiet and secluded, but opening into the sea, as is shown by the numerous teeth and spines of sharks. In this lagoon there had formed a thick deposit of carbonaceous mud, now hardened into a seam of cannel coal, in which are imbedded the remains of some twenty-five species of ganoid fishes, *Cœlacanthus*, *Eurylepis*, *Rhizodus*, etc., and also of an equal number of species of amphibians, as now described by Prof. Cope. This number exceeds that of all the Carboniferous amphibians previously known to science; and we have here a suggestive glimpse of the abundance, in that period, of vertebrate life, of which, at most points, so little is preserved to us. A locality of similar richness is that at Mazon Creek, Illinois, which has likewise yielded a number of interesting species. These batrachians, many of which are closely related to such forms as *Menobranchus*, now living in our western rivers and lakes, flourished in this old lagoon at Linton, and found abundant sustenance in the swarms of ganoid fish, the spines, scales, and teeth of which fairly fill the cannel. Some of them were quite large, attaining a length of several feet.

This seam of cannel was formed from a washed and macerated mass, composed of the soft parts of the vegetation of the coal-marsh into which the lagoon or inlet extended. It is overlaid by one of the important bituminous coal-seams of the Lower Coal Measures, known in Ohio as the "Big Vein," No. 6 of the survey, corresponding to the "Upper Freeport Coal" of Pennsylvania. The record is a plain one; the lagoon that had formed the cannel finally "grew up" with the marshy vegetation of its shores, as so many modern lakes are filling up with peat; the cannel deposit then ceased, and an ordinary coal-seam was formed in its place.

PROF. T. EGLESTON presented an account of the "Systems of Notation of Crystals."

The whole subject of crystallography had, in his judgment, been surrounded with a great deal of mystery and supposed difficulty, which does not really belong to it. In this paper he reviewed the general principles which must enter into the study of crystalline forms, and of the notation of faces; and then traced the several methods adopted by the leaders of crystallographic science, and the successive simplifications which have been developed in notation.

Crystallography must now be regarded as a German science; for although begun by French students, it has been so much advanced and improved during recent years, in Germany, that the latter nation must be credited with its highest development. Hauy, although the father of this science, had yet some important errors and misconceptions. Founding his systems on prisms rather than octahedra, he could not reach the best modes of notation; and his idea of the rhombohedron as equiaxial triclinic, was wholly erroneous, and prevented his ever understanding the real nature of the form, or of its many derivatives.

Prof. Egleston illustrated his paper by blackboard drawings and models, the latter representing seven systems of crystalline forms, as now recognized, three orthometric, three clinometric, and the hexagonal, with its four axes, standing alone as the seventh. The second clinometric system, the Diclinic, has not been generally recognized, and is not included in Prof. Dana's enumeration. Its characters, however, are perfectly distinct, having the two transverse axes at right-angles to each other, as in the monoclinic system, but both inclined to the vertical axis.

THE PRESIDENT gave the second paper announced for the evening, "On the Structure and Origin of the Great Lakes," of which the following is a brief abstract.

The surface-contour of a country at any given time is the result of the counter-action of two ever-contending forces, elevation and erosion. After sketching the character of the Laurentian Highlands of Canada, which represent the oldest land on our continent, as everywhere planed down and worn away, from their ancient height, into low, smooth, rolling hills, he traced the formation of the great plain-country which borders them all around. The wear of untold ages, and the repeated invasions of the Palæozoic seas [see page 123], have formed from these primeval mountains the broad area of sedimentary rocks, Silurian, Devonian, and Carboniferous, which spreads away southward and westward from their base, for the most part unaltered and undisturbed.

These Laurentian hills must have been anciently snow-capped and ice-clad. Of course this was the case in the glacial epoch; but it may, perhaps often, have occurred before. If we study the action of glaciers now, we find that the head of the ice-mass, on reaching the lowland, or the sea-bottom, if it strikes the coast—tends to plow out a valley or depression in the soft material of the soil or the sea-bed. If the glacial action is long-continued or oft-repeated, such valleys may become very deep; this we know is the case on the Greenland coast, even where the force of the glaciers is lessened and limited by the buoying-up and breaking off of their outer ends by the sea.

In the light of such considerations, we may now observe the characters of our Western Lakes.

The whole chain of the Great North American Lakes may be seen to occupy a series of basins excavated in the plateau which skirts the base of the Canadian Highlands. Save in the case of Lake Superior, the outlines of which are partially determined by upheaval, all the lake basins are excavated in nearly horizontal sedimentary rocks. Their sides and bottoms, so far as can be examined, are planed and grooved in a manner which is produced only by glacial action; and the proof is conclusive that each of these basins has been filled, and at least partly excavated, by a mass of moving ice. The direction of the furrows on the rock, and the trail, left behind masses which have offered unusual resistance to this ice action, indicate the directions in which these glaciers moved. The course of the one which produced the basin of Lake Ontario, was from the north and north-east toward the south and south-west. The Lake Erie glacier moved in the line of the major axis of the lake, from east to west, or more accurately, from north 75° east to south 75° west. The islands at the western end of the lake, are remnants of the hard Corniferous limestone beds raised in the line of the great Cincinnati anticlinal. These interposed considerable resistance to the action of the glacier, and portions of them were left, forming the islands, which are grooved, fluted and planed on all sides by the moving ice. The Lake Huron glacier had a course nearly north and south; that of Lake Michigan moved from the north with a direction a little west of south. On the rocky margin of Lake Superior, the scratches indicate a motion of the ice-mass from the north and north-east. The direction of the glacial striæ about the more northerly lakes, Lake of the Woods, Slave Lake, Great Bear Lake, etc., has not been accurately ascertained.

The geographical relation of this series of basins to the Canadian Highlands is not accidental, but is significant of their mode of formation; and there can be no reasonable doubt that each of them was excavated by a glacier descending from the Eozoic highlands, and ploughing into the plain by which these are surrounded. All the region about the Great Lakes was once covered by a moving ice-sheet, or continental glacier, which over-rode and disregarded all minor irregularities of the surface. This great glacier existed during the maximum of cold; and the effect of such an agent would be rather to obliterate than to form local basins. In the earlier part of the ice period, however, it is probable that the excavation of the lake-basins was begun by local glaciers, and again resumed and completed by the same agency at a later period, when the amelioration of climate had caused the continental ice-sheet to disappear. Still later, when the glaciers which had filled and formed the separate lake-beds, were melted away, a great inland sea occupied the general basin of all the lower lakes. Of this sea, the shore lines are easily and widely traceable, and they are now known as the old lake ridges or beaches. At one period in the retreat of the glaciers, they capped the Canadian Highlands, and formed the northern shore of this inland sea. From this ice-wall, masses were from time to time detached and floated away southward, carrying loads of boulders and gravel, which they strewed broadcast over the southern margin of the lake basin, where the bergs stranded and melted. The record of this, the iceberg epoch of the glacial period, is found in the boulders of Canadian rocks scattered over Ohio, Indiana, etc., and often resting upon fine stratified clays and sands, which are perfectly undisturbed, and were laid down by the same waters across which the bergs drifted. This is a state of things which never could occur, unless the boulders had been floated down and quietly dropped upon their present resting-places.

PROF. D. S. MARTIN, who had announced a paper "On the Rhombic Crystallization of Graphite," said that, as the hour was late, he would read the paper in full at the next meeting of the section, giving at present only a general summary of its contents, with a description of the drawings which he had placed upon the board, and of the specimens on the table.

Graphite has almost invariably been regarded as hexagonal; but he had recently obtained a large number of very perfect crystals from Ticonderoga, exhibiting with great distinctness a peculiar series of striations, which led him to regard them as orthorhombic macles. He dwelt upon the recent determinations of Prof. J. P. Cooke, in his paper on "The Vermiculites," as bearing very closely on this point, and showing that much of what has been regarded as hexagonal crystallization is, or may be, orthorhombic twinning. The hexagonal system is at best an anomaly, in having four axes, while there are but three possible dimensions of matter; and it may be, in the light of Prof. Cooke's researches, that we shall be able to dispense with it entirely. If so, the facts here presented with respect to graphite, would afford a new link in the chain of evidence; and he desired to put them on record now, reserving for another meeting the fuller statement of his observations.

[The striæ referred to were pointed out in the specimens, and drawn and explained on the board.]

PROF. EGLESTON expressed a strong interest in the views of the paper, and hoped that it would be presented at the first opportunity when there would be time for full and careful discussion. If true, the discovery was important.

April 27th.

President Newberry in the chair. Twelve persons present.

A large number of specimens in mineralogy and zoölogy were exhibited by members, among which,—

The President showed a specimen of the rare mineral scorodite, which had lately been received at the School of Mines, from Zacatecas, Mexico. It is said to occur there in large masses, similar in character to the piece shown, which has but indistinct indications of crystalline faces. Crystals of scorodite may perhaps be found there; and if so, they would possess much interest.

Prof. D. S. Martin showed three large bones, apparently femora, but unfortunately with the extremities gone, from a Miocene marl in Virginia. The shafts are respectively 5¾, 8, and 8¾ inches in length, evidently belonging to some large animal; but they are hollow, and peculiarly interesting from the great proportionate size of the cavity, which in one is empty, and in the others is partly occupied by a fine diploe.

The aspect of the bones is highly ornithic, the relative sizes of the walls and cavities being nearly the same as in the femur of a turkey, which was shown for comparison, though the shaft is much stouter in proportion to its length than in that bird. These curious and interesting fragments, so disappointing from their broken and indeterminable condition, were found in a bed of shell-marl, by Mr. Thomas L. McCready, on his farm a few miles from the head of Mobjack Bay, near Mathews Court House, Virginia. The shells, Prof. Martin stated, he had in his own collection, and had determined as familiar and typical Miocene species,—*Chama corticosa*, *C. congregata*, *Crassatella undulata*, *Venericardia granulata*, *Astarte undulata*, *Pecten Jeffersonius*, and many more; so that the horizon of the bones is unquestionable. Other bones were reported as found with them, but these are all that could now be obtained, and for the loan of them he was indebted to Dr. B. W. McCready, of this city. Whatever their real character may be, they certainly point to some large species, probably undescribed, in the Miocene beds of the East, which as yet have yielded few reptiles or mammals, and no birds, at least of any great size.

The President gave the society some accounts of the session of the National Academy of Science, held during the previous week at Washington, and summed up the principal points of scientific importance. He dwelt particularly on the two series of government explorations in the far West, those of the War Department, under Lieut. Wheeler, and of the U. S. Geological Survey of the Territories, under Dr. Hayden. The results attained, in the knowledge of the physical history and structure of these vast portions of our continent, cannot be at all appreciated in their real value and extent, without an inspection of the many views, sections, maps, etc., which are in preparation for the forthcoming volumes of reports. These he described as of the highest order and of the greatest importance.

The report of Dr. Bessels, of the Polaris expedition, has likewise developed some very remarkable facts. Chief among these are the evidences of great and recent elevation in the far North, and the direction of glacial transportation in Smith's Sound. On Polaris Bay (Hall's Land) occur Champlain beds, with their characteristic fossils, identical species with those now inhabiting the boreal waters, at a hight of 1800 feet. These and other indications show that the coast of northern Greenland has undergone great elevation, and this within a recent period; while the southern portions are well known to be sinking. All Greenland appears therefore to be tilting upon an axis, which crosses it in about the latitude of the Humboldt glacier.

The remarkable fact observed concerning the drift, is that the boulders on the shores of Smith's Sound, between lat. 81° and 82°, came from rocks that lie to the southward, in some cases as much as 20°. This anomalous exception to all familiar facts of the northern drift, may be due simply to local glaciers at the close of the great ice period. Dr. Bessels refers it perhaps to bergs carried by northward currents, such as have been observed in Smith's Sound.

Dr. Newberry also exhibited an extensive series of large photographs of scenery, etc., taken by Lieut. Wheeler's party, showing moraines of extinct Rocky Mountain glaciers, the Mount of the Holy Cross, etc.

PROF. D. S. MARTIN announced the appointment by the naval authorities, of a naturalist to accompany the Transit Expedition, as had been proposed and sought by the Lyceum. Unable to add a civilian to the already crowded party on the ship, the Department had appointed a medical officer of the Navy, himself a naturalist, as Assistant Surgeon, and had committed to him the charge of making observations and collections. This was a highly gratifying piece of intelligence, both in the general interest of science, and especially to the Lyceum as the prime mover in the matter.

DR. O. W. MORRIS read a paper on the Meteorology of the month of March, published with those of April and May, in these Proceedings, June 1st.

May 4th. Business Meeting.

PRESIDENT NEWBERRY in the chair. Ten persons present.

The Committee on Nominations recommended the following gentlemen for election:—

As Resident Members, Dr. D. B. St. John Roosa, Dr. Charles G. Am Ende (of Hoboken), Mr. Charles A. Colton, E. M., Rev. Howard Crosby, D. D., and Messrs. Arnold Hague, Charles T. White, Wm. H. S. Thorburn, Wm. E. Gifford, and S. F. Emmons.

As Corresponding Members, Messrs. C. Hart Merriam, of Locust Grove, N. Y., C. J. Maynard, of Ipswich, Mass., H. A. Purdie, of Boston, Mass., James D. Hague, of Boston, Mass., Ruthven Deane, of Cambridge, Mass., Prof. J. A. Allen, of Cambridge, Mass., Prof. Darius R. Ford, of Elmira,

N. Y., Prof. R. D. Irving, of Madison, Wis., Prof. G. S. Roberts, of Grinnell, Iowa, Prof. T. G. Wormley, of Columbus, Ohio., Prof. A. A. Wright, of Oberlin, Ohio, Prof. J. Aitken Meigs, of Philadelphia, Penn., Dr. Edward Foreman, of Catonsville, Md.

On ballot, these gentlemen were all duly elected.

Mr. J. Waterhouse Hawkins, having informed the Lyceum of his removal from the city, was transferred to the list of corresponding members.

Other business having been finished,—

The President remarked upon the paper of Prof. C. H. Hitchcock, on the geology of New England, in the American Journal of Science for May, and expressed some dissent from the views therein set forth as to glacial action.

Prof. Stevenson and Prof. Wurtz discussed the phenomena presented by the action of ancient glaciers, as observed by them respectively in the southern portion of the Rocky Mountains, and among the trap ranges in the vicinity of New York.

May 11th. Chemical Section.

President Newberry in the chair. Twenty persons present.

Prof. Albert R. Leeds exhibited some specimens, brought from Dakota Territory, of a greenish earth, which the aborigines, and latterly the whites, have used for washing, under the name of '*natural soap.*' It has a greasy feel and soapy taste, and consists of 18 per cent. of water and organic matters, and the remainder of silica, etc. Also some specimens from Copper Falls, Mich., of a yellow metal, sometimes mistaken for gold, which is found there among the stamp copper, and which proves to be an alloy of copper and zinc, in fact a natural brass. A mineral from Conshohocken, Pa., hitherto called Anthophyllite, and so given by Prof. Dana, was shown to be a new variety of Tremolite.

He gave also the result of an examination of a rod of glass, four feet in length and two inches in diameter, formed by a stroke of lightning falling upon a bank of very white sand, near Fayetteville, N. C. The strangely-contorted fragments of the rod were silex, perfectly fused and almost pure. The only foreign body present was a trace of iron. Some of the sand in immediate contact with the fused silex was stained yellow by the same body. It remains to be determined whether the iron contained in the fulgurite, existed originally in the sand composing the bank, or was in any way present in the lightning discharge.

MR. WILLIAM FALKE read a paper on Physical and Vital Theories of Fermentation.

Two fundamentally-different theories exist, to explain the phenomena of fermentation, one a physical or strictly azotic theory, and the other the germ theory. The prevailing opinion, since the discovery of the yeast plant in 1837, by De la Tour, has been that ferments are living organisms, and that fermentation depends upon an exercise of the vital force. On the other hand, Liebig and others have sought to explain fermentation by so-called presence-action, on the ground that the ferment, being unstable, readily breaks up, and in so doing communicates molecular motion to the body in which the fermentation is effected. The necessity of the presence of oxygen is also a disputed point, and one of great importance. Mr. Falke spoke of the exclusiveness of the vital theory, and proceeded to argue in favor of the physical view, strongly maintaining the doctrine of spontaneous generation. He quoted numerous writers who support this view, and described some of his own microscopic observations on the *Torula cerevisiæ*.

DR. ENDEMANN remarked that there are several varieties of *Torula*, with different capacities of fermentation, and spoke of the weighty evidence of Prof. Wyman's experiments on the side of the germ theory.

MR. FALKE replied to some of Dr. Endemann's statements, and then,—

PROF. B. N. MARTIN stated that the experiments of Wyman showed conclusively that if the solutions experimented upon were boiled long enough, no living organisms could subsequently be detected. Prof. Wyman introduced a prepared solution containing organic matter into a series of small tubes, which were then closed and boiled for some time; but after a few days life was found in them all. When, however, similarly prepared tubes had been boiled for an hour, the number in which life afterwards appeared was much less. Every additional hour's boiling still further reduced the proportion; till of a set of twenty, boiled for five hours, not one showed signs of life. The weak point in Bastian's experiments is his assumption that simple boiling will inevitably destroy life. The attestation which two of his friends recently published in "Nature," of the correctness of his statements, affirmed that the boiling was continued for ten minutes. This, however, was not sufficient. The life of the germs undoubtedly survived this brief exposure to heat.

The subject was further debated for some time, by PROF. SEELEY, MR. FALKE, and PROF. WURTZ.

DR. H. C. BOLTON brought forward the proposal that had appeared in the *American Chemist* for April, looking to a celebration of the first century of modern chemistry, dating from the discoveries of Priestley and Scheele in 1774. He said that the suggestion had already called forth many letters from chemists in various parts of the country, expressing interest and approval. From several of these letters he read portions; and in particular from that of Miss Rachel L. Bodley, Professor of Chemistry in the Woman's Medical College of Pennsylvania, who suggested that the most appropriate spot for the proposed re-union would doubtless be the village of Northumberland, Penn., where Dr. Priestley spent the later years of his life, and where he now lies buried.

After some discussion, Dr. Bolton presented the following resolutions, which were adopted:—

Whereas,—The discovery of Oxygen by Joseph Priestley, on the 1st of August, 1774, was a momentous and significant event in the history of chemistry, being the immediate forerunner of Lavoisier's generalizations, on which are based the principles of modern chemical science; and

Whereas,—A public recognition of the one hundredth anniversary of this brilliant discovery is both proper and eminently desirable; and

Whereas,—A social re-union of American Chemists, for mutual exchange of ideas and observations, would promote good fellowship in the brotherhood of chemists, therefore

Resolved,—That a committee of five be appointed by the Chair, whose duty it shall be to correspond with the chemists of the country, with a view to secure the observance of a Centennial Anniversary of Chemistry during the year 1874.*

May 18th. Geological Section.

PRES. NEWBERRY in the chair. Twenty-four persons present.

DR. FEUCHTWANGER, MR. FALKE, DR. BOLTON, and MR. COLLINGWOOD exhibited various specimens in mineralogy, geology, and entomology.

The following paper was read by title; "An Annotated List of the Birds of Utah," by H. W. HENSHAW; (published in the Annals, Vol. XI, No. 1).

PROF. D. S. MARTIN read his paper "On the Rhombic Crystallization of Graphite," which was briefly presented at the meeting of April 20th.

Graphite crystals are usually more or less definite six-sided plates, which are said by Prof. Dana to be "often striated

---

* President Newberry subsequently appointed the following gentlemen:—

Dr. H. C. Bolton, *Chairman*,
Prof. C. F. Chandler,
Prof. Henry Wurtz,
Prof. Albert R. Leeds,
Prof. Charles A. Seeley.

This committee obtained the signatures, and prepared and issued the circular, which resulted in the Centennial Meeting at Northumberland, Penn.

parallel to the alternate edges" of the hexagon. In a number of large crystals from Ticonderoga, however, he had found, as their especial peculiarity, two triple sets of striæ, one like that referred to, and the other precisely the reverse, crossing the crystal at right angles to each pair of opposite edges, and inclined 30° to the two intervening pairs. In either case, the intersections of the striæ of each set with one another, form angles of 60°, covering the crystal with figures of rhombs and equilateral triangles, which are often sharply reproduced on the smooth surfaces of the felspar matrix.

These two sets of striæ never occur together on the same surface, but appear to alternate throughout the crystal, on opposite sides of its cleavage laminæ; though this alternation does not seem always regular.

Prof. Martin described and drew these striations particularly, regarding them as showing that the crystal of graphite is really an orthorhombic prism of 60° and 120°, twinned by threes into an apparent hexagon, on the same principles as those developed by Prof. J. P. Cooke in his recent paper on the Vermiculites.

In such case, the striæ mentioned by Prof. Dana are probably brachydiagonal, while those that he had now discovered would be macrodiagonal. The two series might alternate on the opposite sides of each lamina; or they might all be macrodiagonal, if the macro-axes of all the rhombic, or elliptical, molecules in a given lamina were alternate with those in the adjacent lamina. The obscurely hexagonal, and sometimes accurately circular, outline of many of the crystals would favor the latter view. In some cases, however, the crystals present strongly rhombic forms, in one instance with well-marked reëntering angles.

[The whole paper was so largely dependent upon illustrations, and upon citations from the views of Prof. Cooke, as to be difficult of reproduction in an abstract. It will probably appear further in the Annals, Vol. XI].

Prof. Egleston and Prof. Leeds expressed much interest, and hoped that the subject would be carried on to a still fuller investigation, as the discovery would be highly important in mineralogy, should it be positively established.

Prof. Egleston followed with a paper "On the Striations of Crystals." He dwelt at some length upon the nature and causes of this phenomenon, of which little is generally known.

The principal cause, though not the only one, is what may be termed "oscillation" between two distinct crystalline forms, a tendency towards each of which may be present during the formation of a crystal, but one more powerful than the other.

The stronger tendency determines the general form, while the weaker one leaves its record in a series of attempted faces, which usually appear only as fine striæ; at times, however, and indeed almost always with a magnifier, these lines are seen to be the mere edges of faces belonging to a different form. Thus the horizontal striation on the faces of quartz crystals is usually due to oscillation between the prism and one or both of the terminal pyramids; as may be seen with a strong glass. Sometimes, moreover, quartz crystals plainly exhibit a succession of numerous pyramids, one above another; most collectors are acquainted with this peculiar structure, which is in fact simply an exaggerated degree of the familiar striation. Ordinary iron pyrites, also, is one of the best species in which to observe these phenomena. Here the two forms between which this interaction most frequently occurs, are the cube and the pentagonal dodecahedron,—one holohedral, the other hemihedral. Cubes of pyrite bear the striæ of the pentagonal dodecahedron, the tendency toward the cubical form having in this case prevailed over the other. Conversely, when the hemihedral tendency succeeds in determining the general figure, we find the pentagonal dodecahedron bearing the striæ of the cube.

In similar ways, we find these oscillations occurring between two hemihedral forms, as e. g., the pentagonal dodecahedron and diploid, or between two holohedral forms, as in some garnets, etc., between the rhombic dodecahedron and the octahedron or the cube.

In the orthorhombic system, the oscillation of the basal and pyramidal planes is a frequent source of striation. So also macrodome or brachydome striæ are produced on the basal planes by oscillation of the latter with one or other of the former. In monoclinic crystals, the corresponding striations are, of course, those of the orthodome and clinodome.

With regard to the previous paper, Prof. Egleston remarked upon the close relation between the hexagonal and the orthorhombic systems, and the frequency of hexagonal twinning in the latter. In these cases, and many others, striation bears a most valuable part in determining both the fact and the manner of twinning; and indeed it is often the only evidence proving such a relation.

Prof. Egleston reviewed the different systems in order, pointing out the principal modes of striation in each, and the importance which attaches to them in the study of crystallography. Like the preceding, this paper was largely illustrated, and cannot be readily presented otherwise.

PROF. H. WURTZ gave an account, under the title of "Products of Alteration in the Palisade Rocks," of several peculiar altered minerals, mainly amorphous, from the trap-ridge of Hudson City and Weehawken. He exhibited numerous specimens, with observations and analyses. Some of these substances may prove worthy to rank as new species.

PROF. LEEDS and Prof. D. S. MARTIN discussed the paper of Dr. Wurtz, and showed a number of other specimens of the same or similar minerals, for comparison, also from the Bergen Ridge.

The last paper announced for the evening was prepared by MR. I. C. WHITE, and entitled "Notes on the Upper Coal Measures of Pennsylvania and West Virginia;" but the hour being late, it was deferred.

May 25th.

PRES. NEWBERRY in the chair. Twenty-three persons present.

DR. FEUCHTWANGER showed specimens of bismuth ochre, lately discovered near Silver City, Utah.

The following paper was read by title:—

"On the Genitalia and Lingual Dentition of Pulmonata, by W. G. BINNEY, with six plates;" (published in the Annals, Vol. XI. No. 1).

The author gives descriptions, with figures, of the genitalia and lingual dentition of a considerable number of species not hitherto examined, of the following genera,—*Limax*, *Zonites*, *Helix*, *Strophia*, *Geomalacus*, *Bulimus*, *Cylindrella*, *Bulimulus*, *Orthalicus*, *Liguus*, *and Succinea*. He also describes *Pallifera Wetherbyi*, a new species recently found near the mouth of

Laurel River, Whitley County, Kentucky, by Mr. A. G. Wetherby.

The species, with one exception (*Geomalacus*), belong to the American fauna.

The author, impressed with a sense of the value of such anatomical details as are afforded in his paper, as aids to classification, takes the opportunity of strongly urging upon conchologists the study of the genital system, as a most reliable specific character in the Terrestrial Pulmonata.

The deferred paper of MR. I. C. WHITE, on the Upper Coal Measures of West Virginia and Pennsylvania, was read in the absence of its author, by Prof. J. J. Stevenson. (Published in the Annals, Vol. XI, No. 2).

The region covered by Mr. White's observations includes portions of Monongalia, Marion, Marshall, and Ohio Counties, in West Virginia, and Greene County, Pennsylvania. The section extends from the Monongahela river, near Morgantown, W. Va., to the Ohio river, at Wheeling. The part of the coal-measures chiefly discussed, is that known as the Upper Barren Group.

The extended observations of the author of this paper are very minutely and carefully recorded. Among the numerous points developed, perhaps that of most interest is the entire absence, so far as particular search could reveal, of any indication of Permian affinities in either the fauna or flora, even where the upper coal rocks present their fullest developement at the highest horizon. Prof. H. D. Rogers had suggested the possible occurrence of such types in this region, as a matter for investigation; but none have yet been obtained.

THE PRESIDENT welcomed the paper warmly as one of high value, covering a district and a horizon of which little was previously known. Especially interesting is the determination concerning the non-appearance of any Permian types of fossils.

THE PRESIDENT gave an account of a second species of *Dinichthys* recently discovered in Ohio, which he names *D.*

Terrelli, after Mr. J. Terrell, who has secured the finest series of specimens.

This genus of gigantic bony-cased fishes has heretofore been represented only by the species *D. Hertzeri*, Newb., discovered and procured with great pains by the Rev. Mr. Hertzer, a Methodist missionary at Delaware, Ohio. Many specimens of this species have now been obtained, and the characters of its enormous jaws and massive shield-like plates are well known. They all occur near the base of the Huron shale of Ohio, corresponding to the upper Hamilton of New York, or more precisely, the Genesee shale.

Plates and fragments of jaws have more recently been found at a horizon near the top of the Huron shale, at Sheffield, Ohio, indicating for the species a length of some 10 to 15 feet. A cranium two feet across was obtained by Mr. Terrell, which rivals in size that of the older species. Subsequently, the discovery of perfect jaws has shown beyond doubt that the Sheffield species is distinct. These jaws are a foot and a half long, somewhat less than those of *D. Hertzeri*; but their chief difference lies in the fact that instead of having a series of small teeth or denticles set along the front portion of the side, as is the case in the other, their edges are raised into a sharp, cutting blade—the maxillary and pre-maxillary shutting down upon the mandible like scissors. These and other differences afford ample grounds for regarding the species as new.

Quite recently, almost the entire bony structure of a large individual of *Dinichthys Terrelli*—the new species—has been found by Mr. Terrell, in the Huron shale near Avon Point, Lorain County, Ohio. In this specimen, the median plate of of the back has a diameter of 30 inches, measured over the arch, and weighs 30 pounds; the cranium is two feet wide at its posterior extremity; the fins are composed of strong bony rays as large as a man's little finger.

This interesting series of bones has been purchased for the cabinet of the School of Mines of Columbia College, where nearly all the remains of *Dinichthys* yet found are now centered.

The genus *Dinichthys*, which is thus shown to have ranged through probably the entire period of the Huron shale, belongs to the group of placoderm ganoids, which are eminently Devonian forms; it is most nearly allied to the little *Coccosteus* and *Pterichthys*, which Hugh Miller has made so familiar, from the Old Red sandstone of Scotland. But the largest of these fishes was not longer than an average-sized mandible of the giant *Dinichthys*.

Among living types, the Siluroids are probably most nearly akin to *Dinichthys.* This group includes our cat-fishes, which have, instead of bony armor, only a hard, tough skin, and certain East Indian species, which possess, to some extent, a plated covering.

This paper was illustrated by drawings of natural size, and by a series of photographs of the remains of the new specimen found by Mr. Terrell.

PROF. LOUIS ELSBERG read a paper entitled, Notes on Physical Regeneration—a Contribution to the Doctrine of Evolution.

This paper discoursed of what may be termed Hereditary Molecules, and was designed to show the modifications which, according to the author, must be made in the doctrine of evolution.

To simplify the subject as much as possible, the genealogy of a child was traced. The impregnated ovum from which it grows consists of matter derived from the bodies of its parents; and it is assumed that some of the particles of this matter are retained in the child's body until, later in life, they are contributed to the formation of a new being, so that the germ of the new being contains some of the very particles of matter originally derived from its grandparents. The objections that might be urged to this assumption were then considered and disposed of. It was said that the transmission of the identical material particles to the grandchild, is a point not absolutely essential to the argument, since the transmission by the parents of particles rendered like those derived from the grandparents, would meet the case; nevertheless actual material transmission of grand-parental molecules was, for reasons given, regarded as most probable. The transmitted molecules were called *plastidules,* meaning plastid-molecules,—*plastids* being the term applied to the ultimate formative elements of organic bodies. To those who can more readily conceive the idea of force being transmitted from generation to generation, than matter, it may make the subject clearer to state that a plastidule is looked upon by the author quite as much as a center or bundle of force as of matter. With the assumption of hereditary molecules, the fact of resemblances in features of children to their grandparents, and of other inheritances, predisposition to diseases, reversion, etc., are quite naturally explained.

Moreover, the germ of a child contains plastidules derived through its parents, not only from grand-parents, but from great-grand-parents, and, in fact, from a long line of ancestors.

Let us start from a primitive "Adam and Eve." Their children came from germs which were wholly derived from their bodies; the germs of the children of these children contained, mixed with the modified plastidules of their immediate progenitors, some of the original plastidules of the first parental pair; and so on in each succeeding generation. The further removed an ancestor is, the smaller is, of course, the quantity of his share in the constitution of the germ, and, other circumstances being equal, the smaller his influence upon the character of the progeny. To express the idea arithmetically: in each succeeding generation, the numerator remaining the same, the denominator of the fraction of the set of plastidules from a particular ancestor increases; while, at the same time, the number of *sets* of ancestral plastidules increases. In the course of a great number of generations, it may be that the plastidules of a particular or primitive ancestor have become exhausted, so that the germ of the progeny no longer contains any of them.

Dr. Elsberg has given to his hypothesis the name of regeneration, because ancestors are assumed to be, to a certain extent, bodily, and to that extent in every other respect, born again in their progeny. He calls it also the preservation of organic molecules, because certain plastidules are supposed to be for a long time preserved, and transmitted from generation to generation; or the preservation of organic forces, for the same reason. Stated without the qualification necessitated by possible exhaustion of plastidules, and applied to all organisms, it is: that the germ of every derivative living being contains plastidules of its whole ancestry.

The modification of the doctrine of evolution which the author attaches to the acceptance of his hypothesis, is chiefly that the organisms now living have not descended from the same individual lower forms, but from similar forms separated in origination by time, and that both origination and evolution have been from the beginning and are still going on. The primary living being which started on its *evolution* (which is regeneration according to the laws of adaptation and heredity) first in time, is, other circumstances being equal, most highly developed;—which means that it may be stated as generally true that the most highly-developed organisms are so, simply because they are the oldest in organic existence.

Furthermore, the difference of rank among existing forms is thus mainly due to the difference of time during which, or the number of times which, regeneration has occurred; the difference of direction in which development has taken place being due to the modifying or adapting influences with which the organism has been surrounded.

The paper concluded as follows: "Man has not been most recently created, but earliest. We are really the descendants, or the ascendants, of the oldest inhabitants of our globe."

June 1st. Business Meeting.

President Newberry in the chair. Twelve persons present.

On the recommendation of the Committee on Nominations, the following gentlemen were elected to membership in the Lyceum:—

As a resident member, Mr. Carlos Cobb.

As corresponding members, Prof. George H. Cook, of New Brunswick, N. J., Prof. Oran Root, of Clinton, N. Y., Prof. Albert H. Chester, also of Clinton, Prof. J. W. Dawson, of Montreal, Canada, and Mr. James Macfarland.

The Committee on Publications laid on the table No. 14 of Vol. X, of the Annals (the closing part, containing index, addenda, etc.), and reported the first number of Vol. XI, as in press. Part 3 of the Proceedings (October to December, 1873, inclusive) was also presented.

The President read a letter from the trustees of the American Museum of Natural History, inviting the members of the Lyceum to attend the ceremony of laying the corner-stone of the building for the museum, in Manhattan Square, on June 2d. On motion, the invitation was accepted.

The meteorological reports for the three spring months, as recorded by Dr. O. W. Morris, at the Cooper Union, may be summed up as follows:—

March, 1874.	Temperature.	Pressure.	Humidity.
Maximum	63.5°	30.291	*Saturation.*
Minimum	17.°	29.338	21.1°
Range	46.5°	.926	78.9°
Mean	39.06°	29.837	62.63°

On the 3d, the temperature reached 89° in the sun.

Snow fell on six days, snow and rain on one, and rain on six. Total amount, 2.2 inches.

One lunar halo and one lunar corona were observed.

April, 1874.	Temperature.	Pressure.	Humidity.
Maximum	63.°	30.475	*Saturation.*
Minimum	25.°	29.368	16.°
Range	38.°	1.107	84.°
Mean	42.41°	29.894	65.42°

The thermometer rose to 92° in the sun, on the 6th and 14th.

Snow fell on one day, snow and rain on four, and rain on ten. Total amount, 8.9 inches. Thunder-showers occurred on the 5th and 20th.

May, 1874.	Temperature.	Pressure.	Humidity.
Maximum	88.°	30.326	*Saturation.*
Minimum	43.°	29.429	19.5°
Range	45.°	.897	80.5°
Mean	60.7°	29.890	53.77°

119° was marked by the thermometer, in the sun, on the 10th.

Rain fell on ten days, but to a total amount of only 2 inches. Thunder-showers occurred on the 21st and 25th.

One aurora was noted, and one lunar halo.

A comparison of the several monthly averages, and also those of the whole Spring, with the deaths in the city for the corresponding periods, shows the following results:—

	March.	April.	May.	Spring.
Mean temperature	39.06°	42.41°	60.7°	47.39°
Mean pressure	29.837	29.894	29.89	29.873
Mean humidity	62.63°	65.42°	53.77°	60.61°
Deaths under one year	501	500	543	1544
Deaths of all ages	2306	2119	2182	6607

Prof. D. S. Martin reported to the society the particulars of the arrangements for natural history observations and collections in connection with the Transit Expedition, now about to sail. As he had mentioned before, the object proposed by the Lyceum, in its memorial, had been substantially met by the appointment of a scientific gentleman as Assistant Surgeon to the expedition. This officer was Dr. J. H. Kidder. Prof.

Martin then stated that he had visited Dr. Kidder at the Brooklyn Navy Yard, and conferred with him freely and at length. The preparations and arrangements were of the most promising character, and far more extensive than he had ventured to expect. Dr. Kidder is a gentleman familiar with naval service at sea, and an enthusiastic student of natural science. He takes out an excellent library and apparatus, and has lately been in conference with some of the most accomplished scientific men in our country, among them Prof. Baird, of the Smithsonian Institution, Dr. Elliott Coues, Count Pourtales, and Prof. Allen, of Cambridge. He will pass several months on Kerguelen's Land, and will probably have excellent opportunities, both there and elsewhere, for important work.

Prof. Martin stated that he had hoped that Dr. Kidder would be present this evening; but in his absence, he could only congratulate the Lyceum on its share in this important enterprise, now so auspiciously begun.

DR. H. C. BOLTON presented some remarkable facts relative to "Paradoxes in Organic Chemistry," illustrating the points by graphic formulæ.

In studying organic bodies, some very singular results appear, when the methods of derivation, substitution, etc., are pushed one step farther than is ordinarily done.

(1) Thus it may be shown that the first alcohol of the series $C_n H_{2n+2}O$ is water; the common difference between successive members of this homologous series is CH_2; ethyl alcohol, for example, less CH_2, yields methyl alcohol,

$$C_2H_6O—CH_2=CH_4O.$$

If now we subtract CH_2 from methyl alcohol, we have water,

$$CH_4O—CH_2=H_2O.$$

(2) A like process will show that the first hydrocarbon of the homologous series $C_n H_{2n}$ is hydrogen; here again, the common difference being CH_2, we have

$$C_2H_6—CH_2=CH_4, \text{ and}$$
$$CH_4—CH_2=H_2.$$

(3) Again, the first acid of the fatty acid series is a molecule of oxygen; for we have as before

$$C_2H_4O_2—CH_2=CH_2O_2, \text{ and}$$
$$CH_2O_2—CH_2=O_2.$$

(4) Moreover, the first aldehyde of the series derived from the alcohols $C_n H_{2n+2}O$ is an atom of oxygen; thus

$$C_2H_4O—CH_2=CH_2O, \text{ and}$$
$$CH_2O—CH_2=O.$$

(5) So also the first ketone of the fatty series is methylic aldehyde. Di-ethyl ketone being $CO \left\{ \begin{matrix} C_2H_5 \\ C_2H_5 \end{matrix} \right.$ or $C_5H_{10}O$, and di-methyl ketone $C\,O \left\{ \begin{matrix} CH_3 \\ CH_3 \end{matrix} \right.$ or C_3H_6O, and the common difference C_2H_4, we have $C_5H_{10}O - C_2H_4 = C_3H_6O$, and by analogy,

$$\underbrace{C_3H_6O}_{\text{Di-methyl ketone.}} - C_2H_4 = \underbrace{CH_2O}_{\text{Methylic aldehyde.}}$$

Dr. Bolton then referred to the derivation of alcohols and acids from hydrocarbons, by successive substitutions of $(OH)'$ for H, and of O'' for H_2. After showing the importance of the group COOH (*carboxyl*) to the formation of an acid, he maintained that the group CHOH is equally necessary to the existence of an alcohol, and proposed for this group the name of *carbhydryl.*

He then explained, using Kekule's six-carbon-atom-ring, why the so-called carbolic acid, or phenol, is no true alcohol, the group carbhydryl being wanting. Phenols therefore are bodies peculiar to the aromatic group, and have no analogues in the fatty group. Ringing the changes on the graphic formulæ, he showed how the true alcohols and acids of the aromatic group are derived, viz.: by effecting the substitutions in the methyl group. Thus benzoic acid is really derived from toluol, which is methyl-benzol. He alluded to the relation which phthalic and salicylic acids bear to this series.

PROF. SEELEY made some remarks on the importance of Dr. Bolton's communication, saying that speculations of a similar character have been a fruitful source of discovery in organic chemistry.

After some conference on the work done by the society during the past year, the Lyceum adjourned, as usual, till the first Monday evening in October.

PROCEEDINGS

OF THE

LYCEUM OF NATURAL HISTORY

IN THE

CITY OF NEW YORK.

SECOND SERIES.

No. 4.

JANUARY 5TH TO JUNE 1ST, 1874.

NEW YORK:

ANGELL, BOOK AND PAMPHLET PRINTER, 410 FOURTH AVENUE.

1874.

COMMITTEE OF PUBLICATION.

THOMAS BLAND, *Chairman.*

GEORGE N. LAWRENCE,	JOHN S. NEWBERRY,
DANIEL S. MARTIN,	H. CARRINGTON BOLTON.

Editor of Proceedings.

PROF. D. S. MARTIN.

OFFICERS OF THE LYCEUM.

President:

JOHN S. NEWBERRY.

Vice-Presidents:

THOMAS EGLESTON,
HENRY MORTON.

Corresponding Secretary:

ROBERT DINWIDDIE.

Recording Secretary:

ROBERT H. BROWNNE.

Treasurer:

JOHN H. HINTON.

Librarian:

BERNARD G. AMEND.

Curators:

WILLIAM J. HAYS, HENRY WURTZ,
LEWIS FEUCHTWANGER, WILLIAM H. LEGGETT,
JOHN J. STEVENSON.

Committee on Nominations:

CHARLES A. JOY, *Chairman;*
ROBERT DINWIDDIE, CHARLES A. SEELEY,
BENJAMIN N. MARTIN, ALBERT H. GALLATIN.

Committee on Publications.

THOMAS BLAND, *Chairman;*
JOHN S. NEWBERRY, GEORGE N. LAWRENCE,
DANIEL S. MARTIN, H. CARRINGTON BOLTON.

Finance Committee.

BENJAMIN N. MARTIN, *Chairman,*
J. CARSON BREVOORT, D. JACKSON STEWARD.

Library Committee:

ROBERT H. BROWNNE, *Chairman;*
LOUIS ELSBERG, ORAN W. MORRIS.

www.ingramcontent.com/pod-product-compliance
Lightning Source LLC
LaVergne TN
LVHW011300110826
845149LV00001B/203

* 9 7 8 1 4 1 8 1 8 8 6 2 7 *